BITTER HARVEST

BITTER HARVEST

Palestine between 1914-1967

by

Sami Hadawi

WITH A FOREWORD BY DR. JOHN H. DAVIS
Former Commissioner-General of U.N.R.W.A.

THE NEW WORLD PRESS
New York

PUBLISHED BY THE NEW WORLD PRESS

135 East 44th Street, New York, N.Y. 10017

Library of Congress Catalogue Card No. 67-28543

First edition, July 1967

Second printing, August 1967

Third printing, October 1967

By the same author :

Palestine : Loss of a Heritage
(San Antonio, Texas: The Naylor Company, 1963)

Dedication

To the Memory of the Arabs who lost their lives in the 1967 War.

Acknowledgements

I gratefully acknowledge the great help I received from Mr. Zahi Khuri of Beirut, Lebanon, in taking over responsibility for the arrangements connected with the printing of this book, the drawing of the maps and the designing of the dust-cover.

I also like to express my gratitude to Mrs. Eve French, of Beirut, for the proof-reading, preparation of the index and generally in assisting me.

Contents

Maps

Foreword

by John H. Davis B.A., M.A., PH.D.
Former Commissioner-General of United Nations Relief and Works Agency (UNRWA) for Palestine Refugees in the Near East.

I RECOMMEND this book as important reading for all persons interested in the subject of Arab-Israeli conflict; a struggle that even pre-dates the establishment of Israel as a State by more than thirty years. Mr. Hadawi is an educated Palestine Arab who as a young man distinguished himself in the service of the Mandate Government of Palestine. Then after becoming a refugee in 1948 he lived for a number of years in the United States where he travelled extensively and spoke to hundreds of American audiences. Drawing on this valuable experience Mr. Hadawi has set forth here what he believes Americans and others want to know and need to know, but what, in fact, few do know about the problem.

The fundamental issue on which Arab-Israeli conflict now centres and has centred is on the basic claims and rights of two peoples in Palestine. The author of this book has attempted to chronicle the major events of the fifty year struggle over such claims and rights in a manner that is factual, well written and well documented. In doing this, he, of course, has included an explanation as to how these events and happenings are viewed by Arab people. It is this, in fact, that enhances the value of the book, since so little has been written from this standpoint. Still further adding to the merit of the publication is the objectivity with which the author views the total problem and the absence of bitterness towards the Jews as people or Judaism as a religion.

The reading of this book will add to one's depth of understanding of the subject and particularly of the thinking and feelings of tens of millions of Arab people, scattered throughout the Middle East.

I urge every one who has opportunity to read this publication.

Preface by the Author

WHEN MY BOOK *Palestine: Loss of a Heritage* appeared in 1963, many of my friends urged me to follow it up with a second book presenting the Arab point of view on various aspects of the Palestine Problem.

They pointed out that, while many worthy books have already been written on the subject by impartial non-Arab authors, an Arab answer to Zionist and Israeli allegations and accusations would shed significant light on the thorny Problem. Many objective writers had felt morally committed to disclose the injustices inflicted upon the Palestine Arabs. These recognized the dangers inherent in the foreign policy of the state of Israel: dangers that threaten the Jews living in Israel, the national interests of Jews who are citizens of other countries, the stability of the vital and strategically situated oil-rich region of the Middle East, and finally the peace of the world.

I was at first reluctant to embark on this project. The experience of publishing my first book, and the difficulties we are encountering at present in finding a publisher for a manuscript of some size of which I am a co-author, have not been encouraging. My Publishers, the Naylor Company of San Antonio, Texas, had been unable to place *Palestine: Loss of a Heritage* in any bookstore in the United States. But individual efforts were well rewarded that convinced me that there were still people who were anxious to hear both sides of the Palestine story. So I decided to meet the wishes of my friends.

This book is no malicious attack on those who broke faith with the Arabs for independence after World War I; or on those who for either material benefits or political advantages used methods which James Forrestal, former U.S. Minister of Defence, described as "bordering closely onto scandal"; or even on those who took advantage of human weaknesses and reached their goal no matter what the cost to other people. It is a chronicle of events which make up the Palestine tragedy.

The Palestine tragedy needs thorough investigating. Men of goodwill should get to the truth of the matter; fix responsibility for the crimes committed against humanity; and adopt the long overdue measures of righting the wrong and bringing 'peace with justice' to the Holy Land – The land which has done so much to bring mankind to God.

Beirut *S.H.*

Lebanon

I | *Introduction*

It is not the first time in history that partition has been resorted to as a solution to a problem. In ancient times, King Solomon ruled: If you cannot give one child to each of the two who claim to be the mother, then split the child into two and give one-half to one and the second half to the other.

An analogous scene was re-enacted in Palestine three-thousand years later, except that the wisdom of Solomon in the judgment was lacking in this case. Like the false mother who welcomed the bisection of the child who was not hers, the Zionists accepted partition of the Holy Land because it gave them something they did not own and to which they were not entitled either in justice or in equity.

Partition of countries against the will of the people is not only wrong in principle; it has been proved to be inhuman too. Wherever applied, partition has brought tragedy, destruction and suffering to millions of human beings. War came to Korea only because of the partition of the land into North and South; the fierce battles raging in Vietnam also have their origin in the partition of that country between North and South; and Germany, with its East and West zones, should not be discounted as another likely source of danger from which the first spark might once again be ignited signalling the beginning of a third world war.

The Powers which resist the will of the people of these three countries to unity and impose upon them a partition that can only be maintained by force of arms, are the same Powers which have inflicted the tragedy of partition on Palestine, with one additional iniquity – they first gave equal validity to the *claim* of the Zionists to Palestine and the *right* of the Arabs to their homeland in order to justify their plans of partition, then went a step further by encouraging the dislodgement of the Arabs from their homes and property.

There is probably no subject fraught with so many distortions and misrepresentations as the Palestine Problem. It has been widely discussed, debated, lectured upon and written about in the past five decades, but still it is far from being correctly understood.

Early in this period, the Zionists succeeded in shaping world opinion into the belief that Palestine was their 'Promised Land' that it was their 'historical' homeland, that it was a country without a people and the Jews were a people without a country. The Jewish endeavour and skill would bring civilization and prosperity to the few 'nomad' Arabs who roamed its countryside.

With unerring skill, the Zionists adapted their arguments to the special circumstances of each situation: They appealed to the Christians, using biblical language to awaken in them deep emotional undertones; to the humanitarians, they urged a permanent solution of the vexatious Jewish problem; to the anti-semites, they showed the way to get rid of the Jew from their midst; and to lure British politicians, an extension of imperial power was vividly portrayed through the establishment of a Jewish commonwealth in Palestine.

The thirty years which followed the ambiguous and ill-fated promise which the Zionists were able to extract from the British Government in 1917 "to view with favour the establishment in Palestine of a national home for the Jewish people", was a period of sweat and blood for the indigenous Arab inhabitants as they tried to defend their homes and homeland against an invasion the nature of which is unprecedented in the annals of modern history.

There are many, while still sympathetic to and concerned over the fate of world Jewry, have begun to doubt the morality and justice of the Zionist claim to Palestine. The dangerous situations arising in the Middle East from time to time since the creation of the state of Israel in 1948, and their effect on world peace, have aroused deep suspicion in the minds of many as to the wisdom of continuing the hitherto unqualified moral, financial and military support of the 'Jewish state'.

It is now suspected that something is basically wrong; that people have been deliberately kept in the dark and given distorted facts; that the stability and peace of the vital Middle East area are at stake.

World opinion has been led to believe that the Palestine problem is a conflict between Israel and the Arab States over the sovereignty of territory which the Arab States regard as part of the Arab homeland. The Israelis, on the other hand, claim Palestine as theirs by reason of the Balfour Declaration of 1917, the United Nations Partition Resolution of 1947, subsequent military conquests and what is commonly referred to as the 'Biblical Promises'. In other words, it is presumed to be a territorial dispute between nations, similar in some respects to the dispute between India and Pakistan over Kashmir.

This Zionist approach is not without a motive. It is intended to confuse the issue and to obliterate the memories of the crimes committed against the Palestine Arabs - crimes which have been described by British historian Arnold Toynbee as no less heinous than the Nazi crimes against the Jews. Its purpose is also to by-pass standing United Nations resolutions calling upon the Israelis to surrender the extra territory they occupied by force of arms beyond the area assigned to the 'Jewish state' under the Partition Plan of 1947; to give the refugees the choice between repatriation and compensation; and to permit the internationalization of Jerusalem. To label the conflict as a dispute between nations, divests it of its human and just elements and puts it in the same category as other world territorial issues where the parties proffer claims and counter-claims perhaps of equal strength.

The truth of the matter is that the Palestine problem must be called first and foremost a dispute between the Palestine Arabs and the Israelis before it can be labelled as an Arab States-Israeli conflict. The issue is fundamentally one of individual rights and principles, as well as of territory and must be treated as a moral and political issue.

No matter what language diplomacy uses in defining the rights of the Palestine Arabs, the fact remains that the major portion of the territory now called 'Israel' is legitimately owned by individual Arabs. Their rights derive from the universally accepted principle that a country belongs to its indigenous inhabitants. The fact that the Arabs fled in terror, because of real fear of a repetition of the 1948 Zionist massacres, is no reason for denying them their homes, fields and livelihoods. Civilians caught in an area of military activity generally panic. But they have always been able to return to their homes when the danger subsides. Military conquest does not abolish private rights to property; nor does it entitle the victor to confiscate the homes, property and personal belongings of the non-combatant civilian population. The seizure of Arab property by the Israelis was an outrage. It was described by many distinguished writers as 'robbery'.

The position of the Arab States fully supports the Palestine Arabs' demand for rights to homes and country. Any solution agreed to by the Palestine Arabs would be acceptable to the Arab States. Conversely, the Arab States cannot conclude a settlement that is unacceptable to the Palestine Arabs.

A solution of the Palestine problem, however, does not necessarily mean a settlement of the Arab States-Israeli conflict. While the former may have some influence on the latter, the Arab States – Israeli conflict arises out of the danger which Zionist ambitions for expansion pose to the territorial integrity of the Arab States. Israel's mass immigration policy and land acquisition goals constitute a serious threat to the peace and stability of the Middle East region. Israeli leaders have repeatedly declared the need for a larger land area. Actions, such as the planned invasion of Egypt in 1956 and the attempted annexation of the Sinai Peninsula and the Gaza Strip territory - which inspired David Ben Gurion to proclaim the areas as having been 'freed' and 'liberated' - provide ample proof of Israeli future aspirations.

It will be recalled that as early as 1948, the late U.N. Mediator Count Folke Bernadotte - who was assassinated by the Israelis because of his recommendations for a solution of the Palestine problem not in conformity with Israeli policy - warned the Security Council: "It could not be ignored that unrestricted immigration to the Jewish area of Palestine might, over a period of years, give rise to a population pressure and to economic and political disturbances which would justify present Arab fears of ultimate Jewish expansion in the Near East." He added: "It can scarcely be ignored that Jewish immigration into the Jewish area of Palestine concerns not only the Jewish people and territory but also the neighbouring Arab world."[1]

It would, indeed, be suicidal for the Arab States to relax their vigilance and allow themselves to be deceived by the Jekyll and Hyde image of the Zionist-Israel character. While the Israelis claim they want peace, they are actually preparing for war. If expansion is not their ultimate aim, what is the meaning of David Ben Gurion's statement: "To maintain the *status quo* will not do. We have set up a dynamic state, bent upon expansion?"[2] This ambition he reiterated in 1952 when he said: "Israel ... has been established in only a portion of the land of Israel. Even those who are dubious as to the restoration of the historical frontiers, as fixed and crystallised from the beginning of time, will hardly deny the anomaly of the boundaries of the new State." [3]

If these statements by the architect of the 'Jewish state' can be waved aside as pure fantasy, the declaration of the leader of the *Herut* Party - the second largest in the Israeli Parliament and which claimed credit for the ousting of the British from Palestine confirms Zionist intentions that expansion is indeed their ultimate goal. He said: "I deeply believe in launching preventive war against the Arab States without further hesitation. By doing so, we will achieve two targets: firstly, the annihilation of Arab power; and secondly, the expansion of our territory." [4]

Many were the Zionist promises and declarations which sought to lull the Arabs into a false sense of security and to mislead world opinion. When the Zionists promoted settlement of the Holy Land in 1920 as a result of the ill-fated Balfour Declaration, they spoke lavishly of their goodwill towards their Arab neighbours and of the many skills and advantages they would bestow upon the country. For example, at the Zionist Congress in 1921, a resolution was passed which "solemnly declared the desire of the Jewish people to live with the Arab people in relations of friendship and mutual respect and, together with the Arab people, to develop the homeland common to both into a prosperous community which would ensure the growth of the peoples."[5]

The world has seen how, thirty years later, the 'Arab people' of Palestine benefitted from Jewish immigration by expulsions and dispossessions under the most cruel conditions. Instead of peace and tranquility, the Holy Land has been turned into a battlefield; the Middle East is now a cauldron of unrest and instability; misery, hatred and bitterness prevail where previously there was harmony and frienship between Arab and Jew.

The Zionist-Israel propaganda machine has not only succeeded in inducing world opinion to regard the Palestine tragedy as a territorial dispute between nations; it has also managed to manoeuver some of the smaller states into sponsoring draft resolutions before the United Nations calling upon the Arab States and Israel to sit at the conference table and resolve their differences. It is noteworthy that the draft resolutions followed the Israeli pattern of ignoring the existence of the Palestine Arabs, whose fate holds the key to peace in the Holy Land.

In three consecutive years the drafts failed to win a majority vote. Some of the leading American press denounced the nations - including their own - which voted against the resolutions, accusing them of submitting to alleged Arab 'blackmail'. On the other hand, the Israelis were commended for their supposed peaceful intentions and willingness to talk peace. The Arab States were condemned and accused of threatening to destroy Israel, to 'push the Jews into the sea', to annihilate the 'Jewish state'.

But the response of the Arab representatives at the United Nations to the draft resolutions was neither negative nor threatening. It followed the logical procedures that disputes must, first of all, be resolved between the parties immediately concerned and on basis of justice and equity. A third party – in this case the Arab States – could enter the picture once the main issues have been settled between the Palestine Arabs and the Israelis. The Arab delegates unanimously told the Special Political Committee, in clear and unequivocal language, that if the Israelis truly wanted a settlement of the Palestine Problem, they should address themselves first to the leaders of the Palestine Arabs who are the aggrieved party. They declared that any agreement arrived at between the parties would be acceptable to their governments.

The Israeli representative not only flatly refused to countenance any suggestion of contact with the Palestine Arabs; he went so far as to protest the nomenclature of the 'Palestine Arab Delegation', arguing that the entity once known as 'Palestine' has ceased to exist and that the individuals who comprise the Delegation represent nobody but themselves. He also opposed the Delegation's right to a hearing by the Special Political Committee.

The record since 1948 has shown that the Israeli peace offers are neither genuine nor sincere. They are as far from real peace as blatant propaganda is from the truth. They are not made with the object of redressing the wrong committed against the Palestine Arabs, nor are they intended to bring stability and peace to the Middle East. They aim to :

(1) Divert public attention from Israeli defiance of United Nations resolutions;

(2) Win world sympathy for Israel as a so-called peace-loving nation which is a 'victim of Arab aggression';

(3) Raise more funds for Israel through the United Jewish Appeal and the sale of Israeli Bonds.

To the Israelis, peace means recognition by the Arab States of Israeli sovereignty over existing Israeli-occupied territory; the removal of the Arab boycott; the opening of the Suez Canal to Israeli shipping; and Arab acquiescence in the diversion of the waters of the River Jordan even though it is to the detriment of Arab rights and interests. By achieving these objectives, the Israelis hope to improve their economy and provide greater man-power through new immigrants, for ultimate realization of their dream of an 'empire' from the 'Nile to the Euphrates'. As for the Palestine Arabs whom they expelled and dispossessed, this is a matter they claim – which was the result of alleged Arab aggression against the 'Jewish state'. Such being the case, they say, it is for the Arab Governments, not Israel, to find a home for the Palestine Arabs.

Those who believe Israel's repeated proclamations of willingness to talk peace with the Arabs fail to realize that peace, in order to be real, has to be based on justice and equity. Ironically, Israel, while claiming to have a right to exist by reason of an act of the United Nations, refuses to honour her responsibilities to the Organization which created it. According to a declaration by David Ben Gurion in 1953 Israel "considers the United Nations resolution of 29 November, 1947, as null and void."[6] If the Israelis are permitted to discard the United Nations resolution which gave birth to their state, by the same token Arab refusal to recognize the existence of the 'Jewish state' is fully justified.

Peace in order to be lasting, is not something that can be achieved by intrigue, deceit, or political influences as the Israelis have been doing since 1948. It must be won on principles of justice and equity. As long as the Israeli attitude remains unchanged, the chances of a solution and peace, on Israeli terms, simply do not exist.

"Only an internal revolution," wrote Israeli Nathan Chofshi from Tel Aviv, "can have the power to heal our people of their murderous sickness of baseless hatred (for the Arabs). It is bound to bring eventual ruin upon us. Only then will the old and the young in our land realize how great was our responsibility to those miserable wronged Arab refugees in whose towns we have settled Jews who were brought from afar; whose homes we have inherited, whose fields we now sow and harvest; the fruit of whose gardens, orchards and vineyards we gather; and in whose cities that we robbed, we put up houses of education, charity and prayer, while we babble and rave about our being the 'People of the Book' and the 'Light of the Nations'."[7]

II | *Historical Background*

The Land and the People

The territory of Palestine covers a total area of 10,435 square miles and is about the size of the state of Vermont in the United States or about one and one-half times the size of Wales in the United Kingdom.

The land area comprises 10,163 square miles (about 6,589,755 acres) and the water area 272 square miles. The latter includes what used to be Lake Huleh (5 square miles), Lake Tiberias or the Sea of Galilee (62 square miles) and half of the area of the Dead Sea (405 square miles). The other half was in what used to be Transjordan.

Palestine is largely an agricultural country. Generally speaking it may be divided into four distinct soil regions:

a) *The coastal plains* – These consist of first class fertile land with an abundance of underground water and a plentiful rainfall. The plains have always been highly developed and contained large stretches of citrus groves.

b) *The hill region* – This region is predominantly rocky, but with proper terracing is suitable for the planting of deciduous trees. The olive is its principal crop. In winter, the large patches of land are cultivated with wheat and barley; and in summer, maize, tomatoes and other vegetables, are grown under dry-farming cultivation.

c) *The Jordan Valley* – This region lies below sea-level where the soil is good for any kind of cultivation, including citrus and tropical fruits. But owing to lack of sufficient rainfall, cultivation must necessarily depend on irrigation from streams or pumped from the River Jordan.

d) *The Southern Desert (Negeb)* – This region comprises nearly half the lands of Palestine (3,144,246 acres). The northern portion (some 640,000 acres) consists of good soil and is suitable for irrigation. The southern portion (2,500,000 acres) running from about five miles south of Beersheba to its apex at the Gulf of Aqaba -- except for small sporadically distributed localities totalling some 90,000 acres suitable for patch cultivation and only in years when there is sufficient rainfall -- consists of deeply eroded uplands and rift valleys.

Public opinion has been led to believe that Palestine was a neglected, desolate land without a people in need of a people without a country and that all developments and progress were the result of Zionist initiative and skill. This is not true.

The Holy Land, since the Crusades, has been renowned for its olive groves and olive oil industry; and long before Zionist immigration began in 1920, Palestine was known as a citrus exporting country, famous for the *Jaffa Orange*. It is unknown when the citrus industry was first developed in Palestine, but the record shows that in 1912-1913, the Arabs had exported 1,608,570 cases of oranges to Europe for a cost of £ 297,700 ($ 1,488,500). [1]

As regards the hill regions, the country is covered with olive orchards, vineyards and other deciduous fruit trees; while the lands in the South were used for the cultivation of grain, and those in the Jordan Valley for the production of vegetables and fruits. Every inch of fertile soil was used to full capacity; and more and more rocky patches were being turned into orchards and groves. A visit today to the village of Qalqilya, in Jordan, which lost all its citrus groves to the Israelis in 1948, will surprise the visitor how once dead or marginal land has been revived and turned into citrus groves and other plantations - all this without outside financial help and a credit to the tenacity and skill of the Arab farmer.

It is true that the expenditure of $ 150,000,000 on the Israeli River Jordan diversion project can improve agriculture in the south of the country, but let it be understood that this is limited to the 640,000 acre stretch in the *northern* part of the Negeb. It will not -- and could not -- include all the 2,500,000 acres of 'deeply eroded uplands and rift valleys' which comprise the arid wilderness of the *Southern* Negeb. Zionist propaganda will have the world believe that it is the *entire* territory of the Negeb that will be turned into a 'rose garden'. This deception helps serve as a means to extract more contributions for the United Jewish Appeal and boost the sale of Israeli Bonds.

Is it not ironic that Israel should today claim and take pride in the two principal agricultural industries - citrus and olives - started and developed over the centuries by the Arab victims of Israeli aggression?

At the close of World War I in 1918, Palestine was an Arab country similar to other parts of the Arab world. It had a population of about 700,000 of whom 574,000 were Moslems, 70,000 were Christians, and 56,000 were Jews. The latter were mostly Arabs of the Jewish faith. About 12,000 of these Jews lived on the land as farmers the rest carried on business in the principal towns – mainly Jerusalem.

Jewish land holdings in 1918 amounted to 162,500 acres, or about two percent of the total land area of Palestine. These consisted of holdings partly in the principal towns and partly in 59 Jewish settlements in different parts of the country. When the British Mandate terminated in 1948 and the Jewish state had come into existence, Jewish land holdings had increased to only 372,925 acres, or 5.67% of the total land area of Palestine of 6,580,755 acres – still an insignificant figure to justify partition of the country.

Arab-Jewish relations in history

According to Moslem doctrine, Christians and Jews are 'People of the Book,' believers in God, revelation and the day of judgment. As such, they are not to be persecuted or forced to become Moslems. No attempt was made to subject them to the Moslem legal code; they were left free to regulate their own communal and personal life in accordance with their own religious laws.

In general, the principles of Islam were obeyed and in consequence the Jewish community in the different Arab countries flourished throughout the centuries of medieval Arab rule. Although they preserved much of their exclusiveness, they became arabized in their language and culture. In the history of Jewish culture the Arabic period is among the happiest and most brilliant. In Spain, in Egypt and elsewhere, the arabized Jews not only carried on their own life of devotion and learning, but contributed to the general Arabic civilization. In science, medicine, scholarship and speculative thought, Jews helped to enrich the literature of the Arabic tongue; and individual Jews were able to reach the highest positions in the State.

With the fall of Arab power in Spain, North Africa and the Arab Middle East became places of refuge and a haven for the persecuted Jews of Spain and elsewhere, where they could pursue their daily lives in perfect freedom and equality.

Thus, one can leaf through the pages of Middle East history and survey many eras of civilization and still find the same story of mutual respect between Arabs and Jews. In the Holy Land, as elsewhere in Arab lands, they lived together in harmony, a harmony only disrupted when the Zionists began to claim that Palestine was the 'rightful' possession of the 'Jewish people' to the exclusion of its Moslem and Christian inhabitants. Before the advent of Zionism, an atmosphere of goodwill prevailed on all sides in the Holy Land. No community trespassed on the rights of another and each worshipped the One God in its own way.

The first signs of unrest between Arab and Jew occurred in 1920 when Zionist designs on the Holy Land became apparent. Riots broke out in Jerusalem on Easter Sunday in April of that year, as a result of which many people on both sides, who had until recently been living on the best of terms, lost their lives needlessly. This initiated the deterioration of Arab-Jewish relations. As Zionism pushed its mass immigration policy, started an extensive campaign of purchasing Arab lands and excluding Arab labour from orange groves and Jewish enterprises, relations between the two communities became more and more strained, erupting from time to time into bloody disturbances. There followed the riots of 1921, 1926; and in 1929, the most severe disturbances occurred throughout the country, resulting in much damage to property and loss of life. After that period, the Jews isolated themselves into separate areas and began to build up their underground forces to 'seize' the country in due time. From then on , there was little intercourse between the two communities as each drifted its own way, one to plan how to occupy the country, the other to make a feeble effort to defend what rightfully belongs to it .

Despite what happened in Palestine, the friendly relations existing between Arabs and Jews in other Arab countries have not been affected. Significant in this respect is the testimony of Gottfried Neubruger, a prominent member of the American Jewish community who visited the Arab world in 1960. One of the conclusions he drew from his visit was, "Arab anti-Zionism is about universal yet I feel," he said, "that it is a basic fallacy and a grave error to equate this with anti-Semitism." He added, "The majority of the population of such countries as Egypt, Tunisia and Morocco, where Jew and Moslem have long lived side by side, is intuitively friendly to Jews. This does not diminish the fact that those same Arabs are strongly hostile to Israel and are deeply suspicious of Israeli future aims and activities." [2]

British war pledges of Arab independence (1915 - 1916)

The World War I 'war aims' of the Allies in Arab territories, as explicitly expressed from time to time in a number of official declarations and pronouncements, were: ". . . guaranteeing their liberation and the development of their civilization"; to establish, "national governments and administrations deriving their authority from the initiative and the free choice of the native population"; to recognize Arab independence as soon as "effectively established"; and "to ensure impartial and equal justice to all, to facilitate the economic development of the country ... to foster the spread of education ..." [3].

Point XII of President Wilson's famous address of January 8, 1918, was devoted to the Ottoman Empire. The following is pertinent to Palestine: "The Turkish portions of the present Ottoman Empire should be assured a secure sovereignty, but the other nationalities which are under Turkish rule should be assured an undoubted security of life and an absolutely unmolested opportunity of autonomous development ..." [4].

With the outbreak of World War I, the Arabs saw their chance to rid themselves of Turkish domination and regain their political independence. Sherif Hussein of Mecca, as spokesman for the Arab cause, approached Sir Henry McMahon, British High Commissioner in Cairo, on 14 July 1915, offering Arab aid in the war against Turkey if Britain would, in return, pledge its support of Arab independence within a certain territory which he specified as "...bounded on the north by Mersina and Adana up to the 37° of lattitude, on which degree fall Birijik, Urfa, Mardin, Midiat, Jezirat (Ibn 'Umar), Amadia, up to the border of Persia; on the east by the borders of Persia up to the Gulf of Basra; on the south by the Indian Ocean, with the exception of the position of Aden to remain as it is; on the west by the Red sea, the Mediterranean Sea up to Mersina." [5].

A correspondence - later known as the Hussein-McMahon Correspondence - consisting of ten letters, was exchanged during the period July 1915 to March 1916, culminating in a British promise of Arab independence as follows :

> "The two districts of Mersina and Alexandretta and portions of Syria lying to the west of the districts of Damascus, Homs, Hama and Aleppo cannot be said to be purely Arab and should be excluded from the limits demanded.
>
> "With the above modification and without prejudice to our existing treaties with Arab chiefs, we accept those limits."

McMahon went on to say, "As for these regions lying within those frontiers wherein Great Britain is free to act without detriment to the interest of her ally France, I am empowered in the name of the Government of Great Britain to give the following assurances and make the following reply to your letter :

> "Subject to the above modifications, Great Britain is prepared to recognize and support the independence of the Arabs in all the regions within the limits demanded by the Sherif of Mecca."* [6].

* The British Government later contended that Palestine was *not* included in

Area of Arab independence as defined by Sherif Hussein in his letter dated 14 July 1915 to Sir Henry McMahon, British High Commissioner in Egypt.

Area of Arab independence as understood to have been excluded from the Sherif's proposal.

The Sykes-Picot Agreement (1916)

Before the ink was dry on the British pledge of Arab independence. the British Government was busy negotiating secretly with the French and Russian Governments for the division among themselves of the Asiatic provinces of the Ottoman Empire after victory.

The Agreement - named after the two main negotiators - roughly provided, in the Arab areas, for :

(a) an independent Arab state or a confederation of Arab States in a part of what is now geographically known as Saudi Arabia and Yemen ;

(b) France in Lebanon and Syria, and Britain in Iraq and Trans jordan, "to establish such direct or indirect administration or control as they may desire and as they may deem fit to establish after agreement with the Arab States or Confederation of Arab States;"

---

the British pledge of Arab independence and claimed that the area cited as being '*west* of the line Damascus, Homs, Hama, and Aleppo', was excluded.

A Committee was formed in 1939 to study the *Correspondence*. Sir Michael McDonnell, former Chief Justice of Palestine, expressed the opinion that "Palestine *was* included", otherwise why "speak of the districts of Damascus, Homs, Hama and Aleppo, not one of which is east of Palestine and all of which go northward in that order away from Palestine?" "Why say nothing," he enquired, "of the Sanjaqs of Hauran and Maan to the west of which the whole of Palestine lies? Why not," he continued, "if Palestine was to be described, speak of Lake Huleh, the River Jordan, the Lake of Tiberias and the Dead Sea as the eastern boundaries?"

Sir Michael then remarked, "To suggest that an area of the size of Palestine and of the importance of the Holy Land, if not excluded by the act that it did not lie west of the districts of Damascus, Homs, Hama and Aleppo, was intended to be excluded by a side wind by the reference to the interests of France which, at the very time, the British Government was refusing to admit, is an argument that will not hold water."

The Committee's findings were: "In the opinion of the Committee, it is, however, evident from these statements that His Majesty's Government were not free to dispose of Palestine without regard for the wishes and interests of the inhabitants of Palestine and that these statements must all be taken into account in any attempt to estimate the responsibilities which – upon any interpretation of the Correspondence – His Majesty's Government have incurred towards these inhabitants as a result of the Correspondence." [7]

(c) Parts of Palestine to be placed under "an international administration of which the form will be decided upon after consultation with Russia and after subsequent agreement with the other Allies and the representatives of the Sherif of Mecca." [8].

Analysing the provisions of the Agreement, George Antonius, an Arab authority on the subject, said of it: "What the Sykes-Picot Agreement did was, first, to cut up the Arab rectangle in such a manner as to place artificial obstacles in the way of unity ... Whatever gains the Allied Powers may have hoped to derive from the partition of that territory, it showed a lack of perspicacity on their part to have imagined that it could make for peaceful or a lasting settlement."

"Another pecularity of the Agreement," said Antonius, "was that it provided for a topsy-turvy political structure in which the first were to come last and the last first. The inhabitants of Syria and Iraq," he pointed out, "were politically more developed and mature than the inhabitants of the inland regions. Yet the Agreement provided that the greater part of Syria and Iraq might be placed under a regime of direct foreign administration, while the inland regions were in any case to form independent Arab States. The absurdity of these provisions is particularly evident in the case of the regions destined to form the British sphere of influence."

"But more serious even than those errors of judgment, was the breach of faith, Antonius added. "The Agreement," he said, "had been negotiated and concluded without the knowledge of the Sherif Hussein and it contained provisions which were in direct conflict with the terms of Sir Henry McMahon's compact with him. Worse still, the fact of its conclusion was dishonestly concealed from him because it was realized that, were he to have been apprised of it, he would have unhesitatingly denounced his alliance with Great Britain."

Antonius described the Agreement as "a shocking document", adding, "it is not only the product of greed at its worst, that is to say, of greed allied to suspicion and so leading to stupidity; it also stands out as a startling piece of double-dealing." [9].

Others also condemned the Agreement, but naturally for different reasons. Lord Curzon said of it: "When the Sykes-Picot Agreement was drawn up, it was, no doubt, intended by its authors ...as a sort of fancy sketch to suit a situation that had not then arisen and which it was thought extremely unlikely would ever arise; that, I suppose must be the principal explanation of the gross ignorance with which the boundary lines in that Agreement were drawn." [10]

Lloyd George, then Prime Minister, without whose approval the Agreement could not have been concluded, nevertheless described it as 'a foolish document' and thought it 'inexplicable that a man of Sir Mark Sykes' fine intelligence should ever have appended his signature to such an arrangement.' [11]

Yet, after victory was won, the Agreement was implemented to the letter!

The Balfour Declaration (1917)

Since 1897, when the Zionist movement was officially launched, Theodor Herzl and his collaborators were intent on the establishment of a Jewish state in Palestine. Herzl then declared: "Let the sovereignty be granted us over a portion of the globe large enough to satisfy the rightful requirements of a nation; the rest we shall manage for ourselves ..." [12]

The outbreak of World War I gave the Zionists their opportunity: 1916 was a disastrous year for the Allies: Losses on the Western Front were three men for every two German casualties, while German submarines were taking a heavy toll of Allied shipping. The Allies' only hope was for the United States to enter the War on their side.

Into this gloomy picture walked James Malcolm, an Oxford educated Armenian who had many contacts in high British circles. He was particularly friendly with Sir Mark Sykes of the Foreign Office. Sir Mark told him that the Cabinet was looking anxiously for U.S. Government intervention in the War. Malcolm replied: "You are going the wrong way about it . You can win sympathy of certain politically-minded Jews everywhere, and especially in the

United States, in one way only and that is, by offering to try and secure Palestine for them."[13].

From then things began to move. Louis Brandeis, U.S. Supreme Court Judge and a personal confidant of Woodrow Wilson, was influenced to win over the President; and in April 1917, the United States entered the war on the side of the Allies. On 2 November 1917, British Foreign Minister Arthur Balfour issued his ill-fated Declaration which now bears his name.

The part played by the Zionists in bringing the United States into the War has been referred to on many occasions. It is supported by the following admissions:

Winston Churchill -- "The Balfour Declaration must, therefore, not be regarded as a promise given from sentimental motives; it was a practical measure taken in the interests of a common cause at a moment when that cause could afford to neglect no factor of material or moral assistance."[14]

Lloyd George -- "There is no better proof of the value of the Balfour Declaration *as a military move* than the fact that Germany entered into negotiations with Turkey in an endeavour to provide an alternative scheme which would appeal to Zionists."[15] Appearing before the Palestine Royal (Peel) Commission in 1937, Lloyd George was more explicit as to the reasons which prompted his Government to grant the Balfour Declaration. Paragraph 16 of the Report has the following entry :

> "The Zionist leaders (Mr. Lloyd George informed us) gave us a definite promise that, if the Allies committed themselves to giving facilities for the establishment of a national home for the Jews in Palestine, they would do their best to rally Jewish sentiment and support throughout the world to the Allied cause. They kept their word."[16]

The text of the Balfour Declaration, issued on 2 November 1917[17] in the form of a letter addressed to Edmond de Rothschild, may be divided into three parts :

The *first*, applicable to the Jews, provided: "His Majesty's Government view with favour the establishment in Palestine of a national home for the Jewish people and will use their best endeavours to facilitate the achievement of this object."

The *second*, affecting the rights and position of the Moslem and Christian inhabitants, stipulated: "It being clearly understood that nothing shall be done which may prejudice the civil and religious rights of existing non-Jewish communities in Palestine."

The *third*, referring to the position of Jews outside Palestine, ruled: "The rights and political status enjoyed by Jews in any other country" shall not be prejudiced by ' the establishment in Palestine of a national home for the Jewish people.', This latter protective clause gave the Jews the homeland of another people while safeguarding their own rights in their countries of origin!

Reading through the *second* safeguarding clause, it will be observed that the Moslem and Christian inhabitants are mentioned in such a way as to give an entirely false picture of their position in the country and their indubitable right to it. Although constituting, in 1917, 92% of the population, they were referred to as "the existing non-Jewish communities of Palestine." This tended to give the erroneous impression that they were an insignificant minority occupying a position subordinate to the Jews. This clause, by purporting to protect the rights of the Arabs as "the existing non-Jewish communities", in reality aimed at robbing them in due course (as did actually happen) of their right to the country as owners and inhabitants.

But leaving aside this deception and looking at the implications of the safeguarding clause, there is only one possible inference that can be drawn from it and only one possible judgment that can be passed on it, namely, it was sufficient to nullify the rest of the Declaration. The British Government should have known that what the Zionists wanted would have constituted a disastrous encroachment on Arab rights in Palestine. In effect the British Government promised to help the Zionists achieve their aim, provided that nothing was done to enable them to achieve it !

Arabs re-assured of fulfilment of promises

The Arabs were unaware that the British Government, after

promising to support Arab independence, had concluded two secret agreements which conflicted with Arab aspirations - The Sykes-Picot Agreement, dividing Arab territories between Britain and France; and the Balfour Declaration signing away to the Jews Arab rights in Palestine. The texts of the two instruments were disclosed by the Bolsheviks on coming to power in 1917, and widely publicized by the Turkish military commander as a sign of British betrayal of pledges to the Arabs.

The disclosure caused great anxiety in Arab circles and the Sherif Hussein requested from the British Government an explanation. The assurances given at various times, while they remained to the Arabs unconvincing, they did not cease to carry out their fight against the Turks. These were :

(1) *The Hogarth Message* of January 1918 - An explicit assurance was given that "Jewish settlement in Palestine would only be allowed in so far as would be consistent with the political and economic freedom of the Arab population." [18] The phrase, 'the political and economic freedom of the population' is very significant in that it represented a fundamental departure from the text of the Balfour Declaration which purported to guarantee only the 'civil and religious rights' of the Arab population and, as will be readily seen, offered a guarantee of Arab independence and sovereignty which the phrase used in the Balfour Declaration did not.

(2) *The Bassett Letter* of 8 February 1918 - This was another reassurance that "His Majesty's Government and their allies remain steadfast to the policy of helping any movement which aims at setting free those nations which are oppressed ..." The letter went on to say, "The Government of His Britannic Majesty repeats its previous promise in respect of the freedom and the emancipation of the Arab peoples." [19]

(3) *The British Declaration to the Seven of 16 June 1918.* This declaration confirmed previous British pledges to the Arabs in plainer language than in former public utterances. The Declaration referred to the proclamations read in Baghdad and Jerusalem on March 19 and December 9, 1917, respectively and stated that these proclamations "define the policy of His Majesty's Government

towards the inhabitants ... which is that the future government ... should be based upon the principle of the consent of the governed. This policy will always be that of His Majesty's Government." [20]

(4) *The Anglo-French Declaration* of 9 November 1918 – If there had been any doubt in the minds of the Arabs, these were dispelled by this last Declaration: "France and Great Britain agree to further and assist in setting up indigenous governments and administrations in Syria (which then included Palestine) and Mesopotamia (Iraq)." [21]

Arab contribution in the war

With these assurances and affirmations, the Arab war against the Turks went on with greater vigour and determination.

The most important contribution of the Arabs in the war was the occupation on 6 July 1916 of the strategic town of Aqaba. Until then, the British army had been unable to cross the Suez Canal and to advance into the Sinai Peninsula. The British High Command were unaware of the Arab attack and occupation of Aqaba until T.E. Lawrence informed them during a subsquent visit to Cairo.

And what followed was no less significant. The Arab army continued to harass enemy lines of communication and to attack on all fronts along the Hejaz railway from Medina to Damascus. The extent of the Arab contribution to allied victory was summed up by Capt. Liddell Hart, Chief Military Commentator with the Allied Forces at the time. He wrote:

> "In the crucial weeks while Allenby's stroke was being prepared and during its delivery, nearly half of the Turkish forces south of Damascus were distracted by the Arab forces ... What the absence of these forces meant to the success of Allenby's stroke, it is easy to see. Nor did the Arab operation end when it had opened the way. For in the issue, it was the Arabs who almost entirely wiped out the Fourth Army, the still intact force that might have barred the way to final victory. The wear and tear, the bodily and mental

> strain on men and material applied by the Arabs... prepared the way that produced their (the Turks') defeat."[22]

The Arab peoples were unware at the time that the result of their participation in the Allied war was not to achieve for them the much sought for independence, but to change masters from Turkish to British and French, despite the latters' promises and pledges supplemented by the declared war aims of the United States. On 11 February 1918, President Wilson declared as essential to any peace settlement, "Peoples are not to be handed about from one sovereignty to another by an international conference or an understanding between rivals and antagonists." And on 4 July 1918, he said: "The settlement of every question, whether of territory, of sovereignty, of economic arrangement, or of political relationship, (be) upon the basis of the free acceptance of that settlement by the people concerned and not upon the basis of material interest or advantage of any other nation or people which may desire a different settlement for the sake of its own exterior influence or mastery."[23]

The Feisal-Weizmann Agreement

Zionists propagandized public opinion into believing that the Arabs at first were not against a Jewish national home in Palestine. They repeatedly quoted – and still do – that an Agreement had been reached between Chaim Weizmann, then head of the newly formed Zionist Organization and Emir Feisal, on behalf of the Arabs, to the effect that the latter had acquiesced in the establishment of a Jewish state in Palestine.

As in the Balfour Declaration, nowhere in the Feisal-Weizmann Agreement of January 1919 is there any mention of a 'Jewish state' in Palestine. The Agreement provided, among other things, for "cordial goodwill and understanding" between Arab and Jew and "to encourage and stimulate immigration of Jews into Palestine on a large scale and as quickly as possible to settle Jewish immigrants upon the land through closer settlement and intensive cultivation of the soil." The Agreement included a protective clause providing, "In taking such measures, the Arab peasant and tenant farmers shall be protected in their rights and shall be assisted in forwarding their economic development."

But the English text of the Agreement also included an all-important reservation written (in Arabic) in Feisal's own handwriting which has been either ignored or grossly misinterpreted. Feisal wrote:

> "Provided the Arabs obtain their independence as demanded in my memorandum dated the 4th of January 1919 to the Foreign Office of the Government of Great Britain, I shall concur in the above articles. But if the slightest modification or departure were to be made, I shall not then be bound by a single word of the present Agreement which shall be deemed void and of no account or validity and I shall not be answerable in any way whatsoever." [24]

No doubt Weizmann was able to secure this agreement from Feisal under promises that he would use his influence toward achieving the independence of all Arab territories (including Palestine) and in return Feisal agreed to immigration of Jews into Palestine. He certainly did not agree to turn Palestine over to the Jews or to establish a 'Jewish state' in Palestine. At any rate, the agreement was nullified by the very fact that Feisal did not achieve the independence he sought and the Palestine "Arab peasants and tenant farmers" were not "protected in their rights" as the agreement stipulated.

The King-Crane Commission

Following the signing of the Armistice and the failure of the appointment of the previously agreed upon Inter–Allied Commission to find out the wishes of the peoples who until then had been under Turkish domination, President Woodrow Wilson dispatched an all–American King–Crane Commission to Syria (including Lebanon and Palestine) to investigate. This Commission toured the area in June and July of 1919 and interviewed people from all sections of the population.

In its analysis of the situation, the King-Crane Commission, it said, was guided by the resolution of the *Council of Four* of 30 January 1919 and the Anglo-French Declaration of 9 November 1918. The first provided that the principle "that the well-being and development" of the peoples involved formed "a sacred trust of civilization and that securities for the performance of this trust shall be embodied in the constitution of the League of Nations" was to be applied. [25] The second document, provided in unequivocal terms for "the complete and definite freeing of the peoples so long oppressed by the Turks and the establishment of national governments and administrations deriving their authority from the initiative and the free choice of the native populations". [26]

For Palestine, the Commission recommended "serious modification of the extreme Zionist Programme for Palestine of unlimited immigration of Jews, looking finally to making Palestine distinctly a Jewish state."

The Commisioners explained that they "began their study of Zionism with minds predisposed in its favour, but the actual facts in Palestine, coupled with the force of the general principles proclaimed by the Allies and accepted by the Syrians have driven them to the recommendation here made."

The Commissioners pointed out that the Balfour Declaration "favouring 'the establishment in Palestine of a national home for the Jewish people', was not equivalent to making Palestine into a Jewish state; nor could the creation of such a state be accomplished without the gravest trespass upon the 'civil and religious rights of existing non-Jewish communities in Palestine'. This fact came out repeatedly in the Commission's conferences with Jewish representatives, that the Zionists looked forward to a practically complete dispossession of the present non-Jewish inhabitants of Palestine, by various forms of purchase."

The Commissioners then referred to President Wilson's address of July 4, 1918, which laid down the following principle as one of the four great 'ends for which the associated peoples of the world were fighting': "The settlement of every question, whether of territory, of sovereignty, of economic arrangement, or of political relationship on the basis of the free acceptance of that settlement by the people immediately concerned and not upon the basis of the material interest or advantage of any other nation or people which may desire a different settlement for the sake of its own exterior influence or mastery. The Tables show," the Commissioners went on to say, "that there was no one thing upon which the population of Palestine were more agreed than upon this. To subject a people so minded to unlimited Jewish immigration and to steady financial and social pressure to surrender the land, would be a gross violation of the principle just quoted, and of the peoples' rights, though it be kept within the forms of law."

The Commissioners then remarked that "the feeling against the Zionist programme is not confined to Palestine, but shared very generally by the people throughout Syria..."

"There is a further consideration," the Commissioners pointed out "that cannot justly be ignored, if the world is to look forward to Palestine becoming a definitely Jewish state, however gradually that may take place, that consideration grows out of the fact that Palestine is 'the Holy Land' for Jews, Christians and Moslems alike. One effect," they said, "of urging the extreme Zionist programme would be an intensification of anti-Jewish feeling both in Palestine and in all other portions of the world which look to Palestine as the Holy Land."

The Commissioners then recommended that "Jewish immigration should be definitely limited", that "the project for making Palestine a Jewish commonwealth should be given up," and that Palestine should be "included in a united Syrian state, just as other portions of the country ..." [27]

III | *Palestine and the Jews*

The 'divine promise'

The Zionist claim to Palestine is primarily based on ancient *Biblical Promises* of four thousand years ago that God promised Abraham that "unto thy seed have I given this land . . ." and that the words 'seed of Abraham' mean only those who today are, by religion, *Jews*, whether or not they are the physical descendants of Abraham.

The supreme tragedy in the Palestine controversy is that Christianity's precepts of brotherly love, charity, human dignity and justice have all been desecrated in the face of a gross misinterpretation of the Holy Bible. Certain church leaders – some with good intentions, others out of ignorance – have fallen prey to Zionist propaganda and influence, believing that by lending their religious support to Zionist political ambitions in Palestine, they would be fulfilling the 'Will of God' and bringing closer the second coming of the Messiah. They misinterpreted the Holy Scriptures and used their pulpits to sway their congregations in favour of the Zionist Movement.

A number of authorities in the Old and New Testaments, both Christian and Jewish, who observed this exploitation of Holy Scriptures, felt concern over the dangers which such misinterpretation held for the basic principles of the Christian and Jewish faiths. They, therefore, took it upon themselves to provide, individually and in their own words, an accurate religious interpretation of the *Divine Promise* to show Christians and Jews the true way. Here is what these scholars and theologians had to say:

Dr. Alfred Guillaume, Professor of Old Testament Studies at the University of London and author of various works on the Old Testament, states: "The first explicit promise of Palestine to the descendants of Abraham was at Shechem (now Nablus) in

Genesis 12:7 – 'Unto thy seed will I give this land.' Chapter 13:15, when Abraham is standing on a hill near Bethel, has the words: 'All the land which thou seest to thee will I give it and to thy seed for ever.' Chapter 15:18 is more explicit – 'Unto thy seed have I given this land, from the river of Egypt unto the great river, the river Euphrates'!"

Guillaume explains that it is "generally supposed that these promises were made to the Jews and to the Jews alone. But, he points out, "that is not what the Bible says. The words 'to thy seed' inevitably include Arabs, both Muslims and Christians, who claim descent from Abraham through his son Ishmael. Ishmael was the reputed father of a large number of Arab tribes and Genesis records that Abraham became the father of many north Arabian tribes through his concubine Keturah. It cannot be argued," he adds, "that the words of Genesis 21:10–12 necessarily cancel the promise made to Abraham's seed as a whole: '(Sarah) said to Abraham, cast out this bondwoman and her son; for the son of this bondwoman shall not be heir with my son Isaac. And the thing was very grievous in Abraham's sight on account of his son. And God said unto Abraham: Let it not be grievous in thy sight because of the lad and because of thy bondwoman; in all that Sarah saith unto thee hearken unto her voice: for in Isaac shall seed be called unto thee. And also of the son of the bondwoman will I make a nation, *because he is thy seed'.*"

It should be noted that when Abraham made a covenant with God through circumcision (Chapter 17:8) and all the land of Canaan was promised to him as 'an everlasting possession', *it was Ishmael who was circumcised; Isaac had not then been born.*

Professor Guillaume goes on to remark, "It is true that henceforth among the descendants of Isaac 'the seed of Abraham' was taken to mean the Israelites; but from the beginning it was not so and *the descendants of Ishmael had every right to call and consider themselves of the seed of Abraham.*"

On the question of whether the 'Promise' was not irrevocable, Guillaume explains that "there never was an unconditional promise of an everlasting possession; though a long and indefinite period was intended ...." He added: "Had we no prophetic messages to guide us, it will be apparent that these promises of possession of the land of Canaan were not unconditional: the covenant relation between Israel and God demanded loyalty from the people, and individual and corporate righteousness. Were the people to fail in these respects, a terrible doom awaited them. The following words spoken by Moses in the 28th Chapter of Deutoronomy apply in parts so easily to the sufferings of Jewry in the past few years that many have seen in them a prophecy of our own times:

> 'It shall come to pass if thou wilt not hearken unto the voice of the Lord they God to observe to do all his commandments and his statutes which I command thee this day; that all those curses shall come upon thee and shall overtake thee...And the Lord shall scatter thee among the peoples, from the one end of the earth even unto the other end of the earth; and there thou shalt serve other gods, which thou hast not known, thou nor thy fathers, even wood and stone. And amongst these nations shalt thou find no ease and there shall be no rest for the sole of thy foot; but the Lord shall give thee there a trembling heart and failing of eyes and pining of souls; and thy life shall hang in doubt before thee.....'"

"It is clear," Guillaume concludes, "that the divine promises to the patriarchs have been annulled by the national apostasy; and when the Assyrian captivity removed the population of Samaria, and the Babylonian captivity of the people of Judah, the prophets saw in the disasters a vindication of the divine justice on a disobedient and gain-saying people. But they taught their people that a remnant would return ... The Jews did return to Judea, they did rebuild the walls of Jerusalem and they did rebuild the temple; and after fluctuating fortunes, they did secure a brief period of political independence and expansion under the Maccabees. Thus the prophecies of the *Return* have been fulfilled, and they *cannot* be fulfilled again. Within the canonical literature of the Old Testament, there is no prophecy of a second return after the return from the Babylonian exile, because:

(i) After the Exile all the Jews who wished to do so had returned to the Holy Land, though a great many more preferred to remain where they were and they formed the *Diaspora* which afterwards became the backbone of the Christian Church; and

(ii) the last of the prophets died centuries before the destruction of Jerusalem in A.D. 70." [1]

Dr. William H. Stinespring, Professor of New Testament and Semitics at Duke University, North Carolina and a Minister in the Presbyterian Church, explains, "there is no basis in either Old or New Testament to support the claim of the Zionists that a modern Jewish state in Palestine is justified or demanded by the Bible or by Biblical prophecy. The 'promises' of Biblical prophecy," he said, "apply to all mankind, and not only to Jews or Zionists; that such terms as 'victory' and 'salvation', in their true Biblical meaning, connote religious and spiritual achievements and not the conquest or degradation of political enemies; and, more specifically, that such terms as 'Israel', 'the new Israel' or 'the Israel of God', in the New Testament apply to the Ideal Christian Church, or to a body of true believers in the religious sense."

Dr. Stinespring goes on to point out, "the evidence is overwhelming that no true Christian, believing in the New Testament, could possibly confuse the modern Israel, brought into being by political machination and military power accompanied by ruthless deprivation of the native inhabitants, with the Israel of God of Christian faith. These two Israels contradict one another completely," Stinespring emphasized.

Dr. Stinespring concludes his study by saying, "Even without the specific statements of the New Testament with regard to the spiritual and religious nature of the promises to Israel, the Old Testament alone in its truest sense and in the hands of its truest interpreters, pointed to a *spiritual* kingdom for all mankind and not to a *political* Israel that occupies territory and homes belonging naturally to another people and reduces some of its inhabitants to second-class citizenship. Moreover, Judaism, like Christianity", he said, "has had a continuous history since Biblical times; and the best insights of this continuing tradition also lead towards an *Israel of the spirit and not of the flesh.*" [2]

Dr. Ovid R. Sellers, former Professor of Old Testament and Dean of McCormick Theological Seminary and Minister in the United Presbyterian Church, is another source which disproves the Zionist claim that the establishment of the state of Israel was in fulfillment of Biblical prophecy. He states: "From its beginning the Christian Church kept the Old Testament as its sacred literature. This was because the Christians believed that their religion was not something entirely new, but a fulfillment of the old. The Ten Commandments still were in effect and the prophecies of a coming Messiah had been fulfilled in Jesus Christ. Early Christian missionaries, particularly Paul, taught that a Gentile by accepting Christ could become heir to the promises made to Israel. 'For in Christ neither circumcision availeth anything, nor uncircumcision, but a new creature. And as many as walk according to this rule, peace be on them and mercy, and upon the Israel of God' (Galatians 6:15–16). This Israel of God, according to Paul, was the community of all believers," Dr. Sellers added.

Dr. Sellers concludes, "a Christian, relying on Christian Scripture, can think of Israel not as a geographical, ethnical, or political unit, but as the body of all believers, 'the Israel of God'." [3]

Dr. Frank Stagg, Professor of New Testament at the Southern Baptist Theological Seminary in New Orleans, arrives at the same conclusions as his colleagues and ends up by pointing out that "to identify modern Israel, the state or the Jewish people, with the 'Israel of God' is to miss the teaching of the New Testament at one of its most vital points." [4]

The Right Reverend Jonathan G. Sherman, Suffragan Bishop of the Episcopal Diocese of Long Island, New York, points out, "The history of Israel demonstrates that God is not primarily concerned with Israel's military conquests or geographical security or economic prosperity: the prophets' predictions are fulfilled when Israel is destroyed as a nation in 722 B.C. and when Judah is driven into exile in 586 B.C. What then? What God is interested in, say the prophets, is a relationship with Israel grounded in God's righteousness, justice and mercy, a relationship between God and man that involves at every point a right relationship between man and man." The Bishop concludes his Study with the statement, "In the Old Covenant God promised to the children of Israel military victory over their enemies in order that they might enter into the land flowing with milk and honey on the condition of Israel's obedience to his commandments. Israel failed to keep the covenant and so forfeited the promises of God. But God promised a New Covenant, to be written not on tables of stone but in the hearts of his people (Jeremiah 31:31–33; Corinthians 3.2f). Of this New Covenant Jesus is the mediator (Hebrews 8:6–13; 9:15). In place of victory over human enemies Jesus gives us victory over sin and death (I Corinthians 15:55–57). In place of the land of Canaan He gives us His kingdom (St. Luke 12:32). In place of milk and honey He gives us the fruit of the Spirit – love and joy and peace and forgiveness. Verily, 'in Him all the promises of God are Yes'!" (II Corinthians 1:20). [5]

Dr. Elmer Berger, a gifted rabbi, and an author of many books on Judaism, came to the same conclusions as did his Christian counterparts. He added, "no Orthodox Jew believes the present state of Israel has come into being in a process which fulfills the injunctions of the Old Testament. There are Orthodox Jews," he said, "who actually repudiate the present Israeli sovereignty as a profanation of the Biblical texts. This attitude is most vigorously and dramatically represented in precisely that part of the state of Israel where the most traditional Judaism is observed – the Mea Shearim quarter of the City of Jerusalem. Here lives the *Netora Karta* who regard the present state of Israel as a subversive phenomenon to their faith and who, themselves, indulge in frequent acts of defiance of the governmental authority of the state of Israel. There are less well known but equally convinced followers of the same position among the Orthodox Jews of the United States. These groups, at times, have made representations to the United Nations. They are particularly agitated over the claims to the New City of Jerusalem advanced by the state of Israel. They prefer internationalization of a Jerusalem once again uniting the old and the new cities."

"This attitude," Rabbi Berger points out, "cannot necessarily be equated with an anti-Israel position, although there are those in these groups who do oppose the present state and who agree it came about, not through fulfillment of the Word of God, but as a result of the secular-political activities of Zionism. It cannot, therefore, be a fulfillment of Old Testament prophecy; and it does not represent, for these people, the Pessianic dream. They regard Israel as a secular state, devoid of Zion."

Rabbi Berger concludes by stating, "The most charitable construction which can be put upon the state of Israel therefore, in the context of considering its Biblical legitimacy, is that through methods having no sanction in the Bible at all, a political sovereignty has been established. In a majority population of Jews, a minority is still engaged in a furious, *political* battle to compel the State to adopt a character which *could* be equated with the Biblical prophecies. The equating is *not* accomplished today. The fulfillment is not even remotely near realization. Neither the process which gave birth to Israel nor the result, in the form of the state itself, can – by any theory with the integrity which is central to all genuine religions – be regarded as justified by the magnificent ethical and religious declarations of the spiritual giants whose words are immortalized in Scripture." [6]

The findings of these distinguished scholars in religion leave no doubt that the Zionist claim to Palestine is neither correct nor legitimate. Besides, one can go a step further to prove the absurdity of the Zionist claim: Nowhere is the notion found that being a Jew is synonymous with physical descent from Abraham. Many Jews in history have been converts from other stock. There were the Black Jews of Malabar, and the Falashas of Ethiopia. The current political leaders of Israel, as well as the Jewish immigrants who hail from Central Europe, Poland, Russia and the United States, are mostly of Khazar extraction, descendants of Caucasian Russians whom Byzantine Jews converted to Judaism in the mid-Eighth century.

Palestine may be associated with those who today profess the

Jewish religion, but this association is only spiritual, not physical. Sir Edwin S. Montagu, Secretary of State for India in the Lloyd George Cabinet which approved the Balfour Declaration in 1917, told his Christian colleagues at the time, as a Jew, "I deny that Palestine is today associated with the Jews . . . It is quite true," he said, "that Palestine plays a large part in Jewish history, but so it does in modern Mohammedan history and, after the time of the Jews, surely it plays a larger part than any other country in Christian history. The Temple," he pointed out, "may have been in Palestine, but so was the Sermon on the Mount and the Crucifixion."

Sir Edwin warned, "Zionism has always seemed to me to be a mischievous political creed, untenable by any patriotic citizen of the United Kingdom. If a Jewish Englishman," he said, "sets his eyes on the Mount of Olives and longs for the day when he will shake British soil from his shoes and go back to agricultural pursuits in Palestine, he has always seemed to me to have acknowledged aims inconsistent with British citizenship and to have admitted that he is unfit for a share in public life in Great Britain, or to be treated as an Englishman."

Montagu then asserted, with emphasis, "there is not a Jewish nation." He referred to members of his own family, whom, he said, had been in the country for generations, as having "no sort or kind of community or views or of desire with any Jewish family in any other country beyond the fact that they profess to a greater or less degree the same religion. It is no more true," he pointed out, "to say that a Jewish Englishman and a Jewish Moor are of the same nation than it is to say that a Christian Englishman and a Christian Frenchman are of the same nation." [7]

Are present-day Jews descendants of the early Hebrews ?

Significantly, in this respect, Harry L. Shapiro, Chairman of the Department of Anthropology at the American Museum of Natural History, states, in a study of the biological history of the *Jewish people*, that the Jews "are not a clan, a tribe, or in a strict sense, a nation." After briefly tracing their history, Dr. Shapiro declares: "It is odd, in the light of their past, that the Jews are often considered and much effort expended to prove them to be a distinct race ... These (biological) comparisons ... prove that the fundamental requirement for any claim that the Jews form a racial entity cannot be met, at least by those traditional standards of racial classification ... The wide range of variation between Jewish populations in their physical characteristics and the diversity of the gene frequence of their blood groups, render any unified racial classification for them a contradiction in terms." [8]

Another distinguished anthropologist dispels 'the myth of the Jewish race.' Professor Juan Comas of the National University of Mexico, comments, "though the idea of 'racialism' evokes in most a negative response, it is curious how the idea survives, because various groups find it useful. Zionist Jews, for example, speak constantly of a 'Jewish people', with distinct racist-like overtones, by which they mean a continuity not only of history but of blood, culture and destiny as well. Such an approach," he points out, "is the more remarkable after the terrible treatment their co-religionists in Germany endured in the name of racialism. They do so," he presumed, "to justify their establishment of a 'homeland' in Israel, and to strengthen the ties with and the support from, Jews by religion in other countries."

Professor Comas then explains, "The anthropological fact is that Jews are racially heterogeneous and there is no foundation for the claim that there is a Jewish race. Their constant migrations through history and their relations - voluntary or otherwise - with the widest variety of nations and peoples have brought about such a degree of cross-breeding that the so-called people of Israel can produce examples of traits typical of every people. For proof, it will suffice to compare the rubicond, sturdy, heavily-built Rotterdam Jew with his co-religionist, say in Salonika with gleaming eyes in a sickly face and skinny, high-strung physique ..."

Comas then classifies the Jews, according to origin, into the following separate groups :

(a) Descendants of Jewish emigrants from Palestine (very few);

(b) descendants of unions between Jews of mixed Asiatic descent or between Jews and other groups, who might be called cross-crossbreeds;

(c) Jews by religion but having anthropologically no connection whatsoever with the Jews of Palestine and consisting simply of individuals of other human strains converted to the Hebrew religion.

Under the last classification, he gives as 'a typical example' Bulan, King of the Khazars, converted to Judaism in A.D. 740 with many of his nobles and peoples.

In support of his argument, Professor Comas points out that in Germany, between 1921 and 1925, for every 100 Jewish marriages, there were 58 all-Jewish and 42 mixed. In Berlin, in 1926, there were 861 all-Jewish marriages and 554 mixed. He then states, "the figures speak for themselves, especially if we take into account the large number of partners who became Jews by religion although there was nothing 'Semitic' about them."

One further proof he cites in support of his argument is, "49 per cent of Polish Jews are light-haired and 51 per cent dark-haired, while there are only 32 per cent of blonds among German Jews and 30 per cent of the Jews of Vienna have light coloured eyes. The hooked nose, which seems so typically Jewish occurs in 44 per cent only of the individuals of certain groups while straight noses are found in 40 per cent, the so-called 'roman' nose in 9 per cent and tip-tilted in 7 per cent."

To confirm his analysis, Professor Comas solicits the views of two other authorities on the subject: R.N. Salman says, "The purity of the Jewish race is imaginary; the widest variety of ethnic types is found among Jews ranging, as regard cranial conformation only, from brachycephalics (broadheaded) to hyperdolichocephalics (longheaded). More particularly, in Germany and Russia, there are Jews who do not display the smallest Semitic characteristics."

To this, M. Fishberg adds: "The percentage of light-eyed blonds and their irregular distribution in the various centres of Jewish population, the extreme variability of the cranial index – at least as great as that observable between any of the peoples of

Europe – the existence among Jews of negroid, monoloid and teutonic types, the variations in stature, etc., are other proofs of the non-existence of one Semitic race unmodified since Biblical times..." Fishberg concludes, "The claims of Jews to purity of descent are so vain and baseless as the allegations of a radical difference between Jews and the so-called Aryan race on which anti-semitism is based." [9]

One further point in support of this argument is that the Jews' own definition of 'who is a Jew' has always been, "a Jew is the son of a Jewish mother, or, alternately, is a person who has been accepted into Judaism through the recognized process of proselytization." [10]

But on the emergence of the Jewish state, the question of 'who is a Jew today' created quite a problem for the Israelis. Jewish immigration – particularly from Poland – brought in "a high proportion of mixed marriages, i.e., marriages in which one of the couples maintained a non–Jewish identity." In most cases, it was pointed out, "the non–Jewish partner was the mother and hence the offspring, by Jewish law, was non–Jewish."[11]

It is, therefore, a sheer fallacy to say that the descendants of Jews of all lands are of one blood and that they are related to the early Hebrews and, as such, 'heirs according to the promise'. The absurdity of the Zionist claim and the accuracy of the findings of the distinguished anthropologists – if further proof is needed – is best illustrated – to quote one example – in the case of United States negro actor Sammy Davis Jr. who embraced Judaism some years ago. According to Zionist logic, as legislated in the Israeli *Status Law* and *Law of the Return,* Davis is considered to be now living in 'exile' in his homeland America, pining for the day to return 'home' to Palestine! Ironically, while a total stranger in language, colour, culture and race can acquire a right to go to Palestine by merely adopting Judaism, the Moslem and Christian inhabitants of the Holy Land – whose physical descent from Abraham can hardly be questioned – if the 'Biblical' promises have any legitimacy in the

20th century at all – are denied the right to live in the country of their birth!

If Christians can, in the face of all these facts still regard the Zionist claim to Palestine as conforming to Biblical prophecies, to the exclusion of its Moslem and Christian inhabitants, then it is suggested that Christ's coming and His Supreme Sacrifice on the Cross to save humanity was in vain and Christianity has, apparently, no heavenly purpose to fulfill. It is indeed inconceivable that a Christian born and reared in Palestine, is not regarded as an 'heir according to the Promise' and must forego his home and homeland to make room for an alien people who are known to have no physical connection whatever with Palestine and who have renounced Christ.

Zionism's 'historical' claim

Another angle of the Zionist claim to Palestine is that the early Hebrews (or Israelites) were in previous occupation of the land.

The only real title which any people has to its country comes from *birth and long and continued possession*. It is these that give the British their right to Britain, the French their right to France and the Americans their right to America. This is a criterion which the common accèptance of mankind has set up as a universal principle. It is recognized as the basis of the integrity and security of all nations and no just international order can be established in the world today on any other foundation.

If such a formula can apply to a new country like America with its only four-hundred and fifty years of history, how much sounder in comparison is the right of the Palestine Arabs to their country which dates back to the dawn of history? The Palestine Arabs of today – Moslems and Christians – are not, as is popularly believed, all exclusively the descendants of the Islamic desert conquerors of 1300 years ago; they are, in fact, mainly the descendants of the original native population – Philistines, Canaanites, etc. They were there when the early Hebrews invaded the land in about 1,500 B.C., survived the Israelite occupation, retained possession of a large part of the country throughout the Israelite period and remained in the country after the Hebrew 'dispersion', to be intermingled first with the Arabs in the seventh century, then with the Crusaders in the 11th Century and continued the occupation of the land in their new arabized character until the Zionist invasion in 1948.

The historical connection of the early Hebrews (or Israelites) with Palestine is not one based on *birth* and *long possession* – as is the case with the Palestine Arabs – but upon *occupation through invasion.* The duration of this occupation is little known; a brief description is given below:

1. In the second millenium B.C., a Semite tribe invaded the East coast of the Mediterranean. Its members became known as Hebrews and later as Israelites since they claimed descent from Abraham through his son Jacob, otherwise known as Israel.
2. Their tradition has it that they migrated to Egypt and eventually were led back by Moses.
3. By 1100 B.C., they had conquered most of the hill-country of Palestine and had done so with the ferocity common to all early conquerors.
4. There was much disunion among them, until the hostility of the Philistines – the original inhabitants of the country – forced them into solidarity and led them to establish a monarchy, first under David (1010–970 B.C.), then under Solomon (970–930 B.C.) who managed to enlarge his territory. But his death ushered the Hebrews' decline.
5. Soon the kingdom was divided into two, which were sometimes at war with each other: In the North, the Kingdom of Israel centered around Samaria; in the South, the Kingdom of Judah.
6. Between 721 and 715 B.C., the northern Kingdom was incorporated into Assyria, and the southern one acknowledged Assyrian suzerainty.
7. In 585 B.C., the new Babylonian Empire under Nebuchadnezzar sacked Jerusalem and took many of its people into captivity to Babylon.

8. In 539 B.C., Cyrus occupied Babylon and freed the Jews, of whom some 40,000 returned to Palestine, the larger part choosing to remain in Babylon.
9. Under the Persians then the Ptolemies, Jewish recorded history is obscure, although modern scholars claim that the period saw the flowering of Hebrew culture.
10. When the Greeks tried to impose their gods, the Hebrews revolted and from about 150 B.C. onwards they recovered most of what Solomon had once ruled.
11. But in 63 B.C., Pompey stormed Jerusalem, and Palestine became virtually a Roman province. There were several revolts, but in A.D., 135 the Romans put an end to Jewish Palestine by destroying Jerusalem.

Such at best is the connection of the early Hebrews (or Israelites) with Palestine. It was short–lived, unstable, intermittent, long extinct, based on nothing better than the right of conquest and subject to the condition that there should have been national or racial affinity between the Hebrews of 4,000 years ago and the Russian, Polish, American and European Jews of today.

If this transitory occupation can give the Zionists a 'historic right' to the country, then it may be argued that the Arabs, who occupied Spain continuously for 800 years, could claim that country today, while the Italians could claim the British Isles and the Red Indians demand the withdrawal from the Americas of all those who settled in the Western hemisphere and now call themselves Americans, Canadians and Latin Americans. If all nations were to adopt this strange Zionist logic, the world would be in utter chaos.

The so-called 'miracle of Israel's restoration' in 1948 was not according to God's Will as the Zionists and some misguided Christians would have the world believe, but as a very un-Christlike human international crime against the Moslem and Christian inhabitants of the Holy Land. It is sheer irony to talk of Jewish aliens 'coming home' to a land they had never seen and taking it from the population who have been born and live there. If the restoration had 'overtones of the eternal', it was of eternal human frailty, not of Divine power.

That such un-Christian treatment of the Moslem and Christian inhabitants should have occurred in the Holy Land unopposed, under the cloak of religion, is bad enough; that it should have happened in a land held sacred by the world's three great religions, is distressing. All Christianity must decry such injustices and the subsequent discriminatory closing of the Holy Land to Moslem and Christian Arabs. It is the responsibility of churches and religious organizations, to educate their members in the true interpretation of Holy Scriptures; they should apprise them of the deplorable situation and its causes; and work toward righting of the wrongs done to a suffering people before the problem imperils world peace and christianity becomes a mockery.

Sir John Bagot Glubb, who was Officer Commanding the Arab Legion in Jordan until 1956, inserted in the Epilogue to his book *A Soldier with the Arabs*, this reminder to the world: "In the land – which has been caused so much suffering and bloodshed during the past forty years – sprang the three great religions of mankind – Judaism, Christianity and Islam. This little country," Glubb Pasha pointed out, "has done more to bring the human race to God than have all the continents by which it is surrounded."[12]

If the world feels it owes nothing to the people of the Holy Land, it should owe it at least to its own conscience and to the land which gave birth to Our Lord and the Prophets. What is required is for all men and women of goodwill to weigh their responsibilities as good Christians and Jews and to resist Zionist attempts to use them to serve their political motives in the erroneous belief that they would be fulfilling the 'Will of God'. Such slogans as 'Biblical prophecies' and 'historic rights' have brought much suffering to human beings and will eventually lead to greater disaster. It is therefore the solemn duty of every conscientious human being – individually and collectively – to fight distortion of God's Holy Word; to expose those who do so for material gains; and to impress upon their political leaders, governments, and congregations the need for 'peace with justice' in the Holy Land. It is only in this way that they will be pleasing God and fulfilling His Will.

IV The Zionist Movement

Principles and Objectives

The basic issue in the Palestine question is the uprooting and dispossession of an entire nation in order to make room for the 'ingathering' in Palestine of Jews from all parts of the world. Whereas some of these Jews may have been victims of terror and injustice, nonetheless, they are being used as pawns in the political programme of Jewish nationalism. The building up of a Jewish population in Palestine was not inspired purely by humanitarian considerations, but achieved principally in order to fulfill the political aspirations of a major ideological movement – Zionism.

The Zionist movement which began in the nineteenth century, took official shape in 1897 with the holding of the First Zionist Congress in Basle, Switzerland. The leader of the movement was Theodor Herzl, an Austrian lawyer, who died in 1904.

The aims of the movement, as formulated by that first Congress, were:

> "Zionism strives to create for the Jewish people a home in Palestine secured by public law. The congress contemplates the following means to the attainment of this end:
> 1. The promotion on suitable lines of the colonization of Palestine by Jewish agricultural and industrial workers.
> 2. The organization and binding together of the whole of Jewry by means of appropriate institutions, local and international, in accordance with the laws of each country.
> 3. The strengthening and fostering of Jewish national sentiment and consciousness.
> 4. Preparatory steps towards obtaining Government consent where necessary to the attainment of the aim of Zionism." [1]

Zionism, as a political philosophy, preaches that the Jews are one people and one nation requiring their own land, to which all Jews must eventually return. Zionism thus spurns the concept of religious fellowship and seeks to endow them with national attributes. For those Jews who choose not to be 'ingathered', Zionism attempts to thwart their civic, cultural and social integration in lands outside of Israel, in order to attach them to a common 'nationhood' of Jews. It seeks the deepening of a *Jewish* national consciousness for strengthening the economic, political and cultural ties that bind world Jewry to the sovereign national center in Israel. Thus, while Christians and Moslems live in many nations and owe allegiance to various flags, Jews, according to Zionist dogma, are only *one* nation. Though they live in many countries, they are considered to be in the *Diaspora* ('exile'), and are supposed to be longing to live in *Eretz Israel* (Palestine) alone.

Zionists have always recognized that, in order to attain their primary goal of 'ingathering' all Jews in their own 'homeland', two campaigns will have to be successfully waged: one, the creation of a legal-political entity known as 'the Jewish people'; the other, recognition of this 'Jewish people' concept in international law.

Judaism versus Zionism

Many people make the simple mistake in believing that Judaism and Zionism are the same. This is not so. *Judaism* is a religion of universal values. Jews are regarded as members of a religious fellowship, who have no national or ethnic ties with their co-religionists of other lands. In the countries of their citizenship, Jews, like Christians and Moslems, have national ties with their fellow-citizens, irrespective of their religious faith. *Zionism*, on the other hand, is an international political movement which aspires to link all Jews, by means of ethnic, nationalistic bonds into a world-wide nation, a peoplehood, having as its political and cultural centre the state of Israel.

Commenting in 1944 on the effect of Zionism on Jewish interests, Professor William E. Hocking, said, he believes "political Zionists are the chief enemies of the Jewish interest in the world of tomorrow." He enquires, "What can they hope to gain by extricating their brethern from the prejudices of Europe only to build a community in Palestine which has to be protected by Western force because it is cradled in an environment of sedulously cultivated distrust and fear." [2]

Recognition of Zionism

In 1917, the British Government became the first Power to recognize 'the Jewish people', in granting the World Zionist Organization the Balfour Declaration. To be sure, even then, British and American anti-Zionist Jews saw in the Declaration a danger to their own security, and forced the inclusion of a safeguard clause, designed to protect the "rights and political status enjoyed by Jews in any other country" (outside Palestine). And in 1924, the United States Government, in accepting the British Mandate over Palestine in a Covenant signed with Britain, supported the incorporation of the safeguard clause in the entire Declaration.

Thus, the stage was set for Zionist exploitation of these and other formal documents. The safeguard clause was blithely disregarded, while emphasis was placed, whenever and wherever possible, on a legal–political relationship for all Jews, through the Jewish Agency for Palestine, with Zionism acting as a public body and internationally recognized as spokesman for a legal-political entity known as 'the Jewish people'. As time passed, the world appears to have accepted this Zionist formula, while those Jews who opposed it became fewer and weaker.

Zionist-Israeli condominium

In 1948, the new state of Israel legislated 'the Jewish people' concept into legal form. The *Law of Return* and the *Nationality Act* granted "every Jew ... certain rights." In 1952, the Israeli Parliament enacted the *Status Law*, which defined the tasks assigned to Zionism throughout the world and inside Israel, as a quasi-governmental agent of the state of Israel. These 'tasks' were set forth in 1954 in a 'Covenant' signed by the Israeli Government and the World Zionist Organization.[3] The Statute and Covenant legally directed the World Zionist Organization to do for the state of Israel, beyond its own boundaries, what the state neither can nor may do itself. These include: exertion of political pressure on governments,* the financing and recruiting of mass emigration to Israel, conducting and directing propaganda on behalf of Israel** in times of crisis, etc.

The connection between Israel and the World Zionist Organization was reiterated in 1959 by a new government coming to power and further strengthened on March 15, 1964, when a communiqué was signed. The Prime Minister explained that the purpose of the communiqué was to bolster Zionist programmes which were in the 'vital interest' of his Government. The purpose, he said, was the classic Zionist goal of 'conquering the communities' of Jews in the areas outside Israel.

The Israeli judiciary as well advances the concept of 'the Jewish people'. In the Eichmann Trial Judgements, the Supreme Court stated that the state of Israel is recognized in international law as the 'sovereign state of the Jewish people'.

The Israeli Government persistently uses international or domestic events to deepen its claim of legal-political linkage with all Jews. For example, in 1959 and 1960, when 'swastika' markings appeared in many countries, Israel took upon itself the responsibility to send formal notes to some twenty governments, including the United States, expressing concern for the safety of their citizens of the Jewish faith. The Israeli attitude was criticized in certain Jewish circles in England as 'interference in the internal affairs of British Jewry'. To this former Foreign Minister Mrs. Golda Meir retorted, "Israel is determined not to yield the right to speak on any Jewish subject. If there are Jews abroad who find themselves

---

* For the methods and extent of Zionist pressure groups on the U.S. Government, see Senator William Fulbrights' statement before the Senate on April 29, 1960.[4]

** See the Investigation of the Foreign Relations Committee into the activities of the Zionist Organization of America.[5]

embarrassed by this attitude, let them be embarrassed," Mrs. Meir added.[6]

On 15 March 1964, the Israeli Cabinet and the Jewish Agency Executive held a joint session and issued a 'communiqué' in which they expressed their joint concern for the 'enhancement of the Zionist spirit in Jewish life.' At this meeting, the 1954 'Covenant' was ratified which included the 'Basic Principle of Government Programme' approved by the Israeli Parliament on 17 December 1959.

Paragraph 59 of this 'Programme', entitled *Chapter VII: Ties with Jewry and the Zionist Movement,* provides, among other things, for "the fight against all signs of assimilation (of Jews in their countries of origin) and denial of Jewish peoplehood."[7]

This unique racist provision, which attempts to block the integration of the Jews of different countries in their respective gentile communities, was attacked by Dr. Elmer Berger, Executive Vice-President of the American Council for Judaism, who said: "What is incomprehensible, illogical, absurd, is that the state of Israel, with seeming impunity, is permitted to operate part of its government in the United States, in direct impact upon United States citizens and in support of this conflicting policy. What is further incomprehensible, illogical and absurd is that the United States Government leaves United States citizens vulnerable to exploitation by the foreign sovereignty for extracting funds and political support to operate the machine and program which is admittedly designed to persuade these Americans to support the policy of the foreign state and ultimately to expatriate themselves."[8]

Relationship of Israel to World Jewry

David Ben Gurion, the architect of the 'Jewish state', outlined the relationship of world Jewry to Israel as follows:

> "On the world scene and in the Middle East, Israel's endeavours must be the same – military and moral, but its destiny depends wholly upon the third domain,

the Jewish people in all its dispersion. The state of Israel is a part of the Middle East only in geography, which is, in the main, a static element. From the more decisive standpoints of dynamism, creation and growth, Israel is a part of world Jewry. From that Jewry it will draw all the resources and the means necessary for the upbuilding of the nation of Israel and the development of the Land; through the might of world Jewry it will be built and built again. A community of destiny and destination joins together indissolubly the state of Israel and the Jewish people. There is an indestructible bond, a bond of life and death between them."[9]

Addressing the 25th World Zionist Congress in the Israeli-occupied part of Jerusalem in January 1961, David Ben Gurion told his audience that "Since the day the Jewish state was established and the gates of Israel were flung open to every Jew who wanted to come, every religious Jew has daily violated the precepts of Judaism and the Torah of Israel by remaining in the *Diaspora*." He denounced all Jews outside of Israel as 'godless'. [10]

Later, speaking before the Israeli Parliament, he said: "Being an American and being a Jew are two different things. I know of only one Zionist in America whom I would call a Zionist and I will not give his name. He does not think of himself as an American. He thinks of himself only as a Jew." [11] And on another occasion, Ben Gurion said: "When a Jew in America or South Africa speaks of 'our government' to his fellow Jews, he usually means the government of Israel, while the Jewish public in various countries view the Israeli ambassador as their own representative." [12]

Nahum Goldmann, President of the World Zionist Organization, was no less emphatic on the relationship between world Jewry and Israel. Speaking before the 25th Zionist Congress, he said:

"*Diaspora* Jewry must have the courage to proclaim and defend its relationship of partnership and responsibility *vis-a-vis* Israel. It has to overcome the conscious or subconscious fear of so-called double loyalty. It has to be convinced that it is fully justified in tying up its destiny with Israel's. It has to have the courage to

> reject the idea that Jewish communities owe loyalty to the states where they live." [13]

In March 1961, Dr. Goldmann is quoted as having said: "To allow people many loyalities was the essence of democracy. To demand a single loyalty was Nazism." [14]

Jewish opposition to Zionism

The American Council for Judaism, an anti–Zionist Organization, protested to the U.S. Government Israel's self–appointed role of speaking for the Jews of the United States. After four years of private discussion, the U.S. Department of State, in a letter dated 20 April 1964, finally made its stand clear by informing the Council that "It does not recognize a legal–political relationship based upon the religious identification of American citizens. It does not in any way discriminate among American citizens upon the basis of their religion. Accordingly, it should be clear that the Department of State does not regard the 'Jewish people' concept as a concept of international law." [15]

This statement has been interpreted as separating Zionism from the state of Israel; limiting Israel's sovereignty to its own legal citizens and nationals; shifting U.S. policy from acquiescence, or seeming acquiescence, to outright rejection of the 'Jewish people' claim; stamping Zionist-Israel claims as being inconsistent with the fundamental constitutional rights of U.S. citizens; and initiating a step which might have significance in the interpretation of international law.

The statement might have had some value if it had been addressed to the Israeli Government in the form of a protest against Israeli legislation involving American citizens; also American Zionists should have been reminded by their Government that the 'Covenant' they signed with the Israeli leaders was in conflict with their responsibilities as American citizens. Instead, the statement remained a 'dead letter'; and Zionist activities in the United States in behalf of Israel did not diminish, even where these activities are detrimental to U.S. interests in the Middle East. On the contrary, evidence is abundant that they have been stepped up with greater participation of the White House, the Government and policy-makers.

Arab rejection of Zionism

The entry of individual Jews into Palestine was never questioned by the Arabs prior to the advent of Zionism, beyond the normal investigations conducted with respect to aliens seeking to settle in any country. Jews were expected to integrate and share in the responsibilities, rights and privileges of citizenship. But when the Zionists attempted in the early part of this century to obtain possession of the country through bribery and the offer of generous advantages, this was resisted by the Ottoman Sultan on the grounds that it was detrimental to the interests of the Arab population.

The fundamental reason for Arab opposition to Zionism is based upon the fact that the Moslem and Christian inhabitants of the country could not be expected to yield to an ideology which sought to wrest – as later events proved – their homeland from them. The Arabs rejected absolutely and unanimously any attempt to destroy the Arab character of Palestine. They still do. The Arabs claim the right of a population to decide the fate of the country which they had occupied throughout history. To them it is obvious that this right of immemorial possession is inalienable; and that it could not be over-ruled either by the circumstances that Palestine had been governed by the Ottomans for 400 years, or that Britain had conquered the land during World War I, or that a 'Jewish state' has been established in part of it by brute force.

Zionism and anti-Semitism

An impression existed at one time that "Zionism would diminish anti-Semitism in the world. We are witness to the opposite," declared Dr. Judah Magnes, the late President of the Hebrew University in Jerusalem. [16]

There is a principle which has guided enquiries into crimes

and disturbances from Roman times to the present day. The Romans asked *Cui bono?* For whose benefit is it? And today, detectives will start an investigation by determining who stood to benefit from a crime. We may therefore consider: Who derives the most advantage from anti–Semitism? Do the Arabs? the Jews? or the Zionists?

The Arabs have nothing to gain and much to lose from anti-Semitic practices. Firstly, were it not for Hitler's inhuman policy of racial discrimination and persecution, the Jews of Europe would never have left their homes in significant numbers; the Palestine tragedy would not have occurred; and the present tension and instability in the Middle East would not have arisen. Secondly, the aims of the anti-Semites run contrary to Arab interests and security. Anti-Semitic practices mean insecurity for Jews in their countries of origin, inducing greater immigration to Palestine, thereby creating a population problem in that country and the inevitable need for territorial expansion. Such conditions can only aggravate the Arab-Israeli conflict still further; make it more difficult for the Palestine Arabs to regain their homes peacefully; and increase conflict in the Middle East.

But the Zionists have much to gain and nothing to lose from the creation of a feeling of insecurity among world Jewry. Without the constant threat of anti-Semitism there could be no Zionism; Jewish immigration to Israel would diminish if not cease altogether; Israel would lose the colossal financial aid it now receives from United States and world Jewry; and the 'Jewish state' would cease to became the nationalist empire and fulcrum for international political influence and economic control envisaged by the Zionists.

The close relationship between Zionism and anti-Semitism was commented upon by British historian Arnold Toynbee in May 1961. Speaking at the annual meeting of the American Council for Judaism in Philadelphia, Toynbee stated: "Zionism and anti-Semitism are expressions of an identical point of view. The assumption underlying both ideologies is that it is impossible for Jews and non-Jews to grow together into a single community and that therefore a physical separation is the only practical way out.

The watchword of anti-Semistism," he said "is 'Back to medieval apartheid'; the watchword of Zionism is 'Back to the medieval ghetto'. All the far-flung ghettos in the world are to be gathered into one patch of soil in Palestine to create a single consolidated ghetto there," Toynbee concluded. [17]

The Zionist smear of anti-Semitism is being used extensively and indiscriminately against all those who disagree with Zionist policy. An American citizen, in a letter to the press, complained that he was "weary of being labelled an anti-Semite for expressing views about the foreign state of Israel which are contrary to those of 'American' Zionists. Do the concepts of 'brotherhood' and 'tolerance'", he asks, "apply only in one direction? I suspect," he said, "it is the threat of being called anti-Semitic by the very vocal Zionists which prevents American politicians from objectively debating the issues of American foreign policy *vis-a-vis* the Middle East." [18]

Anti-Semitism is being used by the Zionist movement as a double-edged weapon: On the one hand, it serves to silence any person who opposes Zionism and Israeli policy; on the other hand, it is used to discourage Jews from becoming assimilated into the lives of the countries of their origin.

Commenting on the first point, Professor David Riesman, of Harvard University, said: "The Zionists can muster not merely the threat of the Jewish vote and the no less important Jewish financial and organizational skills, but also the blackmail of attacking anyone who opposes their political aims for Israel as an anti-Semite." [19]

On the question of assimilation, Dr. Nahum Goldman, President of the World Zionist Organization, in a speech he delivered on 23 July 1958 at the opening of the World Jewish Congress in Geneva, Switzerland, is reported by the *New York Times* to have warned world Jewry that "a current decline of overt anti-Semitism might constitute a new danger to Jewish survival ... Jews nearly everywhere are equal citizens, both politically and economically," Goldman said. "However," he asserted, "the disappearance of anti-Semitism in its classical meaning, while beneficial to the political and material situation of Jewish communities, has had a very negative effect on our internal life . . ." [20]

Another expression of the values of anti-Semitism as a deterrent to Jewish assimilation, comes from a report from the Israeli-occupied sector of Jerusalem. Speaking before the Zionist General Council held in January 1966, Rabbi Mordechai Kershblum, of New York, stressed the importance of fighting assimilation. "I always fear," the Rabbi said, "lest the anti-Semites have adopted a new method. Instead of torture and persecution, they say, 'Give them peace and they will disappear of their own accord'." [21]

Perhaps the most important exploitation of anti-Semitism, as a device to achieve Zionist ends, was revealed in an article in *Davar,* the official organ of the Socialist Labour (*Mapai*) Party, the newspaper of Israel's governing party. Editor Sharun wrote: "I shall not be ashamed to confess that, if I had the power as I have the will, I would select a score of efficient young men – intelligent, decent, devoted to our ideal and burning with desire to help redeem Jews – and I would send them to the countries where Jews are absorbed in sinful self-satisfaction, plague these Jews with anti-Semitic slogans, such as 'Bloody Jew', 'Jew go to Palestine' and similar intimacies. I can vouch that the results, in terms of considerable immigration to Israel from these countries, would be ten thousand times larger than the results brought by thousands of emissaries who have been preaching for decades to deaf ears." [22]

The aims of the Zionist movement, apart from 'ingathering' the Jews of the world into the Palestine area, are to 'shake-down' Jews who do not go to Israel for contributions toward its support, solicit United States and United Nations assistance to Israel and promote the idea of Israel as the representative and guardian of the rights and interests of Jews wherever they may be. The letters of protest sent by the Israeli Government to the more than twenty states where 'swastikas' appeared and the Adolph Eichmann trial, indicate the role which the 'Jewish state' has assigned to itself. Israel speaks out on behalf of world Jewry, defends the interests of all Jews, whether they seek it or not.

The pro-Zionist Kimche brothers wrote that it was the Hitlerite catastrophe that gave post-war Zionism "a moral argument to which the Gentile world could have no answer"; and that when the British Navy turned immigrant ships away from the Palestine coast in the 1940s, it gave "the Jews a great moral weapon." [23]

Commenting, author Erskine H. Childers, wrote, "one of the most massively important features of the entire Palestine struggle was that Zionism deliberately arranged that the plight of the wretched survivors of Hitlerism should be a 'moral argument' which the West had to accept. This was done by seeing to it that Western countries did not open their doors, widely and immediately, to the inmates of the DP. (displaced persons) camps." "it is incredible," Childers continued, "that so grave and grim a campaign has received so little attention in accounts of the Palestine struggle – it was a campaign that literally shaped all subsequent history. It was done by sabotaging specific Western schemes to admit Jewish DPs," [24] for when President Roosevelt, during the war, was considering the feasibility of helping Jewish refugees to settle in America and elsewhere, his plan, which would have absorbed all the DPs of Europe, was scotched by Zionists, not by anti-Semites. [25]

Speaking at the Sixth Annual National Conference of the American Council for Judaism, Morris L. Ernst revealed the extent of opposition to the efforts of President Roosevelt "to give relief to the people pushed around by Hitler." Mr. Ernst disclosed that as the representative of the President, he was "thrown out of parlours of friends of mine" when he discussed with them his plan of relief for DPs, who very frankly warned him: "Morris, this is treason – you're undermining the Zionist movement," to which he replied : "Yes, maybe I am. But I'm much more interested in a haven for a half a million or a million people – oppressed throughout the world." [26]

Childers then stated: "With the West's doors thus closed, the salvation of the DPs was presented to the world solely, desperately and morally as lying in and through a Jewish state in Palestine. Creaking ships were loaded with DPs and sent to Palestine in the certain knowledge that they would be turned back; but, as the

Kimches obliquely admit, the very turning-back would add a 'moral weapon' to the already prepared 'moral argument'."

Childers went on to say: "The very basis of the post-war Palestine struggle was an appeal to the world's humanitarianism over a situation deliberately designed to canalize that humane instinct into one premise: Jewish statehood in Palestine." He added: "None of us who remember the emotional atmosphere of the time can dismiss the role this Zionist campaign played in all that followed. The evidence of the campaign, though suppressed by Zionists and conveniently forgotten by Western liberals who knew about it, is overwhelming. It is detailed in White House conversations. It was publicly acknowledged, for example, by Sulzberger of the *New York Times*, who asked in 1946, 'In God's name why should the fate of all these unhappy people be subordinated to the single cry of Statehood'? " [27]

Richard Crossman, the champion of the Zionist cause on the Anglo-American Committee of Inquiry, writing in his 1946 Washington Diary, said: "The Zionists are terrific . . . their main preoccupation is not to save Jews alive out of Europe but to get Jews into Palestine and to establish a Jewish state." [28]

This discriminatory policy was again made clear in 1959, when Jews were allowed to leave Rumania. Those who signed to go to Israel were assisted in every way; those who elected to resettle in other countries, were not only refused the assistance of the United Jewish Appeal funds collected for needy Jews, but were made to refund money given for travel between Rumania and Austria.

A shocking disclosure of Zionist opposition to Jewish immigration to the U.S.A. was made in an article published in the May 1959 issue of *Unser Tzait*, a monthly publication of the Jewish Labour Bund, entitled 'A Secret Document about Rumanian Jews'. The document was a transcript of the minutes of a meeting held by the Presidents' Conference on 25 February 1959, at which the question of Jewish emigration from Rumania was discussed. The Presidents' Conference – an organization consisting of the heads of nineteen leading Zionist and pro-Zionist bodies in the United States, organized by the Jewish Agency for Israel to exert political pressure on the American Government in favour of Israel – met to formulate opposition to measures favouring the admission of Rumanian Jews into the United States. Nothing was to obstruct their immigration to Israel. The Presidents' Conference also sought to persuade Senator Jacob K. Javits of New York not to introduce an immigration bill which would admit some Rumanian immigrants to the United States as refugees. [29]

Another exposure of Zionist methods this time concerning Arab countries appeared in an article by Ian Gilmour, who said: "Since the basis of Zionism is that Jewish assimilation in other countries is in the long run impossible and that anti-Semitism and persecution are bound to break out sooner or later, Zionism has almost a vested interest in racial discrimination. The Israelis mount 'rescue operations' to save allegedly threatened Jews in other countries. . . ." He added: "In the Arab countries, Jewish difficulties and emigration to Israel were the result not of anti-Semitism but of Zionist activities and the existence of the state of Israel. Zionism aggravated the disease that it professed to cure," [30] he remarked.

V | *Palestine under Mandate (1920-1948)*

The Mandate System

Fighting with the Turks was ended by the Armistice of 30 October 1918; and on 30 January 1919, the Supreme Council of the Peace Conference decided that the conquered Arab provinces, including Palestine, were not to be restored to Turkish rule. To circumvent the fulfilment of their promises of Arab independence, and to implement the secret Sykes-Picot Agreement of 1916, the Allied Powers devised what became known as the mandate system. This turned out to be disguised colonialism.

On 28 June 1919, the Treaty of Versailles and the Covenant of the newly established League of Nations were signed. Article 22 of the Covenant provided, "To those colonies and territories which as a consequence of the late war have ceased to be under the sovereignty of the States which formerly governed them and which are inhabited by peoples not yet able to stand by themselves under the strenuous conditions of the modern world, there should be applied the principle that the well-being and development of such peoples form a sacred trust of civilization and that securities for the performance of this trust be embodied in this Covenant. The best method of giving practical effect to this principle", the Covenant went on to say, "is that the tutelage of such peoples should be entrusted to advanced nations ... and that this tutelage should be exercised by them as mandatories on behalf of the League."

In regard to "certain communities formerly belonging to the Turkish Empire, (which) have reached a stage of development.. their existence as separate nations can be provisionally recognized subject to the rendering of administrative advice and assistance by a Mandatory until such time as they are able to stand alone. The wishes of these communities," the Covenant stressed, "must be a principal consideration in the selection of the Mandatory."[1]

A draft Mandate for Palestine was submitted by Britain to the Council of the League of Nations on 24 July 1922 and an agreed text was not confirmed by the Council until 29 September 1923 when it came formally into operation.

The Mandate included in the *Preamble* a text of the Balfour Declaration providing for the establishment of a Jewish national home with safeguards for the 'non-Jewish communities' and Jews outside Palestine; in *Article 2*, responsibility "for placing the country under such political, administrative and economic conditions as will secure the establishment of the Jewish national home"; in *Article 4*, provision was made for a 'Jewish Agency' to be recognized "as a public body for the purpose of advising and cooperating with the Administration of Palestine in such economic, social and other matters as may affect the establishment of the Jewish-national home"; and in *Article 11*, the Administration was authorized to arrange with the Jewish Agency "to construct or operate, upon fair and equitable terms, any public works, services and utilities, and to develop any of the natural resources of the country."[2]

The Mandate failed to recognize the principles stipulated in *Article 22* of the Covenant of the League of Nations, namely, that Palestine – like Lebanon, Syria and Iraq – by reason of "the geographical situation of its territory, its economic conditions and other similar circumstances," had reached a stage of development where its existence as a nation "can be provisionally recognized subject to the rendering of administrative advice and assistance by a Mandatory until such time as (the inhabitants) are able to stand alone." Nor did the Mandate take into account the pledges of independence made previously to the Arabs by the Allies.

This failure can only be explained by the fact that, as in the case of the Balfour Declaration, the Arabs were not consulted in the preparation of the Mandate. The Mandate, which ostensibly at least, contained two sets of obligations to be undertaken by Britain – one towards the Jews and the other towards the Arabs – was drawn up jointly by the British Government and the Zionists without regard to the rights of the third party. The Zionists believed that they, and they alone, have rights in Palestine and that the presence of the Moslem and Christian inhabitants was a passing phase.

The first interference by the Zionists in the administration of the country occurred in 1919 when it was still under military occupation. On his arrival in Jerusalem in July of that year, U.S. Court Judge Louis Brandeis – who was instrumental in obtaining the Balfour Declaration in return for bringing the United States into the War on the side of the Allies – visited British Military Headquarters on the Mount of Olives in Jerusalem. He is reported to have told General Louis Bols, the Chief Administrator, that "ordinances of the military authorities should be submitted first to the Zionist Commission." The General's Aide-de-Camp is purported to have replied: "For a government to do that would be to derogate its position. As a lawyer you realize this." But Brandeis proceeded to lay down the law as he saw it almost as if Palestine were under his jurisdiction. "It must be understood," he warned, "the British Government is committed to the support of the Zionist cause. Unless this is accepted as a guiding principle, I shall have to report it to the Foreign Office." [3]

Apparently this was too much for General Bols to take. In March 1920, he complained to London, "my own authority and that of every department of my Administration is claimed or impinged upon by the Zionist Commission and I am definitely of opinion that this state of affairs cannot continue without grave danger to the public peace and to the prejudice of my Administration."

Sir Louis then warned, "It is no use saying to the Moslem and Christian elements of the population that our declaration as to the maintenance of the *status quo* on our entry into Jerusalem has been observed. Facts witnesss otherwise: The introduction of the Hebrew tongue as an official language; the setting-up of a Jewish judicature; the whole fabric of government of the Zionist Commission, of which they are well aware; the special travelling privileges to members of the Zionist Commission; these have firmly and absolutely convinced the non-Jewish elements of our partiality. On the other hand, the Zionist Commission accuses me and my officers of anti-Zionism. The situation is intolerable, and in justice to my officers and myself, must be fairly faced."

The Chief Administrator then pointed out, "It is manifestly impossible to please partisans who officially claim nothing more than a 'National Home' but in reality will be satisfied with nothing less than a Jewish state and all that it politically implies." [4]

Civil Administration established

On 1 July 1920, a civil administration was established in Palestine; and the first officials to arrive in the country included British Zionist Jews who were placed in key positions. Some of these were: Herbert Samuel, one of the framers of the Balfour Declaration and a scion of the Zionist movement – High Commissioner; Norman Bentwich, Attorney General and chief legislator of Palestine laws; Albert Hyamson, Director of Immigration; and Max Nurock, Principal Assistant Secretary to the Government with access to all matters pertaining to policy in Palestine.

One of the early actions of this consortium was to enact the first Immigration Ordinance on 26 August 1920, fixing a quota of 16,500 immigrant Jews for the first year.

Other legislation followed – all designed to further the 'Jewish national home' policy, as if the British Government had no obligations to the Arab section of the community. Significant among these, next to the Immigration Law, were laws affecting land disposition, registration and settlement, to hasten Jewish acquisition of Arab land. One of these laws – disguised as a law to protect cultivators against eviction by their landlords – had the opposite effect, ostensibly because almost all of the large tracts of land were owned by absentee land-owners living in Lebanon and Syria. Whereas relations between landlord and tenant had until then been on the best of terms, the new law gave the tenant the impression (and this was encouraged by Jewish land brokers) that he no longer needed to pay his rentals since the law gave him certain 'tenancy rights' and protected him against eviction. Even 'squatters' were soon able to establish 'tenancy rights' under certain

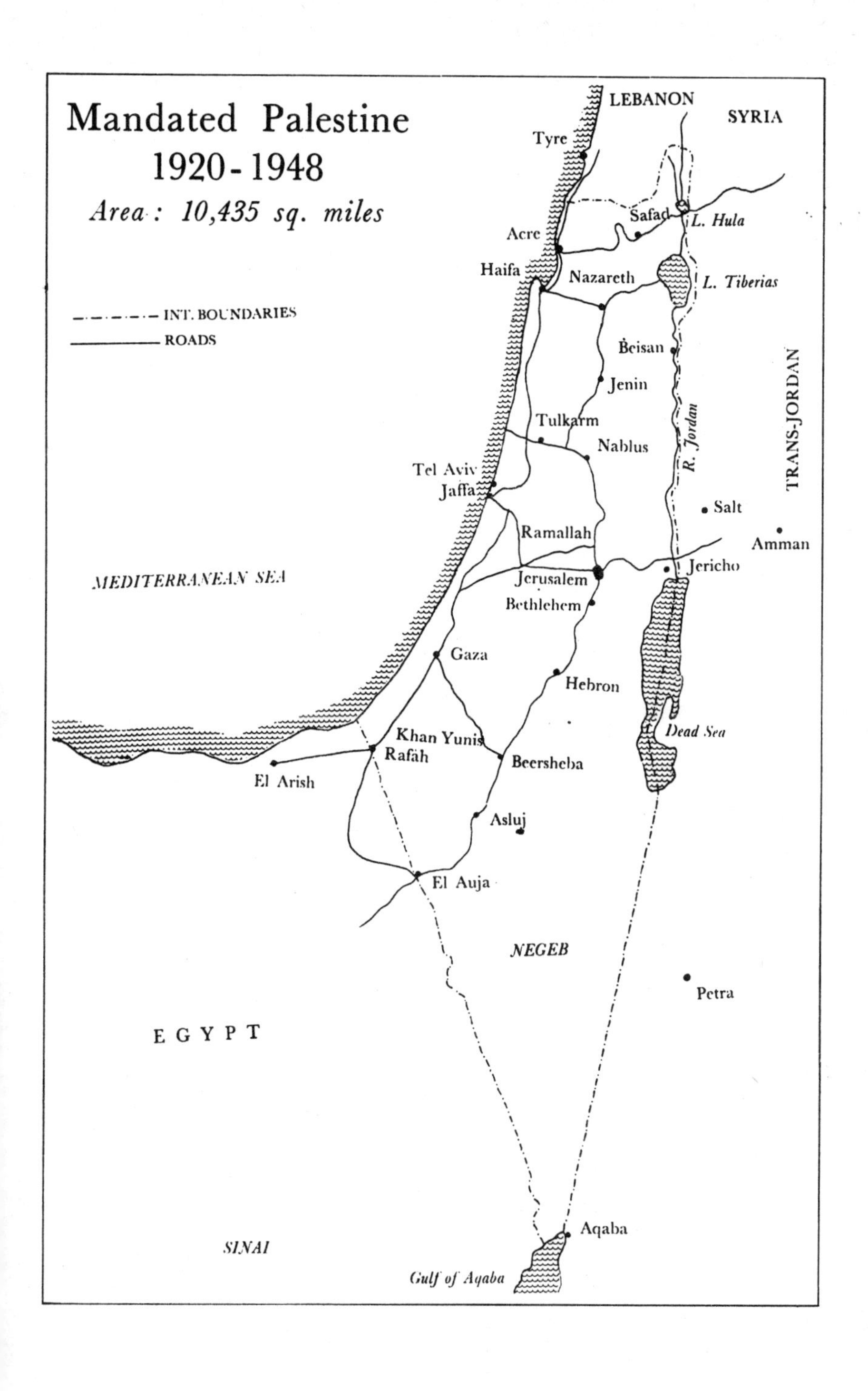
Mandated Palestine
1920-1948
Area: 10,435 sq. miles
INT. BOUNDARIES
ROADS
LEBANON
SYRIA
Tyre
Safad
L. Hula
Acre
Haifa
Nazareth
L. Tiberias
Beisan
Jenin
Tulkarm
Nablus
R. Jordan
TRANS-JORDAN
Tel Aviv
Jaffa
Salt
Ramallah
Amman
Jericho
MEDITERRANEAN SEA
Jerusalem
Bethlehem
Gaza
Hebron
Khan Yunis
Rafah
Dead Sea
Beersheba
El Arish
Asluj
El Auja
NEGEB
Petra
EGYPT
Aqaba
SINAI
Gulf of Aqaba

ambiguously worded provisions of the law. The landlord, placed in the unenviable position of owning land but getting hardly anything out of it, and burdened with taxation beyond his means, found himself in a critical situation. Here is where the Jewish land broker stepped in and offered to buy the land and rid the landlord of his problems. In one instance, over 40,000 acres, comprising 18 villages were sold, resulting in the eviction of 688 Arab agricultural families. Of these 309 families joined the landless classes, while the remainder drifted either into towns and cities or became hired ploughmen and labourers in other villages. Although eviction took place in 1922, the problem remained with the Palestine Government to find land for some of these displaced persons until the termination of the Mandate in 1948.

Other measures favouring Jews were the granting to Jewish companies of concessions over state lands and the natural resources of the country, such as irrigation, electricity and the extraction of potash and other minerals from the Dead Sea.

Faced with its dual and incompatible obligations under the Mandate, and with Arab insistence that the establishment of a Jewish national home was itself an infringement of their rights, the British Government adopted two lines of policy: The *first* was to try to interpret the concept of a national home in such a way as to reassure the Arabs that it did not imply a Jewish state. The Government denied that it was the intention of His Majesty's Government to help in the establishment of anything more than a national home as a centre in which the Jews of the world could take an interest and a pride. Yet all the signs indicated that a 'Jewish state' was envisaged as soon as the Jews became a majority, or at least a sizable minority capable of taking over: The *second* line of policy was that the Government lived from 1922 in the hope that sooner or later the Arabs would give up their opposition to Zionism and become reconciled with the Jewish national home policy. Although the development of self-governing institutions was enjoined in the Mandate, in practice it was deliberately postponed because the Arab majority was known to be opposed to the other provisions of the Mandate. If genuine self-government was established immediately while the Arab majority was inflexibly opposed to Zionism, that would make impossible the fulfilment of British obligations to the Zionists. If, however, its establishment were postponed for some time, then the Arabs might be reconciled to Zionist settlement and representative institutions could thus be established without any danger of a conflict.

Ironically, the majority was to be denied the right of controlling its political destiny until it should change its policy in deference to the will of the minority, or until the minority had itself become a majority !

Arab opposition to Mandate

Arab opposition to the Mandate and the policy of the Balfour Declaration remained obstinate and unrelenting throughout the period of the Mandate.

When appeals, protests, arguments, demonstrations and strikes failed to move the British Government to fulfil its pledges to the Arabs and follow a policy of justice and equity, the Palestine Arabs resorted from time to time to violence. The first violent expression of Arab feeling occurred on Easter Sunday in April 1920; the second in May 1921; the third in August 1929; and between 1936 and 1939, an allout rebellion broke out which was preceded by an unprecedented six-months strike.

Four principal commissions of enquiry were appointed directly as a result of the riots.* Their findings were invariably the same, namely,

(a) Arab disappointment at the non-fulfilment of the promises of independence which had been given to them during the First World War; and

(b) Arab belief that the Balfour Declaration implied a denial of the right of self-determination and their fear that the

* The *Palin* Commission of 1920; [5]
The *Haycraft* Commission of 1921; [6]
The *Shaw* Commission of 1930; [7]
The Royal (*Peel*) Commission of 1937; [8]

establishment of 'a national home for the Jews' in Palestine will lead to their ultimate dispossession of their homes and homeland.

The Zionists made no secret of their intentions, for as early as 1921, Dr. Eder, a member of the Zionist Commission, 'boldly told the Court of Enquiry', "there can be only one National Home in Palestine, and that a Jewish one, and no equality in the partnership between Jews and Arabs, but a Jewish preponderance as soon as the numbers of the race are sufficiently increased." [9] He then asked that only Jews should be allowed to bear arms.

British 'Statements of Policy'

The Commissions of Enquiry which were appointed to establish the causes for the riots were each followed by the issue of a 'Statement of Policy', each attempting to interpret the meaning of 'a national home'.

On 3 June 1922, the British Government issued what became known as 'The Churchill Memorandum' stating that "Phrases have been used such as that 'Palestine is to become as Jewish as England is English'." The Statement went to point out that "His Majesty's Government regard any such expectation as impracticable and have no such aim in view. Nor have they at any time contemplated ... the disappearance or the subordination of the Arabic population, language or culture in Palestine. They would draw attention to the fact that the terms of the (Balfour) Declaration referred to do not contemplate that Palestine as a whole should be converted into a Jewish National Home, but that such a Home should be founded in Palestine." [10]

Although the White Paper repudiated the idea of Jewish domination over the Arabs, it established a principle for the regulation of immigration which would in time make such domination possible if not inevitable. Moreover, it was no more than a statement of formal principles and did not take into account one of the essential facts of the situation: that although the British Government might lay down a general policy which respected the idea of a dual obligation, the Zionists were so much better organized than the Arabs and had so many more ways of putting pressure upon the Government both from within Palestine and through outside Governments and organizations through the privileged status of the Jewish Agency, and in other ways, that they could always tilt the balance in their favour. While the Arabs were not reassured by statements of principle which failed to face the implications of incessant immigration and of Zionist influence, yet they still hoped that a change of British policy to ensure justice for their Arab wards would in time take place.

The riots of 1929 were followed by yet another pronouncement. This took the form of a White Paper which became known as 'The Passfield Memoradum'. In view of the importance of this second 'Statement', it is reproduced at greater length:

> "Many of the misunderstandings which have unhappily arisen on both sides appear to be the result of a failure to appreciate the nature of the duty imposed upon His Majesty's Government by the terms of the Mandate. The next point therefore which His Majesty's Government feel it necessary to emphasize, in the strongest manner possible, is that in the words of the Prime Minister's statement in the House of Commons on the 3rd April last, 'a double undertaking is involved, to the Jewish people on the one hand and to the non-Jewish population on the other'."

And again:

> "These points are emphasized because claims have been made on behalf of the Jewish Agency to a position in regard to the general administration of the country which His Majesty's Government cannot but regard as going far beyond the clear intention of the Mandate. Moreover, attempts have been made to argue, in support of Zionist claims, that the principal feature of the Mandate is the passages regarding the Jewish national home, and that the passages designed to safeguard the rights of the non-Jewish community are merely secondary considerations, qualifying, to some extent, what is claimed to be the primary object for which the Mandate has been framed.
>
> This is a conception which H.M.G. have always

regarded as totally erroneous. However difficult the task may be, it would, in their view, be impossible, consistently with the plain intention of the Mandate, to attempt to solve the problem by subordinating one of these obligations to the other. The British accredited representative, when appearing before the Permanent Mandates Commission on the 9th June last, endeavoured to make clear the attitude of H.M.G. towards the difficulties inherent in the Mandate. In commenting on his statements in their report to the Council the Permanent Mandates Commission made the following important pronouncement:

> 'From all these statements, two assertions emerge, which should be emphasized:
>
> (1) That the obligations laid down by the Mandate in regard to the two sections of the population are of equal weight;
>
> (2) That the two obligations imposed on the Mandatory are in no sense irreconcilable.
>
> The Mandate Commission has no objection to rise to these two assertions which, in its view, accurately express what it conceives to be the essence of the Mandate for Palestine and ensure its future'." [11]

The Arabs, who had never recognized the legality of the Mandate imposed upon them without their consent, could not subscribe to the thesis that the two obligations contained in it were of equal weight. The Zionists proffered a *claim* to Palestine based on questionable ancient biblical and historical theories which the Arabs resisted and continue to resist; the Arabs, on the other hand, have a *right* to Palestine based on *birth* and *uninterrupted possession.*

As a result of the 1936–1939 Arab rebellion, the British Government, on 17 May 1939, issued yet another but final 'Statement of Policy' which became known as 'The MacDonald White Paper'. After referring to the terms of the Mandate, the 'Statement' pointed out, "the Royal Commission and previous Commissions of Enquiry have drawn attention to the ambiguity of certain expressions in the Mandate, such as the expression 'a national home for the Jewish people', and they have found in this ambiguity and the resulting uncertainty as to the objectives of policy a fundamental cause of unrest and hostility between Arabs and Jews." The Government was convinced that, in the interests of peace and well-being of the whole people of Palestine, a clear definition of policy and objectives was essential. Consequently, the British Government declared that neither their undertakings to the Jews nor the national interests of Britain warranted that they should continue to develop the Jewish national home beyond the point already reached. The Government therefore decided:

1. That the Jewish National Home as envisaged in the Balfour Declaration and in previous statements of British policy had been established;
2. That to develop it further against Arab wishes would be a violation of Britain's undertakings to the Arabs, and that such a policy could only be carried out by the use of unjustifiable force;
3. That, therefore, after the admission of a final quota of 75,000 more Jewish immigrants over a period of five years, Jewish immigration should stop;
4. That during this period of five years, a restriction should be placed on the acquisition of further land in Palestine by the Jews; and
5. That at the end of the period of five years, self-governing institutions should be set up in the country. [12]

Arab and Jewish reaction to 1939 White Paper

Arab reaction to the new policy of the 1939 White Paper was mixed. A certain section of the population was willing to accept it but doubted the sincerity of the British Government; the other decided to reject it as not meeting fully the aspirations of the Palestine Arabs which was the abrogation of the Balfour Declaration and the Mandate and the granting of independence to the country.

Zionist reaction, on the other hand, was one of unanimous rejection and condemnation. A general strike was called for the following day of its announcement, when violent and inflammatory speeches were made by Zionist leaders. In Jerusalem, Arab shops were looted, the police stoned when they tried to maintain order, and a British constable was shot. [13]

But on the outbreak of World War II, both parties decided not to embarrass the British Government and to cease all acts of violence. As attested by the Palestine Government, "The Arabs of Palestine demonstrated their support of Democracy at the outbreak of war, and there were spontaneous appeals in the Arab press to Arabs to rally to the side of Great Britain and set aside local issues; acts of terrorism were roundly condemned",[14] while Arab notables called on the High Commissioner to assure him of their loyality. [15] It was later admitted that the British Government was thus "able to build up the comprehensive military organization based on Cairo which was to serve them so well." [16]

The Jews in Palestine also unanimously agreed to put aside their opposition to British policy in Palestine and demonstrated their loyalty to the cause of the democracies. Jewish terrorist acts ceased and the illegal broadcasting station which had previously been operating closed down. The Jewish Agency issued an appeal calling on all Jews in Palestine to close their ranks and offer their full assistance to Britain. But all this proved not to be without a purpose.

The first three years of the war were however profitably used by the Zionists in their plans for Palestine. They employed all means to procure arms; bring in illegal immigrants; recruit and train them for their own fight after the war. In the political field, great activity was observed. In May 1942, a conference of American, European and Palestinian Zionists was held at the Biltmore Hotel in New York under the sponsorship of an Emergency Committe on Zionist affairs. The 'Platform' included an affirmation by the conference of "its unalterable rejection of the White Paper of May 1939, and denies its moral or legal validity. The White Paper," it said, "seeks to limit, and in fact to nullify Jewish rights to immigration and settlement in its denial of sanctuary to Jews fleeing from Nazi persecution..."

The conference then demanded, "In the struggle against the

forces of aggression and tyranny, of which Jews were the earliest victims, and which now menace the Jewish National Home, recognition must be given to the right of the Jews of Palestine to play their full part in the war effort and in the defence of their country, through a Jewish military force fighting under its own flag and under the high command of the United Nations." It urged "that the gates of Palestine be opened; that the Jewish Agency be vested with control of immigration into Palestine and with the necessary authority for upbuilding the country, including the development of its unoccupied and uncultivated lands; and that Palestine be established as a Jewish commonwealth integrated in the structure of the new democratic world." [17]

On the basis of this 'Program', the Jewish Agency presented the British Government on 22 May 1945 – a fortnight after VE Day – with the following demands:

(1) That an immediate decision be announced to establish Palestine 'undivided and undiminished' as a Jewish state;

(2) That the Jewish Agency be invested with the control of Jewish immigration into Palestine;

(3) That an international loan be raised to finance the immigration of the 'first million' Jews to Palestine;

(4) That reparations in kind from Germany be granted to the Jewish people for the 'rebuilding' of Palestine; and – as a first instalment – that all German property in Palestine be used for the resettlement of Jews from Europe;

(5) That free international facilities be provided for the exit and transit of all Jews who wish to settle in Palestine. [18]

Zionist acts of violence

Responsibility for the acts of violence in Palestine between 1943 and 1948 rested entirely with the *Hagana* (meaning 'Defence') and its two splinter groups, the *Irgun Zvei Leumi* (meaning 'National Military Organization') and the *Stern Gang* (self-styled 'Freedom Fighters of Israel'). The Irgun split from the 'mother' organization –

Hagana – in 1935, and the Stern Gang in turn split from the Irgun in 1939.

Whereas the Hagana adhered to a socialist philosophy and obeyed the orders of the Jewish Agency for Palestine, the Irgun Zvei Leumi owed political allegiance to the Revisionists, the extreme nationalist wing of the Zionist movement.

All three groups cooperated when they found this more profitable, but each in its own way. Their objective, however, was the same, namely, the establishment of a 'Jewish state', but they differed in method of achieving this objective. The Hagana at first showed restraint because of its relationship to the Jewish Agency. The Irgun Zvei Leumi, on the other hand, had no need for caution and could therefore afford to be more ruthless. From the beginning it was organized on the strictly conspiratorial lines of a terrorist underground movement; and its recruits were mostly from among the Yemenite and Sephardic Jews who were taught Polish underground tactics. In this manner, the Jewish Agency could – as it always did – disclaim responsibility for any action which shocked the world by reason of its brutality.

The origin of the Hagana – the illegal military arm of the Zionist movement, established and maintained by the officially-recognized Jewish Agency – goes back to the 1870s when the first Jewish agricultural colonies were established in Palestine as the forerunners of the envisaged 'Jewish state'. At first, the duties of these *Hashomer* (Watchmen), as they were then named, were to provide protection against possible stealing. There was then no other reason because the aims of these early settlers were generally still unknown to the Arab inhabitants.

The transformation of the *Hagana* into a fighting force began only after World War I when mass immigration started in earnest and the political Zionist movement had received the recognition of the Allied Powers. Eliahu Colomb, one of the first 'Watchmen', became the Commander of the Hagana and its new role as a para-military organization was to recruit, train and equip all able-bodied young men and women for the day when it would be possible to seize the country by force and establish the 'Jewish State'.

The disturbances of the 1920s enabled Jewish settlements to obtain a limited quantity of arms from the Government for self-protection. These were placed in sealed armouries in charge of the village *Mukhtar* (headman) to be opened only in case of a serious emergency. But it gave the Hagana – whose existence was supposedly unknown to Government – the opportunity to augment its Government issues with illicit arms and ammunition and to start training in attack as in defence.

By 1946, the Hagana had become a strong military establishment. A 'White Paper', published by the Mandatory Government that year, described the Hagana as an illegal and well-armed military organization, organized under a central command with subsidiary territorial commands, in three branches, each of which includes women, viz:

a static force composed of settlers and townsfolk, with an estimated strength of 40,000;
a field army, based on the Jewish Settlement Police and trained in more mobile operations, with an estimated strength of 16,000;
a full-time force (Palmach), permanently mobilized and provided with transport, with an estimated peace establishment of 2,000 and war establishment of some 6,000.

The 'White Paper' added that something in the nature of conscription is in force; a year's service being obligatory for senior school children, male and female, between the ages of 17 and 18. The Jewish publication, *Haboker*, stated that prior to 11th November, 1945, 'every Movement must submit to the Jewish Agency's Recruiting Department in Tel Aviv a roster of its members, male and female, who must enlist'.

The same 'White Paper' added that the Irgun had a strength estimated at between 3,000 and 5,000; while the Stern Gang had between 200 and 300 dangerous fanatics. [19]

The first signs of Zionist acquisition of illicit arms came to light in October 1935 when "a large quantity of arms and ammunition smuggled in a consignment of cement from Belgium was discovered at Jaffa port and led to rumours among Arabs that the Jews were extensively arming themselves." [20]

With the increase in the Jewish population as a result of mass immigration and the entry of elements brought into the country with the sole purpose of creating a Jewish majority and establishing a 'Jewish state', the ranks of those for whom arms and training had to be found obviously swelled. The second World War brought about just that opportunity. While the British Government was engaged with the war against Germany, the Zionist Organization was busy acquiring arms and training its underground forces.

As early in the War as 5 October 1939, forty-three Jews, wearing uniforms, were arrested while engaged in military manouvers and carrying rifles and bombs; on 18 November of the same year, thirty-eight Revisionist Jews, engaged in manouvers and carrying arms, bombs, gelignite, etc., were arrested; and on 22 January 1940, a search of the Jewish settlement of Ben Shemen revealed a hoard of arms and ammunition.[21]

According to the Palestine Government: "During March 1943, there was a notable increase in the number and magnitude of thefts of arms and explosives from military establishments, and shortly afterwards there was revealed the existence of a large scale stealing racket connected with the *Hagana* and with ramifications throughout the Middle East. Jewish feeling against action by Government and the military authorities to stop this traffic was roused by the trial by military court of two Jews who had taken part in the traffic. The 'arms trial', as it came to be known, was preceded by the trial of two British military deserters (Privates Harris and Stoner) who were sentenced each to fifteen years' imprisonment for complicity in the thefts..."

"In passing sentence the President of the court stated that the trial had shown 'that there is in existence in Palestine a dangerous and widespread conspiracy for obtaining arms and ammunition from His Majesty's Forces' and that the organization behind the activities of the two accused 'seems to have had considerable funds at its disposal and to possess wide knowledge of military matters, including military organization'.

"The trial caused considerable bitterness on the part of the Jewish community against Government who, they thought, should recognize that the Jews had a moral right to arm; feeling was aggravated by the fact that the trial was held in public and that the Jewish official bodies had been mentioned in the course of the proceedings." [22]

With signs that the Nazi menace to Palestine was over and that the Allies would finally be winning the war, the Zionist campaign of terror began in earnest at the end of January 1944 and continued until the end of the Mandate in 1948. These acts of violence and sabotage coming as they did at a time when England's hands were still full with the war against Germany and therefore least able to maintain law and order, harassed the Government. Consequently, on 10 October 1944, the Officer Administering the Government and the Commander-in-Chief, Middle East, issued a joint official communique in which it was clearly stated that the terrorists and "their active and passive sympathizers are directly impeding the war effort of Great Britain" and "assisting the enemy." The communique called upon "the Jewish community as a whole to do their utmost to assist the forces of law and order in eradicating this evil thing within their midst"; it added that "verbal condemnation of outrages on the platform and in the press may have its effect but is not in itself enough; what is required is actual collaboration with the forces of law and order, especially the giving of information leading to the apprehension of the assassins and their accomplices." The communique then demanded "of the Jewish community in Palestine, their leaders and representative bodies to recognize and discharge their responsibilities and not to allow the good name of the *Yishuv* to be prejudiced by acts which can only bring shame and dishonour on the Jewish people as a whole." [23]

The situation did not alter. Government buildings continued to be blown up, railway tracks and telephone lines were cut, British personnel assassinated; but the most outstanding acts of terror were:

(1) On 6 November 1944, two Zionist gunmen of the Stern

Gang murdered Secretary of State Lord Moyne in Cairo. It is generally held that the assassination was an act of revenge for the anti-Zionist policy he was believed to have advocated. [24] A Zionist writer had listed the charge: he had been 'busy rigging up' the Arab League as a counter-force to Zionism; as Colonial Secretary in 1941 and 1942, he 'vehemently' opposed Jewish immigration; he had made a declaration in the House of Lords on 9 June 1942 that the Jews were not the descendants of the ancient Hebrews with no 'legitimate claim' to the Holy Land; and he was 'an implacable enemy of Hebrew independance'. [25]

On 17 November, Sir Winston Churchill then Prime Minister and an ardent Zionist, made a revealing statement in the House of Commons regarding the assassination: "If our dreams for Zionism", he said, "are to end in the smoke of assassins' pistols and our labours for its future are to produce a new set of gangsters worthy of Nazi Germany, many like myself will have to reconsider the position we have maintained so consistently and so long in the past. If there is to be any hope of a peaceful and successful future for Zionism, these wicked activities must cease and those responsible for them must be destroyed, root and branch." [26]

(2) On 22 July 1946, a wing of the King David Hotel in which the Government Secretariat and part of the military headquarters were housed, was blown up causing the death of about 100 Government officials –British, Arab and Jewish. [27]

Indignant at the cowardly act, the General Officer Commanding in Palestine, circulated a letter on 26 July to his troops in which he stated, "The Jewish community of Palestine cannot be absolved from responsibility for the long series of outrages culminating in the blowing up of a large part of the Government Offices in the King David Hotel causing grievous loss of life. Without the support, active and passive, of the general public," he said, "the terrorist gangs who actually carry out these criminal acts would soon be unearthed, and in this measure the Jews in this country are accomplices and bear a share in the guilt."

The General then decided "to put out of bounds to all ranks all Jewish places of entertainment, cafés, restaurants, shops and private dwellings. No soldier," he ordered, "is to have any intercourse with any Jew; and intercourse in the way of duty should be as brief as possible and kept strictly to the business in hand." [28]

(3) On 29 December, a British army major and three British non-commissioned officers were abducted and flogged as a reprisal for the execution of a sentence of 18 strokes imposed by a military court on a Jewish terrorist; [29]

(4) On 30 July 1947, two British sergeants (Martin and Paice), spending the afternoon innocently on the beach in the Jewish town of Natanya, were dragged and hanged in a citrus grove on the outskirts of the town and their bodies made into 'booby traps', said to be in reprisal for the execution of two Jewish terrorists. A notice reading "This is the sentence of Irgun's High Command" was attached to the bodies. [30]

Jewish Agency directs violence

On 24 July 1946, the Mandatory Government issued a 'Statement of Information relating to Acts of Violence (Jewish)' in which it declared that the information which was in the possession of His Majesty's Government has led them to the conclusion that "the Hagana and its associated force the Palmach (working under the political control of prominent members of the Jewish Agency), have been engaging in carefully planned movements of sabotage and violence under the guise of 'the Jewish Resistence Movement'; that the Irgun Zvei Leumi and the Stern Gang have worked since last Autumn in co-operation with the Hagana High Command on certain of these operations; and that the broadcasting station 'Kol Israel', which claims to be 'the Voice of the Resistence Movement' and which was working under the general direction of the Jewish Agency, has been supporting these organizations." [31]

The revelation that the Jewish Agency was not only in touch with Hagana, Irgun and the Stern Gang but actually coordinated and directed their activities of murder, destruction and sabotage, did not come as a surprise. The Jewish Agency however challenged the British Government, alleging that the information in the possession of His Majesty's Government was not authentic. In answer to a complaint on the subject made to the United Nations Special Committee which visited Palestine in 1947 to consider the 'future government of Palestine', the Government described Hagana as "not a purely 'defensive' organization." It said, "In its attack on Givat Olga, the sabotage of the railways, the ambushing of the police during the attack on Athlit camp, and the attacks on the radar stations on Mount Carmel and at Sarona, the Hagana was used for coercive 'terrorist' purposes. Its difference from the dissident Irgun Zvei Leumi and Stern Groups was not in any principle, but only in regard to choice of strategic moments to apply force." [32]

In a report to the Secretary of State, the High Commissioner described the situation in Palestine in May 1947 in the following terms:

> "The first and most important element in the situation is that, because of political differences with the mandatory administration on account of the inability of His Majesty's Government to accede to Jewish demands, the Jewish community, whose dissident members are responsible for these outrages, have declined and still decline to give any assistance to the police and military forces in the maintenance of law and order, These forces are thus working in and among a population of over 600,000 whose leaders have refused to call for cooperation with the police against the extremists and have thus, however much they themselves may not have wished it, in effect encouraged the terrorist groups to further lawlessness and wanton

> assaults by all available means upon constituted authority in almost any form. [33]

In July 1947, the Palestine Government, in a supplementary memorandum to the U.N. Special Committee, said: "When the war against Germany and Japan was seen to be approaching a successful conclusion, the Jews brought into action their weapons of lawlessness and terrorism in support of their own political aims and ambitions." The memorandum pointed out, "The right of any community to use force as a means of gaining its political ends is not admitted in the British Commonwealth. Since the beginning of 1945, the Jews have implicitly claimed this right and have supported, by an organized campaign of lawlessness, murder and sabotage, their contention that, whatever other interests might be concerned, nothing should be allowed to stand in the way of a Jewish state and free Jewish immigration into Palestine." [34]

Sympathy and support for the Jewish terrorists was not confined to the Jewish community in Palestine. The terrorists had many sympathizers and supporters in the United States without whose contributions terrorism and sabotage would not have been possible. At the time when Zionist terrorism was at its highest, Ben Hecht, a rich and influential Jewish Hollywood scenario writer, published an encouraging 'Letter to the Terrorists of Palestine' in the *New York Herald Tribune* of 15 May 1947, He said "The Jews of America are for you. You are their champions. You are the grin they wear. You are the feather in their hats."

"In the past fifteen hundred years", he added, "every nation of Europe has taken a crack at the Jews. This time the British are at bat. You are the first answer that makes sense – to the New World."

"Every time you blow up a British arsenal, or wreck a British jail, or send a British railroad-train sky high, or rob a British bank, or let go with your guns and bombs at the British betrayers and invaders of your homeland," he gloated, "the Jews of America make a little holiday in their hearts." He concluded by assuring his "brave friends, we are working to help you. We are raising funds for you . . ." [35]

Is it not ironic that in 1917 Zionism was seeking the favours of Britain which were generously given against its better interests of friendship with the Arabs. Now that the Jews became a sizable minority capable of looking after itself through British benevolence and assistance, they called them 'betrayers and invaders'?

Despite this record, the Zionists claim that their contribution to the war effort helped the British to liberate North Africa and bring about the surrender of Nazi Germany!

Termination of Mandate

In 1947, at the height of Zionist acts of terrorism and sabotage, the Mandatory Government made one last attempt to settle the Palestine Problem by suggesting to both Arabs and Jews that British trusteeship over Palestine should continue for another five years with the declared object of preparing the country as a whole for independence. [36]

The Arabs presented their own proposals for independence with guarantees for Jewish minority rights which were unacceptable to the British Government; the Jewish Agency, on the other hand, rejected the Government's proposals out-right and intensified its terrorist and sabotage activities.

On 18 February 1947, the British Foreign Secretary announced in the House of Commons that His Majesty's Government had found, "the Mandate has proved to be unworkable in practice, that the obligations undertaken to the two communities had been shown to be irreconcilable," [37] and therefore announced its intention of giving it up.

VI | *The Palestine Problem before the United Nations*

General Assembly seized with Problem

On 2 April 1947, the United Kingdom delegation to the United Nations addressed a letter to the Secretary-General of the United Nations requesting that the question of Palestine be placed on the agenda of the next regular session of the General Assembly, and, further, that a special session of the General Assembly be summoned as soon as possible for the purpose of constituting and instructing a special committee to prepare for the consideration of the question by the Assembly at its next regular session. [1]

On 21 and 22 April 1947, five Member States (Egypt, Iraq, Syria, Lebanon and Saudi Arabia) communicated to the Secretary-General the request that the following additional item be placed on the agenda of the special session:

> "The termination of the Mandate over Palestine and the declaration of its independence." [2]

On 29 April 1947, the General Committee of the Assembly recommended the inclusion in the agenda of the item submitted by the United Kingdom; [3] and on 30 April 1947, decided by a vote of eight to one, with five abstentions, not to recommend the inclusion in the agenda of the item demanded by the Arab States. [4]

Notwithstanding this rejection, the item was included for discussion by the General Assembly under rule 18. At its 70th meeting on 1 May 1947, the General Assembly approved the inclusion in the agenda of the item submitted by the United Kingdom Government; [5] and at its 71st meeting of the same date, rejected by a vote of 24 to 15 with 10 abstentions the inclusion of the item proposed by the Arab States. [6]

Thus, the sole item on the agenda of the special session was that submitted by the United Kingdom Government, viz: "Constituting and instructing a special committee to prepare for the consideration of the question of Palestine at the second regular session." The item was then referred to the First Committee of the General Assembly for its consideration.

The manner in which the British Government had referred the Palestine problem to the United Nations, and the action taken by the latter as described above, left much to be desired from the point of view of the Arab States and the Arabs of Palestine. The Arabs felt that both the British action and that of the United Nations were not in conformity with the provisions on self-determination prescribed in the United Nations Charter.

On 5 May 1947, the General Assembly decided that the First Committee should grant a hearing to the Jewish Agency; [7] and on 7 May 1947, a similar decision was adopted with regard to the Arab Higher Committee for Palestine. [8]

At the meeting of the General Assembly held on 15 May 1947, the Representative of the United Kingdom declared: "We have tried for years to solve the problem of Palestine. Having failed so far, we now bring it to the United Nations in the hope that it can succeed where we have not. All we say," he added, "is that we should not have the sole responsibility for enforcing a solution which is not accepted by both parties and which we cannot reconcile with our conscience." [9]

To have taken the British Government thirty years to find out that the Mandate for Palestine was 'unworkable' and Britain's obligations 'irreconcilable' – as the British Foreign Minister declared in the House of Commons – after having created a prolem in 1917 where none existed before, and after flooding the country with Jewish immigrants until they became strong enough to wrest the country from its original Arab inhabitants; and then to wash its hands at this late hour and declare its unwillingness to enforce a solution "not accepted by both parties" under the pretext of 'conscience', does not speak well of either the British conscience or intelligence.

The Palestine Problem before the First Committee of the General Assembly

The First Committee devoted twelve meetings to the consideration of the question of constituting and instructing a special committee on Palestine. At its 57th meeting on 13 May 1947, the First Committee, by a vote of 13 to 11, with 29 abstentions, [10] recommended the following composition of the Special Committee which was subsequently approved in the General Assembly by a vote of 39 to 3, with 10 abstentions:

Australia, Canada, Czechoslovakia, Guatemala, India, Iran, Netherlands, Peru, Sweden, Uruguay, Yugoslavia.

The report of the First Committee, including its final resolution concerning the composition and terms of reference of the Special Committee on Palestine, was discussed by the General Assembly at its 77th, 78th and 79th plenary meetings. The Assembly adopted the recommendations of the First Committee at the 79th meeting on 15 May 1947 by a final vote of 45 to 7 with 1 abstention. [11]

The Palestine Arabs strongly objected to the whole idea of forming yet another committee of enquiry into the Palestine problem. The Arab States all voted against the Assembly resolution and were supported by the Moslem States of Afghanistan and Turkey, with Siam abstaining.

The Palestine Problem before the United Nations Special Committee on Palestine (UNSCOP)

The members of the Special Committee arrived in Palestine on 14 and 15 June 1947, and during their stay in the Middle East, held 36 meetings. It was evident to the Palestine Arabs that the majority of the members of the Special Committee had arrived in Palestine predisposed to accepting a Zionist 'solution' of the Palestine problem based on partition of the Holy Land. Consequently, the Arab Higher Committee, as the spokesman of the Palestine Arabs, cabled the Secretary-General of the United Nations informing him that after a thorough study of the deliberations and circumstances under which the Palestine fact-finding committee had been formed and the discussions leading up to its terms of reference, the Palestine Arabs had decided to abstain from collaboration with the Special Committee and to desist from appearing before it for the following main reasons:

Firstly, United Nations refusal to adopt the natural course of inserting the termination of the Mandate and the declaration of independence of Palestine in the agenda of the special session of the General Assembly and in the terms of reference of the Special Committee;

Secondly, United Nations failure to detach the Jewish world refugee question from the Palestine problem;

Thirdly, the transgression of the interests of the Palestine inhabitants in the name of world religious interests although these latter were not the subject of contention.

The Arab Higher Committee then pointed out that the Palestine Arabs' natural rights to their country were self-evident and could not continue to be subject to investigation but deserved to be recognized on the basis of the principles of the United Nations Charter. [12]

After completing its investigations in Palestine, the Special Committee retired to Geneva to start its deliberations and prepare its report. But before doing so, it formed a sub-committee – in spite of Arab protests – to visit displaced persons camps in Germany and Austria to look into the situation of the inmates of certain assembly centres. Among their observations was one in regard to the propaganda to which the Jewish refugees had been subjected. They reported that "some actual evidence was seen in the form of posters and written material at some of the centres. In particular, at one centre," the sub-committee pointed out, "a poster was noted with the inscription 'Palestine – a Jewish State for the Jewish People' and also a large pictorial design showing Jews from eastern Europe on the march towards Palestine shown as a much larger area than the present geographical limits."

The sub-committee went on to say, "our enquiries, so far as they went, indicated that in the schools in the various centres children are being taught Hebrew and given an intimate historical and geographical knowledge of Palestine."

The sub-committee then commented: "Naturally, also, the continual presence in the centres of representatives of such bodies as the Central Committee of Liberated Jews, the Jewish Agency, the American Joint Distribution Committee, and other voluntary organizations gives every opportunity for general indoctrination of the idea of settlement in Palestine . . ." [13]

On 31 August 1947, the Special Committee completed its report [14] and submitted it to the General Assembly. This embodied twelve general recommendations. Eleven of these were approved unanimously, and the twelfth (with two members dissenting and one recording no opinion) provided that "In the appraisal of the Palestine question, it be accepted as incontrovertible that any solution for Palestine cannot be considered as a solution of the Jewish problem in general."

The eleven recommendations approved unanimously, provided for the termination of the Mandate, independence for Palestine after a transitional period during which administration of the country would be the responsibility of the United Nations, and for the preservation of the Holy Places. The General Assembly was to undertake immediately the initiation and execution of an international arrangement whereby the problem of the distressed European Jews, of whom approximately 250,000 were in assembly centres, should be dealt with as a matter of extreme urgency for the alleviation of their plight and of the Palestine Problem. Minority rights were to be protected, peaceful relations were to be a prerequisite to independence, provision was to be made for economic unity, and the abolition of the capitulations, and lastly, an appeal was to be made to both parties to end acts of violence.

The Committee then presented two alternatives:

(1) *A Plan of Partition with Economic Union* supported by seven members of the Committee: Canada, Czechoslovakia, Guatemala, Netherlands, Peru, Sweden and Uruguay. This plan, which became known as the *Majority Plan*, divided Palestine into an Arab State, a Jewish State, and an international zone of Jeru-

salem and its environs under United Nations jurisdiction. In area, the Arab State was to comprise 4,476 square miles or 42.88 percent of the total; the Jewish State 5,893 square miles or 56.47 percent; and the Jerusalem International Zone 68 square miles or 0.65 percent. As regards population, the Jewish State was to contain 498,000 Jews and 497,000 Arabs, and the Jerusalem International Zone 105,000 Arabs and 100,000 Jews. Jewish land ownership within the frontiers of the proposed Jewish State was less than 10 percent and less than 6 percent in the whole of Palestine.

(2) *A Federal-State Plan* supported by three members: India, Iran and Yugoslavia. This plan, which became known as the *Minority Plan,* provided, *inter alia,* that an independent state of Palestine would be established which would comprise an Arab State and a Jewish State. Jerusalem would be its capital. The federal state would comprise a federal government and governments of the Arab and Jewish states respectively. The federal government would exercise full powers over such matters as national defence, foreign relations, immigration, currency, inter-state waterways, transport and communications. The Arab and Jewish States would enjoy full power over local self-government in its various aspects. There was to be a single Palestinian nationality and citizenship, with guaranteed equal rights for all minorities and fundamental human rights and freedoms, as well as free access to the Holy Places.

The Zionists received the *Majority Plan* with keenness and enthusiasm since it fully accorded with their aspirations for a Jewish state. To the Arabs, both plans were totally unacceptable for obvious reasons: The *Majority Plan,* because it blatantly destroyed the territorial integrity of their homeland; placed a 50 percent Arab population in the proposed Jewish state as an official and permanent minority at the mercy of the other 50 percent comprising the Jewish population; and gave the latter control over Arab lands. The *Minority Plan* was equally rejected primarily because of its implicitly partitionist content.

Report of UNSCOP before the Ad Hoc Committee of the General Assembly

On 23 September 1947, the General Assembly established an *Ad Hoc* Committee to consider the report of UNSCOP.

On 25 September 1947, the *Ad Hoc* Committee began its deliberations, and on 29 September 1947, the Representative of the Arab Higher Committee was invited to address the Committee. He began by stating that it was the sacred duty of the Arabs of Palestine to defend their country against all aggression, including the aggressive campaign being waged by the Zionists with the object of securing by force a country – Palestine – which was not theirs by right. The *raison d'être* of the United Nations was, he said, to assist self-defence against aggression.

The rights and patrimony of the Arabs of Palestine had been the subject of no fewer than eighteen investigations within 25 years, and all to no purpose. Commissions of inquiry had either reduced the national and legal rights of the Palestine Arabs or had glossed them over. The few recommendations, he said, favourable to the Arabs had been ignored by the Mandatory Power. For these and for other reasons already communicated to the United Nations, it was not surprising that the Arab Higher Committee should have abstained from the nineteenth investigation (i.e., UNSCOP's) and refused to appear before it.

The Representative of the Arab Higher Committee then pointed out that the struggle of the Arabs of Palestine against Zionism had nothing in common with anti-semitism. The Arab world, he said, had for centuries been one of the rare havens of refuge for the Jews of the world until the atmosphere of neighbourliness had been poisoned by the Balfour Declaration and by the aggressive spirit the latter had engendered in the Jewish community.

He disputed the claims of world Zionism to Palestine as having no legal or moral basis. The religious connection of the Jews with Palestine, which he noted was shared by Moslems and Christians, gave them no secular claim to the country. As for the Balfour Declaration, the British Government had no right to dispose of

Palestine, which it had occupied in the name of the Allies as a liberator and not as a conqueror. The Declaration was in contradiction to the Covenant of the League of Nations and was an immoral, unjust and illegal promise.

The Palestine spokesman then said that no people would be more pleased than the Arabs to see the distressed Jews of Europe given permanent relief. But Palestine, he pointed out, had already absorbed far more Jews than its just share, and the Jews could not impose their will on other nations by choosing the place and the manner of their relief, particularly if that choice was inconsistent with the principles of international law and justice, and prejudicial to the interests of the nation directly concerned.

He noted that the solution of the Palestine problem was simple. It lay in the Charter of the United Nations in accordance with which the Arabs of Palestine, constituting the majority of the population, were entitled to a free and independent state. The United Nations, he pointed out, was not legally competent to decide or impose Palestine's constitutional organization, and he went on to outline the following principles as the basis for the future constitutional organization of the Holy Land:

1. That an Arab State in the whole of Palestine be established on democratic lines.
2. That the Arab State of Palestine respect human rights, fundamental freedoms and equality of all persons before the law.
3. That the Arab State of Palestine protect the legitimate rights and interests of all minorities.
4. That freedom of worship and access to the Holy Places be guaranteed to all.

He then explained that the following steps would have to be taken to give effect to the above-mentioned four principles:

(a) A Constituent Assembly should be elected at the earliest possible time. All genuine and law-abiding nationals of Palestine would be entitled to participate in the elections of the Constituent Assembly.

(b) The Constituent Assembly would, within a fixed time,

formulàte and enact a Constitution for the Arab State of Palestine, which should be of a democratic nature and should embody the above-mentioned four principles.

(c) A Government should be formed within a fixed time, in àccordance with the terms of the Constitution, to take over the administration of Palestine from the Mandatory Power.

Such a program, he stressed, was the only one which the Arabs of Palestine were prepared to accept. The only item on the Committee's agenda with which the Arab Higher Committee would associate itself was item 3, namely, "The termination of the Mandate over Palestine and the recognition of its independence as one State." [15]

On 22 October 1947, the *Ad Hoc* Committee appointed two Sub-Committees to examine and report on the findings of UNSCOP:

Sub-Committee 1, [16] (comprising Canada, Czechoslovakia Guatemala, Poland, South Africa, the United States of America, Uruguay, the U.S.S.R. and Venezuela) recommended the adoption of the *Majority Plan* after slight modifications.

Sub-Committee 2, [17] (comprising Afghanistan, Colombia, Egypt, Iraq, Lebanon, Pakistan, Saudi Arabia, Syria and Yemen), at its first meeting on 23 October 1947, felt that it was somewhat unfortunate that both Sub-Committee 1 and Sub-Committee 2 were so constituted as to include in each of them representatives of only one school of thought, respectively, and that there was insufficient representation of neutral countries. Accordingly, it was proposed that the Chairman of the *Ad Hoc* Committee should be requested to reconstitute Sub-Committee 2 (irrespective of what might be done with regard to Sub-Committee 1) by replacing two of the Arab States on the Sub-Committee (which were prepared to withdraw) by neutrals or countries which had not definitely committed themselves to any particular solution of the Palestine question. The Chairman of the *Ad Hoc* Committee, being approached in this connection, explained to the Sub-Committee that he could not see his way to accepting the recommendation.

To the Arabs, the composition of the membership of the Sub-Committees and the attitude of the Chairman of the *Ad Hoc* Committee, represented one thing, namely, that the partition of Palestine had already been agreed upon by the Great Powers to fit Zionist aspirations and that what was taking place in the United Nations was merely to give the semblance of legality to an illegal operation.

Nevertheless, Sub-Committee 2 proceeded with its investigation and formed three Working Groups:

1. *Legal problems* – Pakistan, Syria and Saudi Arabia
2. *Refugee problem* – Afghanistan, Colombia and Lebanon
3. *Constitutional proposals* – Egypt, Iraq and Yemen.

After considering the reports of the three Working Groups, the Sub-Committee presented its recommendations to the *Ad Hoc* Committee in the form of three draft resolutions. According to the first, the General Assembly, before recommending a solution of the Palestine problem, would request the International Court of Justice for an advisory opinion on certain legal questions connected with or arising from that problem, including questions concerning the competence of the United Nations to recommend or enforce any solution contrary to the wishes of the majority of the people of Palestine. The second resolution recommended an international settlement of the problem of Jewish refugees and displaced persons, and stated principles and proposed machinery for the cooperation of Member States in such a settlement. The third resolution provided for the creation of a provisional government of the people of Palestine to which the authority of the Mandatory Power would be transferred, as a preparatory step to the setting up of an elected Constituent Assembly. The Constitution framed by the latter would, *inter alia,* contain guarantees as regards the Holy Places, human rights and fundamental freedoms. Such guarantees were enumerated in the draft resolution. [18]

On 19 November 1947, the *Ad Hoc* Committee met to consider the reports of its two Sub-Committees. The representative of the Arab Higher Committee was again invited to present the views of the Palestine Arabs. Commenting on the Zionist-inspired *Majority*

Plan proposing the partition of the country, he said: "The two great champions of freedom – the U.S.S.R. and the United States – have joined hands, prompted, they said, by humanitarian motives, to support the monstrous perversion of the principle of self-determination in Palestine. They had agreed on only one thing, namely, the partition of Palestine. They had prepared," he said, "for that destructive policy for divergent motives: the one to please Jewish voters in the United States; the other to permit tens of thousands of immigrants to inundate Palestine in order to propagate its theories and political aims..."

The Palestine Arab spokesman reiterated that the United Nations should "participate in establishing a democratic State as proposed by the Arabs. Nothing," he said, "would come of it but prosperity and peace for all." He referred to the treatment of Jews by Arabs in Arab Spain and in Palestine before the Balfour Declaration as examples of the spirit that could exist in Palestine if such a State were established. [19]

Voting on the recommendations of the two Sub-Committees began on 24 November. First to be put to the vote were the three draft resolutions submitted by Sub-Committee 2:

Draft Resolution No. I, was voted upon in two parts: The first part providing for the reference to the International Court of Justice for an advisory opinion concerning legal questions, was rejected by a vote of 25 to 18 with 11 absentions. The second part, comprising the question of the competence of the United Nations to enforce any plan of partition of Palestine contrary to the wishes, or adopted without the consent of, the inhabitants of Palestine, was rejected by a bare vote of 21 to 20 with 13 abstentions. [20]

Draft Resolution No. II, dealing with Jewish refugees and displaced persons, received 16 votes in favour, 16 against, with 26 abstentions. [21]

Draft Resolution No. III, dealing with the establishment of an independent unitary State of Palestine, was rejected by a vote of 29 to 12, with 14 abstentions. [22] Here the United Nations dealt a severe blow to the principle of self-determination which formed the basis of the United Nations Charter.

The *Ad Hoc* Committee, having disposed of a recommendation which rested on the principles in Article 22 of the Covenant of the League of Nations and the United Nations Charter on self-determination in too obviously perfunctory a manner, then turned its attention to the recommendations of Sub-Committee 1, which dealt with the Plan of Partition with Economic Union. The report of this Sub-Committee was approved by a vote of 25 to 13, with 17 absentions.* [23]

The delegations of Syria, Iraq and Egypt protested against the partition resolution as being unjust, impractical, against the Charter and a threat to peace. The representative of Egypt reserved the right of his Government to consider the resolution as null and void.

The Report of the Ad Hoc Committee before the General Assembly.

Consideration of the report [24] of the *Ad Hoc* Committee by the General Assembly began on 26 November 1947. The general trend appeared to be moving steadily towards the adoption of the *Majority Plan* of partition with economic union. Representatives of Member States who were not influenced by outside pressures warned against the dangers of partition. The Representative of the Philippines expressed his delegation's "profound misgivings" in the wisdom of partition and said: "With interest we have followed the course of the debate since the special session of the General Assembly last April. We have carefully studied the report of the Special Committee on Palestine [25] and pondered the various proposals that have been submitted. As a result of these studies, the Philippines Government has come to the conclusion that it cannot give its support to any proposal for the political

* Voting *against:* Afghanistan, Cuba, Egypt, India, Iran, Iraq, Lebanon, Pakistan, Saudi Arabia, Siam, Syria, Turkey and Yemen.
Abstaining: Argentina, Belgium, China, Colombia, El-Salvador, Ethiopia, France, Greece, Haiti, Honduras, Liberia, Luxemburg, Mexico, Netherlands, New Zealand, United Kingdom, Yugoslavia.

disunion and the territorial dismemberment of Palestine ... We hold that the issue is primarily moral. The issue is whether the United Nations should accept responsibility for the enforcement of a policy which, not being mandatory under any specific provision of the Charter, nor in accordance with its fundamental principles, is clearly repugnant to the valid nationalist aspirations of the people of Palestine. The Philippines Government believes that the United Nations ought not to accept any such responsibility."* [26]

Similar misgivings felt by other Member States which later voted for partition are perhaps best expressed in the words of their delegates: The Swedish delegate admitted that the plan "has its weak sides and some dangerous omissions;" [27] the delegate from Canada said "We support the plan with heavy hearts and many misgivings;" [28] New Zealand's representative talked of the "grave inadequacies of the present proposals;" [29] while Belgium's Foreign Minister Van Langenhove said of it: "We are not certain that it is completely just; we doubt whether it is practical; and we are afraid that it involves great risks ..." [30]

Sir Zufrallah Khan, Representative of Pakistan, warned the Western Powers, which took it upon themselves to push through the partition resolution, "to remember that you may need friends tomorrow, that you may need allies in the Middle East. I beg of of you," he pleaded, "not to ruin and blast your credit in these lands." He questioned the viability of the proposed 'Jewish state' and the sincerity of the United States and the Western Powers. "They who paid lip-service to humanitarian principles," he said, "closed their own doors to the 'homeless Jews', but voted Arab Palestine to be not only a shelter, a refuge, but also a state so that he (the homeless Jew) should rule over the Arab." [31]

On the eve of the final vote, Mr. Camille Chamoun, Representative of Lebanon (who later became President of his country), made the following statement: "To judge by the press reports

* On the orders of his Government, Mr. Romulo was on the s. s. *Queen Elizabeth* bound for Europe within hours after delivering his speech against partition. The Philippines then voted for partition.

which reach us regularly every two or three days, I can well imagine to what pressure, to what manœuvres your sense of justice, equity and democracy has been exposed during the last thirty-six hours. I can also imagine how you have resisted all these attempts in order to preserve what we hold dearest and most sacred in the United Nations, to keep intact the principles of the Charter, and to safeguard democracy and the democratic methods of our Organization. My friends, think of these democratic methods, of the freedom in voting which is sacred to each of our delegations. If we were to abandon this for the tyrannical system of tackling each delegation in hotel rooms, in bed, in corridors and ante-rooms, to threaten them with economic sanctions or to bribe them with promises in order to compel them to vote one way or another, think of what our Organization would become in the future." [32]

Notwithstanding the hesitations of some, the misgivings of others, and the warnings of the Arab and other States, the General Assembly, on 29 November 1947, adopted the *Majority Plan* providing for the partition of Palestine by a vote of 33 in favour, 13 against, with 10 abstentions.* [33]

The Partition Plan divided Palestine into six principal parts. Three were allotted to the *Jewish state*, and three, with the 'enclave of Jaffa,' to the *Arab state*. The purpose behind this extraordinary and unnatural division was to include within the *Jewish state* all areas owned and inhabited by Jews, even though this meant the inclusion of large areas owned and inhabited by Arabs. The *Arab state*, on the other hand, was to include the least possible

*The voting was: *In favour* – Australia, Belgium, Bolivia, Brazil, Byelorussian SSR, Canada, Costa Rica, Czechoslovakia, Denmark, Dominican Republic, Ecuador, France, Guatemala, Haiti, (33) Iceland, Liberia, Luxemburg, Netherlands, New Zealand, Nicaragua, Norway, Panama, Paraguay, Peru, Philippines, Poland, Sweden, Ukrainian SSR, Union of South Africa, U.S.S.R., U.S.A., Uruguay, Venezuela.

(13) *Against* – Afghanistan, Cuba, Egypt, Greece, India, Iran, Iraq, Lebanon, Pakistan, Saudi Arabia, Syria, Turkey, Yemen.

(10) *Abstained* – Argentina, Chile, China, Colombia, El-Salvador, Ethiopia, Honduras, Mexico, United Kingdom, Yugoslavia.

number of Jews and the smallest amount of Jewish property. The City of Jerusalem and the area around it, including Bethlehem, were set aside as an *international zone* to be placed under United Nations jurisdiction.

The Partition Resolution guaranteed the civil, political, economic, religious and property rights of the Arabs. It provided that the stipulations contained in the Declaration on those rights were to be recognized as fundamental laws of the State; and no law, regulation, or official action was to conflict or interfere with these stipulations or take precedence. It also stipulated that "no discrimination of any kind shall be made between the inhabitants on the grounds of race, religion, language or sex"; that "no expropriation of land owned by an Arab in the *Jewish state* shall be allowed except for public purposes"; and that "in all cases of expropriation, full compensation as fixed by the Supreme Court shall be paid previous to dispossession."

The Partition Resolution further stipulated that the Jewish and Arab states were to come into being two months after the date of termination of the Mandate, which the British Government had scheduled for 15 May 1948. In addition, the Resolution provided for the establishment of a Palestine Commission which would progressively take over the administration of the country, for ultimate transfer of responsibility to the envisaged Arab and Jewish governments.

Delegates who voted for partition did so with little or no enthusiasm. Were it not for the extreme pressures to which they and their Governments had been subjected, they would have given the matter more serious consideration and no doubt would have come out with a different resolution. Sir Zufrallah Khan, Representative of Pakistan, summed up the position of these and other delegates when he explained his own negative vote. Because of the wisdom of his words, and their applicability to the situation in the Middle East after the lapse of almost twenty years, Sir Zufrallah Khan's statement is reproduced in full:

"A fateful decision has been taken. The die has been cast. In the words of the greatest American: 'We have striven to

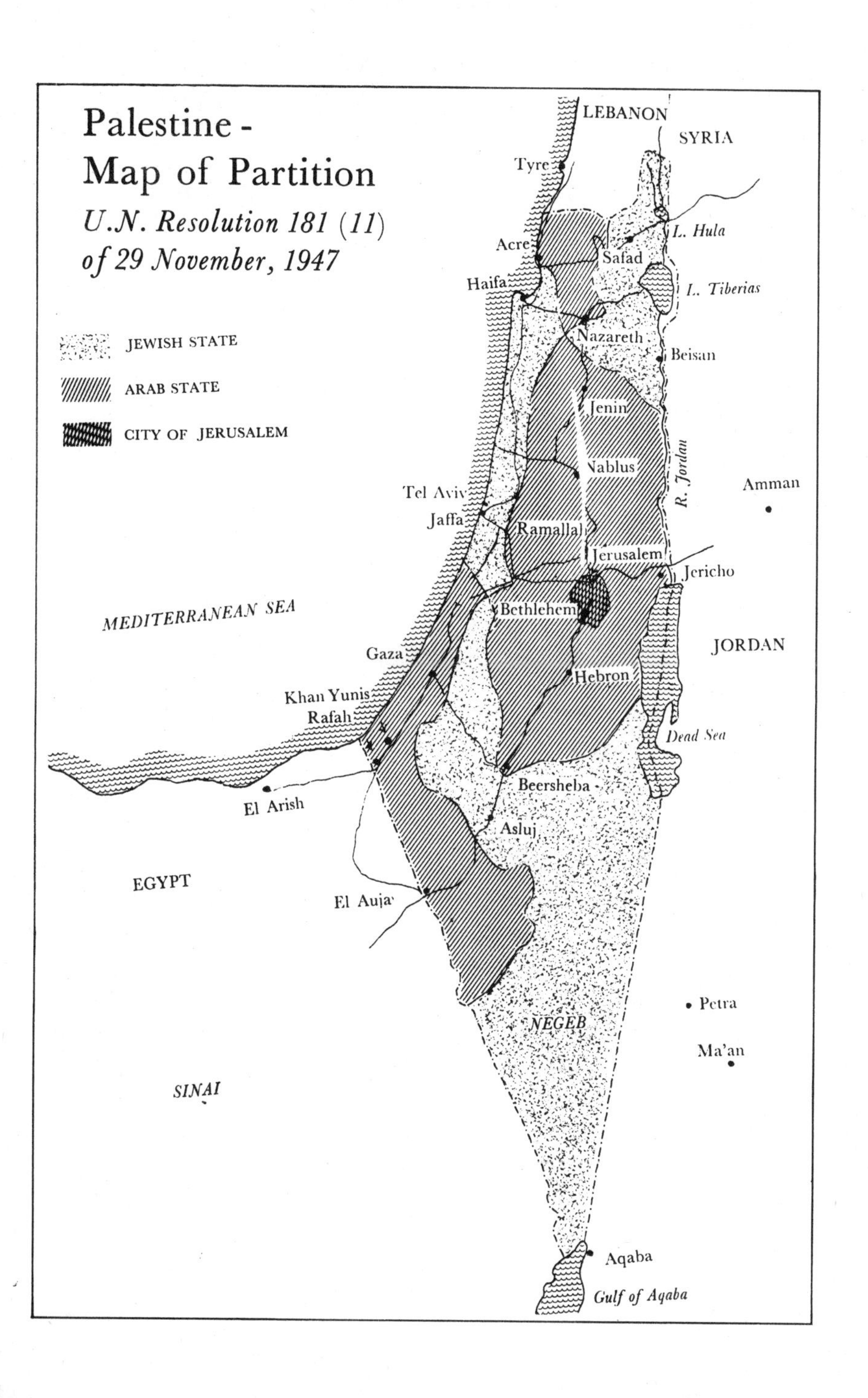
Palestine -
Map of Partition
U.N. Resolution 181 (11)
of 29 November, 1947
JEWISH STATE
ARAB STATE
CITY OF JERUSALEM
LEBANON
SYRIA
Tyre
Acre
Safad
L. Hula
Haifa
L. Tiberias
Nazareth
Beisan
Jenin
Nablus
R. Jordan
Amman
Tel Aviv
Jaffa
Ramallah
Jerusalem
Jericho
MEDITERRANEAN SEA
Bethlehem
JORDAN
Gaza
Hebron
Khan Yunis
Rafah
Dead Sea
Beersheba
El Arish
Asluj
EGYPT
El Auja
Petra
NEGEB
Ma'an
SINAI
Aqaba
Gulf of Aqaba

Jerusalem International Zone

As Resolved by General Assembly Resolution No. 181(11) of 29 November, 1947

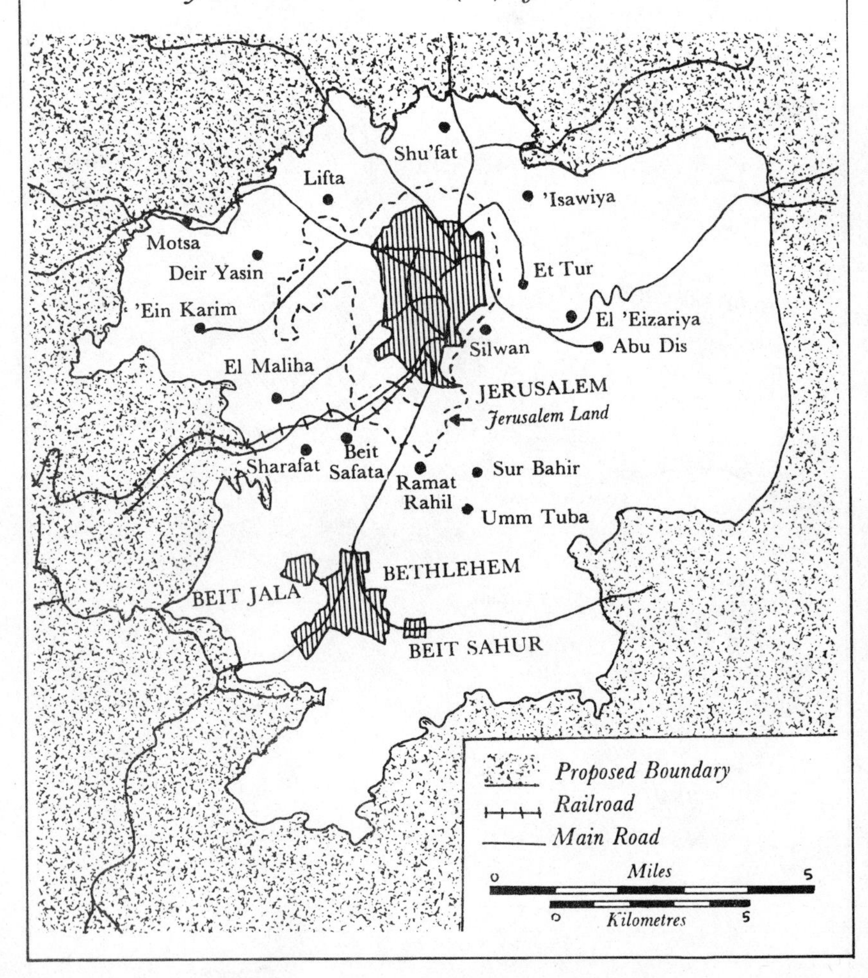

do the right as God gives us to see the right.' We did succeed in persuading a sufficient number of our fellow representatives to see the right as we saw it, but they were not permitted to stand by the right as they saw it. Our hearts are sad but our conscience is easy. We would not have it the other way round.

"Empires rise and fall. History tells us of the empires of the Babylonians, the Egyptians, the Greeks and the Romans, the Arabs, the Persians and the Spaniards. Today, most of the talk is about the Americans and the Russians. The Holy Koran says: 'We shall see the periods of rise and fall as between nations, and that cycle draws attention to the universal law. What endures on earth is that which is beneficent for God's creatures.'

"No man can today predict whether the proposal which these two great countries have sponsored and supported will prove beneficent or the contrary in its actual working.

"We much fear that the beneficence, if any, to which partition may lead will be small in comparison to the mischief which it might inaugurate. It totally lacks legal validity. We entertain no sense of grievance against those of our friends and fellow representatives who have been compelled, under heavy presure, to change sides and to cast their votes in support of a proposal the justice and fairness of which do not commend themselves to them. Our feeling for them is one of sympathy that they should have been placed in a position of such embarrassment between their judgement and conscience, on the one side, and the pressure to which they and their Governments were being subjected, on the other." [34]

A pertinent criticism of the manner in which the Partition Resolution was obtained came from author Alfred Lilienthal. He wrote: "The United Nations dealt a severe blow to the prestige of international law and organization by its hasty, frivolous, and arrogant treatment of the Palestine question. The General Assembly turned down the only reasonable suggestions – a referendum in Palestine and submission of the legal problems to the International Court of Justice. The Displaced Persons Problem was handled with outrageous thoughtlessness," Lilienthal pointed out. "For persons displaced by World War II, whatever their faith, were surely a responsibility of international welfare organizations – not pawns in a whimsical power play of Jewish nationalists," Lilienthal concluded. [35]

Pressures inside and outside the United Nations

During the period when the future of the Holy Land was in the balance, Zionist pressures inside and outside the United Nations increased. To the American public, the Zionist approach was through the Bible and the sufferings of European Jewry. To those who frowned on Zionist acts of terror and sabotage in Palestine, the Zionists made believe that their underground movement was engaged in the same kind of struggle that the American Revolutionists had waged against the very same British imperialist Power, and that the establishment of a Jewish state would be one of the loftiest acts of humanitarianism. [36]

To the United States policy-maker, the Zionists waved the 'Jewish vote'. This is confirmed by a conversation between then Secretary of Defence James Forrestal and Senator Howard J. McGrath, from Rhode Island and Democratic Chairman. Forrestal argued, "No group in this country should be permitted to influence our policy to the point where it could endanger our national security." To this McGrath replied, "There were two or three pivotal states which could not be carried without the support of people who were deeply interested in the Palestine question." [37] On another occasion, McGrath stressed the fact that a substantial part of the contributions to the Democratic National Committee were made "with a distinct idea on the part of the givers that they will have an opportunity to express their views and have them seriously considered on such questions as the present Palestine question." [38]

On the other hand, those United Nations Member States, and others, who were opposed to partition, were threatened, intimidated or black-mailed. For example, the Liberian delegate to the United Nations when approached to support partition replied that he considered the method of approach as "attempted intimidation" and so reported to the U.S. State Department. [39] But when the vote came, Liberia – like Haiti and the Philippines which also had opposed partition in the first instance – changed its vote to 'yes'.

Arthur Hayes Sulzberger, publisher of the *New York Times,* describing the situation, said publicly: "I dislike the coercive methods of Zionists who in this country have not hesitated to use economic means to silence persons who have different views. I object to the attempts at character assassination of those who do not agree with them." [40]

A leading Zionist, summing up Zionist activities at the time, admitted that "Every clue was meticulously checked and pursued. Not the smallest or the remotest of nations, but was contacted and wooed. Nothing was left to chance." [41]

The part played by the United States – Government and people – in bringing about a majority vote in the General Assembly, can best be illustrated by quoting from American sources:

(1) *The Hon. Lawrence H. Smith,* declared in the U.S. Congress, Let's take a look at the record, Mr. Speaker, and see what happened in the United Nations Assembly meeting prior to the vote on partition. A two-thirds vote was required to pass the resolution. On two occasions the Assembly was to vote and twice it was postponed. It was obvious that the delay was necessary because the proponents (the U.S.A. and the U.S.S.R.), did not have the necessary votes. In the meantime, it is reliably reported that intense pressure was applied to the delegates of three small nations by the United States member and by officials 'at the highest levels in Washington'. Now that is a serious charge. When the matter was finally considered on the 29th, what happened? The decisive votes for partition were cast by Haiti, Liberia and the Philippines. These votes were sufficient to make the two-thirds majority. Previously, these countries opposed the move... The pressure by our delegates, by our officials, and by the private citizens of the United States constitutes reprehensible conduct against them and against us." [42]

(2) *Journalist Drew Pearson* explained in his 'Merry-Go-Round' column that in the end, "a lot of people used their influence to whip voters into line. Harvey Firestone, who owns rubber plantations in Liberia, got busy with the Liberian Government; Adolphe Berle, advisor to the President of Haiti, swung that vote . . . China's Ambassador Wellington Koo warned his Government . . . The French Ambassador pleaded with his crisis-laden Government for partition."

"Few knew it," he wrote after the partition, "but President Truman cracked down harder on his State Department than ever before to swing the United Nations vote for the partition of Palestine. Truman called Acting Secretary Lovett over to the White House on Wednesday and again on Friday warning him he would demand a full explanation if nations which usually line up with the United States failed to do so on Palestine . . ." [43]

(3) *Sumner Welles* affirmed, "By direct order of the White House, every form of pressure, direct or indirect, was brought to bear by American officials upon those countries outside the Moslem world that were known to be either uncertain or opposed to partition. Representatives or intermediaries were employed by the White House to make sure that the necessary majority would at least be secured." [44]

(4) *James Forrestal,* then Secretary of Defence, described "The methods that had been used . . . to bring coercion and duress on other nations in the General Assembly bordered closely onto scandal." [45]

Arab rejection of the Partition

The Arabs rejected the partition on the grounds that it violated the provisions of the U.N. Charter, the principles on which the Universal Declaration of Human Rights were later based, international law and practice, and the right of a people to decide its own destiny.

Arab rejection was also based on the fact that, while the population of the *Jewish state* was to be 497,000 Arabs* and 498,000 Jewish, with the Jews owning less than 10% of the *Jewish state* land area, the Jews were to be established as the ruling body – a settlement which no self-respecting people would accept without protest, to say the least.

Contrary to what public opinion has been led to believe, the General Assembly of the United Nations is not a legislative or a judicial body, and therefore its resolution on the partition of Palestine was no more than a *recommendation*. It did not have the force of a decision and it could not be binding on the majority of the people of Palestine who had opposed it and continue to do so. Besides, the action of the United Nations conflicted with the basic principles for which the world organization was established, namely to uphold the right of all peoples to self-determination. By denying the Palestine Arabs, who formed the two-thirds majority of the country, the right to decide for themselves, the United Nations had violated its own Charter.

The Partition Resolution was also in violation of the principles enunciated in the Joint Declaration of President Roosevelt and Prime Minister Winston Churchill of 12 August 1941 – which became known as the Atlantic Charter – namely:

> "First, their countries seek no aggrandizement, territorial or other;
>
> "Second, they desire to see no territorial changes that do not accord with the freely expressed wishes of the peoples concerned; and
>
> "Third, they respect the right of all peoples to choose the form of government under which they will live; and they wish to see sovereign rights and self-government restored to those who have been forcibly deprived of them . . ."

* As a result of the Armistice signed in 1949, the Israelis now occupy an additional 220 Arab towns and villages beyond the territory assigned to the *Jewish state* under the Partition Plan. The inhabitants of these towns and villages numbered, in 1945, about 400,000.[46] Added to the figure of 497,000 Arabs estimated to be in the *Jewish state* area, the Arabs affected by the Israeli occupation were, in 1948, about 897,000 persons as compared with the U.N. estimate of the Jewish population of 498,000 for the *Jewish state*.

In the light of this joint undertaking, the obvious was to carry out a referendum in Palestine before a vote was taken on partition by the General Assembly. But this proposal was blocked in the United Nations by the Big Powers for vested interests. Even the request to refer the matter to the International Court of Justice for an expression of opinion as to whether the General Assembly was within its rights under the Charter to partition countries, was rejected.

Zionist acceptance of the Partition

The Zionists, on their part, had no reason to reject the Partition Plan which gave them sovereignty over Arab territory and the power to expel and dispossess – as they later did – the Arab inhabitants. The Balfour Declaration gave the Zionists a foothold in Palestine, and the Partition Resolution helped them reach their goal of a *Jewish state.* Those who saw the dangers in the establishment of a Jewish state were the anti-Zionists, but their number was not sufficient to tip the scale.

In his book *The Decadence of Judaism in Our Times,* Moshe Menuhin, who became 'disenchanted with the developments of political Zionism' and left Palestine because he believed 'they implied wàrs of injustice and the degeneration of Judaism', [47] explains why the Zionists had accepted the Partition Plan. He said: "The fanatical 'Jewish' political nationalists, of course, 'accepted' Partition with alacrity, for the Partition Plan was merely a foothold for the full realization of *Eretz Israel* as predatory Ben Gurion and Menachem Beigin had envisioned it all along, openly and unashamedly, quoting the Bible and preparing for the bloody 'redeeming' and 'ingathering'." Menuhin went on to point out, "On October 2, 1947, Ben Gurion had stated before the Elected Assembly in Jerusalem: 'I do not minimize the virtue of statehood even within something less than all the territory of the land of Israel on either bank of the Jordan.' And a little earlier, in 1946, before the Anglo-American Commission of Inquiry, he said: 'Our aim is not a majority. A majority will not solve our problem. The majority is only a stage, not a final one. You need it to establish the commonwealth. We still have to build a national home'." [48]

Mr. Menuhin considers that Menachem Beigin had been more 'honest and frank' when he put it plainly: "The Jewish homeland, the area which covers both sides of the Jordan, is a complete historic and geographic entity. Dissection of the homeland is an unlawful act; agreement to dissection is also unlawful, and is not binding on the Jewish people. It is the duty of this generation to return to Jewish sovereignty these parts of the homeland which were torn from it and given to foreign rule."* [49]

Failure of the United Nations

Recognizing the anomaly and uniqueness of its action, the United Nations tried to protect, but only on paper, the Arabs of the proposed *Jewish state* by providing that their civil, political, economic, religious and property rights were in no way to be prejudiced by the partition. When these rights were encroached upon, the United Nations failed to fulfil its guarantees.

The League of Nations had failed to keep the peace in the world because certain nations refused to honour their obligations to the principles and rules affirmed by the League, whenever these principles conflicted with unilateral interests.

When the United Nations was created in 1945, it was hoped that the impotence of the defunct League would not return, and that nations granted membership would *unreservedly* adhere to the principles and rules of the new Organization. The fact that Red China, while not a member of the United Nations, had, in the opinion of the United States Government, violated the principles of the United Nations Charter to which it was not a party, by her action in Korea, barred her from membership in the World Organization. Yet we find that the state of Israel, which has violated the very resolution which created the *Jewish state* in the first ins-

* The statement "these parts of the homeland which were torn from it and given to foreign rule" refers to Jordan which the Zionists claim is part of *Eretz Israel;* and by "foreign rule", they mean the Jordan Government.

tance, and the obligations it 'unreservedly' accepted when it was admitted into membership of the United Nations, as well as its utter disregard for its international obligations and for subsequent resolutions calling upon Israel to do certain things, continues to enjoy membership in the World Body!

A 'Jewish state' is born

The general impression is that the state of Israel came into being as a result of, and in conformity with, a recommendation of the United Nations General Assembly. This is not so.

The Partition Resolution of 29 November 1947 had recommended the creation of a *Jewish state* on 56% of the territory of *Palestine*; an *Arab state* on 43%; and an *International Zone of Jerusalem and Environs* on the remaining 1%. The resolution decreed that Arabs living in the area set aside for the Jewish state were to continue to reside there and to enjoy their fundamental rights and basic human liberties under the guarantees of the United Nations. The resolution further stipulated that the Jewish and Arab states were to come into being two months after British withdrawal on 15 May 1948. [50]

However, instead of waiting until the United Nations Palestine Commission prescribed in the Partition Resolution took over authority from the British Mandatory, and in turn handed over such authority progressively to the leaders of the Arab and Jewish states, the Zionists proclaimed the state of Israel on 14 May 1948 and faced the world with a *fait accompli*. By this date they had already seized territory beyond that assigned to the Jewish state. Instead of having jurisdiction over 56% of the territory of Palestine, the Israelis presently occupy 77%; instead of Jerusalem being internationalized, the greater part of the Holy City has been Israelized and declared the 'capital' of the Jewish state; instead of Arabs being permitted to remain in their homes and country to lead a normal life, nearly one million men, women and children – Moslems and Christians – were forcibly expelled and dispossessed.

Therefore, what actually emerged as the *Jewish state* on 14 May

1948 was anything but the 'state' planned for under the Partition Plan. The new 'state of Israel' was the product of brute force, created in violation of the principles of the United Nations Charter, the Universal Declaration of Human Rights, and the very resolution under which the Israelis now claim sovereignty.

VII | *Strife, War, Truce (1948-1949)*

Britain hands over authority to Zionists

The British representative at the United Nations informed the Security Council in 1948 that his Government would continue to be responsible for the administration of Palestine and the maintenance of law and order for the duration of the Mandate.

At the same time, the British Government issued a warning that any outside interference in the affairs of Palestine would be met with force of arms. This warning was intended, as later events proved, to keep the Arab States from coming to the aid of the Palestine Arabs who were being subjected to all kinds of attacks.

On the other hand, the Partition Resolution provided that "the administration of Palestine shall, as the Mandatory Power withdraws its armed forces, be progressively turned over to the Palestine Commission ..."[1] This Commission, established especially by the United Nations to take steps preparatory to independence, was not permitted by the Mandatory Power to come into effective being on the grounds that there could not be two governing authorities in one country at the same time. Theoretically, the Commission existed, but it exercised no functions. It was, however, relieved "from the exercise of its responsibilities under resolution 181 (11) of 29 November 1947" on 14 May 1948, the very same day the state of Israel was proclaimed.[2] The Commission's duties were then taken over by U.N. Mediator Count Folke Bernadotte, but the damage to Arab rights and interests had already begun.

The British Mandatory would not hand over authority to a properly established organ of the United Nations; but no sooner was the Partition Resolution adopted when the Government announced its withdrawal from Tel Aviv and environs and handed over administration and security to the local Jewish authorities.

This freed the hands of the Zionists within a significant Jewish area of Palestine and arms and fighting men began to arrive through the port of Tel Aviv to augment the Zionist underground forces.

This was confirmed by Menachem Beigin who declared that at the end of March 1948, the first shipload of arms and ammunition from Czechoslovakia arrived in Palestine, which proved to be a vital factor in the turning of the tide. From then on, militarily, the Zionists never looked back. Tiberias fell on the 18th of April; on the 21st Hagana forces began to attack Haifa. On May 10 Safad fell after more than a week of heavy fighting. At the end of April, Hagana occupied the Katamon Quarter of Jerusalem; and in co-operation with Hagana, the surrender of Jaffa took place on May 13, 1948. [3]

While more and more Jewish areas were evacuated and handed over to the Zionists as the day of British withdrawal approached, British forces remained in Arab areas impeding any preparations of defence which the Arab inhabitants might have had in mind. With each new day, Zionist assaults on Arab areas increased with no Government interference whatsoever. Arab appeals for Government help were rejected on the grounds that there were not sufficient security forces available because of the withdrawal. Even in Jerusalem – a territory set aside to be administered by the United Nations – the British military authorities not only refused to come to the aid of the inhabitants of Katamon Quarter, but prevented the Arab Legion guarding the Iraq Consulate in the area from interfering.

The Arab inhabitants, forsaken by the Government which undertook to maintain 'law and order' and not permitted by their so-called protectors to seek outside aid, had no alternative but to flee before the advancing Zionists – an exodus, for which the Zionists had planned and organized so well, was now assisted by those who originally undertook to ensure the establishment of a Jewish national home in Palestine.

British behaviour towards Arabs and Jews during this critical period, could only be explained that the British Government was determined to the last moment to fulfil its obligations to the Jews in helping them to transfer the 'national home' into a 'state' before they pulled out of the country.

Thus, on the date of the expiration of the Mandate, the Zionist forces were already in occupation of strategic positions well within the territory assigned to the 'Arab state'. Even Jerusalem – reserved as an international city – was not spared. Glubb Pasha, the Commanding Officer of the Arab Legion in 1948, noted, "The Jews were already in the Arab area when the Arab Legion arrived." [4]

United Natios concern over violence

The United Nations became alarmed at the violence to which its Partition Resolution had unwittingly given birth. On 19 March, the Security Council met, and the United States delegation stated that since it had become clear that the Partition Resolution could not be implemented by peaceful means and that the Security Council was not prepared to implement it, the Council should recommend a temporary trusteeship for Palestine.*

The Jewish Agency replied by rejecting a trusteeship, and

* On 25 April 1963, David Ben Gurion recalled: "I was then at Haganah Headquarters at Tel Aviv and could not consult my colleagues on the Zionist Executive, who were in Jerusalem. I saw it my duty immediately to state: 'This stand of the United States in no way alters fundamentally the situation in the country, nor does it undermine the establishment of the Jewish state. Establishment of the State was not, in effect, given in the United Nations resolution of last November 29 – although the resolution was of great moral and political value – but by our ability to bring about a decision in the country by force. Through our own strength – if we will it and succeed in mobilizing it fully – the State will be established even now."

Ben Gurion added: "And the State came into being – and we were forced to fight for its existence. We won and I have no doubt that this was one of the greatest achievements in our history as a nation," He went on to say, "The War of Independence which lasted from the 15th May, 1948 to July 1, 1949, gave us a state larger and more complete than the one delineated by the United Nations General Assembly resolution of 1947. It gave us", he said, "nearly all of Jerusalem, Western Galilee, the entire corridor from Jaffa to Jerusalem and all of the Negev with the exception of the Gaza Strip." [5]

declared that it was the most terrible sell-out since Munich. To thwart any attempt to nullify the Partition, the Zionists stepped up their attacks against Arab towns and villages in order to face the United Nations on 15 May 1948 with a *fait accompli.*

Is it not ironical that while the United States representative was arguing at the United Nations for a shift from partition to trusteeship, former President Harry Truman suddenly recognized the new state of Israel? He did so exactly eleven minutes after Israel had been proclaimed as a state to the utter amazement of the Zionists themselves. This hasty recognition – unprecedented in history – came as a complete surprise to the United States mission to the United Nations, which was first informed of it by the Soviet representative!

Zionist aggression before termination of Mandate

The Israelis have always claimed that the 'Palestine war' was started with the entry of the Arab armies into Palestine after British withdrawal from the country on 14 May 1948. If this is to be accepted as true, then by the same token Britain and France must be held responsible for the start of the Second World War since it was they who had officially declared war on Nazi Germany in 1939. In the case of Palestine, as in that of World War II, it is what took place *before* the two opposing armies met on the battlefield that must fix responsibility.

The war in Palestine, to be understood correctly, must be divided into three distinct phases:

The first the period prior to the Partition Resolution of 29 November 1947 when the Zionists were planning, organizing and carrying out terror and sabotage activities with a view to first expelling the British Mandatory and then the Moslem and Christian inhabitants;

The second, the six-month period between 29 November 1947 (the date of the Partition Resolution) and 14 May 1948 (the date of British withdrawal); and

The third, the period subsquent to 14 May 1948 during which the armies of the Arab states entered Palestine.

The first phase has already been dealt with in Chapter V. It was the second phase, not the third, that really determined responsibility, and knowledge of it should dispel the myth that it was the Arab States that started the Palestine war.

There is ample evidence to show that the Zionists, having achieved British withdrawal following the resolution of partition, were now ready to switch their campaign of terror from the Mandatory Government to the unarmed Arab population. They aimed at two major objectives; first, to confirm Jewish dominance over the fifty per cent Arab inhabitants living within the limits of the proposed 'Jewish state'; and secondly, to expand those limits so as to include the greatest possible area – if not all Palestine – before Britain withdrew from the country on 14 May 1948.

The Zionist plan of *intention* was disclosed during a conversation in December 1947 between a British officer of the Jordan Arab Legion and a Palestine Government Jewish official. The former is reported to have asked the latter "whether the new Jewish state would not have many internal troubles in view of the fact that the Arab inhabitants of the Jewish state would be equal in number to the Jews." The Jewish official is reported to have replied: "Oh no! That will be fixed. A few calculated massacres will soon get rid of them." [6]

This plan was immediately put into effect. The methods used, however, varied. Some of the inhabitants "were driven out by force of arms; others were made to leave by deceit, lying and false promises." [7] Others still were "encouraged to move on by blows or by indecent acts." [8]

But the most outstanding incident which shocked the world and accelerated the panic flight of the Arab inhabitants was the massacre of 250 men, women and children in the village of Deir Yasin on 9 April 1948. Jon Kimche, author and correspondent who was in Jerusalem at the time, described the attack as "the darkest stain on the Jewish record." He added: "It is historically important because it was to become the beginning of a second legend with which the terrorists sought to serve their cause and justify their deeds. Just as they claimed credit for the British decision to leave Palestine as being the result of the terrorists' attacks on British troops, so later they justified the massacre of Deir Yasin because it led to the panic flight of the remaining Arabs in the 'Jewish state' and so lessened the Jewish casualties." [9]

Dov Joseph, one time Governor of the Israeli sector of Jerusalem and later Minister of Justice, called the Deir Yasin massacre a "deliberate and unprovoked attack"; [10] while British historian Arnold Toynbee described it as "comparable to crimes committed against the Jews by the Nazis." [11] But Menachem Beigin, the leader of the attack on Deir Yasin, said, "The massacre was not only justified, but there would not have been a state of Israel without the 'victory' at Deir Yasin." [12]

Unashamed of their deed and unaffected by world condemnation, the Zionist underground forces, using loud-speakers, roamed the streets of cities warning the Arab inhabitants: "The Jericho road is still open," they told the Jerusalem Arabs, "fly from Jerusalem before you are killed." [13]

Another testimony comes from Major Edgar O'Ballance, a competent and objective observer, who wrote: "Many Israeli sympathizers were appalled at the ruthless way in which the Arab inhabitants were outsed from their homes and driven before advancing armies, and this caused many twinges of conscience in the Western world. The Israelis made no excuse for it, as *it was part of* their plan for the reconquest of their *Promised Land*, in which there was no room for large, hostile, alien groups." [14]

The late William Zukerman, Editor of the *Jewish Newsletter* (New York), suming up the situation in Palestine wrote: ". . . the flight of the Palestine Arabs, which created the Arab refugee problem, was not a spontaneous act, nor due entirely to the propaganda call of the Arab leaders as the Zionists have claimed all along. It was a coldly calculated plan executed by the Irgun but with the knowledge of the Hagana and the Jewish Agency of the time." [15]

Another description of the fighting of that six-month period came from Major Edgar O'Ballance. He said:

> "It was the Jewish policy to encourage the Arabs to quit their homes, and they used psychological warfare extensively in urging them to do so. Later, as the war went on, they ejected those Arabs who clung to their villages. This policy, which had such amazing success, had two distinct advantages: first, it gave the Arab countries a vast refugee problem to cope with which their elementary economy and administrative machinery were in no way capable of attacking; and secondly, it ensured that the Jews had no fifth column in their midst." [16]

That the Zionists started war on the Palestine Arabs before the creation of the state of Israel is confirmed by David Ben Gurion himself. He said: "As April (1948) began, our War of Independence swung decisively from defence to attack. Operation 'Nachshon'... was launched with the capture of Arab Khulda near where we stand today and of Deir Muheisin, and culminated in the storming of Qastal, the great hill-fortess near Jerusalem."* [17]

On another occasion, Ben Gurion said: "The primary task of the Hagana was to safeguard our settlements and lines of communications, but here the best defense is attack. Field troops and Palmach in particular were thus deployed and quickly showed the mettle that was soon to animate our army and bring it victory. In operation 'Nachshon' the road to Jerusalem was cleared at the beginning of April, almost all of New Jerusalem occupied, and the guerillas were expelled from Haifa, Jaffa, Tiberias, Safad while still the Mandatory was present. It needed sagacity and self-control not to fall foul of the British army. The Hagana did its job; until a day or two before the Arab invasion not a settlement was lost, no road cut, although movement was seriously dislocated, despite express assurances of the British to keep the roads safe so long as they remained. Arabs started fleeing from the cities almost as soon as disturbances began in the early days of December (1947). As

* The three villages named are part of the territory which was alloted to the 'Arab state' under the Partition Resolution.

fighting spread, the exodus was joined by Beduin and fellahin, but not the remotest Jewish homestead was abandoned and nothing a tottering Administration (meaning the British Mandatory) could unkindly do stopped us from reaching our goal on May 14, 1948 in a State made larger and Jewish by the Hagana."* [18]

That the Zionists warred on the Palestine Arabs *before* the creation of the state of Israel is also admitted by Menachem Beigin, leader of the *Irgun Zvei Leumi* terrorist group. Beigin tells how "In Jerusalem, as elsewhere, we were the first to pass from the defensive to the offensive ... Arabs began to flee in terror ... Hagana was carrying out successful attacks on other fronts, while "All the Jewish forces proceeded to advance through Haifa like a knife through butter. The Arabs began to flee in panic shouting 'Deir Yasin!'" [19] He added: "In the months preceding the Arab invasion, and while the five Arab States were conducting preparations, we continued to make sallies into Arab territory. The conquest of Jaffa stands out as an event of first rate importance in the struggle for Hebrew independence early in May, on the eve of the invasion by the five Arab States ..." [20]

– The following is a list of the major attacks, occupations and expulsions which took place *before* the British left on 14 May 1948, *before* a single soldier from any Arab State entered Palestine and *two months before* Israel could legally be proclaimed according to the Partition Resolution:

(a) *In the territory reserved for the 'Arab state'*

The village of Qazaza was attacked and occupied as

* On 9 March 1964, the *New York Times* reported that "former Premier David Ben-Gurion and two generals who helped forge the state of Israel in 1948 argued publicly this weekend over who was responsible for this 8,000-square-mile country being so small."

In an interview with *Haboker*, a Tel Aviv daily, Ben-Gurion is reported to have said that "Israeli territory might have been greater if Gen. Moshe Dayan had been chief of staff during the war of 1948 against the Arabs of Palestine."

This belated admission removes any doubt that the Zionists had planned to occupy the whole of Palestine before the British left and before the Arab armies entered Palestine soil. It is further admission that the war was waged against the Palestine Arabs before the Arab armies came to the rescue.

early as December 1947; Salameh in March; Saris, Qastal, Biyar 'Adas and the town of Jaffa, in April; and the town of Acre in May 1948, together with many other villages;

(b) *In the territory assigned to the 'Jewish state'*
The towns of Tiberias and Haifa in April; Safad and Beisan in May 1948, besides hundreds of Arab villages;

(c) *Within the area reserved for 'Jerusalem International Zone'*
The village of Deir Yasin was attacked where the massacre of 250 men, women and children took place on April 9, 1948; and the Arab Quarter of Katamon in Jerusalem City on April 29.

During this six-months period over 300,000 Arabs were driven out of their homes and became refugees – contrary to the expressed intentions of the United Nations.

It is, however, worth noting that Chaim Weizmann, who became first President of the state of Israel in 1948, in an effort to impress the members of the United Nations Special Committee who visited Palestine in 1947, then shed 'crocodile tears' over the dastardly crimes that were being perpetrated by his followers against the Arab and British Mandatory which made it possible for the Jews to go to Palestine. "In all humbleness," he declared before the Committee, "*Thou shalt not kill* has been ingrained in us since Mount Sinai. It was inconceivable ten years ago that the Jews should break this commandment. Unfortunately, they are breaking it today, and nobody deplores it more than the vast majority of the Jews. I hang my head in shame when I have to speak of this fact before you." [21]

No doubt the members of the Committee were very much touched at the time by this display of false emotion. But when his forces subsequently massacred innocent people and expelled the Moslem and Christian inhabitants of the country, Dr. Weizman's so-called 'shame' vanished and his quotation of the commandment 'Thou shalt not kill' was suddenly transformed into a declaration of "It was a miraculous clearing of the land; the miraculous simplification of Israel's task."[22]

The Arab-Israeli War

It has already been established that the Arab States were prevented from coming to the aid of the Palestine Arabs before British withdrawal on 14 May 1948. It has also been established that the Zionist underground forces had, prior to 14 May 1948, crossed over and encroached on the territory reserved for the 'Arab state' and the Jerusalem international zone.

The Israelis now allege that the Palestine war began with the entry of the Arab armies into Palestine after 15 May 1948. But that was the second phase of the war; they overlook the massacres, expulsions and dispossessions which took place prior to that date and which necessitated Arab States' intervention.

However, before the Arab States' armies entered Palestine, the Secretary-General of the Arab League cabled the Secretary-General of the United Nations on 14 May informing him that the Arab States "were compelled to intervene for the sole purpose of restoring peace and security and of establishing law and order in Palestine . . ." Their intervention was also "to prevent the spread of disorder and lawlessness into the neighbouring Arab lands; and to fill the vacuum created by the termination of the Mandate." [23]

Had the British Government fulfilled its obligations in Palestine "to maintain law and order" up to the date of the termination of its Mandate; and had the United Nations from then on undertaken its responsibilities of ensuring peace and security for the Arab inhabitants, Arab States intervention would have been unnecessary.

It should also be noted that the armies of the Arab States were at no time inside the area set aside for the 'Jewish state' under the Partition Resolution. Had the Arab States not intervened during the crucial period when the British Administration withdrew, the whole country would have been over-run by the Zionist forces.

The intentions of the Arab States, apart from having been adequately expressed in the telegram to the Secretary-General of the United Nations on 15 May 1948, were attested to by Glubb

Pasha in these words: "In 1948, Trans-Jordan became involved in hostilities with Israel.She did not want to do this. She intended only to occupy that part of Palestine awarded to the Arabs..." [24]

Security Council orders truce

On 22 May, the Security Council adopted a resolution calling upon "all governments and authorities, without prejudice to the rights, claims or positions of the parties concerned, to abstain from any hostile military action in Palestine, and to that end to issue a cease-fire order to their military and para-military forces." [25]

On 29 May, a second directive was issued, this time calling on the parties "to undertake that they will not introduce fighting personnel" into the area "during the cease-fire." The parties were also ordered "to refrain from importing or exporting war material" into the area "during the cease-fire." [26]

The Israelis defied every provision of the cease-fire orders during the four-week interval and emerged from the truce stronger and better equipped to resume the hostilities. This is evident from the reports of the U.N. Mediator, as well as from his Memoirs, *To Jerusalem.*

Israeli defiance of the terms of the truce manifested itself in:

(a) the release from British custody and the bringing into Palestine of thousands of 'illegal immigrants' who had been detained in Cyprus;

(b) the training and arming of these released detainees;

(c) the smuggling into the area of large quantities of arms, ammunition, and military aircraft, mainly from communist Czechoslovakia. Journalist Jon Kimche wrote in his *Seven Fallen Pillars*: "Israeli emissaries scoured the whole of Europe and America for possible supplies. American Jews were contributing generous supplies of dollars and the arms merchants were prepared to deal for dollars. The Czechs were most helpful. A regular airlift began to operate from Prague to 'Aqir in southern

> Palestine. Rifles, ammunition and guns were now arriving. So were the first bombers – Flying Fortresses smuggled from the United States, and the Beaufort Fighter-bombers trickled out of England ... When the truce ended, a coherent Jewish army with a tiny but effective air force and a small and daring navy was ready to give battle." [27]

It can thus be seen that the Israeli acceptance of the truce was not accompanied by a sincere desire to implement the provisions of the order of the Security Council, but merely to gain time. This is evident from the statement of David Ben Gurion on 10 June 1948, of his Government's acceptance of the cease-fire: "... Our bounds are set wider, our forces multiply, we are administering public services, and daily new multitudes arrive ... All that we have taken we shall hold. During the cease-fire, we shall organize administration with fiercer energy, strengthen our footing in town and country, speed up colonization and *Aliyah* (immigration), and look to the army." [28]

Arab expulsion

The Israelis later claimed that they urged the Arab inhabitants to stay; that they were not driven from their homes; and that they fled of their own free will or at the instigation of their leaders who promised them swift victory. In support of their argument, the Israelis quote an appeal made to the Arabs of Haifa.

Admittedly one such appeal was made to the inhabitants of Haifa, not by the Zionist authorities responsible for Jewish affairs, but by the Jewish Mayor of the City on his own initiative. In no other town or area in Palestine did any member of the Jewish community urge the Arab inhabitants to stay. "Later on, when the problem of the Arab refugees became a tragedy which drew the attention of the world, Jewish apologists claimed that the Arabs had voluntarily become refugees, and that they had not been driven out." [29]

If the Haifa appeal had indeed reflected general Zionist policy towards the Arabs, the call would have emanated from the Jewish

Agency as the official body of Palestine Jewry. The Agency had three opportunities to prove its good faith: the first, before the British left, which the Israelis now allege they did; the second when the state of Israel was established and the problem had become a tragedy calling for humane action; and the third since 1948, to answer the call of conscience to allow the refugees to return. Instead, more and more Palestine Arabs were expelled to join the ranks of those who went before them.

The truth of the matter is that it was the concerted policy of the Zionist movement to oust the Palestine Arabs from their homes and country, because they needed Palestine *Arabrein* to make room for their mass immigration policy. Without Arab lands and property it is not clear how the Zionists could establish a 'Jewish state'.

What actually happened in Palestine was truthfully disclosed by Nathan Chofshi, a Jewish immigrant from Russia who arrived in Palestine in 1908 in the same group with David Ben Gurion. He wrote in a rebuttal of an American Zionist rabbi's assertion: "If Rabbi Kaplan really wanted to know what happened, we old Jewish settlers in Palestine who witnessed the flight could tell him how and in what manner we, Jews, forced the Arabs to leave cities and villages ... Here was a people who lived on its own land for 1,300 years. We came and turned the native Arabs into tragic refugees. And still we dare to slander and malign them, to besmirch their name. Instead of being deeply ashamed of what we did and of trying to undo some of the evil we committed by helping these unfortunate refugees, we justify our terrible acts and even attempt to glorify them." [30]

Professor Erich Fromn, a noted Jewish writer and thinker, had this to say on the Zionist argument that the Arab refugees left of their own accord:

> "It is often said that the Arabs fled, that they left the country voluntarily, and that they therefore bear the responsibility for losing their property and their land. it is true that in history there are some instances – in Rome and in France during the Revolutions – when enemies of the State were proscribed and their property confiscated. But in general international law, the

principle holds true that no citizen loses his property or his rights of citizenship; and the citizenship right is *de facto* a right to which the Arabs in Israel have much more legitimacy than the Jews. Just because the Arabs fled? Since when is that punishable by confiscation of property and by being barred from returning to the land on which a people's forefathers have lived for generations? Thus, the claim of the Jews to the land of Israel cannot be a realistic political claim. If all nations would suddenly claim territories in which their forefathers had lived two thousand years ago, this world would be a mad-house."

Dr. Fromn goes on to say:

> "I believe that, politically speaking, there is only one solution for Israel, namely, the unilateral acknowledgement of the obligation of the State toward the Arabs – not to use it as a bargaing point, but to acknowledge the complete moral obligation of the Israeli State to its former inhabitants of Palestine." [31]

Further proof of forced Arab expulsion – if further proof is required in the face of the preceding outright disclosure – comes from Glubb Pasha, who, as Commanding Officer of the Arab Legion, was on the spot at the time and therefore in a position to know what was going on. He said: "The story which Jewish publicity at first persuaded the world to accept, that the Arab refugees left voluntarily, is not true. Voluntary emigrants," he pointed out, "do not leave their homes with only the clothes they stand in. People," he said, "who have decided to move house do not do so in such a hurry that they lose other members of their family – husband losing sight of his wife, or parents of their children. The fact is that the majority left in panic flight, to escape massacre. They were in fact helped on their way by the occasional massacres – not of very many at a time, but just enough to keep them running." [32]

Notwithstanding, the Israelis have not ceased to use the argument that the Arabs had not been driven out, but they have never been able to produce documentary evidence to prove their contention. Erskine B. Childers, a British writer much interested in the subject, took the trouble to investigate the situation. This is what he came up with:

> "Examining every official Israeli statement about the Arab exodus, I was struck by the fact that no primary evidence of evacuation orders was ever produced. The charge, Israel claimed, was 'documented'; but where were the documents? There had allegedly been Arab radio broadcasts ordering the evacuation; but no dates, names of station, or texts of messages were ever cited. In Israel in 1958, as a guest of the Foreign Office and therefore doubly hopeful of serious assistance, I asked to be shown the proofs. I was assured they existed, and was promised them. None had been offered when I left, but I was assured again. I asked to have the material sent to me. I am still waiting."

Childers continues: "I next decided to test the undocumented charge that the Arab evacuation orders were broadcast by Arab radio – which could be done thoroughly because the BBC (British Broadcasting Corporation) monitored all Middle Eastern broadcasts throughout 1948. The records, and companion ones by a United States monitoring unit, can be seen at the British Museum." He explained: "There was not a single order or appeal, or suggestion about evacuation from Palestine from any Arab radio station, inside or outside Palestine, in 1948. There is repeated monitored record of Arab appeals, even flat orders, to the civilians of Palestine to stay put. To select only two examples: On April 4, as the first great wave of flight began, Damascus Radio broadcast an appeal to everyone to stay at their homes and jobs. On April 24, with the exodus now a flood, Palestine Arab leaders warned that:

> 'Certain elements and Jewish agents are spreading defeatist news to create chaos and panic among the peaceful population. Some cowards are deserting their houses, villages or cities .... Zionist agents and corrupt cowards will be severely punished (*Al-Inqaz* – the Arab Liberation Radio – at 1200 hours)'."*

---

* Under letter No. 808 (file S/132) dated 8 March 1948 addressed by the Arab Higher Committee to the Prime Minister of Egypt, the Committee urged:
"In view of the events which are taking place in Palestine, certain of the Arab inhabitants have begun to leave the country for the neighbouring Arab States... The Arab Higher Committee has resolved that it is in the interests of Palestine

"Even Jewish broadcasts (in Hebrew)," Erskine Childers continues, "mentioned such Arab appeals to stay put. Zionist newspapers in Palestine reported the same; none so much as hinted at any Arab evacuation orders." [33]

---

that no Palestinian should be permitted to leave the country except in special circumstances . . .
The national interest demands that these persons should return to Palestine. . . and the Arab Higher Committee requests that their residence permits should not be renewed and that they should return to Palestine . . ."

VIII | *The Armistice*

Open hostilities between the Arab States and the Israelis, which began after the withdrawal of the British Administration from Palestine on 14 May 1948, came to an end on the orders of the Security Council contained in its resolution dated 15 July 1948. [1]

On 16 November 1948, the Security Council, after "taking note that the General Assembly is continuing its consideration of the future government of Palestine in response to the request of the Security Council of 1st April 1948 (S/714)," decided that, "in order to eliminate the threat to the peace in Palestine and to facilitate the transition from the present truce to permanent peace in Palestine, an armistice shall be established in all sectors of Palestine." The Council then called upon "the parties directly involved in the conflict in Palestine, as a further provisional measure under Article 40 of the Charter, to seek agreement forthwith, by negotiations conducted either directly or through the Acting Mediator on Palestine, with a view to the immediate establishment of the armistice, including:

(a) The delineation of permanent armistice demarcation lines beyond which the armed forces of the respective parties shall not move;

(b) Such withdrawal and reduction of their armed forces as will ensure the maintenance of the armistice during the transition to permanent peace in Palestine." [2]

General Armistice Agreements were consequently concluded between the Arab States of Egypt, Lebanon, Jordan and Syria, on the one hand, and the Israeli authorities, on the other, under the auspices of the Acting U.N. Mediator Dr. Ralph Bunche. [3]

No sooner were the Agreements signed, when the Israelis began to argue that the Arab States could no longer claim the right of 'belligerency', hoping in this way to force the Arab States into a permanent peace on the basis of the accomplished fact. Although the Security Council, in its resolution of 16 November 1948, had made it clear that the armistice was a "provisional measure under Article 40 of the Charter" pending reconsideration by the General Assembly of the question of "the future government of Palestine," the Israelis insisted that the signing of the Agreements had terminated the 'state of war' between the Arab States and Israel and all that remained to be done was to conclude peace treaties.

The position of the Arab States was – and still is – that the Agreements were merely armistice agreements which did not terminate the 'state of war' existing between them and the Israelis. This attitude is reinforced by international law which prescribes: "Armistices or truces in the wider sense of the term, are all agreements between belligerent forces for a temporary cessation of hostilities. They are in no wise to be compared with peace and ought not to be called temporary peace, because the condition of war remains between belligerents and neutrals on all points beyond the mere cessation of hostilities." [4]

In taking note of the conclusion of the Armistice Agreements, the Security Council further noted that "the Armistice Agreements provide that the execution of those Agreements shall be supervised by Mixed Armistice Commissions whose Chairman in each case shall be the United Nations Chief of Staff of the Truce Supervision Organization or a senior of that organization designated by him following consultation with the parties to the Agreements." [5]

The fundamental provisions in the four Agreements which are worth bearing in mind when dealing with the situation arising on the 'armistice demarcation line' from time to time, are:

(a) The principle is affirmed in the Agreements that "no military or political advantage should be gained under the truce ordered by the Security Council;"

(b) "The basic purpose of the armistice demarcation line is to delineate the line beyond which the armed forces of the respective Parties shall not move . . ."

(c) "No aggressive action by the armed forces – land, sea or air – of either Party shall be undertaken, planned or threatened. . ."

(d) "The armistice demarcation line is not to be construed in any sense as a political or territorial boundary and is delineated without prejudice to rights, claims and positions of either Party to the Armistice as regards the ultimate settlement of the Palestine question;"

(e) "The provisions of this Agreement are dictated exclusively by military and not by political, considerations;"

(f) "Where interpretation of the meaning of a particular provision of this Agreement, except Articles I and II, is at issue, the (Mixed Armistice) Commission's interpretation shall prevail."

The Agreements also provided for the creation of ***demilitarized zones*** and *no-man's land* areas. Four demilitarized zones were created along the armistice demarcation line: One (of three sections) in the north on the Palestine-Syrian border;* [6] a second encircling the Hebrew University and Hadassah Hospital buildings on Mount Scopus in Jerusalem; a third on Jabal el-Mukabbir in Jerusalem, comprising the old Government House and Arab College buildings and environs, was assigned a special status as headquarters of the Truce Supervision Organization and thus removed from Arab or Israeli jurisdiction; and a fourth diamond-shaped area around El-Auja in the south on the borders with Egypt. In addition, two no-man's land areas were established: one in Jerusalem to separate the Arab from the Israeli-held Sectors of the City; the other in the Latrun area on the Jaffa-Jerusalem road.

For all intents and purposes, the Armistice Agreements established two rules to be observed by the Parties during the armistice and placed on the representative of the United Nations in the area responsiblity for their implementation.

The first rule is that there is no such thing as a 'border', a 'frontier' or a 'boundary' in the international sense of the word separating the territories of the Arab States from the Israeli-held part of Palestine. What the Armistice Agreements created were:

---

* *Northern Sector* – Khan ed-Duweir and El–'Abasiya area;
Central Sector – Mazari' ed-Daraja to 'Arab el-Shamalina;
Southern Sector – Nuqaib-Samakh-El Himmeh area.

an armistice demarcation line that did not necessarily follow the international boundary of Mandated Palestine; areas between the international boundary and the armistice demarcation line known as 'demilitarized zones'; 'defensive areas' between the demilitarized zones and the territory in which the Israelis were free to act. Thus, Israeli military personnel were free to move in one area; restricted to defensive forces in the second; and totally excluded from the third. It should be noted that the United Nations recognizes the state of Israel's conditional presence in Palestine; its maps still carry the name "Palestine" with the connotation "Israel" marked against the western portion of the country. It is therefore wrong to refer to the 'borders', 'frontiers' or 'boundaries' of Israel so long as the General Armistice Agreements are in existence.

The second rule is that the Armistice Agreements give a special status to the Demilitarized Zones over which neither party can claim sovereignty.

The Arab States accepted their obligations under the General Armistice Agreements with every goodwill, in the belief that the agreements were a temporary measure to give the General Assembly the opportunity to review its hasty recommendation of partition and to find an equitable solution "for the future government of Palestine" compatible with the principles on self-determination embodied in the United Nations Charter.

But subsequent events showed that the Israeli signature was with certain covert aims in view. They needed time to consolidate their military gains in Palestine and the General Armistice Agreements gave them just that. Once their objective was achieved, they had little use for the Armistice Agreements except where they could be manipulated to their further advantage. The following pages give a brief history of conditions on the armistice demarcation line since the General Armistice Agreements were concluded in 1949:

1. Demilitarized Zone along the Syrian border

Article V of the Israeli-Syrian Armistice Agreement deals

with the status of the demilitarized zone. Paragraph 1, "emphasizes that the Armistice Demarcation Line between the Israeli and Syrian armed forces and for the Demilitarized Zone are not to be interpreted as having any relation whatsoever to ultimate territorial arrangements affecting the two Parties to this Agreement."

The Article proceeds to provide in paragraph 2: "In pursuance of the spirit of the Security Council resolution of 16 November 1948, the Armistice Demarcation Line and the Demilitarized Zone have been defined with a view toward separating the armed forces of the two Parties in such manner as to minimize the possibility of friction and incident, while providing for the gradual restoration of normal civilian life in the area of the Demilitarized Zone, without prejudice to the ultimate settlement."

The Article further stipulates in paragraph 5 (a), "Where the Armistice Demarcation Line does not correspond to the international boundary between Syria and Palestine, the area between the Armistice Demarcation Line and the boundary, pending final territorial settlement between the Parties, shall be established as a Demilitarized Zone from which the armed forces of both Parties shall be totally excluded and in which no activities by military, or para-military forces shall be permitted." Sub-paragraph (b) regards "any advance by the armed forces, military or para-military, of either Party into any part of the Demilitarized Zone, when confirmed by the United Nations representative," as constituting "a flagrant violation" of the Agreement.

Sub-paragraph (c) places responsibility for "ensuring the full implementation of this Article" on the Chairman of the Mixed Armistice Commission; and Sub-paragraph (e) empowers the Chairman of the Mixed Armistice Commission "to authorize the return of civilians to villages and settlements in the Demilitarized Zone and the employment of limited numbers of locally recruited civilian police in the zone for internal security purposes."

Paragraph 6 of Article V provides for a 'defensive area' on "each side of the demilitarized zone ... in which defensive forces only shall be maintained ..." The compliments of Syrian and Israeli forces in these defensive areas are clearly defined in Annex

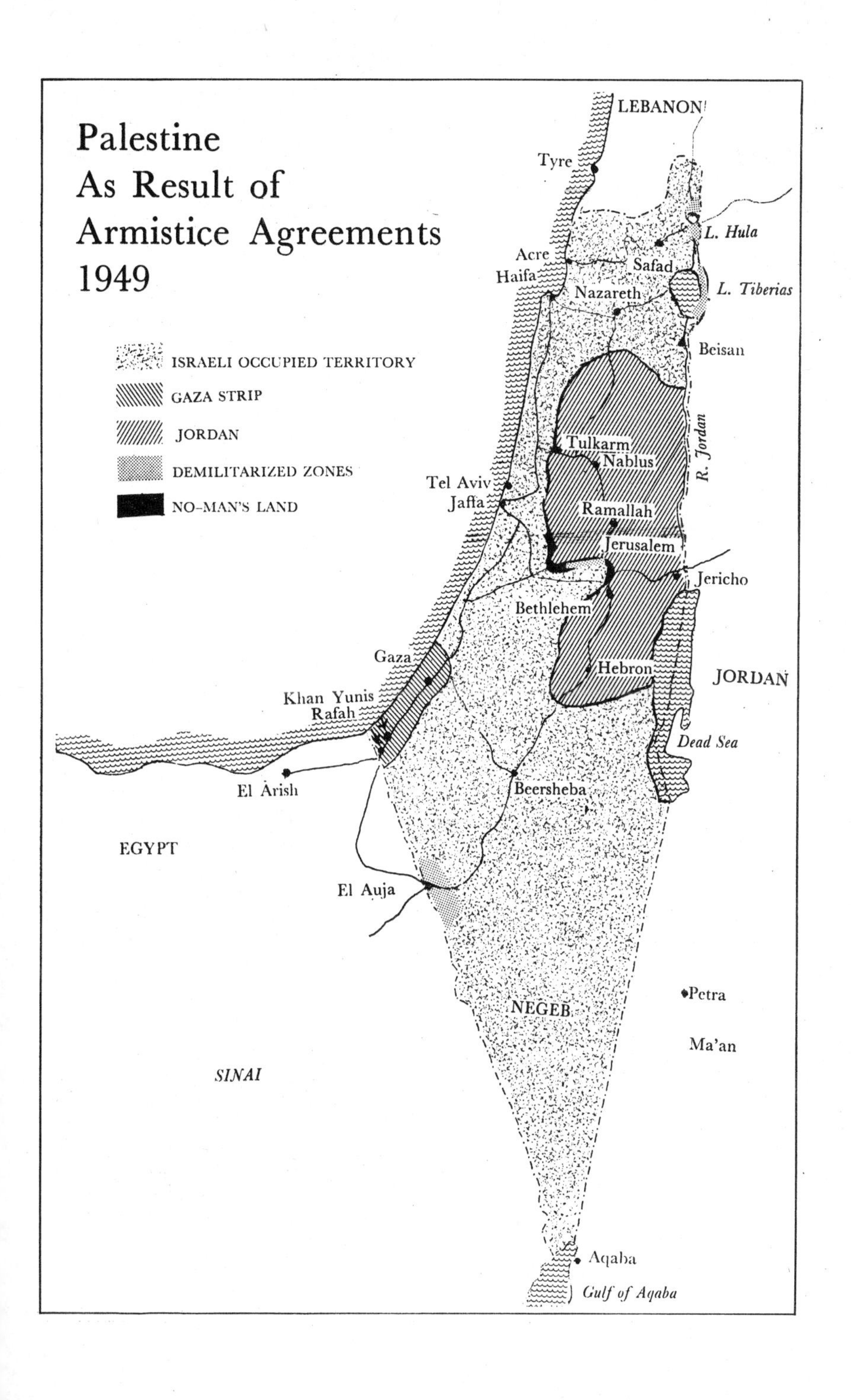

Palestine
As Result of
Armistice Agreements
1949
ISRAELI OCCUPIED TERRITORY
GAZA STRIP
JORDAN
DEMILITARIZED ZONES
NO-MAN'S LAND
LEBANON
Tyre
Acre
Haifa
Safad
L. Hula
L. Tiberias
Nazareth
Beisan
R. Jordan
Tulkarm
Nablus
Tel Aviv
Jaffa
Ramallah
Jerusalem
Jericho
Bethlehem
Gaza
Hebron
JORDAN
Khan Yunis
Rafah
Dead Sea
El Arish
Beersheba
EGYPT
El Auja
Petra
NEGEB
Ma'an
SINAI
Aqaba
Gulf of Aqaba

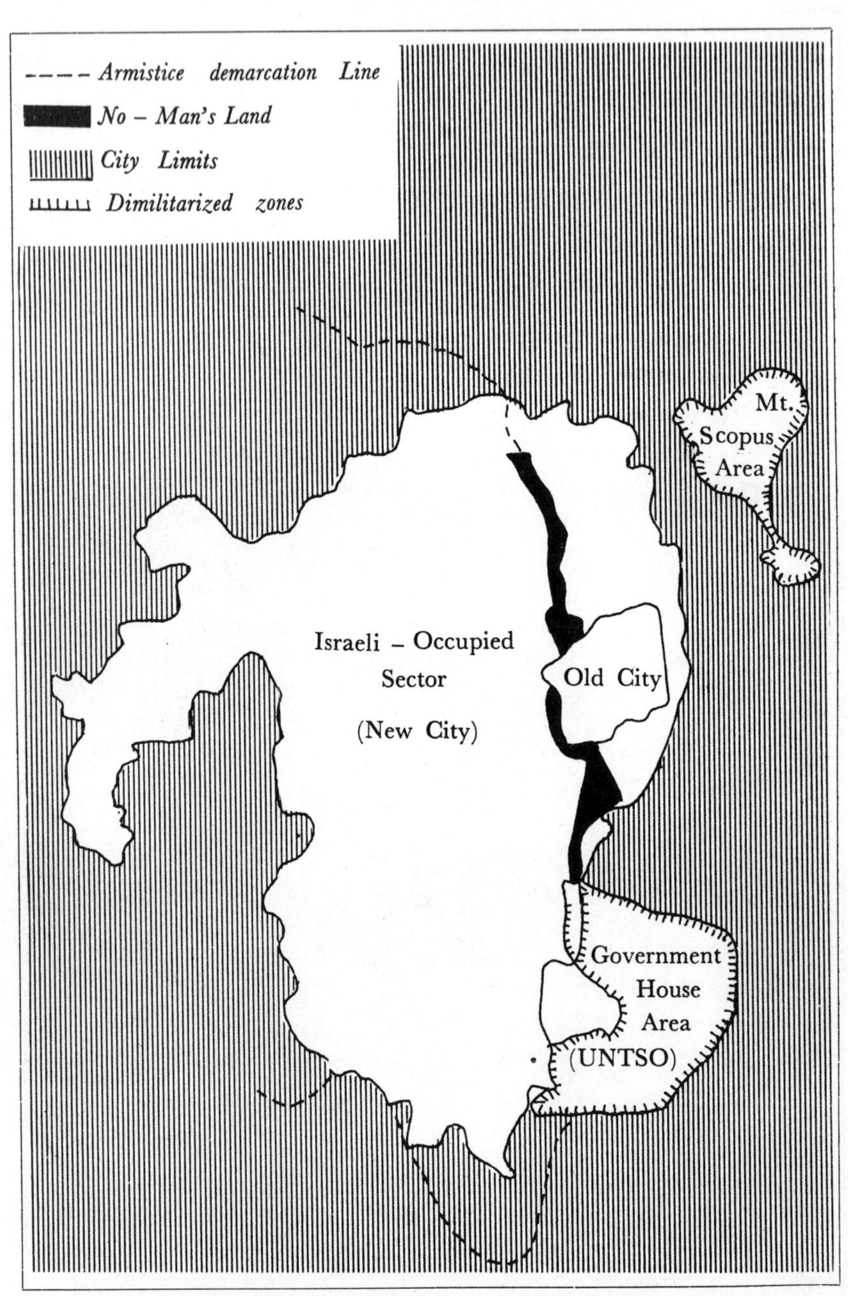

Jerusalem According to the General Armistice Agreement 1949

IV to the Agreement. These areas are seldom referred to in discussions of the problem and are little understood as to their significance.

Article VII, paragraph 8, prescribes, "Where interpretation of the meaning of a particular provision of this Agreement, other than the preamble and Articles I and II, is at issue, the Commission's interpretation shall prevail."

It should be noted that until the signing of the General Armistice Agreement, the Syrian army had been in occupation of the greater part of the Demilitarized Zone and that it was only after the arrangements agreed upon in Article V of the Agreement had been concluded, did the Syrian troops withdraw from the area.

But shortly after the signing of the Armistice Agreement, the Syrian Government had occasion to complain that the Israeli authorities were contravening their undertakings under Article V. The Israelis, the Syrian Government complained, had not only refused to allow the return of the Arab civilian inhabitants to their homes, but also, among other things, had banished into the interior those who had remained in their homes in the central sector of the zone.* [7] When summoned by the Chairman of the Mixed Armistice Commission to a meeting of the Commission to consider the Syrian complaint, the Israeli authorities refused to attend, claiming that the demilitarized zone was in Israeli territory and as such was not subject to discussion with the Syrian Government.

This Israeli attitude was reported to the Security Council in a memorandum dated 7 March 1951. At the same time, the Chief of Staff gave his own interpretation of the provisions of the Armistice Agreement. He explained that the demilitarized zone was "defined with a view toward separating the armed forces of both parties while providing for the gradual restoration of normal civilian life in the area of the demilitarized zone." He pointed out that "the

---

* General Vagn Bennike, the Chief of Staff who replaced General William Riley, stated before the Security Council on 9 November 1953: "785 Arabs were removed from their homes" on the night of 30-31 March 1951 in the demilitarized zone.

Chairman of the Mixed Armistice Commission was charged with the responsibility of ensuring that the provisions of the Armistice Agreement with respect to the demilitarized zone were implemented;" and concluded by saying, "It follows that neither party to the Armistice Agreement therefore enjoys rights of sovereignty within the zone." [8]

In a follow-up cable to the Security Council on 12 April 1951, the Acting Chief of Staff stated that in his discussion of the Israeli attitude with the Acting Israeli Foreign Minister, the latter is said to have informed him that "The Government of Israel considered that the demilitarized zone was in Israel territory," and "insisted upon the non-interference by Syria in the internal affairs of Israel." To this, the Acting Chief of Staff replied: "As long as the Israel-Syrian General Armistice Agreement was in force, the territory controlled by Israel was west of the demilitarized zone demarcation line, the demilitarized zone having special status." [9]

The Security Council convened to consider the Syrian complaint and the reports of the Chief of Staff. On 18 May 1951, the Council adopted a resolution confirming that "Article V of the General Armistice Agreement gives to the Chairman (of the Mixed Armistice Commission) the responsibility for the general supervision of the demilitarized zone." The Council considered it "inconsistent with the objectives and intent of the Armistice Agreement to refuse to participate in meetings of the Mixed Armistice Commission or to fail to respect requests of the Chairman of the Mixed Armistice Commission as they relate to his obligations under Article V . . ."

The Council then called upon the parties to give effect to the following which, it pointed out, had already been agreed to by the parties at the conference held on 3 July 1949 at which the articles of the draft armistice agreement were being considered, as being "an authoritative comment on Article V of the Syrian-Israeli Armistice Agreement":

> "The question of civil administration in villages and settlements in the demilitarized zone is provided for, within the framework of an armistice agreement, in sub-paragraphs 5 (b)

and 5 (f) of the draft article. Such civil administration, including policing, will be on a local basis, without raising general questions of administration, jurisdiction, citizenship and sovereignty.

"Where Israel civilians return to or remain in an Israel village or settlement, the civil administration and policing of the village or settlement will be Israelis. Similarly, where Arab civilians return to or remain in an Arab village, a local Arab administration and police unit will be authorized.

"As civilian life is gradually restored, administration will take shape on a local basis under the general supervision of the Chairman of the Mixed Armistice Commission.

"The Chairman of the Mixed Armistice Commission, in consultation and co-operation with the local communities, will be in a position to authorize all necessary arrangements for restoration and protection of civilian life. He will not assume responsibility for direct administration of the zone." * [10]

With regard to the evacuation of the Arab residents from the demilitarized zone, the Security Council decided that "Arab civilians who have been removed from the demilitarized zone by the Government of Israel should be permitted to return to their homes and that the Mixed Armistice Commission should supervise their return and rehabilitation in a manner to be determined by the Commission." The Council further held that "no action involving the transfer of persons across international frontiers, armistice lines or within the demilitarized zone should be undertaken without prior decision of the Chairman of the Mixed Armistice Commission." [11]

While the Security Council resolution correctly interpreted the status of the demilitarized zone, the obligations of the parties

---

* Cited by the Chief of Staff at the 542nd meeting of the Security Council on 25 April 1951, as being from the summary record of the Syria-Israel Armistice Conference of 3 July 1949 – at which Acting Mediator Ralph Bunche was present – which culminated in the signing of the Israeli-Syrian Armistice Agreement on 20 July 1949. The text was embodied in Council resolution 93 (1951) of 18 May 1951.

under the Agreement and the responsibilities of the Mixed Armistice Commission, its provisions remained unimplemented and the United Nations took no action to enforce compliance. The Israelis continued to refuse to attend meetings of the Mixed Armistice Commission pertaining to the zone; they persisted in preventing the return of the Arab civilian inhabitants to their villages; they failed to appoint 'locally recruited Arab civilian police' for internal security purposes which obviously became unnecessary after the Arab inhabitants had either been banished into the interior or expelled across the armistice demarcation line into Syria; they seized Arab lands and established Jewish settlements thereon; militarized the zone; and blocked admission of United Nations personnel into the zone – claiming absolute sovereignty over it as an integral part of Israel, despite the Security Council ruling to the contrary.

During the rest of 1951 and the whole of 1952, there was no change in the Israeli attitude of defiance. In four separate reports, the Chief of Staff drew the attention of the Security Council that the Israeli authorities have refused to implement the Council's resolution of 18 May 1951; [12] that Israeli police continue to occupy and to exercise general control over the demilitarized zone; [13] that Israeli police control the movements of the Arabs and interfere with the freedom of movement of the Chairman of the Mixed Armistice Commission and United Nations observers; [14] and that the Israeli police continue to maintain a check-post on the main road of Mishmar ha Yarden in the central sector of the demilitarized zone. Although removal of the check-post was requested by the Chairman, it has not been removed. [15]

On 27 October 1953, General Vagn Bennike, the new Chief of Staff, appeared before the Security Council to report on the situation along the armistice demarcation line. In regard to the Israeli-Syrian General Armistice Agreement, General Bennike reiterated the difficulties reported upon by General Riley during the previous two years. He listed these as "the economic situation of the Arabs in the demilitarized zone, encroachments on Arab lands, control exercised by the Israeli police over the greater part of the zone, Israeli opposition to the fulfilment by the Chairman and United Nations observers of their responsibility for ensuring the implementation of Article V of the General Armistice Agreement."

The Chief of Staff then suggested that "These difficulties can be solved if the provisions of Article V of the General Armistice Agreement are applied in the light of the Acting Mediator's authoritative comment, accepted by both Parties in 1949." [16] General Bennike then referred to a later statement which his predecessor, General Riley, had read at the Security Council meeting on 25 April 1951, i.e., Dr. Ralph Bunche, Acting Mediator, wrote, *inter alia*: "In the nature of the case, therefore, under the provisions of the Armistice Agreement, neither party could validly claim to have a free hand in the demilitarized zone over civilian activity, while military activity was totally excluded."

General Bennike then expressed the opinion that "total adhesion to these two principles would greatly ease the situation. It would mean, in particular, he said, recognition of the special powers of the Chairman of the Mixed Armistice Commission and the observers in the demilitarized zone." [17]

Despite all these reports of Israeli violations, no change in the situation took place; and at its 72nd Emergency Meeting held on 12 December 1954, the Israeli-Syrian Mixed Armistice Commission condemned "the presence of a regular Israel police force in the southern demilitarized zone as a flagrant violation of Article V of the General Armistice Agreement" and requested "the Israel authorities to take promptly the necessary steps to . . . withdraw definitely Israel regular police from the southern demilitarized zone." [18]

On 6 January 1955, the new Chief of Staff, Lt-General E.L.M. Burns, also was obliged to report to the Security Council that "police from the state of Israel, acting under orders from police headquarters outside the demilitarized zone, dominated the zone;" adding that "The Chairman of the Mixed Armistice Commission was unable to implement the provision of the General Armistice Agreement requiring the employment of 'locally recruited civilian police' in the zone. Repeated requests by the Chairman of the Mixed Armistice Commission," he said, "to remove the non-local police from the demilitarized zone were rejected." [19] In May 1956, General Burns drew the attention of the Secretary-General of the United Nations to the effect that "the position had not changed in any essential since his last report." [20]

In January 1958, General Carl Von Horn, of Sweden, replaced General Burns as fourth Chief of Staff of the United Nations Truce Supervision Organization for Palestine. During his first courtesy visit to the Israeli Foreign Office, writes Von Horn, "he was left in no doubt that the United Nations had failed regrettably to co-operate with Israel's sincere desire for a peaceful settlement, had entirely neglected in fact to show the understanding and sympathetic tolerance for a small, oppressed State which would have been in keeping with its role as a world force dedicated to peace." The General concludes that "the gist of the advice 'to assist me in my task' was that I should refrain from sticking to the rules of the Armistice Agreement." [21]

Soon after this social meeting, the situation in the demilitarized zone flared up at Et-Tawafiq. The Chairman of the Mixed Armistice Commission invited the parties to attend a meeting of the Commission to consider the situation. The Syrians replied "they were ready to meet the Israelis at any time within the framework of the Mixed Armistice Commission to discuss the recent incidents and aggressive actions which had arisen through Israel breaking the General Armistice Agreement. But in order to ensure the tranquility of the area, problems affecting the demilitarized zone *must* be discussed." General Von Horn said he put this to the Israeli authorities but "met a blank wall of refusal." He remarked, "I was very angry. And with reason. The Israelis had broken the Armistice Agreement, broken their word, ignored my ruling of 20 January and were now blatantly disregarding the Security Council's ruling that they should attend meetings called by the Chairman of the Mixed Armistice Commission. It was stalemate; there was no alternative but to convene a meeting without them," decided General Von Horn. [22]

The meeting was convened; and once the Syrian complaints had been considered and the observers' reports examined, the events which had led up to the incident were summed up in careful detail. The meeting recalled that "the Israelis had broken the agreement reached in November 1957, had opposed the Chief of Staff of U.N.T.S.O.'s findings of 20 January 1960 by using force against the Arabs and had used their regular armed forces to attack Lower Tawafiq which had no fortifications other than a trench and some barbed-wire entanglements. As a result of this premeditated attack serious tension had been aroused in the area." [23]

The Et-Tawafiq incident reached the Security Council and General Von Horn arrived in New York to appear before the Council on 3 April, 1962. Sitting in his temporary office on the 38th floor of the United Nations building, the General received a visit by Michel Comay, the Israeli representative. The conversation which followed gives a true picture of the Israeli character and the methods used to achieve an objective. "It would be best," advised Comay, "to forget all about that out-dated United Nations idea of running a patrol boat on Lake Tiberias; the idea was stillborn," he said, "and ought to be abandoned, because the Lake was essentially Israeli sovereign territory." Comay then pointed out that "he understood that this had already been made clear in Jerusalem. After all," he said, "why did I waste my time insisting on so many things which I knew the Israelis were opposed to?" He concluded: "It would be wise to listen to his advice–otherwise my life was bound to become a great deal more uncomfortable." [24]

General Von Horn replied that he "appreciated his thinly-veiled threats," and pointed out, "it was really a waste of breath to attempt to intimidate the Chief of Staff of U.N.T.S.O. – especially on United Nations territory." General Von Horn then borrowed a phrase of Mrs. Meir's * [25] and told him, "I did not

---

* At a meeting with Mrs. Meir in Jerusalem to protest the barring of the General's path by Jewish guards on Mount Scopus from entering the demilitarized zone, Mrs. Meir is reported to have retorted: We, Jews, do not like to be pushed around."

want to be pushed around." [26]

On 3 April 1962, General Von Horn appeared before the Security Council and reminded its members that "when, in 1956, the late Secretary-General had requested a specific assurance from both sides that the principle of United Nations freedom of movement should be recognized, assurances to this effect had been given by all the Arab States whilst Israel had come up with the proviso that it would 'continue to afford United Nations observers the same degree of freedom of movement inside Israel which all visitors to the country normally enjoy'." [27]

From that date on, the Israeli authorities doggedly persisted in their attitude of refusal to abide by their obligations under the General Armistice Agreement; the United Nations did nothing to compel the Israelis to comply; while the situation within the zone had gone from bad to worse. The clashes which took place in the area during 1966 and the fierce air and land battles early in 1967, should serve as a reminder to the United Nations that unless Israeli aggression is arrested and Israeli leaders are compelled to respect their obligations under the General Armistice Agreement, the future may spell disaster.

2. Mount Scopus Demilitarized Zone

The Mount Scopus demilitarized zone runs along the crest of a hill to the north of Jerusalem. It commands a general view of the City and dominates its east and north approaches. The entire hill is inside Jordan territory and its strategic importance is recognized.

The zone comprises the Hebrew University and Hadassah Hospital compound, as well as the Augusta Victoria building which is presently being used as a hospital for the Palestine Arab refugees.

Under an agreement signed on 7 July 1948 between the Jordan and Israeli Military Commanders of Jerusalem – to which the United Nations was a third party – the area was demilitarized and officially designated to be under "United Nations protection until hostilities cease or a new agreement is entered upon."

The Agreement provided for U.N. check-posts to be established by the U.N. Commander; for Arab and Jewish civilian police to be placed on duty under the U.N. Commander; the U.N. flag to fly on the main buildings; all military personnel to be withdrawn together with such of their equipment and other supplies as are not required by the U.N. Commander; the U.N. to arrange that both parties receive adequate supplies of food and water, and replacements of necessary personnel in residence on Mount Scopus. Under an Annex to the Agreement of the same date, it was agreed that the United Nations Observers would be responsible to arrange for the relief of 50% of the Jewish personnel on Mount Scopus during the first and third weeks of each month.

The General Armistice Agreement signed between the Jordan Government and the Israeli authorities which followed on 3 April 1949, did not supersede the 1948 Agreement; and the map of Jerusalem attached to the Armistice Agreement shows the demilitarized zone to be on the Jordan side of the armistice demarcation line and therefore outside Israeli jurisdiction.

The United Nations flag was hoisted – and still flies – over the Hebrew University and Hadassah Hospital buildings, while Jewish policemen were allowed to guard Jewish-owned property within the zone. Similarly, the United Nations flag continues to fly over the Augusta Victoria building and only Arab policemen are allowed into the area.

The intent and spirit of the two Agreements are obvious. The demilitarized zone was supposed to be under the direct control of the Chief of Staff of the United Nations Truce Supervision Organization and that the civilian policemen (Arab and Jewish) who were to guard Arab and Jewish properties respectively in the zone, were supposed to obey his orders.

But in actual practice, this has not been the case in the Jewish section since the Agreement of 7 July 1948 was signed. Although the United Nations flag still flies over the buildings, United Nations personnel are not permitted to come anywhere close to the area which the Israelis define as 'an enclave of Israel'; Arab farmers tending their fields in the vicinty are periodically fired upon with impunity; pedestrians crossing Arab lands on the western fringes of the zone to the village of Isawiya beyond are molested; and the United Nations does nothing to assert its authority in a territory over which its own flag flies.

With conditions being what they were, it soon became apparent to the Jordan Government that, apart from violating their obligations under the Military Agreement of 1948, the Israelis were using the convoys authorized under the Annex Agreement to reinforce the supposedly 'Jewish police guards' on Mount Scopus and to militarize the zone. Jordan suspicions were confirmed with the disclosure of two incidents. The first became known as "The Barrel Incident". U.S. Commander Elmo Hutchison, who served with the United Nations Truce Supervision Organization in Palestine from 1951 to 1955 first as observer and later as Chairman of the Israel-Jordan Mixed Armistice Commission, reports that on June 4 1952, while the fortnightly convoy to Mount Scopus was being checked before entering Jordan territory, the United Nations guard observed that his test rod struck a metal object in the centre of one of the drums. He ordered the drum taken off the truck; and while he sent for the tools to have the drum opened, the Israelis pushed the truck carrying the rest of the drums towards the Israeli check-post outside the reach of the United Nations observers to escape further detection.

Commander Hutchison adds: "Before the cutting tools could be obtained, the Israelis, in direct violation of the Armistice Agreement, moved soldiers into no-man's land and demanded the return of the remaining barrel." But the barrel was removed into the close-by office of the Mixed Armistice Commission to be held until a decision on its future could be obtained from the Chief of Staff, General William Riley, who was then in New York.

The Israelis, continued Commander Hutchison, demanded the return of the barrel without further inspection. The Jordanians in the meantime claimed that it was the duty of the UNTSO to check it thoroughly before it went on to Mount Scopus or was returned to Israel. All members of the Mission who were present agreed, he said, that the barrel should be opened. General Riley was contacted, and after a few days he sent a message granting permission to open the barrel. The opening was set for 12:30 hours local time on June 20.

At 12:00 on the day scheduled, the door of the Mixed Armistice Commission office burst open and three Israeli officers, with pistols drawn and escorted by two enlisted men who were holding Thompson sub-machine guns at the ready, marched into the room and stationed themselves outside the barrel-room door. The Jordan Military delegate, who arrived soon after appraised the situation and enquired how much of this the United Nations would tolerate. He then left in protest stating that no further MAC meetings would be held in that building.

Attempts were made by the United Nations observers at the appointed time to open the door but they were prevented by the Israeli soldiers. The Israeli authorities refused to recognize the inviolability of the United Nations Office; took over the offices; placed another lock on the barrel-room door and took away the key to the MAC building in the possession of the United Nations. What transpired in the interval to tamper with the contents of the barrel is a matter of conjecture.

However, on his return from New York, General Riley condemned the Israeli action of allowing their soldiers to enter no-man's land and for taking over the MAC building. He then arranged to have the barrel checked. What happened to make him change his mind from having the barrel opened to dipping a rod into its unknown contents, it is not difficult to surmise. In the end he remarked: "There is extraneous matter in this barrel and I don't believe it contains the 50 gallons of fuel oil as required by the manifest. I am, therefore, returning the barrel to Israeli control." The Jordan representative immediately protested and demanded that the barrel be opened, but General Riley over-ruled and the matter of the barrel was considered closed much to the consternation of the Jordan Government and the disappointment of the United Nations personnel who went to so much trouble to carry out their duties faithfully.

Commander Hutchison summed up the situation in those

words: "Israel was guilty of falsifying records submitted to the United Nations; Israel was guilty of attempted smuggling and had revealed to the world it was contravening the Mount Scopus Agreement; Israel had ignored the inviolability of the United Nations Mixed Armistice Commission Headquarters and had taken it over by armed force; Israel had broken the General Armistice Agreement by ordering troops into no-man's land. All of this should have been flashed around the world – not only by Jordan but by the United Nations. Instead, the United Nations kept quiet . . ." [29]

The second incident occurred on 13 December 1952. A group of Israelis attempted to make an end run to the north of Jerusalem with a good-sized load of ammunition for Mount Scopus. Six U.S. Army manpacks were used for the haul. They included 1,000 rounds of rifle ammunition, 2,000 rounds of Sten-gun ammunition, six 81mm. mortar shells, six 2" mortar shells, three 90 volt dry batteries and 24 hand grenades with a tine of detonators. Commander Hutchison states, "The Israelis had almost reached their objective when they were surprised by Jordanian National Guardsmen. They fled, leaving the loaded manpacks on the ground. Three of the men lost their fatigue caps bearing names and numbers. One of the men must have been wounded, as blood-stains and a bandage were found near one of the packs. Twice during the night the Israelis tried to retrieve the equipment, but on both occasions they were driven back."

"The next day," Hutchison states, "the Israelis entered a counter-complaint, alleging that a group of Arabs had entered an ammunition supply camp in Jerusalem and stolen the manpacks. They also claimed that an Israeli guard had been wounded during the Arab raid." [30]

This Israeli attempt at distortion did not impress the Mixed Armistice Commission which condemned Israel for trying to smuggle ammunition to Mount Scopus.

The Jordan Government did not cease to express its deep concern to the successive Chiefs of Staff of the United Nations Truce Supervision Organization over what was happening on Mount

Scopus. General Riley did little to assert United Nations authority over the demilitarized zone after the Military Agreement had been concluded on 7 July 1948; and when he made his belated and feeble effort in 1952 to inspect the area, "the Israelis could not furnish the keys to several rooms." In the Fall of 1953, General Bennike, who replaced General Riley and inherited an unsatisfactory situation on Mount Scopus, made a similar attempt, but the Jewish officer in charge informed him that he had no orders to allow the inspection. After contact with the Israeli authorities, the inspection was permitted, only to be disallowed to continue thirty minutes after it had started. [31]

General E.L.M. Burns, who replaced General Bennike in 1954, had no better luck. He said he considered it perfectly understandable that Jordan should be deeply concerned about Israeli encroachments on Mount Scopus. The zone, he explained, absolutely dominates the roads into Jerusalem which is the nexus of all important roads connecting the larger towns of Arab-held Palestine. "If the Israelis," the General pointed out, "could connect up with the sort of fortess held by the detachment of Israeli police (who were probably regular soldiers), they would dominate and could eventually compel the surrender of Jerusalem and probably cause the collapse of Jordanian control of the area west of the Jordan River." He added, "the seizure or occupation of it by Israel would be a disaster for Jordan." [32]

3. **Jabal el-Mukabbir Demilitarized Zone**

Besides being a demilitarized zone, this area, comprising the old Government House, the Arab College, a Jewish Agricultural School and the lands around, has a special status.

The Government House building is being used as the headquarters of the United Nations Truce Supervision Organization for Palestine, the Arab College is empty and neglected after having been sacked by the Israelis in an attempt to occupy it, while the Jewish Agricultural School is in operation.

The Israelis made several attempts to exert sovereignty over the area; and on 22 January 1958, the Security Council was obliged to draw their attention that "the status of the zone is affected by the provisions of the Israel-Jordan General Armistice Agreement and that neither Israel nor Jordan enjoys sovereignty over any part of the zone (the zone being beyond the respective demarcation lines.)" [33]

The fact that no forceful entrance has been made so far can only be explained as due to the physical presence of the United Nations Truce Supervision Organization on the spot.

4. **No-Man's Land between the Arab and Israeli-held Sectors of Jerusalem**

This area consists of open fields and demolished or damaged buildings. Where a building is only partly damaged and the entrance is on the Israeli side, the Israelis have occupied such buildings against the protests of the Jordan Government and the directives of the United Nations Truce Supervision Organization. The Tannous building near the Jaffa Gate is a case in point. Every effort of the Mixed Armistice Commission to dislodge the Israelis has failed and the United Nations did nothing about it.

5. **The Latrun area (on the Jaffa-Jerusalem road)**

This No-Man's Land area consists of agricultural land comprising approximately 15,500 acres wholly owned by the Arab farmers of the surrounding villages.

The Israelis first attempted to eliminate its status by suggesting its division between Jordan and themselves or exchanging it for territory further north; and when both these proposals failed, the Israelis began to encroach on the land through cultivation of as many plots as they could in an effort to establish a precedent, as they did in the demilitarized zones. Clashes ensued which necessitated Security Council intervention.

The natural and obvious thing to do is to permit the Arab farmers to cultivate their lands under United Nations protection. To leave the land fallow is to invite trouble.

6. **Villages severed by the Armistice Demarcation Line**

When hostilities between Jordan and the Israeli authorities ceased, there were certain Arab villages within the 'Little Triangle' in the central sector of Palestine where the inhabitants had successfully defended themselves, their homes and lands against Zionist attacks until the cease-fire order of the Security Council became effective. Some of these villages and localities were later ceded to the Israelis under certain specific conditions explicitly prescribed in the General Armistice Agreement.

Article VI, paragraph 6, stipulated, "Where villages may be affected by the establishment of the Armistice Demarcation Line provided for in paragraph 2 of this article, the inhabitants of such villages shall be entitled to maintain and shall be protected in, their full rights of residence, property and freedom."

In the case of Arab villages located on the Israeli side of the demarcation line, the Article prescribed, "It shall be prohibited for Israeli forces to enter or to be stationed in such villages, in which locally recruited Arab police shall be organized and stationed for internal security purposes."

There is no ambiguity in the intent and meaning of these two provisions. The first applies to Arab villages situated on both sides of the armistice demarcation line and whose lands are severed by the line. In this case, the farmers were guaranteed their 'full rights' in homes and property. This also meant that the villagers were to be allowed to cross over the line, cultivate their lands, gather their crops and remove them to their villages as they had been doing since time immemorial. In the case of Arab villages falling on the Israeli side of the armistice line, the provision is clear that internal security was to be the responsibility of 'locally recruited Arab police', and that Israeli forces were to be 'prohibited' from entering or being stationed in these villages.

After signature of the Armistice Agreement, the farmers of Arab villages on the Jordan side were in fact permitted to cross over and to cultivate their lands. But when it came to harvesting their crops, the farmers were prevented from doing so under the threat of military force, which resulted in clashes and in some instances in the loss of life. The Arab crops that year were gathered by the Israelis; and soon after, also the lands were seized and distributed among existing Jewish settlements or used for the establishment of new fortified frontier settlements.

As regards the second provision, the Israelis failed to establish the 'locally recruited Arab police' which they undertook under the Agreement to do. Instead they stationed their own Jewish frontier force and applied the same discriminatory and emergency regulations in force in Arab villages in the Galilee area. Some of the Arab lands were confiscated and the villagers could not move about freely, along with other restrictions. On 29 October 1956 – the day the Israelis invaded Egypt – a curfew was imposed on the village of Kafr Qasem while the farmers were absent in their fields; and when they returned to their homes, they were met with bursts of gun fire for no apparent reason which resulted in the death of 51 men, women and children and the wounding of 13 others. Among the dead were 12 women and girls, ten boys between the ages of 14 and 17 and seven between the ages of 8 and 13 years. This dastardly deed was not only in 'flagrant violation' of the Armistice Agreement; it was 'deliberate murder' by those who were supposed to 'protect' the Arab inhabitants.

The Arab inhabitants believed that the arrangements affecting them in the Armistice Agreement were only temporary measures for the period of the armistice. Had it been suspected that the situation would develop into incorporating their villages and lands into Israeli territory, it is certain that the Jordan Government would not have agreed to the arrangement and more than likely that the villagers would have continued to fight.

7. Functions of the Special Committee

Article VIII of the Israeli-Jordan General Armistice Agreement provides for the establishment of a Special Committee to formulate "agreed plans and arrangements":

1. designed to enlarge the scope and improve the application

of the Armistice;

2. for such matters as either Party may submit to it, "which, in any case, shall include the following:
   (a) free movement of traffic on vital roads, including the Bethlehem and Latrun-Jerusalem roads;
   (b) resumption of the normal functioning of the cultural and humanitarian institutions on Mount Scopus and free access thereto;
   (c) free access to the Holy Places and cultural institutions and use of the cemetery on the Mount of Olives;
   (d) resumption of operation of the Latrun pumping station;
   (e) provision of electricity for the Old City; and
   (f) resumption of operation of the railroad to Jerusalem."

The Special Committee had its first meetings in 1949* under the chairmanship of General William Riley, Chief of Staff of the United Nations Truce Supervision Organization at the time.

The Israeli position throughout the 1949 meetings of the Special Committee was – and still is – that Article VIII was, with two exceptions, entirely in their favour. They claimed it gave them the right of access to Mount Scopus, the Jewish cemetery on the Mount of Olives, the Wailing Wall in the Old City, free movement of traffic on the Latrun-Jerusalem road, resumption of operation of the Latrun water pumping station and resumption of the railroad to Jerusalem.

The Special Committee's functions under Article VIII, they maintained, were merely to decide on the procedure to be adopted for the implementation of the points cited above, with no right for the Arab side to raise new issues.

In return, the Israelis said, Jordan would have access to Bethlehem through the occupied part of Jerusalem; and the Old

---

* The Jordan Delegation was composed of Hamad el-Farhan and Abdullah el-Tal, with Capt. (later General) Ali Abu Nuwwar acting as military adviser and Sami Hadawi acting as civilian adviser.
The Israeli Delegation was composed of Moshe Dayan and Avraham Biran.

City would be supplied with electricity from the main plant in the Israeli-held Sector.

The Jordan Delegation pointed out that its own interpretation of the meaning of Article VIII was far wider in scope and spirit than the Israelis allege. It maintained that the intent and purpose of the said Article were to provide for normal civilian life to return to the Holy City for *all* sections of the population without exception. It is inconceivable, the Delegation explained, that the Article could have been designed to serve the interests of the Israelis in full and utterly disregard the interests of the Arab inhabitants of Jerusalem.

The Jordan Delegation then proceeded to present its point of view, as follows:

(1) The first paragraph of Article VIII stipulates that a Special Committee shall be established "for the purpose of formulating agreed plans and arrangements designed to enlarge the scope of this Agreement." The words "to enlarge the scope" can only mean that the door is left open for both Parties to proffer claims and counter-claims before the Special Committee which they had no time to formulate during the hurried interval the Armistice Agreement was prepared.

(2) The first sentence of paragraph 2 of the said Article lays down that the Special Committee "shall direct its attention to the formulation of agreed plans and arrangements *for such matters as either Party may submit to it.*" This provision reinforces the first argument that the Parties are not restricted to the six specific items enumerated in the Article, but are at liberty to 'enlarge' on them, particularly since the words which follow make it clear that such matters, '*in any case, shall include*' the items specified, 'on which agreement in principle already exists.' The words 'in any case' are very significant because they indicate that whatever is decided upon by the Special Committee, the enlarged programme *must* include the items enumerated in the Article.

(3) The meaning of the item on "free movement of traffic on vital roads, including the Bethlehem and Latrun-Jerusalem roads," is quite obvious that the Special Committee is empowered to establish what in its judgement are roads *vital to both Parties*, but that

such vital roads *must* include the Bethlehem and Latrun-Jerusalem roads. If only the two roads were intended, the Article would have stated so without needing to prefix the words 'vital roads'.

(4) The Article also provided for "free access to the Holy Places." Here again it did not limit this free access to *Jewish* Holy Places, nor did it specify that 'Holy Places' means the Wailing Wall, as the Israeli claim alluded. If it had meant either or both these cases, it would have said so explicitly.

The Jordan Delegation maintained that free access to the Holy Places meant for Moslems, Christians and Jews over the whole territory of Palestine; not made available to Jews in both Arab and Israeli-held territories and out-of-bounds to Moslems and Christians in the Israeli-held area. If Jews are to be accorded rights and privileges in the Arab area, then it is only reasonable to demand that Moslems and Christians should be accorded the same treatment in a land which is theirs by right of birth and occupation until expelled.

The Jordan Delegation then presented the following 'plans and arrangements' to the Israeli side and suggested that they form a package deal and the basis for the discussion:

(1) *The Jordan Government* agrees to permit access to the Jewish buildings on Mount Scopus, the Jewish cemetery on the Mount of Olives, the Wailing Wall in the Old City, free movement of traffic on the Latrun-Jerusalem road, resumption of operation of the Latrun water pumping station and resumption of operation of the railroad to Jerusalem.

(2) *The Israeli Government*, on its part, agrees to permit the return of the Moslem and Christian inhabitants of Jerusalem to their homes; to grant free access to the Holy Places in Israeli-held territory, such as, Nazareth and Nabi Rubin in Jaffa; free movement of traffic on vital roads, such as, to Nazareth and Jaffa on festival occasions; to Gaza to provide a link between Arab families living in Jordan and the Gaza Strip; and free movement of traffic to Bethlehem. The question of providing the Old City with electricity from the Israeli Sector was dropped as it was neither practical nor necessary any more.

(3) *Jerusalem* will continue to be administered as a divided city, the Israelis having jurisdiction over the Jewish populated areas and the Jordan over the Arab quarters.

The Israeli Delegation ridiculed the proposals and described them as 'fantastic'. The Israeli representatives were reminded that if they demanded for their citizens the right to lead a normal civilian life, they must not deny the same right to the Moslem and Christian inhabitants. With Israeli refusal to discuss Arab claims, the meetings came to an end. Further meetings were held in 1950 and again they bogged down in barren wrangling over the agenda, as a result of the extremely restricted scope of action which the Israeli delegation sought to impose on it.

8. **Demilitarized Zone on the Egyptian Border**

The Armistice Agreement with Egypt provides in Article VIII, paragraph 1, "The area comprising the village of El-Auja and vicinity shall be demilitarized, and both Egyptian and Israeli armed forces shall be totally excluded thereform." The Article goes on to say, "The Chairman of the Mixed Armistice Commission and United Nations Observers attached to the Commission shall be responsible for ensuring the full implementation of this provision."

Paragraph 5 stipulates, "The movement of armed forces of either Party to this Agreement into any part of the area defined in paragraph 2 of this Article, for any purpose, or failure by either Party to respect or fulfill any of the other provisions of this Article, when confirmed by the United Nations representative, shall constitute a flagrant violation of this Agreement."

Article X, paragraph 2, provides, "The Mixed Armistice Commission shall maintain its headquarters at El-Auja . . ." And paragraph 8 states, "Where interpretation of the meaning of a particular provision of this Agreement is at issue, the Commission's interpretation shall prevail, subject to appeal . . ."

As in the case of the demilitarized zone on the Syrian border, the Israeli authorities, no sooner was the Armistice Agreement signed, when they began to exert control over El-Auja. They expelled the Arab inhabitants, seized their lands, established Jewish settlements and started to militarize the zone, claiming sovereignty over the entire area. It is noteworthy that not one inch of land within the zone is Jewish-owned, and no Jewish settlement had ever existed therein prior to the date of its seizure by the Israelis.

On 20 March 1950, the Mixed Armistice Commission decided that the occupation by the Israeli forces of Bir Qattar within the zone was a violation of the Armistice Agreement. Upon appeal by Israel, the Special Committee of the Mixed Armistice Commission, whose decisions are final, confirmed the decision. But Israeli forces continued to occupy the area. [34] The matter was reported to the Security Council and on 13 November, the Chief of Staff affirmed that the decision of the Special Committee was final and that Israel had not carried it out. [35] The representative of Israel then announced that his Government was prepared to comply with the decision.[36] On the strength of this promise, the Security Council, in its resolution dated 17 November 1950, took note of the statement "that Israel armed forces will evacuate Bir Qattar pursuant to the 20 March 1950 decision of the Special Committee" and that "the Israel armed forces will withdraw to positions authorized by the Armistice Agreement." * [37]

On 18 September 1950, General Riley, then Chief of Staff, reported to the Security Council on the Israeli explusion of the Arab inhabitants of the El-Auja demilitarized zone. He stated: "On 2 September 1950, Israeli military rounded up some 4,000 Bedouins who have been living in the Negeb in and around the demilitarized zone of El-Auja, and drove them out of Israel-controlled territory across the Egyptian international boundary into Egyptian territory ..."

"An investigation of the above incident by the Chairman of the Egyptian-Israel Mixed Armistice Commission on 6 September revealed," he said, "that refugee Arabs representing five Bedouin

* The zone was, however, re-occupied by the Israelis in September 1955 and served as a springboard for the invasion of Egypt in October 1956.

tribes concur in statements: (a) that they had lived in the Beersheba area under the British Mandate but had moved to El-Auja about two years ago because of Israeli pressure; (b) that since 20 August, Israelis had conducted operations to clear the Bedouins, employing army troops with armored cars and guided by reconnaissance aircraft; (c) that after driving the bedouins across the border, the Israelis burnt tents, crops and possessions; and (d) that thirteen Bedouins were killed by Israelis during these operations . . ." [38]

On 17 November 1950, the Security Council took a decision, and among other things, requested the Israel-Egyptian Mixed Armistice Commission to give urgent attention to the Egyptian complaint of expulsion of thousands of Palestine Arabs; called upon both parties to give effect to any finding of the Israel-Egyptian Mixed Armistice Commission regarding the repatriation of any such Arabs who in the Commission's opinion are entitled to return; authorized the Chief of Staff of the Truce Supervision Organization with regard to the movement of nomadic Arabs to recommend to Israel, Egypt and to such other Arab States as may be appropriate, such steps as he may consider necessary to control the movement of such nomadic Arabs across international frontiers or armistice lines by mutual agreement; and called upon the Governments concerned to take in the future no action involving the transfer of persons across international frontiers or armistice lines without prior consultation through the Mixed Armistice Commission. [39]

Like other Security Council decisions affecting the demilitarized zones, the latter resolution was ignored by the Israelis, as more and more Arabs were expelled from their homes and lands. According to General Bennike, then Chief of Staff, between 6,000 and 7,000 Arabs were expelled from El-Auja demilitarized zone before May 1951 when the Mixed Armistice Commission examined the matter and decided against Israel's action; 200 to 250 more were expelled in 1953. [40]

This Arab expulsion was not without a purpose; it was made in order to make room for new Jewish immigrants. For on 28 September 1953, the Israelis proceeded to establish their first settlement in the

El-Auja area. The Mixed Armistice Commission, in an emergency meeting held on 2 October 1953, decided that "the existence of an Israel police in the new *Kibbutz* (Settlement) established in the demilitarized zone is a violation of Article IV, paragraph 1, and Article VIII of the General Armistice Agreement." [41] (The Mixed Armistice Commission did not deal with the question of the establishment of the Jewish settlement because it maintained that civilian matters were outside its jurisdiction). The non-withdrawal of the Israeli police from the demilitarized zone was reported to the Security Council on 3 February 1954, but the question was never discussed. [42]

The attitude of the Israeli authorities towards the demilitarized zone was conveyed by General Bennike to the Security Council on 9 November 1953. In his report, he drew attention to a letter dated 21 September which the Chairman of the Egyptian-Israel Mixed Armistice Commission had received from the Senior Israeli Delegate. The latter had stated, *inter alia,* "The demilitarized zone being an integral part of Israel, the term 'Palestinian Bedouin' does not exist." He went on to point out that "Any Israeli activity in the demilitarized zone (beside the penetration of military forces) is an internal Israel affair and of no concern of anybody, including Egypt." [43]

On 21 September 1955, the Chief of Staff reported to the Security Council that the Israeli army had re-occupied the demilitarized zone; [44] on 21 August 1956, he reported "Israel opposes any meeting of the Mixed Armistice Commission at its Headquarters at El-Auja situated in the demilitarized zone which is now occupied by Israel troops; [45] and on 5 September 1956, the Chief of Staff re-affirmed his previous reports to the effect that "the Israeli army continue to occupy the El-Auja demilitarized zone." He stressed, "El-Auja is not only the centre of the demilitarized zone... it is also, under Article X, paragraph 2, the Headquarters of the Mixed Armistice Commission. Because of her military occupation of the demilitarized zone, Israel refuses access to El-Auja to the Egyptian members of the Mixed Armistice Commission," he added. The Chief of Staff went on to report that on 3 September 1956,

"Mr. Ben Gurion repeated his refusal to allow meetings of the Mixed Armistice Commission at El-Auja." [46]

Thus were expelled from the demilitarized zone, not only the Arab inhabitants, but also the United Nations personnel and organization responsible for the implementation of the provisions of the General Armistice Agreement. Had the United Nations exerted its authority within the demilitarized zone and insisted upon the withdrawal of Israeli troops and the non-encroachment on Arab rights and property within the zone, the invasion of Egypt in October 1956 might not have taken place – an aggression which brought the world to the brink of a third world war.

8. Invasion of Egypt

The invasion of Egypt is discussed here only insofar as it relates to Israeli violations of the provisions of the Egyptian-Israeli General Armistice Agreement.

The said Agreement prescribes that no element of the forces of either party shall commit any warlike or hostile act against the forces of the other, or shall advance beyond or pass over the armistice demarcation line. [47] Yet, on 29 October 1956, the Israelis committed their most flagrant violation since 1949 by crossing the armistice demarcation line into the Sinai Peninsula in full military strength; they attacked Egyptian positions; and later occupied the Gaza Strip in their bid to annex both territories to their 'state'.

The reasons the Israelis gave for their action varied. In a communiqué issued on the eve of the invasion, the Israeli Ministry of Foreign Affairs described the campaign in terms of both a preventive war and a retaliatory raid.[48] General Moshe Dayan's order to his troops read: "Today the Southern forces will fight across the border and will enclose the Nile army in its own country." [49] When asked to explain the Israeli action, the Liaison Officer for Armistice Affairs at the Ministry of Foreign Affairs contradicted the terms of the official communiqué and confirmed that "this was not just a retaliatory raid, but that the Israel forces were going to stay in Sinai." [50]

In announcing the invasion of Egypt to the Israeli Parliament, David Ben Gurion was more explicit. He said: "The army did not make an effort to occupy enemy territory in Egypt proper and limited its operations to free the area from northern Sinai to the tip of the Red Sea." Referring to the occupation of the Island of Tiran, south of the Gulf of 'Aqaba, he described it as "the Island of *Yotvat*, south of the Gulf of *Elath*, which was liberated by the Israeli army." [51]

Mr. Ben Gurion's statement that his troops did not attack "territory in Egypt *proper*," the selection of the words 'free' and 'liberated' and the use of Hebrew terminology for centuries-old Arabic names, leave no doubt that the purpose of the Israeli attack was in fact neither a 'preventive war' nor a 'retaliatory raid' as was first claimed, but a well planned campaign to occupy the whole of the Sinai Peninsula and the Gaza Strip in the Israeli program of expansion.

On the question of the Armistice Agreement with Egypt, Mr. Ben Gurion stated: "The Armistice with Egypt is dead, as are the armistice lines, and no wizards or magicians can resurrect these lines." [52] Implementation of this policy was attempted in the Gaza Strip. General Burns reported that on the occupation of Gaza, Lt-Col. Nursella "asked for the UN personnel of the Gaza Strip to be withdrawn from the Strip, on the grounds that as the armistice no longer existed, there were no functions for them." General Burns writes: "My first reaction was to agree with this proposal, but when I reported it to the Secretary-General, he took a very strong stand against any withdrawal, pointing out that since the duties of UNTSO under the GAA were not suspended by the 'present state of affairs', the personnel of UNTSO were required to remain at their posts." The Israeli authorities when so informed, imposed restrictions on the movement of the members on the grounds of "security" and the General then reported that there was even an attempt to close down the EIMAC radio-station. When the officer in charge refused to hand over the equipment, Israeli soldiers broke down the door and took the transmitter away." [53]

On 2 November 1956, the General Assembly, meeting in

special emergency session to consider the British-French-Israeli aggression, adopted a resolution urging "as a matter of priority that all parties now involved in hostilities in the area agree to an immediate cease-fire and, as part thereof, halt the movement of military forces and arms into the area." The resolution further urged the Parties to the Armistice Agreement "promptly to withdraw all forces behind the Armistice Lines, to desist from raids across the armistice lines into neighbouring territory, and to observe scrupulously the provisions of the Armistice Agreements." [54]

The Israelis resisted the General Assembly order every inch of the way; and it was not until another five resolutions had been passed calling upon Israel to withdraw and the threat of economic sanctions that the Israeli army finally retired on 6 March 1957 to behind the armistice demarcation line. In the meantime, an United Nations Emergency Force was formed and stationed along the line around the Gaza Strip and at Sharm Esh-Sheikh on the extreme south-eastern tip of the Sinai Peninsula.

The Israelis did not withdraw from the Sinai Peninsula peacefully. General Burns reported: "As the Israelis withdrew across the Sinai, they began a systematic destruction of the surfaced roads, the railway, the telephone-lines, and what few buildings there were along the railway, and at one or two road-junction points." The General's reaction was: "God had scorched the Sinai earth, and His chosen people removed whatever stood above it." He then added: "When UNEF found out what was going on, Mr. Hammarskjold protested vigorously to the Israel Government, that this destruction was a breach of the undertaking they had given to facilitate the efforts of UNEF directed towards maintaining peaceful conditions and it certainly was not co-operation to destroy the roads by which we had to advance." By the time the destruction had ceased, the Israelis had already "thoroughly demolished" about 70 kilometres of roads. [55]

9. **The Gulf of Aqaba**

The Israeli invasion of Egypt in 1956 was launched with two

objectives in view: The first, was in order to annex the Sinai Peninsula in conformity with the Israeli policy of expansion; the second was, if for any reason the Israelis failed in gaining their first objective, they would at least have opened the Strait of Tiran to Israeli shipping.

During the discussion of the 1956 Israeli aggression in the General Assembly, the stand of the United States Government, supported by repeated pronouncements of President Eisenhower and his Secretary of State, was to the effect that *Israel must withdraw unconditionally and that she must not be allowed to benefit from her attack against Egypt.*

With these assurances in mind, and anxious to lessen tension in the Middle East, President Nasser cooperated with the United Nations. While the Israelis refused to allow the United Nations Emergency Force to have freedom of movement on their side of the armistice demarcation line, President Nasser permitted them to be stationed on the Arab side, on the understanding that they would be immediately withdrawn when required to do so.

Little was it then realized that these forces would be instrumental in defeating the very aims and spirit of the resolution which called upon the Israelis to withdraw from Egyptian territory and the principle that they must not be allowed to benefit from their aggression. For no sooner were U.N. forces stationed at Sharm Esh-Sheikh, when Israeli shipping and merchandise began to pass freely through the Strait of Tiran. To lend legality and provide a precedent for the operation, an amendment to the Maritime Law was adopted in 1958 (by a vote of 62 to 1 with the Arab States abstaining). Article 16 (as amended) reads:

> "There shall be no suspension of the innocent passage of foreign ships through straits that are used for international navigation between one part of the high sea and another part of the high seas or the territorial sea of a foreign state."

The Israeli delegation described the article at the time as a "clear-cut decision preventing suspension on any legal ground of the free passage of ships of all nationalities through the Strait of Tiran to and from the Gulf of Aqaba." The Saudi Arabian Representative declared that his Government would not recognize the article which he described as "specially tailored to fit a special case."

It should be noted that the decision was merely a *recommendation* and is binding only on those nations that ratify it. Refusal by any nation to recognize the agreement can in no way be construed to be a violation of the United Nations Charter. The United Arab Republic made it clear that so long as the United Nations Emergency Force remained at Sham Esh-Sheikh, Israeli shipping will be able to pass through the Strait of Tiran. This does not mean, however, that the U.A.R. has accepted the changed situation or that a precedent has been established that would alter the *status quo* existing up to 1956.

The attitude of the Western Powers towards the Gulf of Aqaba has been one of unqualified support for the Israeli point of view that the Strait of Tiran was an international waterway that must be kept open to Israeli shipping at all times, notwithstanding the state of war which still exists between the United Arab Republic and the Israelis.

The Arab stand is that the Strait of Tiran has been Arab territorial waters from time immemorial; that there is no international agreement to which Egypt is a party declaring it otherwise; that the U.A.R. is technically at war with the Israelis; that the U.A.R. is obligated to take all measures to defend its security; and that the U.A.R. cannot permit the approach of its enemy to within 500 yards of its shores.* Such a situation would be preposterous!

These principles are not foreign to either Britain or the United States. During both World Wars, the German navy was excluded from the Suez Canal which was then under British control; while

* The mouth of the Gulf of Aqaba is bordered by the United Arab Republic on the west and Saudi Arabia on the east. The passageway into the Gulf is interrupted in the centre by the islands of Tiran and Sanafir. The passageway between the islands and the Saudi Arabian coast is not navigable; that between the islands and the U. A. R. coast is three miles in width, but only some 500 yards are navigable, and these closer to the U. A. R. coast.

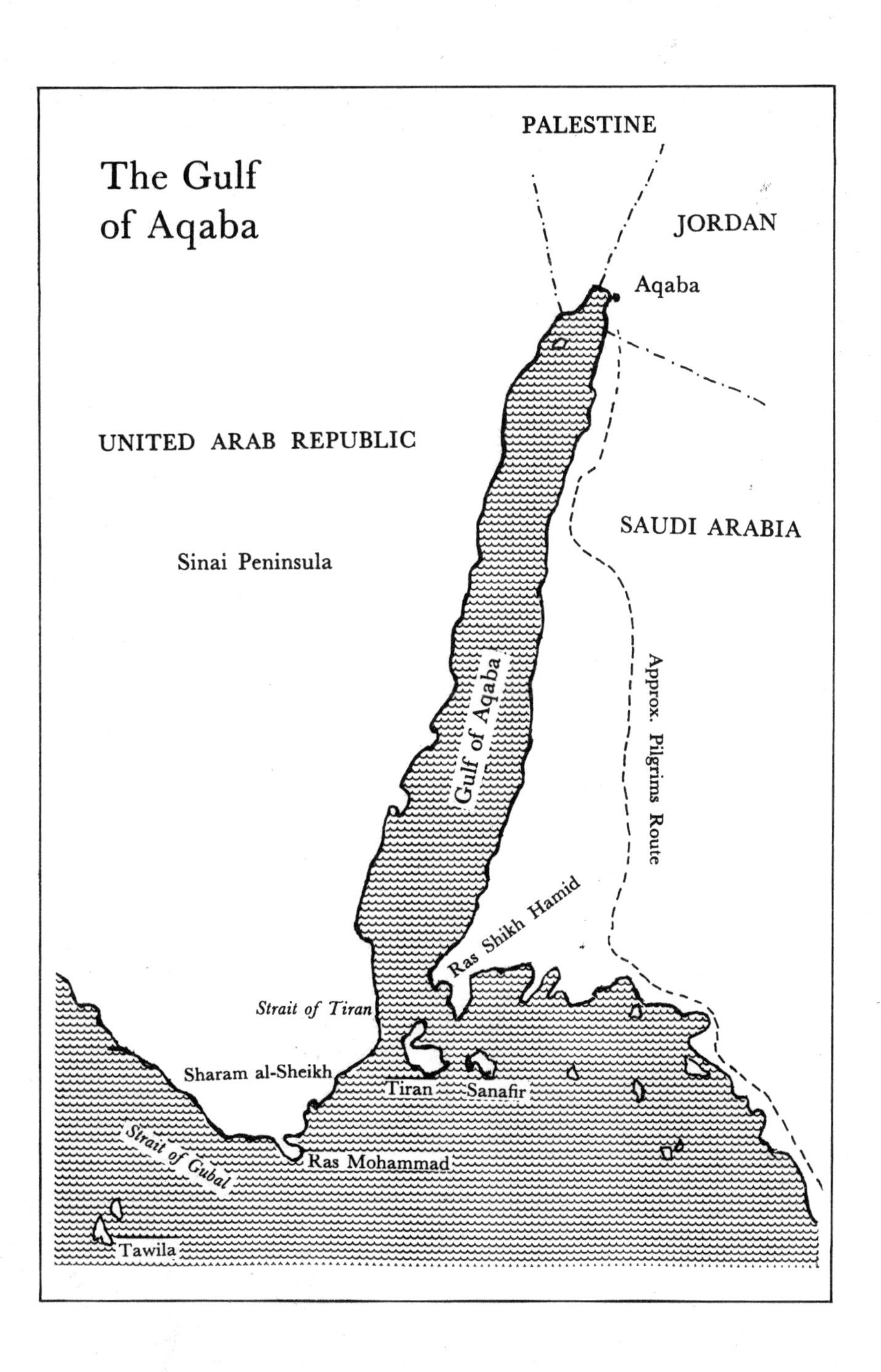

The Gulf of Aqaba
PALESTINE
JORDAN
Aqaba
UNITED ARAB REPUBLIC
SAUDI ARABIA
Sinai Peninsula
Gulf of Aqaba
Approx. Pilgrims Route
Ras Shikh Hamid
Strait of Tiran
Sharam al-Sheikh
Tiran
Sanafir
Strait of Gubal
Ras Mohammad
Tawila

the United States Government prohibits ships belonging to Red China from passing through the Panama Canal with whom it is not at war. Another illustration is the blockade imposed in 1962 against Cuba with whom the United States was not at war. The United States Government then did not feel perturbed or even concerned over public opinion when it was accused of 'piracy on the high seas'. All its interest then was – and perhaps quite rightly so – how to remove the alleged danger to "the security of the United States." [56] If the United States can impose a blockade on the high seas to defend its security, surely the United Arab Republic is entitled to defend its security from an enemy that passes at a distance of a stone's throw from its coastline !

An argument the Israelis use to support their claim of free passage through the Gulf of Aqaba is that they are the successors of the Palestine Government in the area, and any rights that Government exercised were automatically transferred to them. In normal circumstances that may be so. But Israeli presence on the waterfront is illegal and in violation of international instruments. To understand the problem, it is necessary to review the situation since the Security Council issued its truce order of 15 July 1948. The resolution ordered "the Government and authorities concerned, pursuant to Article 40 of the Charter of the United Nations, to desist from further military and para-military action and, to this end to issue cease-fire orders to their military and para-military forces." The resolution further declared, "failure by any of the Governments or authorities concerned to comply ... would demonstrate the existence of a breach of the peace within the meaning of Article 39 of the Charter." The Council then decided, "the truce shall remain in force in accordance with the present resolution and with resolution 50 (1948) of 29 May 1948, until a peaceful adjustment of the future situation of Palestine is reached." [57] The fact that 'a peaceful adjustment' has not been reached to date, means that the cease-fire order is still in force, and any action by either party after 15 July 1948 to alter the situation is a violation of the truce directive.

Despite this explicit Security Council order, on 14 October

1948, the Israelis attacked and occupied the town of Beersheba and the El-Auja area – both of which were assigned to the 'Arab state' under the Partition Resolution of 1947. The Israeli action was obviously naked aggression. On 19 October 1948, the Security Council took a decision ordering the "withdrawal of both parties from any positions not occupied at the time of the outbreak;" [58] and on 4 November 1948, the Council once again called upon the parties "to withdraw those of their forces which have advanced beyond the positions held on 14 October . . ." [59] This was a clear-cut order that Israel's presence in territory not held on 14 October was illegal and in violation of the truce order.

The Israelis ignored the Security Council directives, and the United Nations took no action to compel them to comply. On 24 February 1949, an armistice was concluded between Egypt and the Israeli authorities, whereby the Israelis were permitted to hold what they had acquired in violation of the truce order. But in the direction of the Gulf of Aqaba, they were limited to within half the distance between the Gulf shoreline and the area they then actually held. This is quite explicit from the provisions of Annex II (b) to the General Armistice Agreement which prescribe that the armistice demarcation line in the south shall run "from point 402 down to the southernmost tip of Palestine, by a straight line marking half the distance between Egypt-Palestine and Transjordan-Palestine frontiers." [60] The Israelis were thereby excluded from access to the Gulf. But on 10 March 1949 – thirteen days after they had signed the General Armistice Agreement – the Israelis launched an attack on the southern Negeb which brought their forces up to the Gulf of Aqaba.

Another provision of the General Armistice Agreement pertinent to the situation of the Gulf of Aqaba is contained in Article IV (1) and (3) which stipulates:

> "The principle that no military or political advantage should be gained under the truce ordered by the Security Council is recognized.
>
> "It is further recognized that rights, claims or interests of a non-military character in the area of Palestine covered by this Agreement may be asserted by either

> Party and that these, by mutual agreement being excluded from the Armistice negotiations, shall be, at the discretion of the Parties, the subject of later settlement. It is emphasized that it is not the purpose of this Agreement to establish, to recognize, to strengthen, or to weaken or nullify, in any way, any rights, claims or interests which may be asserted by either party in the area of Palestine or any part or locality thereof covered by this Agreement . . . The provisions of this Agreement are dictated exclusively by military considerations and are valid only for the period of the armistice." [61]

The United Nations took no steps to dislodge the Israelis. Notwithstanding, their presence there is illegal. The Arab village of Umm Rashrash on the Gulf was occupied, the Arab villagers were expelled and dispossessed, and Eilat was established on Arab-owned land. To lend permanence to their newly acquired so-called 'right,' and face the world with a *fait accompli,* the Israelis immediately embarked on a scheme to construct port facilities; an eight inch oil pipeline was laid linking the Red Sea with the Mediterranean; and Eilat, with a population of 13,000 in 1966, has been developed as a resort which, it is claimed, will in time receive some 100,000 visitors per annum. Between 1948 and 1956, Eilat handled only 600 tons of commerce per annum; in 1957, after the Gulf had been opened to Israeli shipping, 40,000 tons went through; and by the end of 1966, it is claimed that 260,000 tons of merchandise were handled. These figures do not, however, include Eilat's role as an oil port, which are not being divulged for obvious reasons.

The proper thing to do is:

(1) to desist from attempting to impose a political solution on the U.A.R. and to refer the matter to the World Court of Justice for an expression of opinion as to whether or not the Strait of Tiran is, in fact, an international waterway; and whether in time of war, the U.A.R. has the right to close it in the face of its enemy.

(2) to call upon the Israelis to comply with the directives of the Security Council and implement the provisions of the General Armistice Agreement. Once this is carried out, the Israelis would

be obliged to withdraw from the Gulf of Aqaba as their presence there is in violation of the international instruments just mentioned. The problem of passage through the Strait of Tiran would then be automatically solved, and the peace of the world would not be jeopardized.

10. Conclusion

To sum up: A study of the texts of the General Armistice Agreements, the reports of the Secretary-General and those of the various Chiefs of Staff of the United Nations Truce Supervision Organization, as well as the resolutions of the Security Council on incidents occurring along the armistice demarcation line since 1949, lead to the following conclusions:

(1) The General Armistice Agreements signed between the Arab States and the Israeli authorities are not peace treaties but only agreements intended to stop the fighting.

(2) The Agreements were designed as a temporary measure to deal with the situation which had arisen in Palestine as a result of the establishment of the state of Israel.

(3) Both parties to the Agreements, having voluntarily undertaken to do certain things, they are obligated to abide unreservedly by their undertakings.

(4) The armistice demarcation line is not an international boundary, a frontier or border limit; its objective is merely to separate the military forces of the disputing parties.

(5) The Security Council has accepted the interpretation of the U.N. Acting Mediator and the Chairmen of the Mixed Armistice Commissions that the provisions of the General Armistice Agreements preclude the parties from claiming sovereignty over the demilitarized zones and no-man's land. This interpretation was made clear in one instance and acquiesced in by the Syrian Government and the Israeli authorities at the Armistice Conference held on 3 July 1949, prior to the signing of the Armistice Agreement on 20 July 1949, and on the strength of which the Syrian troops pulled out of the areas they then occupied.

(6) While sovereignty over the 'defensive areas' by the parties concerned is not questioned, certain limitations have been placed on military personnel and equipment within the areas. These are restricted to 'defensive forces' only.

(7) Military and para-military forces were to be totally excluded from the demilitarized zones; while normal civilian life for *both Arabs and Jews* was to be permitted under local administrations under the supervision of the Mixed Armistice Commissions.

(8) The Mixed Armistice Commissions were empowered to arrange for "the return of civilians to villages and settlements in the demilitarized zone, and for the employment of limited numbers of locally recruited civilian police in the zone for internal security purposes."

(9) The inhabitants of villages affected by the armistice demarcation line are entitled "to maintain, and shall be protected in, their full rights of residence, property and freedom." Israeli forces are "prohibited" from entering or being stationed in such villages in which "locally recruited Arab police shall be organized and stationed for internal security purposes."

(10) The Military Agreement on the Mount Scopus demilitarized zone in Jerusalem places the zone under "United Nations protection"; while the General Armistice Agreement with Jordan places the zone east of the armistice demarcation line in Jordan territory. Jurisdiction over the zone is the responsibility of the "U.N. Commander."

(11) The Mixed Armistice Commissions were entrusted with the task of ensuring the observance and implementation of certain provisions of the General Armistice Agreements; and in regard to the meanings of certain clauses, the interpretation of the Mixed Armistice Commissions shall prevail.

(12) The Armistice Agreements provide authority for the free movement of the United Nations Truce Observers within the demilitarized zones and along the armistice demarcation line in order to carry out their duties.

(13) Israeli presence on the Gulf of Aqaba is illegal and in violation of the Security Council directives of 15 July 1948, of

4 November 1948 and the provisions of the General Armistice Agreement with Egypt.

(14) Neither party has the right to repudiate the Armistice Agreements or any of their provisions.

An objective comparison between these basic provisions and the actions of the Arab States, on the one hand, and the Israelis, on the other, since 1949 will reveal that the Arab States have faithfully carried out their obligations whereas the Israelis have violated every provision cited and that the United Nations failed to assert its presence in the area by enforcing compliance.

Israeli attitude in Palestine can best be illustrated by drawing upon the experiences of General Carl Von Horn during the period he was Chief of Staff of the United Nations Truce Supervision Organization. The General stated, "time and time again in the course of frank discussions with Israeli officers and officials, I had heard them openly repudiate the idea of objectivity. Their flat statement," he said, "was 'You are either for or against us'. Even nastier," he added, "was an Israeli tendency to immediately brand objectivity as anti-Semitic; a convenient label which could be smeared on to any U.N. soldier whose impartial report did not weigh down in favour of the Israelis."

In reviewing his relations with Arabs and Israelis, General Von Horn remarked that UNTSO personnel had "from time to time incurred a certain degree of animosity" in their dealings with the Arabs, but never, he said, "in the same implacable and frenetic way." He went on to testify that "the Arabs could be difficult, intolerant, and indeed often impossible, but their code of behaviour was on an infinitely higher and more civilized level." He then pointed out that "all came to this conclusion in UNTSO," which he described as "strange, because there was hardly a man among us who had not originally arrived in the Holy Land without the most positive and sympathetic attitude towards the Israelis and their ambitions for their country."

General Von Horn went on to explain, "after two or three years in daily contact with officials, soldiers and private individuals on *both* sides, there had been a remarkable change in their attitude."

He found it, he said, "sad but very significent" that when he asked what their most negative experiences had been during their service with UNTSO, the reply was almost invariably: "The consistent cheating and deception of the Israelis." [62]

IX United Nations Efforts for a Settlement

Appointment of a Mediator

With the abolition of the Palestine Commission which was supposed to take over the administration of the country progressively from the departing Mandatory Power, Count Folke Bernadotte was appointed U.N. Mediator and entrusted with the task of bringing about a settlement.

After surveying the situation and arranging for a truce, the U.N. Mediator presented the parties on 28 June 1948, with a tentative plan, the salient points of which were:

(a) The Arab areas of Palestine be united to Jordan and that Jordan, so constituted, should form a union with Israel.

(b) The union should handle economic affairs, foreign policy and defence for both Israel and Jordan.

(c) Subject to the instrument of union, Jordan and Israel would each control its own internal affairs.

Attached to the proposals was an annex dealing with territorial matters. In it, Bernadotte suggested that all or part of the Negeb be included in Jordan, in return for which all or part of Western Galilee would go to Israel. He further proposed that Jerusalem should be Arab, that Haifa be a free port and Lydda a free airport.[1]

Bernadotte's proposals were rejected by both parties; and on 17 September 1948, together with his French aide Colonel Serot, Bernadotte was assassinated in the Israeli-occupied sector of Jerusalem by men wearing the uniform of the Israeli army. "No action was taken by the Israeli authorities for twenty-four hours to apprehend the murderers. Then Ben Gurion roused himself and took action. Most of the members of the Stern Group were rounded up and many were arrested, but the assassins were never caught." * [2]

* Bernadotte's assassination is reminiscent of the murder of Lord Moyne in Cairo in 1944, because the British policy in Palestine he had suggested was contrary to Zionist aspirations.

Moshe Menuhin, commenting on the assassination, said: "And thus Israel got away with murder. The United Nations demanded that Israel bring the assassins to justice; the answer was that she could not find the murderers." Menuhin then points out, "Count Bernadotte was the first martyr in the service of United Nations reconciliation efforts in Palestine – a saint to the Arabs and, perhaps as is usually the case, an anti-Semite in the eyes of the fanatical 'Jewish' political nationalists." He goes on to say, "The saddest part is that Count Bernadotte's plan was the only answer to the Arab-Israeli war. And another thought: To this day it is almost a crime to recall the murder of Count Bernadotte because 'it may be a disservice to the best interests of poor little Israel'. Forgotten is the name of the noble man who was a victim of ungrateful, land-hungry jingoists." [3]

On 16 September 1948 – one day before his assassination – Count Bernadotte presented to the General Assembly his final recommendations for a solution of the Palestine problem. He drew the attention of the General Assembly that "The Jewish state was not born in peace as was hoped for in the Resolution of November 29, but rather ... in violence and bloodshed."

The main point in his Report was his insistence on the necessity for prompt and firm action by the United Nations. He then advised the General Assembly that the refugees' "Unconditional right to make a free choice (between return and compensation) should be fully respected." He added: "It is, however, undeniable that no settlement can be just and complete if recognition is not accorded to the right of the Arab refugee to return to the home from which he has been dislodged. It will be an offence," he continued, "against the principles of elemental justice if these innocent victims of the conflict were denied the right of return to their homes while Jewish immigrants flow into Palestine, and indeed, at least offer the threat of permanent replacement of the Arab refugees who have been rooted in the land for centuries."

On the question of property, Bernadotte remarked that "There have been numerous reports from reliable sources of large scale looting, pillaging and plundering, and of instances of destruction of villages without apparent military necessity. The liability of the Provisional Government of Israel to restore private property to its Arab owners and to indemnify those owners for property wantonly destroyed, is clear," he said.

The Mediator's report also recommended the modification of the Partition Plan in such a way as to include the Negeb in the 'Arab state' area and in return, Galilee and the enclave of Jaffa in the 'Jewish state'.[4] His intention was apparently to give each side a solid and homogeneous block of territory, instead of the cross-overs, pockets and corridors in the United Nations plan. The towns of Lydda and Ramle were to return to the Arabs, and Jerusalem was to be placed under United Nations jurisdiction.

The report caused much consternation among the Israelis. By this time they had experienced the taste of victory and were not going to allow it to slip through their fingers. Bernadotte was highly respected in United Nations and international circles, and the Israelis feared that his recommendations would receive universal support. His murder removed any chance of approval of his recommendations.

General Assembly Resolution

On 11 December 1948, the General Assembly met and, among other things, resolved "that refugees wishing to return to their homes and live at peace with their neighbours should be permitted to do so at the earliest practicable date, and that compensation should be paid for the property of those choosing not to return and for loss of or damage to property which, under principles of international law or in equity, should be made good by the Governments or authorities responsible."

At the same time the General Assembly established a Conciliation Commission and instructed it "to facilitate the repatriation, re-settlement and economic and social rehabilitation of the refugees and the payment of compensation..."

It also instructed the Commission "to take steps to assist the Governments and authorities concerned to achieve a final settlement of all questions outstanding between them." [5]

The tragedy of this resolution was threefold: its lateness; the absence of effective machinery for execution; and the absence of any admission of United Nations responsibility, thus leaving compliance to the pleasure of the parties concerned. The intervening period of seven months between the date the state of Israel was proclaimed and the adoption of the resolution, saw nearly one million homeless and destitute Palestine Arabs still searching for safety, shelter and food, while many died from starvation or exposure. On the other hand, the Israelis were given ample opportunity to consolidate and strengthen their hold over Palestine. Once confident that the United Nations did not possess the power or willingness to assert its authority and enforce compliance, the Israelis simply ignored it – and continue to do so – claiming in 1965 that the resolution was "obsolete by the course of events." [6]

On 14 December 1950, the General Assembly met once again, and this time, "*noting with concern* that agreement has not been reached ... repatriation, resettlement, economic and social rehabilitation of the refugees and the payment of compensation have not been effected, *recognizing* that... the refugee question should be dealt with as a matter of urgency ... *directs* the United Nations Conciliation Commission for Palestine to ... continue consultations with the parties concerned regarding measures for the protection of the rights, property and interests of the refugees." [7]

The vagueness and mildness of this belated resolution, though it recognized the 'urgency' of the refugee problem, did nothing to bring it to an end. This was added encouragement to the Israelis in their intransigence. They were now certain – if they doubted it before – that the United Nations was incapable of doing anything not acceptable to them.

From this date on, no further action was taken except to affirm and reaffirm annually the right of the refugees to repatriation or compensation under the resolution of 11 December 1948, leaving the Palestine Arabs in the squalor of refugee camps and the Israelis in occupation of Arab homes and property.

Palestine Conciliation Commission

The Commission began its functions soon after its appointment by first meeting in Beirut, Lebanon and later in Lausanne, Switzerland. It then reported to the General Assembly that "the exchange of views ... must be considered not only as bearing upon one of the specific tasks entrusted to the Commission by the General Assembly resolution of 11 December 1948, such as the refugee question or the status of Jerusalem, but also as bearing upon its general task of conciliation of the points of view of the parties with a view to achieving a final settlement of all questions outstanding between them." [8]

The Commission also reported that it had presented the parties with a *Protocol* "which would constitute the basis of work" and asked them to sign it. The 'Protocol', signed on 12 May 1949, provided that the Commission, "anxious to achieve as quickly as possible the objectives of the General Assembly Resolution of 11 December 1948, regarding refugees, the respect for their rights and the preservation of their property, as well as territorial and other questions, has proposed to the delegations of the Arab States and to the delegation of Israel that the working document attached hereto (map of partition) be taken as a basis for discussions with the the Commission."

The Commission added that "the interested delegations have accepted this proposal with the understanding that the exchange of views which will be carried on by the Commission with the two parties will bear upon the territorial adjustments to the above indicated objectives." [9]

At this stage, things looked as if one possible solution of the Palestine Problem might be in sight. But the Commission went on to report that when it then asked the two parties to make known their views on outstanding questions, the Delegation of Israel submitted proposals regarding the territorial questions, according to which it demanded that *the international frontiers of Mandatory Palestine be considered the frontiers of Israel,* with one provisional and temporary exception, namely, the central area of Palestine then under Jordanian military authority, in which the Israelis consented to "recognize the Hashemite Kingdom of Jordan as the *de facto* military occupying Power," without entering into "the future status of the area" for the time being. [10]

When the Arab Delegations protested that these unique proposals constituted a repudiation by the Israelis of the terms of the 'Protocol' signed on 12 May 1949, the Israeli Delegation retorted, "*it could not accept a certain proportionate distribution of territory agreed upon in 1947 as a criterion for a territorial settlement in present circumstances.*" [11]

It is worth recording in this respect that during the debate on the report of the U.N. Mediator in November 1948, in which he suggested certain territorial changes, it was the Israeli representative who strongly objected to any alteration in the boundaries as resolved in the Partition Resolution of 1947 and argued that "It was logical that any conciliation effort should make the 29th November resolution its basis." At a subsequent meeting, the Israeli representative said, "in the view of his Delegation, the Assembly's resolution of 29th November 1947, is a valid international instrument of international law, while the conclusions in the Mediator's report were merely the views of a distinguished individual which were not embodied in any decision of a United Nations organ." [12]

Is it not ironic that the U.N. Partition Resolution should be regarded as a 'logical' basis for 'any conciliation effort' and 'a valid international instrument of international law' in November 1948 and no longer so hardly a year later because the Israelis had achieved their objectives?

Concerning the refugee and Jerusalem issues, the Delegation of Israel adopted similar inflexible attitudes incompatible with the provisions of the General Assembly resolution of 29 November 1947 (on partition) and 11 December 1948 (on repatriation and compensation), the acceptance of which the Israelis had indicated – by signing the 'Lausanne Protocol' of 12 May 1949.

When its initial efforts for a political settlement failed, the Commission retired to United Nations Headquarters in New York and concerned itself with the less important duties of preparing lists of individual Arab property in Israeli hands and valuing it; arranging for the release of blocked Arab bank accounts in Israel; and reiterating from time to time that its services were available to the parties if called upon.

Lacking power and not possessing the machinery to enforce its wishes, the Commission was unable to carry out its task of protecting "the rights, property and interests of the refugees" pending a final settlement.

This callous attitude of the United Nations has one and only one explanation, that the Palestine Problem was by now regarded as one of those chronic problems to be shelved for time – not justice and equity – to solve.

On 23 March 1953, representatives of the Arab States to the United Nations submitted to the Conciliation Commission a joint memorandum concerning Israel's wrongful disposal of Arab property in the territory under its control. The Arab representatives called on the Commission to take expeditious and effective measures to safeguard the property of the refugees.

The Commission later reported that the Israeli representative to the United Nations had stated orally that any action taken would not impair any legal claims of the Arab refugees, and that his Government would provide the Commission with further information.

On the face of it, such a statement appeared satisfactory, but, on 7 July 1953, the Israeli representative informed the Commission in writing that His Government was prepared to discuss the payment of compensation in practical terms.

On 29 July 1953, the Commission rightly replied, "It was on the question of the manner in which Arab property was being dealt with and not on the question of compensation that the Commission sought information." The letter went on "to recall that in its resolutions of 11 December 1948 and 14 December 1950, the General Assembly had given the Commission a responsibility in connection with the property rights of the refugees." These remarks are significant because they indicate clearly that the Commission fully recognized and accurately interpreted the nature of the tasks entrusted to it. The Commission's letter to the Israeli representative also included certain specific questions, amongst which was whether "the necessary measures have been taken to ensure the restitution of their property to such refugees as might be repatriated."

The Israeli representative's reply on 23 August 1953 was that the disposal of property had been authorized by the Government of Israel under the Absentee Property Law, the funds realized being credited to the property for which it had been received; and that the policy of the Government of Israel was to ensure integration of those refugees who were legally authorized to enter Israel.

The ambiguity and evasiveness of the Israeli replies to the clear questions of the Commission are apparent. Even the words 'integration of those refugees who were legally authorized to enter Israel' – intended to give the impression that they applied to the *Arab* refugees – actually meant new *Jewish immigrants.*

Arab protests were directed specifically to the Absentee Property Law, on which the Israelis relied. They regarded this 'law' as a violation of the provisions of the Partition Resolution. The Israeli attitude should have prompted the Commission to investigate whether the 'laws and regulations' enacted and the 'official actions' taken by the Israelis were indeed in conformity with the stipulations and guarantees in the Partition Resolution. Unfortunately, the matter was not pursued further by the Commission and the Israelis were permitted to proceed unhindered in their policy of confiscation and liquidation of Arab rights, property and interests.

The Arab States have not ceased to demand of the Conciliation Commission to carry out the tasks entrusted to it by the General Assembly, and to raise at every session of the United Nations the question of the appointment of a custodian to administer Arab refugee property pending a settlement.

On 1 March 1956, representatives of the Arab States to the United Nations once again submitted a joint memorandum to the Commission requesting it to assume its full responsibilities and to adopt a policy of vigorous and effective action for "the protection of the rights, property and interests of the refugees." The Delegations pointed out that the Commission in discharging this task should take into consideration the points raised by the Arab Delegations in the debates at General Assembly sessions on the question of the appointment of a trusteeship over Arab refugee property. The Commission was also requested to report to the General Assembly "on the causes and various forms of Israeli infringements and actions which affect the legitimate and inherent rights, property and interests of the refugees, and are in any way prejudicial to them."

In addition, the Commission was asked to prepare and submit to the General Assembly a complete report on Arab property in the territory occupied by Israel. This report should include, among other things, how the property is controlled and managed and what measures are being taken to preserve it; a complete statement of account, showing the income and rental derived from the different types of properties; and an appraisal of the manner followed by the Israeli authorities for fixing the rent, as well as the basis upon which the rent is calculated.

The joint communication concluded with the statement that the Commission was duty-bound, more than ever before, to take vigorous and effective action with the view of protecting the rights, property and interests of the refugees without further delay. It pointed out that until the problem of the refugees is finally settled to their complete satisfaction, the protection of their rights, property and interests constituted a sacred trust of the Conciliation Commission, and was a matter of most vital importance to the refugees as well as for the peace and tranquility of the whole Middle East.

What action the Commission took on this communication beside acknowledging it has never been known. No Progress Report was published for either 1956 or 1957, and the matter was allowed to lapse as if it were of no importance.*

---

* For a full study of the work of the Palestine Conciliation Commission, See *Palestine: Loss of a Heritage,* by Sami Hadawi.

With this attitude of indifference on the part of the Commission, the Arab States no longer communicated with it, but their Representatives at the United Nations raised the issue of the appointment of a custodian at every session of the General Assembly.

Israeli membership in United Nations

The Israelis had no intention from the start of giving up one inch of territory or allowing the return of a single refugee to his home. They signed the 'Lausanne Protocol' for the purpose of gaining admission to membership of the United Nations. Without that, the new state's sovereignty and acceptance into the community of nations would have remained shaky.

It should be noted that Israel's first application for membership was rejected in December 1948 because it was then felt that the 'Jewish state' did not fulfill the requirements of the United Nations Charter. At that time, the Israelis had encroached upon and were still in occupation of, territory assigned to the proposed 'Arab state' and the 'International zone of Jerusalem'; while hundreds of thousands of Palestinian Arabs swarmed the surrounding Arab countries as refugees.

In 1949, the Israelis once again sought admission. Concurrently, the Conciliation Commission was conducting negotiations for a settlement in Lausanne, Switzerland. Anxious to gain admission, the Israelis could not again afford to display patent disregard for the will of the United Nations. The signing of the 'Lausanne Protocol' on 12 May 1949 coincided almost to the hour with the approval of Israel's admission into membership of the United Nations on 11 May 1949, if the time difference between Lausanne and New York is taken into account. The signature, of which member-states were informed, gave the impression to the opposing members that the Israelis were now ready to surrender the extra territory occupied beyond that assigned to the 'Jewish state' under the Partition Plan, and to allow the Palestine Arabs to return to their homes.

This deception was later officially admitted with impunity,

by the Israelis in these words: "Some members of the United Nations wished at this opportunity to test Israel's intentions with regard to the refugees, boundaries and Jerusalem issues, before approving its application for admission. In a way, Israel's attitude at the Lausanne talks aided its Delegation at Lake Success in its endeavour to obtain the majority required for admission." [13]

Once admission was secured by such a ruse, Israel had no further need to honour her pledges to the United Nations.

It is significant to note that, in approving Israel's second application for membership, the General Assembly did not overlook the special relationship between Israel's existence and previous resolutions of the Assembly. Nor was Israel's special obligations to implement these resolutions ignored.

Of some seventy-six states admitted into membership since 1949, Israel was the only state that was accepted on the understanding that specific resolutions of the General Assembly would be implemented.

Despite the verbal assurances of the Israeli representative before the Assembly, the *Preamble* of the resolution of admission included a safeguarding clause as follows: "Recalling its resolution of 29 November 1947 (on partition) and 11 December 1948 (on repatriation and compensation), and taking note of the declarations and explanations made by the representative of the Government of Israel before the *ad hoc* Political Committee *in respect of the implementation of the said resolutions,* the General Assembly . . . decides to admit Israel into membership in the United Nations." [14]

Here, it must be observed, is a condition and an undertaking *to implement* the resolutions mentioned. There was no question of such implementation being conditional on the conclusion of peace on Israeli terms as the Israelis now claim to justify their non-compliance.

It should further be noted that, in the Israeli Proclamation of Independence dated 14 May 1948, the Israeli leaders promised that they would be "ready to cooperate with the organs and representatives of the United Nations in the implementation of the Resolution of the Assembly of November 29, 1947." [15]

Israel today claims sovereignty by reason of the Partition Resolution; it also claims that its sovereignty cannot now be touched even by the United Nations. The fact that Israel has not fulfilled the stipulations in the resolution which gave it birth and has failed to live up to the promises and obligations it undertook when admitted into membership of the United Nations, makes that sovereignty – legally and morally – null and void and leaves Israel's presence in Palestine based on brute force which, in other cases, has been condemned by Western democracy.

Internationalization of Jerusalem

Efforts were also made by the Conciliation Commission to obtain agreement of the parties on the internationalization of Jerusalem.

The Israeli attitude has been from the beginning to resist to the utmost the internationalization of the City. When the Trusteeship Council called upon Israel in 1949 to submit to United Nations authority "in the light of her obligations as member of the United Nations", the Israeli answer was to transfer their parliament and government from Tel Aviv to Jerusalem and to declare the City their capital. In response to the request of the Trusteeship Council "to revoke these measures and to abstain from any action liable to hinder the implementation of the General Assembly resolution of 9 December 1949," [16] the then Prime Minister, David Ben Gurion, countered with a declaration, "the United Nations ... saw fit ... this year to decide that our eternal city should become a *corpus separatum* under international control. Our rebuttal of this wicked counsel," he said, "was unequivocal and resolute: The Government and Knesset at once moved their seat to Jerusalem and made Israel's crown and capital irrevocably and for all men to see." [17]

This challenge to world authority and to all Moslems and Christians throughout the world who look towards the Holy City for inspiration, was allowed to stand. It might be regarded today as contributing to the tension and instability in the area. So instead of peace, brotherhood and love coming out of Jerusalem, the Holy City has been turned into a hot-bed of hatred and strife between the three communities.

X | *The Arab Refugee Problem*

When the Palestine tragedy occurred in 1948, the conscience of the world was moved and prompt action was taken to bring relief to the victims. But through political obstruction inside and outside the United Nations, the injustice has been allowed to linger and the distress has been prolonged until now it may be included in the category of 'problems' which the world tends to accept as chronic and something it must learn to live with. Thus, the initial impulse of conscience became blunted and the calamity was allowed to continue indefinitely. Instead of a just solution being imposed by the United Nations on the defaulting party under at least the threat of sanctions if compliance could not be effected by other means, meagre relief is doled out to the victims in the hope that time will solve the problem.

Statements have been heard from time to time that, after all, the Palestine Arabs are not the only refugees in the world; that there is no reason for granting them preferential treatment.

There is one basic difference, however, which few recognize, between the refugees from European countries, Red China, Cuba and those who migrated when India and Pakistan became independent, on one side and the Palestine Arabs, on the other. The former were *not* ousted by their governments but left of their own free will because they either disagreed with, or did not wish to live under the changed political conditions. There is no law or policy in all these countries to prevent their returning if they wished to do so. The Palestine Arabs, on the other hand, were *forcibly expelled and dispossessed* by an alien people who established themselves as a government; they are still eager to return to their homeland and are only prevented from doing so by those who now occupy their homes and lands.

United Nations failure to protect the Arab inhabitants and to fulfill the guarantees it voluntarily undertook to uphold Arab rights, property and interests in the territory set aside for the 'Jewish state', has, by its inaction, encouraged the aggressor and removed all chances of a peaceful settlement.

Solutions have been offered from time to time, but all invariably ignored the Palestine Arabs' natural rights to their country. One of the proposals made was resettlement of the refugees in Arab countries. The obvious answer to this suggestion was given by the late U.N. Secretary-General in his Report for 1959. Dag Hammorskjold warned: "No reintegration would be satisfactory, or even possible, were it to be brought about by forcing people into their new positions against their will. It must be freely accepted, if it is to yield lasting results in the form of economic and political stability." [1]

Attitude of the refugees

The attitude of the refugees has been made clear since 1948. They are unwilling to accept anything short of their full rights to their homes and country. This expression of desire has not altered during the years and has been conveyed annually to the General Assembly by the Agency responsible for their relief (UNRWA). Here are some examples:

In one instance, the Director reported, "the great mass of the refugees continues to believe that a grave injustice has been done to them and to express a desire to return to their homeland." On the question of the Israeli stand, he said: "The Government of Israel has taken no affirmative action in the matter of repatriation and compensation . . ." [2]

In another instance, the Director told the General Assembly, "the past and present drove home to each of us, even more forcibly, the truly tragic plight of the Palestine refugees . . . They have existed," he said, "by virtue of charity meted out on a meagre scale." He then drew attention that "for the most part they have lived without opportunity for self-advancement and – worst of all – their hopes for the future have tended to grow dimmer than brighter." He ended by pointing out that, "viewed by any standard, the plight of these people stands out as a dark stain on human history." [3]

One would imagine that such reports would spur the General Assembly to action in order to alleviate the sufferings of these unfortunate victims of a political conspiracy. But four years later, the new Commissioner-General of UNRWA had occasion to report, "All that he has so far seen and heard since assuming his present responsibilities confirms the view recorded in previous reports that the refugees in general strongly maintain their insistence on the idea and aspiration of returning to their homes . . . The refugees", he added, "have also expressed the wish that they should be enabled to receive redress for the loss they have suffered without prejudicing their claims to repatriation or any other political rights mentioned in resolution 194 (III). The modalities of implementing that paragraph of the General Assembly resolution may be differently conceived by the refugees," he said, "but what is not in doubt is that their longing to return home is intense and widespread." The Commissioner - General went on to say, the refugees "express their feeling of embitterment at their long exile and at the failure of the international community, year after year, to implement the resolution so often reaffirmed. They feel that they have been betrayed and their resentment is directed not only against those whom they regard as the chief authors of their exile, but also against the international community at large whom they hold responsible for the partition and loss of their homeland, which they regard as an offence against natural justice."

"One further point," the Commissioner-General said, "should be made regarding the general attitude of the refugees. In their own eyes they are not refugees at all in the sense in which that term is used to describe persons who have uprooted themselves and broken with their past in order to seek a new life in new surroundings and in a new country. The Palestine refugees regard themselves rather as temporary wards of the international community whom they hold responsible for the upheaval which resulted in their having to leave their homes. As they see it, the international community has a duty to enable them to return to their homes and meanwhile, to provide for their maintenance and welfare." [4]

In 1965, the Commissioner-General once again drew attention to the attitudes and feelings of the refugees which, he said, continue unchanged. "From their standpoint, a nation has been obliterated and a population arbitrarily deprived of its birthright. This injustice," he pointed out, "still festers in their minds and they hold the United Nations responsible for their lot and for extending assistance to them until a solution can be found to their problems. Their longing to return to their homes, encouraged by the General Assembly's declaration on repatriation and compensation in paragraph 11 of resolution 194 (III) and referred to in many subsequent resolutions, remains unabated. During the past year," the Commissioner-General added, "their emotions have, if anything, increased with the additional focus for their feelings provided by the Palestine Liberation Organization which came into being in June 1964. According to a declaration of September 1964 by the Council of Kings and Heads of State of the League of Arab States, the Organization was established 'to consolidate the Palestine entity and as a vanguard for the collective Arab struggle for the liberation of Palestine'." The Commissioner-General pointed out that "Apart from the view expressed by that Organization and by the Arab Governments, the refugees themselves use every opportunity to stress the intensity of their aspirations and hopes to return to their former homeland and to urge the Commissioner-General to convey their views to the General Assembly. From this stand point and from such information as has come to his attention, the Commissioner-General believes that the refugee problem has not grown any less complex or less dangerous to the peace and stability of the region." [5]

In his report for 1965-1966, the Commissioner-General emphasized, "As year succeeds year, there is no sign that the refugees are becoming any less embittered by their conviction that a grave injustice has been done to them through the loss of their homes and country and the continued deprivation of any benefit from the property they left behind. The implications for peace and stability in the Middle East of the continued existence of the Palestine refugee problem thus remain as grave as ever." [6]

It is neither surprising nor the work of politicians, as the Israelis claim, that the Palestine Arabs – old and young – should, after this lapse of time, still insist upon their right of return to their homes and country. The demand is genuine. Apart from the need to redress the injustice inflicted upon them, it should be noted that it is part of the Arab character to be attached to the soil where their ancestors had lived and are buried. Their removal has created in them a spiritual emptiness which no amount of material compensation can satisfy.

It is perhaps difficult for a westerner to understand this Arab mentality. A dialogue which took place in 1966 between an American reporter and a young Palestinian refugee who was about to leave for Sweden for vocational training, will explain that the feelings and attitudes of the younger generations towards Palestine are no less strong and determined than those of the older folks. Asked if he might elect to remain there to make a new life, the youth replied: "I must come back because my country needs me." The American reporter said: "I asked the question because my own country was created by men who found life not worthwhile in their own land." When this comment had been translated into Arabic, the young refugee looked troubled. "You mean," he enquired, "by men who abandoned their homeland?" The American said, "Yes." "Then," remarked the young Palestinian, "America is based on a bad principle." [7]

What is significant about this conversation is the amazement and disbelief – rightly or wrongly – shown by the youth that people would give up their love for home and country when offered a more congenial and lucrative way of life abroad. With the new generations of Palestinians growing up imbued with such ardent love for their usurped homeland that transends the amenities and opportunities which foreign lands may have to offer, it is easy to discern why the chances are remote for the Palestine problem to be solved on the basis of the *status quo*.

Refugee living conditions

The conditions under which the refugees presently live remain inadequate and deplorable. By 1966, the problem had not grown any less intractable or less dangerous to the peace and stability of the Middle East. The Commissioner-General of the United Nations Relief and Works Agency described the life of the refugees as one of "bitterness, frustration and disappointed hopes. During the long period of their dependence on international charity," he said, "their life has been one of hardship and privation. The relief accorded by UNRWA, though indispensable," he pointed out, "has been no more than a bare minimum... The rations are meagre and unvarying and would hardly sustain a person who depended solely on them for any long period. . ." the Commissioner-General added.

He then stressed, "whatever differences of opinion there may be about certain aspects of the problem, it is clear that a large part of the refugee community is still living today in dire poverty, often under pathetic and in some cases appalling conditions. Despite the sustained efforts of UNRWA and of the host Governments and other collaborating agencies, there are families," he pointed out, "who still live in dwellings which are unfit for human habitation: some in dark cellars, others in crumbling tenements, others in grossly over-crowded barracks and shacks . . . Nearly all the UNRWA camps are extremely over-crowded with five or more persons living in one small room. They lack adequate roads and pathways and many camps are deep in mud in winter and in dust in summer. There are rarely any sewers or stormwater drainage. The water supplies are communal and often inadequate, particularly during the hot summer months. Yet the refugees living in the camps (who constitute about two-fifths of the total number of refugees receiving relief) are, on the whole, probably better housed and better cared for than many of the remaining three-fifths living outside the camps in such dwellings as they have been able to provide for themselves. Understandably, UNRWA is under constant pressure from these less fortunate refugees to expand its camps and build more shelters."

"I am in no doubt," continued the Commissioner-General, "that a large category of refugees is genuinely in need of the relief dispensed by the Agency and that these refugees would face starvation or at least extreme privation if this relief ceased. Their dependence on help from others is not due to unwillingness to work, but to the simple lack of jobs which they can do. As to the attitude of the Arab Governments towards the employment of the refugees, the Commissioner-General has seen much to show that the authorities in the host countries are adopting a helpful and humane attitude to the question of enabling the refugees to find work and support themselves, even though this reduces the opportunities open to the local population."

It seemed to the Commissioner-General that it would be useful to consider what future awaits the Palestine refugees if the present deadlock over repatriation continues. Without attempting a detailed forecast, he offers three general observations:

(1) A large 'hard core' of refugees will continue to live in poverty and dependence on the charity of their fellowmen for the indefinite future. How large this 'hard core' may be is conjectural but even years hence (assuming that no solution of the refugee problem is found) it would seem that it must still include most of the refugees now living in the Gaza Strip, a substantial part of those living in Jordan and a significant number of those in the other host countries. If it seems intolerable that so large a number of human beings should spend their lives in perpetual dependence and that their fellow men should be asked to shoulder indefinitely the burden of supporting them, then it should be remembered that this would appear to be part of the price that has to be paid for the continuing lack of a solution to this problem. It should be remembered also that, however heavy the load imposed on others may be, the cruelest burden is that borne by the refugees themselves;

(2) The remaining refugees, not included in this 'hard core', will probably continue to improve their ability to support themselves at a rate depending on (a) the general economic develop-

ment of the region and the creation of new opportunities of employment and (b) the employability of individual refugees (the latter depending in large measure on the education and training which they receive); until their self-support is securely established, they (as well as the 'hard core') will continue to need assistance of the kind provided by the Agency;

(3) There is a danger that bitterness and resentment may continue among the refugees against those whom they hold responsible for the tragedy that befell them and against the international community in general for its failure to provide a remedy; that this bitterness and resentment may be diffused more widely and rooted more deeply throughout the Arab world as the *diaspora* of the Palestine refugees continues; and that, as a result, hope of a solution of the refugee and other related problems may diminish rather than increase as time goes on.

The Commissioner-General concludes by pointing out that the refugees regard the UNRWA rations not merely as a form of assistance from the international community which they are entitled to receive so long as their problem remains unsolved, but also as a recognition of their status and position while they await repatriation or compensation. [8]

Number of persons affected by the Palestine tragedy

According to United Nations records, the number of persons who left their homes by 14 May 1948 was in the neighborhood of 900,000. The years which followed saw more and more Arabs expelled particularly from the Beersheba Sub-District into Jordan and the Sinai Peninsula.

The latest report of the United Nations Relief and Works Agency (UNRWA) for Palestine shows that the number of refugees registered with the Agency as on 30 June 1966, was 1,317,749, as compared with 1,280,823 for the previous year. The refugees are distributed as follows:

Jordan	–	706,568	
Gaza Strip	–	307,245	
Lebanon	–	163,904	
Syria	–	140,032	1,317,749 [9]

These figures do not include, however, Palestinians who have lost their means of livelihood but not their homes and as such, do not quality for relief under the United Nations definition of 'refugee'. They also do not include persons who have been able to re-establish themselves in the host countries and are therefore not in need of relief; or Palestinians who are now scattered throughout the world.

The total number of Palestinians affected by the Palestine tragedy, after including the following categories, is about 1,858,000:

Persons in Jordan and Gaza Strip who do not qualify for rations	–	325,000 [10]	
Non-registered self-supporting in			
Jordan	–	50,000	
Lebanon	–	50,000	
Iraq	–	10,000	
Kuweit	–	60,000	
Syria	–	10,000	
U.A.R., Libya, etc.	–	20,000	
Europe, the Americas, Asia and Africa		15,000	540,000

Basis of relief rations

The refugees are presently maintained by the United Nations on a diet made up of the following basic rations and other supplies:

1. *Basic dry rations*

A monthly ration for one person consists of:

10,000 grams of flour
600 grams of pulses
600 grams of sugar
500 grams of rice
375 grams of oils and fats.

This ration provides about 1500 calories per day per person. In winter, the monthly ration is increased by

300 grams of pulses
400 grams of flour

It then provides about 1600 calories per day per person.

2. *Other supplies*

One piece of soap (150 grams) per month to each ration beneficiary. One and one-half litres of kerosene have hitherto been allocated to ration beneficiaries and to babies and children registered for services, in camps in Jordan, Lebanon and Syria during five winter months. In Gaza, one litre has been allocated to these beneficiaries, whether or not they live in camps, during five winter months. For the future, it is planned to issue kerosene only on a hardship basis in all host countries.[11]

The 1500 calories provided the refugees per day in summer and the 1600 calories in winter are below the minimum required for an individual. These do not include meat, vegetables or fruits, which the refugee must either find elsewhere or learn to do without.

UNRWA annual budget

The Agency's budget estimates for 1967, as compared with the estimates for 1966 and the actuals of 1965, are:

	1967 *budget estimates*	1966 *estimated expenditure*	1965 *actual expenditure*
	(in thousands of U.S. dollars)		
Part I – Relief services			
Basic rations	12,165	12,163	12,304
Supplementary feeding	1,421	1,361	1,315
Shelter	472	350	502
Special hardship assistance	493	461	516
Share of common costs from part IV	3,013	2,922	3,139
Total, Part I	17,564	17,327	17,776

Part II – Health services			
Medical services	3,243	3,089	3,037
Environmental sanitation	1,032	941	921
Share of common costs from part IV	939	935	991
Total, Part II	5,205	4,965	4,949
Part III – Education services			
General education	11,324	10,324	9,209
Vocational education	2,595	2,571	2,851
University education	351	351	399
Share of common costs from part IV	2,299	2,293	2,435
Total, Part III	16,569	15,539	14,894
Part IV – Common costs			
Supply and transport services	3,079	3,040	3,136
Other internal services	2,006	2,010	2,151
General administration	1,166	1,170	1,278
Total, Part IV	6,251	6,220	6,565
Costs allocated to operations	(6,251)	(6,220)	(6,565)
Net, Part IV	–	–	–
Total, all parts	39,338	37,831	37,619 [12]

Voluntary relief agencies

In addition to the relief provided by the United Nations, there are 14 voluntary agencies in the area of UNRWA operations giving active help to the refugees. There have also been generous donations of used clothing made available to UNRWA by 17 institutions to meet the needs of the refugees. During 1965, 675 tons of donated clothing were received and distributed in Jordan, Lebanon and the Syrian Arab Republic to refugee families in special need. In Gaza, general distribution continued. Some $ 50,000 were spent by UNRWA to meet inland transport costs and freight for clothing shipped from countries other than the United States of America.[13]

This help is gratefully received by the refugees and much appreciated by the Arab world. It is a tangible sign of man's humanity to man.

Arab host Governments contribution to refugee relief

Little in the past was known of the Arab States' contributions to the refugees, apart from the fact that the host countries have had to carry the burden of a big refugee population out of all proportion to their economic and social abilities. But due acknowledgement of this assistance has been made by UNRWA itself. The Commissioner-General told the General Assembly, "The host Governments have, as in past years, performed notable services on behalf of the refugees. . . . they finance certain levels of education for the refugees in an amount greater than that spent for the purpose by UNRWA; they also give substantial direct assistance to the refugees in the fields of health and welfare and through the provision of building sites, water supplies and security protection for the Agency's camps and other installations. "The host Governments report," the Commissioner-General said, "that the cost of this direct assistance totalled $ 7,603,700 in 1965-1966." [14]

In reporting on Arab help to the Palestine refugees, the former Commissioner-General of the United Nations Relief and Works Agency told the General Assembly, "The severe strain which the refugee problem places on the whole structure – political, economic and social – of the host countries and their natural concern with the scope and complexity of the Agency's operations, must be borne in mind." [15]

Significant is the total absence of any material contribution by the Israelis to UNRWA relief programmes. They have 'seized' Arab property; they unashamedly continue to enjoy without payment the fruits of Arab labour; and they will not share in paying charity to their Arab victims who are barely subsisting in refugee camps.

Problem before United Nations

The Palestine Arabs have repeatedly expressed their resentment at having to receive charity. They have considerable property in the Israeli-occupied part of Palestine, the income from which would be sufficient to maintain them on a more decent standard of living than the meagre seven cents per person per day level doled out to them by the United Nations. The income from this property – the patrimony of an entire nation – runs into the hundreds of millions of dollars. The capital value of the agricultural lands, farmsteads, cattle, machinery, city properties, contents of private homes and businesses, motor vehicles, etc., which the Israelis 'seized', adds up to billions of dollars. Some of these properties have been sold, others are leased; and the proceeds from the transactions are being used for the settlement of new Jewish immigrants, of whom few were ever 'refugees'.

The annual debates of the Palestine Question in the Special Political Committee are generally intense, but the ultimate result is the adoption of a resolution of extended help, leaving the cause of the problem to fester and grow. A spokesman of the Palestine Arabs told the Committee, in unequivocal terms, "The establishment of the Palestine Liberation Organization was an expression of the Palestinian Arabs' determination to continue the struggle for those rights, which had been taken away from them by invading British colonialists and Zionists and by the United Nations, and given to total strangers from all parts of the world. Although the Organization had the support of the Arab Governments, it had not been established by them but was a manifestation of the vitality, initiative and spirit of sacrifice of the people of Palestine themselves in dealing with their problem. Its formation had been proclaimed by the First Palestine Arab National Congress held at Jerusalem on 28 May 1964 and attended by 424 Palestinian representatives. The Congress had declared the unequivocal determination of the people of Palestine to liberate their homeland from foreign occupation and domination. The establishment of the Organization had constituted the turning-point in the history of the Palestinian Arabs and a repudiation of the claims of those who would have the United Nations believe that the question of Palestine no longer existed and that it was only the refugee problem which was on the agenda."

"After seventeen years of patient waiting," the spokesman went on to say, "they had lost all faith in the United Nations, but the establishment of the Organization had re-awakened their hopes and afforded them an opportunity to renew the struggle for their homeland, their strong and genuine attachment to which could not be shaken by the lapse of time. Wherever they were now residing," he said, "the more than two million Arabs of Palestine formed a single national entity which had its home in Palestine from time immemorial." [16]

Another spokesman was no less emphatic and determined on the rights of the Palestine Arabs. He warned that "The Palestine Arabs, the lawful owners of the country, continued to exist and they had one goal: to repossess their homeland and exercise their right to self-determination. Whether the refugees became self-supporting or not, whether UNRWA continued to function or not, nothing would deflect them from their determination to achieve that objective. Their rights and their national identity would not be weakened by the passage of time and their just cause was supported by all the Moslem and Arab peoples and by freedom-loving nations throughout the world. The Palestine problem," he pointed out, "was an example of colonialism in its ugliest form and a case of genocide in the era of the United Nations. It constituted a violation of human rights and a denial of the right of self-determination." [17]

During the debates of 1964, the Representatives of Afghanistan and Malaysia introduced a draft resolution (A SPC/L. 116) calling for the appointment of a custodian to administer Arab property in Israeli-occupied territory.* The sponsors explained that the provisions of the draft were humanitarian and not political. It was designed solely to enable the Arab refugees from Palestine to receive the income from the property which they owned in their ancestral land. "That was simply a matter of common sense and justice," they said. The Representative of Afghanistan pointed out, "he could not see any reason why Moslem or Christian Arabs should

---

* A similar proposal to appoint a custodian of Arab property in Israeli-occupied territory, sponsored by Afghanistan, Malaysia, Pakistan and Somalia, was again made in 1966. It was defeated by 38 votes to 36, with 36 abstentions. [18]

not continue their ownership of property which belonged to them in a town or village in Palestine, even if the town or village had been occupied by the Israeli authorities since 1948. To refuse them that right," he added, "would be an act of racial and religious discrimination condemned by the whole world." [19]

The Israeli representative opposed the draft resolution on the grounds that the Arabs had rejected the Partition Plan and they could not now claim its implementation; that the proposed measure would constitute a limitation upon Israel's sovereignty; that the United Nations could not intervene in the internal affairs of any state; and that the Arabs have been unwilling to conclude a peace treaty with Israel.

The Representative of Malaysia replied that, in the first place, he wished to explain, "It was essential to bear in mind that the proposed text did not call upon the Committee or the General Assembly to come to a decision on the substance of the matter, or to pass any kind of judgment, but merely requested, in accordance with international practice and custom, the appointment of a custodian to administer the disputed property in the best interests of its owners."

Commenting on the four objections raised by the Israeli representative, the Representative of Malaysia replied as follows:

First, "Whether they (the Arabs) accepted partition or not, the situation was a *fait accompli* and the new state occupied land which had not previously belonged to it, so that the question whether the property now belonged to its own nationals, to aliens or to enemies was still in debate."

Secondly, "The question of Israel's sovereignty had to be viewed in the context of international principles and the obligations placed on that state, when it was created by a United Nations resolution."

Thirdly, "If a state had certain obligations that it refused to fulfill, it was the duty of the General Assembly to ask it to do so."

Fourthly, "In fact, the property in question should be treated as enemy property which was subject to duly established *International Law,* which drew a distinction between what was called the acquired rights of a new state, rights that were already in existence before the new state came into existence and rights of enemy property. The question whether a belligerent might confiscate the private property of enemy nationals on its own soil was controversial. The state of Israel," he added, "claimed precisely to have a right, under its domestic laws, to expropriate and confiscate all property within its territory. However," he pointed out, "since the end of the eighteenth century and after the Second World War, the outright confiscation of enemy property had been eschewed, and the principle of indemnification had been affirmed by treaty.* The purpose of the immunity of private property from confiscation was to avoid throwing the burdens of war upon private individuals. Furthermore," he went on, "there was some doubt as to whether the confiscations that might have been made would be recognized by other states or by international tribunals." [20]

It is obvious from the annual debates in the Special Political Committee that the majority of the members of the United Nations have the desire to do in Palestine what they know is right and what is just; but the World Organization, when acting as a body, is generally influenced to remain equivocal in pressing for Israeli compliance. Instead of facing the facts squarely and placing responsibility for the deadlock where it belongs, the United Nations contends itself each year with applying palliatives in the form of charity to the victims of its ill-conceived decision of partition of 1947 and a superficial call to both parties "to settle their differences either by direct negotiation or through the Conciliation Commission" – as if the Arabs are equally to blame for the tragedy.

According to the Israelis, they claim there is nothing to settle: the Palestine Arabs are out and must remain out; their properties have been confiscated for the use of new Jewish immigrants and cannot be returned; and all that remains to be done is for the Arab States to settle for peace with Israel on the basis of the *fait accompli.*

---

* For details of laws on indemnification, reparation and restitution, enacted by the Allied Nations after the surrender of Nazi Germany see *Palestine : Loss of a Heritage*, by Sami Hadawi, pp. 87-98

Misconceptions about the problem

The Arab States are accused of keeping the dispute alive because of their refusal to resettle the refugees in their own territories. It must be realized that there is *no* resolution of the United Nations calling on the Arab States to do so; but there *are* resolutions calling on the Israelis to permit the refugees to return to their homes and compensate those who do not wish to return. Nevertheless, the Arab States have shown every willingness to open their countries to those refugees who wish to settle in Arab lands after they have been allowed to exercise their right of free choice between repatriation and compensation, as laid down in paragraph 11 of resolution 194 (III). This willingness was clearly expressed by Ambassador Kamil Abdel Rahim on behalf of the other Arab States. He told the General Assembly: "The Arab countries would be quite prepared to welcome all those who preferred to stay out of Israel, but they had no power over the overwhelming majority of refugees who want to go back." [21]

There prevails in certain circles an assumption that the Arab States are using the refugees as pawns in the game of power politics with Israel. The additional charge is that the Arab States have both mistreated and neglected the refugees and have made no effort to alleviate their sufferings.

The real facts have long been obscured by Israeli propaganda. But Dr. John H. Davis, former Commissioner-General of the United Nations Relief and Works Agency (UNRWA), who could speak with authority on the subject, has exploded the misconceptions about the situation.

In a speech delivered before the Conference of Voluntary Agencies in Geneva, Switzerland, on 18 January 1961, Dr. Davis declared that "the Palestine refugee problem has defied political solution, not because of alleged 'whims' of Arab politicians or the reputed 'shiftless' nature of the refugees, but because of the 'depth and universality' of the conflict of basic feeling between Arabs and Israelis."

"The reason," he pointed out, "is a 'widespread lack of understanding' of the problem." He listed what he termed as five major 'misconceptions' about the situation:

1. 'That the Palestine Arab people are shiftless and prefer international charity to working for a living.'
   Dr. Davis countered that this is not true – The Palestinians are "generally industrially inclined and have a strong desire to be self-supporting. As of 1948, the Palestine economy and culture were about the most advanced of any in the Middle East."
2. 'That the Arab host Governments have mistreated the refugees by neglecting them and even holding them as hostages in their struggle with Israel.'
   Dr. Davis replied that "the truth is that in general the host governments have been sympathetic and generous within their means."
3. 'That the conniving of unprincipled Arab politicians had held the refugees idle.'
   Dr. Davis declared that Arab politicians "quite accurately voice the deep feelings and aspirations" of their peoples, refugees and non-refugees alike, when they refuse to "accept Israel as a permanent component of the Middle East. It is the basic feelings of the peoples on both sides of the Palestine issue rather than politicians' whims, that have prevented and still prevent a political solution to the Palestine Problem."
4. 'That a political solution would mean an end to the refugee problem.'
   Dr. Davis pointed out that, politics aside, there is the human aspect of the problem – namely, that a large portion of the adult male refugee population is unemployable. The older generations were farmers or unskilled labourers and the younger are untrained and all of them are now living in countries where the demand for such workers is already fully met.
5. 'That internal pressure should now be applied to host governments to force them to solve the refugee problem more quickly.'
   Dr. Davis said, "in view of the human aspect of the problem

alone and without regard to political factors (important as they are), the host governments cannot themselves solve the Palestine refugee problem. To pressure them to do so would tend to increase economic and political instability in these countries, which in turn, would tend to delay rather then facilitate a permanent solution." [22]

Right of Refugees to homes and property

The Partition Resolution provides that the Arab inhabitants of the 'Jewish state' shall be protected in their rights and property. In addition, the *Israeli Proclamation of Independence* of 14 May 1948, while guaranteeing political equality and other freedoms for all its citizens, provided, "The state of Israel will be ready to cooperate with the organs and representatives of the United Nations in the implementation of the resolution of the Assembly of November 29, 1947 and will take steps to bring about the economic union over the whole of Palestine." [23] Ironically, this 'Proclamation' was made *after* the Zionists had already expelled and dispossessed at least 300,000 Arabs, but still needed world opinion on their side.

Now, Israel disclaims any responsibility for the Palestine tragedy and has consistently refused to comply with United Nations resolutions. The former Director of UNRWA reported to the General Assembly in 1958, the "reintegration of the refugees into the economic life of the Near East either by repatriation or by resettlement" will continue to be hampered so long as the Government of Israel will take no "affirmative action to facilitate the implementation of General Assembly resolution 194 (III) of 11 December 1948 concerning repatriation and compensation." [24]

Israel's refusal to allow the refugees a choice between return to their homes and compensation is part and parcel of the political policy which motivated the decision of expulsion and dispossession in 1948.

The immorality of the Zionist treatment of the Palestine Arabs has been amply recorded for all time by British historian Arnold Toynbee in his *A Study of History*. He wrote:

> "If the heinousness of sin is to be measured by the degree to which the sinner is sinning against the light that God has vouchsafed to him, the Jews had even less excuse in A.D. 1948 for evicting Palestinian Arabs from their homes than Nebuchadnezzar and Titus and Hadrian and the Spanish and Portugese Inquisition had had for uprooting, persecuting and exterminating Jews in Palestine and elsewhere at divers times in the past. In A.D. 1948 the Jews knew, from personal experience, what they were doing; and it was their supreme tragedy that the lesson learned by them from their encounter with the Nazi Gentiles should have been not to eschew but to imitate some of the evil deeds that the Nazis had committed against the Jews." [25]

In a lecture at McGill University in Montreal, Canada, Professor Toynbee told his Jewish audience "The Jewish treatment of the Arabs in 1947 was as morally indefensible as the slaughter by the Nazis of 6,000,000 Jews." He also pointed out, "The most tragic thing in human life is when people who have suffered impose suffering in their turn." When told during a subsequent debate with the Israeli ambassador that the Nazi action was planned and carried out in cold blood, Toynbee retorted: "I still feel that the massacres of Arab civilians by the Israeli armed forces were carried out cold-bloodedly and with a purpose. It is impossible," he said, "to be more than 100% wicked. A murder is a murder. If I murder one man," he pointed out, "that makes me a murderer. I don't have to reach 6,000,000 or even 1,000," he added.

On the question of the return of the refugees, Professor Toynbee drew attention to the fact that the Jews had acquired most of the land in Israel by dispossessing the Arabs. "To put it bluntly," he said, "that is robbery and I am sure it is on the Jewish conscience. What I have said has given the Jews a bit of a shock treatment. I have said aloud a bit of what is being said inside your conscience. I say listen to your own inner voices," Toynbee advised his Jewish audience. [26]

The attitude of the Israelis towards their Arab victims has been condemned repeatedly by people of conscience inside and outside Israel. In one instance, Rabbi R. Benjamin, writing from Israel, said: "In the end we must come out publicly with the truth: That we have no moral right whatever to oppose the return of the Arab refugees to their land . . . that until we have begun to redeem our sin against the Arab refugees, we have no right to continue the Ingathering of the Exiles. We have no right to demand that American Jews leave their country to which they have become attached and settle in a land that has been stolen from others, while the owners of it are homeless and miserable."

The Rabbi went on to say, "We had no right to occupy the house of an Arab if we had not paid for it at its value. The same goes for fields, gardens, stores, workshops. We had no right to build a settlement and to realize the ideal of Zionism with other people's property. To do this is robbery. I am surprised that Rabbi Herzog and all those who speak in the name of Jewish ethics and who always quote the Ten Commandments should consent to such a state of affairs." [27]

Another case of condemnation comes from the late William Zukerman, Editor of the *Jewish Newsletter* (New York). He declared: "The fact that they (the Arab refugees) fled in panic because of a real, or imaginery, danger is no excuse for depriving them of their homes, fields and livelihoods." He pointed out, "No people is exempt from panic in war time; least of all the Jews . . . To deprive them (the Arabs) of their homes and property because they, like most humans, sought safety for themselves and their children, is a grave act of injustice . . . It is a reversal," he said, "of all the moral principles upon which the Jews have based their civilization and their way of life from the days of the Prophets to the present." Zukerman then enquires: "How can a people which has for centuries led a life as refugees and experienced all the bitter pain of exile, begin its political renaissance with an act of injustice against other refugees? The most tragic aspect of this entire affair," he added, "is not only that a grave collective injustice has been committed, but that the majority of Israelis and *Diaspora* Jews justify and glorify it as an act of patriotic pride, historic justice and heroism. Not until this appalling spiritual confusion is cleared up, can any practical measures be undertaken," [28] he concluded.

XI | *Arabs under Israeli Rule*

Israel claims it is the only democratic nation in the Middle East where all citizens enjoy full and equal rights without distinction as to race, colour, or religion. Accordingly, Israel poses as a freedom-loving nation, fulfilling all the requirements of the United Nations Charter, the Universal Declaration of Human Rights and the United Nations Partition Resolution which gave birth to the 'Jewish state.'

That this claim has gone unchallenged does not substantiate it. While the Jewish majority in the country may enjoy full rights and liberties, it is certainly not true of the Arab minority – Moslem and Christian. A nation's democracy is judged not by the form of government it has or by the method of its voting or the number of its political parties, but by the manner and extent of the equalities and freedoms enjoyed by all of its citizens without discrimination.

The creation of Israel was made possible as a result of the United Nations Partition Resolution of 29 November, 1947, which explicitly laid down the conditions under which the 'Jewish state' and 'Arab state' were to come into existence. The Resolution stipulates in Section B (10) (d) and Section C (1) and (2) that the Consitution of the proposed state shall, *inter alia,* embody provisions which shall guarantee "to all persons equal and non-discriminatory rights in civil, political, economic and religious matters and the enjoyment of human rights and fundamental freedoms;" and shall make "no discrimination of any kind between the inhabitants on the ground of race, religion, language, or sex."

The use of the imperative word 'shall' in the Resolution was not accidental but deliberate, in order to ensure full freedom and equality for Moslem, Christian and Jew.

In addition, complete equality was guaranteed to the Arab inhabitants in the countless statements of Zionist leaders in their demand for a 'Jewish state.' David Ben-Gurion, arguing the Zionist case for a 'Jewish state' before the Anglo-American Committee of Enquiry on Palestine in 1946, made the following statement: "We will have to treat our Arab and other non-Jewish neighbours ... as if they were Jews but make every effort that they should preserve their Arab characteristics, their language, their Arab culture, their Arab religion, their Arab way of life, while making every effort to.. gradually raise their standard of life." [1]

The zeal and enthusiasm which Mr. Ben-Gurion – who was later to become the first Prime Minister of Israel – displayed as Chairman of the Zionist Organization in Palestine, may have persuaded the Committee that the Arabs had nothing to fear from a 'Jewish state' whose leaders promise not only that "nothing shall be done which may prejudice the civil and religious rights of the non-Jewish communities in Palestine" but also that every phase of Arab life and culture will be perserved and improved.

In 1948, the 'Jewish state' still needed international support. To assure the United Nations and world opinion that the attitude of Zionist leaders towards the Arab minority had not altered, Israel's Proclamation of Independence *guaranteed* that the State "will be based on principles of liberty, justice and peace as conceived by the Prophets of Israel; will uphold the full social and political equality of all its citizens, without distinction of religion, race, or sex." [2]

These laudable principles proved to be mere lip-service after the state was established. The Arabs living in the Israeli-occupied territory of Palestine have been condemned to a life of deprivation, restriction, confiscation of property, degradation and second-class citizenship within their ancestral homeland since 1948.

Visitors to the Holy Land have drawn attention to the plight of the Moslem and Christian Arab inhabitants, while representatives of the oppressed citizens have not ceased to appeal in one form or another to the conscience of the world. But all of their efforts have been in vain, like 'a voice crying in the wilderness.'

At the 15th session (1960) of the United Nations, the Arab States, disturbed by the deplorable situation of the Arabs in Israel, once again called the attention of the General Assembly to their plight and urged that "an impartial commission of enquiry be appointed to examine the conditions under which Arabs in Israel are living."

The Israeli representative replied by claiming that the Arabs in Israel possess the same economic, social and political rights as Jews and were even better off than the Arabs in adjacent countries.

The Israeli representative failed to explain the Israeli *Nationality Act* which confers citizenship rights on a Jew the moment he steps onto Palestine soil but denies the same rights to an Arab born and living in the country. He also failed to explain why the Arab community which constitutes more than 10% of the total population is denied a fair share in Cabinet appointments.

The question may be asked: Why is it that the Israelis became "persecutors in their turn for the first time since A.D. 135 – this at the first opportunity that had arisen for them to inflict on other human beings who had done the Jews no injury, but who happened to be weaker then they were, some of the wrongs and sufferings that had been inflicted on the Jews by their many successive Gentile persecutors?"[3] The answer is clear and simple: They wanted Palestine rid of its Moslem and Christian owners. Those who remained behind constituted a thorn in the side of the 'Jewish state'. The Israeli Government decided to make life for them unbearable in the hope that they would depart, foregoing homes, farmsteads, lands and other possessions as a free handout to Jewish occupation.

The denial of the Israeli representative that there exists any discrimination, produced a protest from the Arab community in the Israeli-held territory in the form of an appeal to the President of the United Nations General Assembly.* The appeal requested that "a committee be appointed and entrusted with the task of enquiring into the conditions of the Arab minority in Israel and of recommending the necessary measures to ensure the elimination of all oppressive, discriminatory and humiliating designs and to remedy the numerous injustices and grievances from which they suffer."[4]

* This was later published by the Arab Information Center, 757 Third Avenue, New York, N.Y. 10017 under the title *Violation of Human Rights*.

The urgency of this plea reached a climax in September 1961, when the Arabs in Israel demonstrated against their ill-treatment by the government of Israel. In Nazareth, on September 20th, a crowd of 5,000 Arabs marched before the town hall. The next day, more than 2,000 Nazareth schoolboys crowded into a square by the Virgin Mary's Well shouting "down with Ben-Gurion and his government of murderers." Similar demonstrations then spread to other towns, such as Haifa and Acre. The killing of five young Arabs by Israeli border guards, as the youths sought to flee to the U.A.R., was the immediate cause of these riots, but Arab and Israeli officials alike recognized the deeper causes of discontent.

In reporting these incidents from Israeli official sources the *New York Times* correspondent, Lawrence Fellows, stated:

> "The dissatisfaction felt by Arabs in Israel, these (Israeli) officials said, is partly a result of frustration at their inability to find employment that pleases them. Israeli Arabs rarely find good jobs outside their villages and towns.
>
> "The bitterest pill for the Arabs by far is the military government. Perhaps 180,000 of the 220,000 Arabs in Israel live under army rule. They are under curfew restrictions and are confined to certain areas.
>
> "In addition, they are not given access to civilian courts under ordinary circumstances but are subject instead to courts-martial." [5]

This view was later corroborated by the Arab Deputy Mayor of Nazareth, Mr. Abdul Aziz Zubi who felt that the major cause of the Arab revolt was Arab resentment of Israeli military rule and the curtailment of their right to work. In addition, he pointed out "Another source of bad feeling ... is the expropriation of Arab-owned lands by the State. He asserted that 250,000 acres had been taken from Arab citizens in the last thirteen years." [6]

These opinions, and the riots themselves, have demonstrated to the world that severe measures were being used against the Arab minority in Israel, constituting a clear violation of human and minority rights. The petition of ten Arab leaders in Israel to the United Nations is not to be construed merely as an appeal of ten men. The riots substantiate the view that behind this petition and similar protests were thousands of Arabs who are oppressed in Israel.

In contrast to Israeli treatment of their Arab citizens, it is significant that there are no laws in any Arab country which discriminate between citizens on grounds of race, colour or religion. Jews enjoy full and equal rights with their Moslem and Christian brethren. If there was any truth in the Zionist-Israeli propaganda accusations that Jews in Arab countries were being persecuted or discriminated against, the United Nations would have been confronted with the problem under the item 'Protection of Human Rights' and the Zionist-controlled press would have carried on a barrage of attacks and denunciations against the Arabs.

The Arab Population

After hostilities between the Arab States and Israel ceased and Armistice Agreements had been signed, only about 170,000 Arabs remained in the Israeli-occupied territory. Of these 119,000 were Moslems; 35,000 were Christians and 15,000 were Druze. About 32,000 were city and town dwellers, 120,000 were villagers and 18,000 were Bedouins.

In 1965, the Arab population of the occupied territory stood at:

Moslems	–	202,267
Christians	–	55,484
Druze	–	28,634
Total:		286,385 [7]

The Arab inhabitants are concentrated mainly in the Galilee region, originally assigned to the 'Arab state' under the Partition Plan of 1947; the second largest region where Arabs are concentrated is in the 'Little Triangle', in the center of the country bordering Jordan; and in the South, there are 31,687 Bedouins.

Arab minority placed under military rule *

On 15 May 1948, the 'Jewish state' was established and the Great Powers – with the United States jumping the gun – recognized Israel. The Israelis felt confident that they had nothing more to fear from the Arabs who had been reduced to a mere minority. Having a power base in the world media of information, the Zionist leaders felt no longer bound to the promises freely given before the creation of the 'Jewish state' and the guarantees embodied in the Partition Resolution.

The first legislative act of the Israeli authorities was the enactment of the *Law of Administration Ordinance* [8] which empowered the Minister of Defence to issue *Emergency Regulations* [9] that would restrict movement of the Arab minority and control all their other human liberties. Under these *Emergency Regulations,* the Minister of Defence was empowered to establish 'defence areas' within which he could designate 'security zones' and delegate his authority within these 'areas' and 'zones' to military officers of certain ranks.

Israeli authorities also applied to the Arab minority the *Defence (Emergency) Regulations* which had been enacted by the Palestine Government in 1945 [10] to combat Jewish terrorism. The irony is that, whereas these Regulations were vehemently condemned as cruel and undemocratic by the Jews of Palestine, the Jewish Agency and world Jewry at the time they were promulgated; they were now being applied by the Israelis with even greater vigour to an Arab minority. Arab citizens showed no signs of hostility towards the 'Jewish state' after the Armistice had been signed. They remained docile and peaceful. The Arabs have therefore given the Israelis no legitimate excuse to apply to them the harsh measures which

* It is reported that "the Government (of Israel) decided to abolish the Military Government machinery as of December 1, 1966." An official announcement stated, "the areas affected by the decision will now be joined to the three existing military regions into which the country is divided." [11]
Commenting on the decision, Taufiq Toubi, an Arab member of the Israeli Parliament and Mr. Uri Avneri a Jewish member, termed the Government's decision "misleading", claiming "that Military Government in all its ramifications would continue under a different guise." [12]

were enacted by the Mandatory Power to curb Jewish terrorism.

The next step taken divided the regions where the majority of the Arabs lived, into three military zones:

1. *The Northern Sector,* or Galilee, bordering on Lebanon and the Northern Province of Syria, which contained over 130,000 Arabs;
2. *The Central Sector,* or the 'Little Triangle' as it came to be known, bordering on the West Bank of Jordan, where some 35,000 Arabs once lived; and
3. The Beersheba Sub-District, or the 'Negeb', bordering on the West Bank of Jordan in the north and the United Arab Republic and the Gaza Strip in the west, which contained some 14,000 Bedouin Arabs.

No person, except a soldier or a policemam on duty, was allowed to enter these 'security zones.' Any person who was a permanent resident within any of these zones at the time the Emergency Regulations went into effect, was not "required to leave until fourteen days after receiving an order from the authorities to do so." Any person entering a security zone without a military permit could be removed and was also subject, on conviction, to imprisonment for a term not exceeding one year or a fine not exceeding 500 pounds, or to both these penalties.

Military courts were then established to deal with persons accused of violating the provisions of the Emergency Regulations. Violators were brought before these courts within 48 hours of their arrest and summarily tried either in open or closed session as the court saw fit. The verdict of the court was final and could not be questioned or challenged.

Provisions of the Emergency Regulations may be summarized as follows:

1. 'Defense areas' and 'security zones' were established in order to give the military authorities power, at their discretion, to expel the Arab inhabitants from their villages or to transfer them to other localities;
2. The military and police could seize and detain any "goods, articles and things." They could also enter and search any

place and detain any individual;

3. The military commander was authorized to limit individual movements, to impose restrictions upon employment and business, to issue deportation orders, place any person under police supervision for a period not exceeding one year, or impose forced residence in a fixed place of any person as he deems necessary;
4. District commissioners were authorized to take possession of any land if such action was "in the interest of public safety." Both the district commissioner and military commander were empowered to requisition any chattle which "includes any substance, vehicle, animal or small craft" and to "use or deal with, or authorize use in dealing with the chattle or property for such purposes as he thinks expedient ... and hold or sell or otherwise dispose of it;"
5. The military commander could occupy any area where he believes the inhabitants did not assist him in the performance of his duties. Police or troops could be quartered in any village at the expense of the inhabitants;
6. Road movements were also prohibited or controlled. The military commander was authorized to impose curfews, suspend postal services and cut off telephone communications and other public services. Any area under his control could be declared a 'closed area', entrance into which required a military permit. As a result, many villages and farms were closed to their inhabitants and the lands turned over to new Jewish settlers.

American Author Don Peretz sums up the effect of this legislation on the Arab inhabitants as follows:

> "Arabs in these areas lived under a complex of legal restrictions. Their movement into, out of, and within security zones was regulated by the military. Legal residents could be banished and their properties confiscated. Whole villages could be removed from one area to another. The final authority regarding violations of emergency regulations was a military court, whose decisions were not subject to juridiction of the Civil Courts of Appeal." [13]

If the purposes behind these Israeli restrictive and stringent measures against the Arab inhabitants were dictated exclusively by the exigencies of war, one could readily understand the precautions taken. But when these measures are aimed against Arab communities and individuals who do not pose any danger to the security of the state and continue to be generally enforced long after the danger is over, it seems apparent that the motives behind them are other than the regulations imply.*

The Israelis seem determined to have this 'state' of theirs free of all non-Jewish elements. The Zionists successfully planned and executed their policy of expulsion of the Arab population and were now anxious to rid themselves of those Moslems and Christians who obstinately stood by their homes and fields, but they have withstood all pressures to leave. The Emergency Regulations may appear to safeguard the security of the 'state' against a so-called 'fifth-column'; but in actual practice, they are being used to inflict each day a new form of physical or material injustice upon the Arab minority.

In pursuing this ruthless policy toward the Arab minority, the Israelis hope to gain two advantages: *first*, that the Arabs will finally, of their own volition, depart the country and forego their homes and lands to make room for more Jewish immigrants; *second*,

---

* According to a report published in the *Jerusalem Post* (Israel) of 13 January, 1966, Israeli Premier Levi Eshkol, speaking on Israeli policy following the 1965 elections, told his audience that it was the intention of his Government "to grant further relaxations in the Military Government areas. The Beduin in the Negeb," he said, "will be exempted from the need for movement permits and will be able to move freely about the country. The Military Government area in the North," he added, "will be opened, with the exception of closed areas along the borders to free movement in both directions. It is our plan," he promised, "to arrive, in the course of a year, at the abolition of Military Government machinery."

If the future is to be judged by the past when similar statements and promises were made before, during and after elections but never honoured, the 1966 'promises' must be regarded as another piece of propaganda. At any rate the 'year' has passed and no change in the pathetic condition of the Arab minority has been observed.

that it would dissuade the Arab refugees from demanding return to their homes. Neither objective has so far been realized.

Israeli Citizenship

Full and equal rights of citizenship are guaranteed in principle for the Moslem and Christian inhabitants of Palestine, who live in that part of the territory assigned to the 'Jewish state'. Chapter 3, Article 1, of the Partition Resolution stipulates, "Palestinian citizens residing in Palestine outside the City of Jerusalem, as well as Arabs and Jews who, not holding Palestinian citizenship, reside in Palestine outside the City of Jerusalem, shall, upon recognition of independence, become citizens of the State in which they are resident and enjoy full civil and political rights." [14]

In 1950, the Israeli authorities promulgated *The Law of Return*. This was followed in 1952 by *The Nationality Law*. [15]

Under these two laws, the right of entry into Israel is automatically and unconditionally conferred upon a Jew, of whatever nationality, the moment he steps on Israeli soil. The Moslem and Christian Arabs, on the other hand, are not so privileged even within their own country. The fact that the Palestine Arab was born in the territory now under Israeli control is insufficient to confer upon him automatic citizenship, notwithstanding the specific stipulation in the United Nations Resolution and the common practices followed in all civilized countries. To become an Israeli citizen, an Arab must be naturalized. This is only possible by proving that he was born in the country; that he lived in Israeli-occupied territory three out of the five years preceding the date of his application for citizenship; that he is entitled to permanent residence; that he is settled or intends to settle permanently in the country; and that he has a sufficient knowledge of the Hebrew language. Even if the Arab met all these requirements, it was still left to the discretion of the Minister of the Interior to grant or refuse the application.

Arab members of the Israeli Parliament and a section of the Jewish community considered the law discriminating and urged that provision should be made whereby all individuals who were born in the country should automatically be recognized as Israeli nationals, whether or not they had a knowledge of Hebrew. The fact that Arabic was also regarded as an official language did not help the Arab resident in acquiring the citizenship of the country in which he was born and lives. Automatic citizenship, the Parliament members pointed out, was a natural right of the individual; was in conformity with existing practices all over the world; and was guaranteed in the United Nations Partition Resolution of 1947. This request was flatly rejected and the law was enacted with all of its iniquities.

After this law was passed, the Minister of the Interior admitted in Parliament that racial discrimination did exist. But he pointed out that this stemmed, not from the *Nationality Law*, but from the *Law of Return* which endowed only Jews with the right of 'return'. The former law, he argued, intended to distinguish between those whose loyalty to Israel was accepted and those who had to prove it.[16]

Whatever the explanations, the fact remains that discrimination exists - be it under one law or another, or for one reason or another. Whereas an alien is granted citizenship the moment he steps on Palestine soil, provided he is a Jew, an Arab born in the country of Palestinian parents many generations back, can acquire citizenship only by naturalization – and this under certain extraneous conditions.

Commenting on this law, the Hebrew paper *Haaretz* said that the Nationality Law sacrificed an opportunity to establish better rapport between the Arab minority and the State. The demand – the paper continued - that Arabs be required to have some knowledge of Hebrew was unfair; and it supported the grant of automatic citizenship to all Arabs who had Israeli identity cards. The paper concluded by reminding the Israelis of the Jewish struggle for minority rights in other countries. [17]

Derek Tozer, a British correspondent, writing in the *American Mercury*, stated "the official policy of the Government (of Israel) is unequivocal. Arabs, like the Jews in Nazi Germany, are officially

'Class-B' citizens - a fact which is recorded on their identity cards."[18]

William Zukerman, Editor of the *Jewish Newsletter,* said "a more flagrant case of discrimination is hard to find even in the annals of the chauvinistic twentieth century." [19]

That this discrimination exists and is not only racial but religious, is irrefutable. Jews throughout the world maintain that they are citizens entitled to full rights and equalities in the countries in which they have citizenship. They argue that, religiously, they are Jews who follow the teachings of the Holy Writ. Politically, economically and socially, they see themselves as being no different from their fellow-citizens of other faiths. Their religion, they maintain, is a matter of personal conscience. Any attempt at discrimination is labelled as 'anti-semitism'. There is ample proof that Jews in all freedom-loving countries are recognized and accepted as Americans, English, French, etc., 'of the Jewish faith'. *It follows with reason, therefore, that the Jews born in the Arab countries are 'Arabs of the Jewish faith' and they are so treated.*

The fact that automatic citizenship rights are granted to an Iraqi or Yemenite Arab 'of the Jewish faith' the moment he enters Palestine, but denied to a Palestine Arab 'of the Moslem or Christian faith' who has been born and has lived in the country for generations, is a flagrant case of discrimination. No law similar to the Israeli *Nationality Law* is known to exist in any other civilized country. While Zionists insist on equality for Jews living outside Israel, they deny similar equality to non-Jews living inside the 'Jewish state' !

Restriction of Movement

Article 13 of the Universal Declaration of Human Rights provides, "everyone has the right to freedom of movement and residence within the borders of each state," and "everyone has the right to leave any country, including his own, and to return to his country."

However, while Iraqi, Yemenite and other 'Arab Jews' enjoy

complete freedom of movement within their countries, the Moslem and Christian Arabs – no matter how remote their homes may be from the 'armistice demarcation lines' – still live under military rule. Their movements are restricted.

A truly democratic government makes no distinction among its citizens, permitting full freedom to some and restricting the movement of others. Emergency laws, on the other hand, are not generally applied to a particular section of the population as a whole but are restricted to a group or to individuals if it is established that the group or some individuals are actually engaged in the disturbance of the peace or are a source of danger to the 'safety of the state'.

The Arab minority has so far not given the Israeli authorities any reason to suspect them, either as a whole or as individuals, of subversive or hostile activities. The fact that the Arab residents happen to be a part of the expelled population is not sufficient reason for placing them under restrictive measures which would deprive them of their freedom and would interfere with their normal way of life. The Israelis had ample time to distinguish between the peaceful and law-abiding Arabs and those who might be a danger; but they failed to differentiate in their treatment between one and the other. This proves that the Israeli policy is against the Palestinian Arab, as such, whatever his conduct, beliefs, or attitude.

What the Arab residents have experienced under the rule of the 'Jewish state' and what they still suffer at the hands of their Zionist rulers, cannot substantiate the claim of Israel to be a democratic nation.

Whenever confronted with the statement that Israel was discriminating against the Arab minority, the Israelis argue that so long as peace is not concluded between Israel and the neighbouring Arab States, Israel cannot afford to grant freedom of movement to the Moslem and Christian Arab citizens without endangering the security of the State. This caution might be justified if it were limited to the inhabitants of border villages who might have easier access to Arab territory across the 'armistice demarcation lines'; but when

Arabs living in the heart of the country are deprived of travelling a short distance outside the confines of their town or village, restriction of movement no longer becomes a precaution against a so-called 'fifth-column', but is an unjustified act of oppression and discrimination.

Destruction of Arab Villages

The destruction of whole Arab villages by the Israeli authorities was not confined to those villages whose inhabitants fled the country, but included some of the villages not evacuated by their inhabitants.

The following are glaring instances:

(1) In October 1948, the Christian villagers of *Ikret* in western Galilee were removed from their village and told that their removal was necessary for 'security reasons'; that they would be allowed to return to their homes within fifteen days. For this reason, the villagers took only the clothing required for their temporary absence. But the '15 days' period dragged on, first, into months and then into years. Tired of broken promises, the villagers petitioned the courts of justice; and the verdict ordered the Israeli army to permit the return of the villagers. The army responded by destroying every house in the village, choosing Chrismas Day, 1951, for their action. Not even the church was spared; and, to add insult to injury, the church bell was removed to a nearby Jewish settlement and used, not to call people to prayer, but to announce the time for meals.

Archbishop George Hakim, Head of the Greek Catholic community, cabled a strong protest to the Israeli authorities against this unwarranted wholesale destruction of a Catholic village and the desecration of its church. Following a visit to the ruined village, the Archbishop wrote to Rabbi Hertzog, Minister of Religious Affairs and said: "From above the churchyard overlooking the village, I could not but ponder over these atrocities, and ask what would the Righteous God – in Whom we both believe – keep in store for these crimes that are being committed by a people or a state and what would be the verdict of the international conscience?"

(2) On 16 and 17 September 1953, the Christian inhabitants of *Kafr Bir'im*, suffered the same fate. Like *Ikret*, this village is far removed from the 'armistice demarcation line'. There too, the Israelis could not use the pretext that the villagers constituted a threat to the 'safety of the state', especially since hostilities had ceased and the Armistice signed. The Israeli magazine *Ner* described the incident as follows:

> "Further proof of the intensification of the measures against the Arabs of Israel lies in the complete demolition of the village of *Kafr Bir'im*, the Maronite inhabitants of which were expelled by the military authorities in 1948 and are at present dispersed in adjacent Arab villages. The Maronite Patriarch and Bishop Mubarak had interceded on behalf of these villagers. Promises were lavishly made that they would be permitted to return to their homes and lands. In fulfillment of these promises, the village has been razed to the ground." [20]

Other similar expulsions of population and the demolition of Arab villages occurred in *Sha'b*, *Birwa*, *Umm El-Faraj* and *Mujeidal* – all of which are located in the centre of Galilee and distant from adjacent Arab territory.

(3) The Arab village of *Et-Tira*, near Haifa, was subject to a twelve-hour search on 31 July 1953, under the pretext that an Israeli air force plane had been damaged by bullets while flying over the village. A search was carried out in the most ruthless manner as men, women and children were herded like cattle into concentration pens where they were kept for several hours without food or water in the blazing sun. Valuables were looted by the Israeli army. Furniture and windows were smashed. Commenting on this Israeli action, the English daily, *The Jerusalem Post,* wrote: "The suggestion is that it has not been shown that the curfew at *Et-Tira* was justified objectively, that the army plane was in fact fired at from *Et-Tira* village, nor that adequate steps were taken, before proceeding to so harsh a measure as curfew to ascertain definitely whether it was or was not."

The village committee estimated the damages caused by the Israeli army at 10,500 Israeli pounds. No illegal arms were found; no suspects were detained; and no effort was made to compensate the innocent villagers for their losses. It is significant that during the previous four years, there had not been a single incident in which any of the *Et-Tira* villagers had violated the security of the area.

(4) Even the last resting places of the dead were not respected. On Good Friday, 1954, the Christian cemetery in Haifa was desecrated, 73 crosses were smashed and trampled underfoot. The Christian communities were horrified at this wickedness and expressed their condemnation during a demonstration on 2 May 1954, in which the leaders of the Christian communities and prominent Christian citizens of Haifa took part. Other Christian churches, as well as Moslem mosques, were destroyed in other parts of the country, without regard for the sanctity or historical value of these holy places.

Replying to Israeli press charges alleging that he was conducting a campaign of defamation against Israel, the late Monsigneur MacMahon, Head of the Pontifical Mission in the Arab countries, said: "It is neither a campaign nor defamation when the Catholic press throughout the world expresses indignation over the destruction of villages and churches in Israel."

(5) Another act of desecration of the last resting places of the dead occurred in June, 1959. According to a report in the Israeli newspaper *Letzte Nayeś* of Tel-Aviv (15 June, 1959) "the Christian cemetery in Jerusalem was desecrated by vandals and forty-two crosses were destroyed." The newspaper described the incident as "shocking and as an act of barbarism designed not only to desecrate the honour of the dead, but also the good name of Israel." [21]

The Kafr Qasem Massacre

On 29 October 1956, the Israeli army entered the Sinai Peninsula in an act of naked aggression against Egypt. On the same day, an Israeli frontier force moved against the unarmed and unsuspecting village of *Kafr Qasem* – an Arab 'border' village located within the 'Little Triangle', inside Israeli-occupied territory.

As the villagers returned from their day's work in the fields, they were met with machine-gun bullets, which resulted in the cold-blooded murder of 51 men, women and children and the wounding of 13 others. Among the dead were 12 women and girls, ten boys between the ages of 14 and 17 years and seven between the ages of 8 and 13 years.

News of this ghastly massacre committed against innocent citizens which leaked out in an ambiguous and intermittent manner, raised the grave concern of every conscientious person inside and outside Israel.

Realizing the gravity of the crime and disturbed by the manner in which it was received by world public opinion, the Prime Minister's office issued a statement, on November 11, 1956 – two weeks after the crime – in an attempt to minimize the incident and shield the perpetrators.

The statement opened with a reference to the "extensive fedaiyeen activities" – the usual pretext for Israeli aggression – and explained that the curfew was imposed "to safeguard the lives of the inhabitants of those villages." From whom it was intended to 'safeguard' them, the statement did not clarify. It was hardly necessary to expect an explanation in the light of the aggression started against Egypt. To appease public opinion, the statement promised an immediate investigation into the massacre and compensation for the loss of lives suffered. By promising to take such action, the Israeli authorities tried to convince world opinion that the incident had taken place without the knowledge or permission of the Government. They hoped that – like the Count Bernadotte assassination in 1948 – it would soon be forgotten.

Mr. Taufiq Toubi, an Arab member of the Israeli Parliament, carried out a thorough investigation of the incident. In a broadly publicized letter, he described the Prime Minister's statement as 'vague' as an attempt to conceal the vicious deed. He scored the Government's censorship of details of the massacre and gave a full account of what happened in the village on that fateful day, according to eye witnesses, enumerating names, ages and sexes of those killed and wounded.

Mr. Toubi said that on October 29 – the day hostilities against Egypt began – a unit of the Frontier Force arrived after 4 p.m. in the 'Triangle'. The village notables, mukhtars and chairmen of local councils were informed of the curfew imposed on the villages, as of 5 p.m. and consequently advised that the inhabitants should remain indoors. The mukhtar of *Kafr Qasem* told the officer who notified him of the curfew at 4:45 p.m. that there were many labourers working outside the village; that it would be physically impossible for them to return before 5 p.m. The officer answered: "The Frontier Force will 'take care' of these labourers."

An eye witness who was one of the first to be fired upon and miraculously escaped death, related his account of the attack. Samir Budair said: "I arrived at the village entrance in the vicinity of the school together with three other workmen on bicycles, at 4:55 p.m. We were halted by a group of 12 frontier force guardsmen with an officer in their cars. The workmen greeted the officer by saying 'Shalom.' He asked them: 'Are you happy?' The workmen answered 'Yes.' Immediately the guardsmen dismounted and ordered the labourers to stand by. The officer then ordered his men saying 'Mow them down.' As the guardsmen fired, I threw myself on the ground and began to roll towards a pit by the road. I was shouting, but I was not hurt. I then ceased shouting to feign that I was dead. The Guardsmen continued to fire on the labourers who fell. The officer then said 'Enough. They have been killed. It's a pity to waste more bullets on them'."

Another group consisting of 13 women and girls arrived in a truck, Hana Suleiman Amer, a girl of about 16 years of age, was the only survivor who related her experience of the massacre in these words:

> "The Frontier Force guardsmen stopped the truck carrying me at the entrance of the village, ordered the truck driver and 2 men labourers to alight and told them that they intended to kill them. The women began to scream, beseeching the guardsmen to release the labourers. The guardsmen answered:, You, too, we shall kill!

> Having fired at the 2 labourers and the driver and killed them, the guardsmen seemed uncertain as to what they should do with the women."

Hana then related how she heard the officer contact his chief at *Ras el 'Ain* police station over the wireless, seeking guidance as to what should be done with the women. The guardsmen immediately began firing at the women, all of whom (12 in number) were killed. Among those killed was a certain Fatima Sarsour, who was 8 months pregnant, a number of old women between 50 and 60 years old, 2 young girls: Loutfieh Issa and Rashiqa Budeir, 13 years old each.

Kafr Qasem is a 'border' village. Under the terms of the Armistice Agreement with Jordan, Israeli forces are *prohibited* "to enter or to be stationed in such villages, in which locally recruited Arab police shall be organized and stationed for internal security purposes." [22] The Israeli army had no legal right to enter the village; their entry and the massacre that followed could not have occurred without the full knowledge and acquiescence of the Government, as the investigation later proved.

According to the Hebrew daily *Haaretz* of 11 April 1957, "the eleven officers and soldiers who are on trial for the massacre in *Kafr Qasem* have all received a fifty per cent increase in their salaries. A special messenger was sent to Jerusalem to bring the cheques to the accused in time for Passover. A number of the accused had been given a vacation for the holiday." The paper added, "the accused mingle freely with the spectators; the officers smile at them and pat them on the back; some of them shake hands with them. It is obvious, that these people, whether they will be found innocent or guilty, are not treated as criminals, but as heroes," [23] commented the paper.

It transpired at the trial that "Lieutenant Moshe Fodor, one of the two officers accused of shooting the Arabs, testified that at a briefing by Major Malenkoff which he attended, the officers were told that the order to shoot to kill every one found outside his home, came from above. "I want the Arabs to understand that this is serious," the Major added. After the briefing, the following questions were asked and answers given:

Question: What are we to do with women and children?
Answer: They should be treated like others, without sentimentality.
Question: What are we to do with the wounded?
Answer: There should be no wounded.
Question: What are we to do with prisoners?
Answer: There should be no prisoners." [24]

This interrogation corroborates the statement of the girl eye-witness who escaped certain death when her twelve women companions were murdered. She lived to bear witness that the soldiers were, in fact, acting under orders which 'came from above'.

The *Jewish Newsletter* carried an item on the 'hate' attitude of the Israeli security forces toward the Arab residents whose lives it was their duty to protect. Private David Goldfield is reported to have resigned from the Security Police in protest against the trial. When he appeared as a witness, he testified: "I feel that the Arabs are the enemies of our State ... When I went to *Kafr Qasem,* I felt that I went against the enemy and I made no distinction between the Arabs in Israel and those outside its frontiers." When asked by the Judge what he would do if he met an Arab woman who wanted to get into her home and was not in any way a threat to security, the witness replied: "I would shoot her down, I would harbour no sentiments, because I received an order and I had to carry it out."*[25]

---

* This feeling of hatred for the Arab is not engendered in one lone individual but is apparently part of the Israeli policy of indoctrination of the youth of of Israel.

According to an item of news which appeared in the Hebrew weekly, *Haolem Hazeh* of Tel-Aviv, the Editors are reported to have "talked to hundreds of Jewish children, boys and girls, of different social classes and of ages varying from 6-13 years, about the Arabs of Israel and what they thought should be done with them. 95% of these children said that they should be murdered. A small percentage were a little compassionate and human. They opined that the Arabs should be detained in concentration camps or else deported to the Negev."

The Editors, it was stated, "attributed this wicked propensity to the childrens'

In October, 1958, the military tribunal completed the case. Reading the verdict, the judge said: "It was clear from the evidence that Lt. Gavriel Dehan, Commander of the Police platoon at *Kafr Qasem,* had ordered the murder of the villagers in 'cold blood' and has himself shot two of the victims." [26] He added: "The crime committed was not technical murder but deliberate murder." [27]

Consequently, the sentences were:

Major Shmuel Malinki, commander of the local police – 17 years imprisonment. Lt. Gavriel Dehan and his Assistant – 15 years each. Five constables – 7 years each.

Last to be tried for his part in the *Kafr Qasem* crime was Colonel Aluf Mishne Shadmi, Commander of the Border Police. On 26 February 1959, the defendent was sentenced to "a token fine of *two cents* for exceeding his authority by imposing an absolute curfew on an Arab village in Israel in 1956." [28] He was, however, absolved

---

family life, to their social environment and to the education they receive in school."

But "A mother wrote to the Editors saying that her son's reply was due solely to the education he was receiving in school and not to his home life or to his private associations."

"However, this malicious tendancy," the Weekly pointed out, "is not uncommon among Jewish rank and file. The wholesale massacre on the eve of the Sinai campaign of 49 innocent Arab farmers in Kafr Qasem village – boys and girls, men and women some of whom were visibly pregnant – was the outcome of scholastic education, all of which infuse xenophobic feelings against the Arabs."

Another expression of violent hatred for the Arab came from an Israeli Jew studying in the United States. In a letter to Arab lawyer Elias Koussa who lives in Haifa, dated 4 November 1956, Bertram H. Appleby wrote: "As soon as my medical course ends, I shall return to Israel to devote my life to fighting her enemies, especially the enemy within, a people without conscience, morality, humanity, or simple intelligence. We Zionists can easily read your mind, your intentions – to make Israel accept a huge % of Arab refugees, to renounce pieces of territory, the larger the better, to give you special privileges, special schools, special everything. But your evil plans (or should I say plots?) will not succeed, now as in the past. Believe me, everything you do, everything you speak, is being noted and when the day of reckoning comes, all these will be atoned for."

of the crime and was permitted to retain his high office.

The result this absurd sentence had on those previously meted out against the officers and men who executed the orders, was that the five men sentenced to seven years imprisonment each were immediately released and the sentences of the others were considerably reduced. When the wrath of public opinion subsided the latter were released and reinstated.

Commenting on the verdict, the *Jewish Newsletter* said: "There cannot be the slightest doubt that the Government policy of segregating the Israeli Arabs from the Jews and treating them as second-class, inferior citizens, has implanted in the minds of the average Israeli citizen in and outside the Army that the Arabs are the enemies of the State and should be treated as traitors. This is the deeper source of the *Kafr Qasem* crime. The real culprit is the Israeli Government. If Ben Gurion, who waxes so morally indignant over the crime, really wants to atone for this Nazi-like atrocity and wipe out the stain it brought on Israel, he should abolish the military rule which is the cause of this and many other terrible crimes." [29]

Confiscation of Arab Lands*

The United Nations tried to safeguard Arab property by including, in the Partition Resolution, "No expropriation of land owned by an Arab in the Jewish State shall be allowed except for public purposes." The Resolution further stipulated, "In all cases of expropriation, full compensation as fixed by the Supreme Court shall be paid previous to dispossession." [30]

The United Nations may have felt confident that the leaders of the Zionist movement would respect their obligations toward the Arab minority. There was, therefore, no need for measures enforcing compliance, in the event of a violation. It was apparently the mistaken belief of the framers of the Resolution that Zionist

* For a full study, see *Palestine: Loss of a Heritage* by Sami Hadawi (San Antonio, Texas: Naylor Publishing Co., 1963).

leaders would feel so grateful to the United Nations for making possible the creation of the 'Jewish state', and so anxious to demonstrate their appreciation and peaceful intentions towards their Arab neighbours, that there would be whole-hearted respect for the wishes of the World Organization. An international instrument of such magnitude should not have taken anything for granted. The failure of the United Nations to take a vital precaution, encouraged the Israelis to proceed without fear of contradiction or obstruction in their policy of the seizure of Arab lands.

After Israel was established in 1948, the Arab minority was subjected to several legal devices calculated to confiscate Arab land:

(1) *Military Emergency Regulations* established 'security zones' and 'closed areas' into which no Arab was allowed to venture. An Arab who had land within a 'security zone' or a 'closed area' was unable to get to it without a military permit, which was often refused.

In an article published in New York following a visit to the Middle East, Derek Tozer described "the measures adopted as extraordinary, even in modern times. The military governor," he said, "will declare an Arab area a prohibited zone, thus debarring entry to any Arab wishing to tend his land. The 1953 law is then invoked and agricultural lands become liable to confiscation, since the owners have failed to tend and till their lands themselves. This means that the property of the Arabs automatically becomes the property of the State." [31]

(2) *Civil Emergency Laws and Regulations*. The first empowered the authorities to declare any Arab town, village or part thereof to be an 'abandoned area' *whether the area had been abandoned by its inhabitants or not;*

The second defined 'absentee' to *include Arabs who had not left the territory occupied by Israel either before, during, or after the fighting was over.* [32]

Explaining the law, Don Peretz said:

> "Every Arab in Palestine who had left his town or village after November 29, 1947, was liable to be clas-

> sified as an absentee under the regulations. All Arabs who held property in the New City of Acre, regardless of the fact that they may never have travelled farther than the few metres to the Old City, were classified as absentee. The 30,000 Arabs who fled from one place to another within Israel, but who never left the country, were also liable to have their property declared absentee." [33]

The third provision empowered the Minister of Agriculture to take over any land which has not been cultivated by its owner. The law required a warning, ordering the owner to cultivate or ensure cultivation of his land, but no consideration was taken of the circumstances and legal restrictions which prevented the owner from complying with the order even, if he had received the notice. Article 2 (c) provided, "No act done in respect of waste land under these Regulations shall be invalidated on the ground that the warning did not come to the knowledge of the owner of the land."

(3) *Land Acquisition Law.* On 10 March, 1953, the Israeli authorities moved a step further in consolidating their hold over Arab lands. The various emergency regulations and laws were replaced by *The Land Acquisition Law* (*Confirmation of Past Actions and Compensation*). [34] The purposes behind the law were to 'legalize' past seizures of Arab lands and to ensure future acquisitions. The Arab citizens protested this new act of injustice to the Israeli Parliament, to the United Nations, the Western Powers and to world conscience; but to no avail. They were even joined in their protest by individual members and groups of the Jewish community in Israel who condemned the law as oppressive, prejudicial and discriminatory.

David K. Elston, former Mandate official in Palestine and a popular British columnist of the Jewish English daily, *The Jerusalem Post,* who acquired a national reputation for his staunch support of Israel's cause during the Palestine war, attacked the law as "perhaps the most serious factor creating embitterment among all Arabs." Writing in the Hebrew daily *Haaretz,* he pointed out that in Galilee, twenty villages had been deprived of their property by Jewish collectives, which "arrogated to themselves, through long–term leases granted by the Minister of Agriculture, lands of Arabs who were free from any guilt or wrong-doing." [35]

Dr. Shereshevsky of the *Ihud* Party in Israel, protested to a responsible leader in the Israeli Parliament and described the law as "robbery of land from people, inhabitants of the State." He pointed out, "They are agricultural people, like you, citizens like you. There exists only one difference between them and you, they are Arabs and you are a Jew," he said. "This difference," he added, "seemed to you so great and decisive that you were ready to trespass on all that is required by the Law of Israel and its tradition." [36]

Moshe Keren, another Jewish writer, described the law as "wholesale robbery with a legal coating," and added: "The future student of ethnology will wonder how it came to pass that it was the Jewish people, striving to build their state on the foundations of justice and righteousness and having themselves been the victims of unparalleled acts of robbery and expropriation, that should have been capable of doing this to a helpless minority." [37]

Under the 1953 Law and the Emergency Regulations which preceded it, the Israeli authorities had, by 1957, confiscated about 40,000 acres of land belonging to the Arab minority including most of their fertile fields and orchards. The pretext that the land was required for 'public purposes', according to the condition in the Resolution of Partition, could not be used because this land was sold to the 'Development Authority' which in turn transferred it to the Jewish National Fund or to some other organization at a handsome profit, for the settlement of new Jewish immigrants, or extension of existing settlements. In other cases, the land was leased to neighbouring Jewish settlements at a nominal rental. *It is significant that no land belonging to Jewish individuals or companies has been so expropriated or confiscated.*

Although the main objective of the Land Acquisition Law was to legalize the seizure of Arab lands, it also legislated for the payment of compensation. This latter provision, however, did not conform with the stipulation of the Partition Resolution that "full compensation as fixed by the Supreme Court shall be paid previous to dispossession," but gave authority of assessment of such compensation to the Custodian of Absentee Property, whom the Supreme Court in one of its judgments had accused of giving "verdicts favourable to himself."

Although Arab lands had been seized as far back as 1948, little or no compensation has been paid to the Arab farmers. Referring to the provision in the law, Yaacov Aviel, a writer from Israel, said that the least that might have been expected from the perpetrators of this law is that the one constructive paragraph of the law would be implemented with fairness and decency. Official figures disclose, he said, that two years after the passage of the law no more than one thousand compensation claims had been filed, of which only a few hundred have been settled and these concerned mostly the claims of towns-people whose confiscated lands have been merely a small and subsidiary source of their income. Aviel pointed out that not one single *fellah* among the thousands of DPs has so so far been the beneficiary of any measure of agricultural rehabilitation. [38]

(4) *Law of Limitations*. In March 1958, the Israeli Government advanced still another step in providing legislation for the further confiscation of Arab lands by the enactment of the *Law of Limitations*. This law required landowners who do not have a registered title to produce evidence that they have been in continuous undisputed possession of their lands for fifteen years*, or forfeit them to the Israeli Government.

Under the Ottoman Empire and British Mandate laws, landowners had to prove possession and cultivation for ten consecutive years to obtain title deeds. The increase from ten to fifteen years detrimentally affects the rights of a significant number of Arab owners, who have already acquired title under existing land laws by virtue of continuous possession for ten years.

Since Israel was not in existence for more than ten years,

---

* The period appearing in the 'Bill' was originally *fifty* years. It was reduced to fifteen as a result of stormy criticism inside and outside Israel.

prior to the enactment of this new Law, the Arab farmer had difficulty proving that he was in possession of his land, for at least five years prior to the creation of the 'Jewish state'. In the first place, the majority of lands in Palestine were not registered; sales transactions usually took place outside the land registry, by means of either a properly drawn, notarized agreement, or a simple statement attested to by some witnesses in the village, as was customary from the time of the Ottoman Empire. In the second place, since Palestinian Arabs are now refugees living outside the country, finding adequate witnesses is much more difficult. Had the old period of ten years been retained, the Arab farmer would have had little trouble in producing evidence of possession, because the witnesses are available in the country; but to require evidence of occupation of five years prior to the establishment of Israel, places the Arab owner in the impossible position of not being able to obtain the necessary evidence. As a result, his land is forfeited to the state. This, in effect, was the intention of the Israeli authorities.

Most property still held by Arabs living in Israeli-occupied territory, today falls in areas where land settlement operations, started by the Mandate authorities, in 1927, had not been commenced on the date of British withdrawal. Having little more than verbal evidence of possession, if that, Arabs have been affected by this law and are being deprived of their lands.

It was the duty of the United Nations to question the legality and take steps to abrogate these Israeli 'laws', regulations and official actions', since they were in conflict with Section C of the Partition Resolution. The General Provision states, "The stipulations contained in the Declaration are recognized as fundamental laws of the state, and no law, regulation, or official action *shall* conflict or interfere with these stipulations, nor *shall* any law, regulation, or official action prevail over them"; and Chapter 4 provides "The provisions of Chapters 1 (on Holy Places) and 2 (on Religious and Minority Rights), *shall be under the guarantee of the United Nations* and no modifications *shall* be made in them without the assent of the General Assembly of the United Nations."

At no time did the United Nations approve a departure from

these stipulations. Consequently, this failure renders the 'laws , regulations and official actions' of the Israeli authorities illegal. United Nations silence about these oppressive and discriminatory actions had the effect of encouraging the Israelis to proceed in their policy of separating the Arab residents from their lands.

Arab Rights Before the Israeli Courts

The Israeli judiciary system in the early days of Israel's statehood appeared immune to political pressures and free from military intimidation or coercion. This being the case, the Arabs felt that they had at least one venue open to them through which they could recover their property and protect their rights and interests. They took their grievances against the Israeli military and civil authorities to the High Court of Justice, which, in the majority of cases, decided in their favour. On numerous occasions the High Court found it necessary to call Israeli authorities to task; and at times it was obliged to reprimand those responsible for disregard of the law and of minority rights. If the Courts failed to do justice to a wronged Arab minority, it was principally due to the Israeli basic policy of oppression and discrimination which had been adopted against the Arab citizen.

Don Peretz cites the case of one Tannous Elias 'Askar versus the Custodian of Absentee Property as "typical of many cases which reached the courts and thousands that did not."

Tannous 'Askar, Mr. Peretz writes, was a legal resident of Haifa. After the establishment of Israel in May 1948, 'Askar obtained permission from the Custodian to receive rent from his home in Haifa and to lease a shop. Shortly thereafter, he was denounced as an Absentee who had procured his contract under false pretenses. The Custodian certified that he was an absentee and ordered him to evacuate his shop.

'Askar appealed to the High Court which decided that the evidence against him was groundless. The Custodian had recognized his *de facto* exercise of the rights and obligations of citizenship. He had been permitted to receive rent. He was taxed. He possessed an identity card. He participated in the national elections. Exercise of these rights and obligations gave him *de jure* citizenship prerogatives and automatically exempted him from the Custodian's arbitrary authority. The Court called attention to the unusual power of the Custodian to execute administrative justice in cases in which he desired a verdict favourable to himself.

In the opinion of the court, evidence presented by the Custodian showed that 'Askar was classified as an absentee in order to force his removal from his shop. This procedure interrupted the course of justice by depriving 'Askar of elementary citizenship rights. The fact that a person was an absentee did not completely deprive him of property. It merely transferred his rights to the Custodian, who was to use them in conformity with the law. 'Askar should not have been served with an evacuation order without court approval.

The Court concluded by stating that "the certificate (classifying 'Askar as an absentee) was issued only to deprive the claimant of elementary rights and of legal assistance and defense and in this respect the Custodian acted in an untoward manner." [39]

Court procedure is generally lengthy and costly and not every Arab – against whom there is a definite policy of discrimination – can afford to appeal to the courts. For those Arabs who could afford to sue, the Israeli authorities found the ways and means of circumventing an unfavourable court order. Dr. Harold E. Fey, Senior Editor of the *Christian Century* magazine, reported in this connection that "court rulings in favour of the Arabs are frequently by-passed or circumvented. In August 1953, when the people of a northern village got an order from the court that they should be restored to their village, residents of the neighbouring Israeli settlement went and dynamited their homes and uprooted their fruit trees. When a complaint was made to the police, the police said they could do nothing." [40]

Administration of Moslem Waqf * Properties (Benevolent or Religious Endowment)

During the Ottoman Regime in Palestine, laws affecting the constitution, jurisdiction, procedure and internal organization of *Waqf* property were promulgated by the legislative authority of the Ottoman Empire. Before the Turkish Constitution of 1908, this authority was the Sultan, who was also Caliph. After 1908, it was the legislative body created by the Constitution. Since the Ottoman Empire was a Moslem State, that authority was also Moslem.

At the outbreak of the First World War in 1914, the administrative powers in regard to the procedure and organization of the Moslem Religious Courts passed to the control of the Ottoman Ministry of Justice; and the Ministry of *Awqaf* (plural of *Waqf*) supervised the administration of the 'trust property', or administered it directly.

When Palestine became detached from the Ottoman Empire, after the First World War, and fell under the rule of a non-Moslem Government, it became necessary to create a new machinery for Moslem *Waqf* property, and for other religious matters, administered and controlled by a Moslem body in accordance with Moslem tradition and practice of the past centuries.

By Order of the High Commissioner for Palestine in December, 1921, a Supreme Moslem Council was constituted for "the control and management of Moslem *Awqaf* and *Sharia* (Religious) affairs in Palestine." [41] The Palestine Mandate, on the other hand, included in Article 9 a condition that "the control and administration of *Waqf* shall be exercised in accordance with religious law and the dispositions of the founders." [42]

This meant, in effect, that the *status quo* prior to the British Occupation, having the Moslems themselves administer and control Moslem religious affairs and *Waqf* property, was to be maintained.

The main source of revenue of the Supreme Moslem Council

---

* A Turkish term describing *land assured to pious foundations, or revenue from land assured to pious foundations.*

in Palestine was from the *tithe* – a Government tax levied on the lands of certain villages dedicated by the former rulers of the Ottoman Empire for charitable purposes and placed under the control of the *Ottoman Ministry of Awqaf.* The collection of the *tithe* in these villages was credited to the Supreme Moslem Council, less collection charges fixed at six per cent of the actual collections. In 1927, the *tithe* was commuted for an annual payment fixed at the average assessment of a period of three to five years. This measure was followed after 1930 by a series of crop failures which substantially affected the revenue derived from *waqf* villages. In 1935, the Palestine Government decided to replace the *tithe* system of taxation by a fixed rural property tax. Since this new tax was expected to yield considerably less revenue than the *tithe*, the Palestine Government agreed to pay the Supreme Moslem Council the lump sum of 30,000 Palestine pounds, annually, in lieu of the *waqf* share in the *commuted tithe.* When, during the Second World War, the Palestine Government decided, as a war measure, to double and redouble the rates of rural property tax, the Supreme Moslem Council applied for and received a proportionate increase in their share of the tax.

Just as the British Mandatory Government took measures to ensure that control of Moslem religious and *waqf* affairs was to remain in the hands of a Moslem administration in accordance with Moslem tradition and custom, so also it was expected that the 'Jewish state' would honour and respect the customs and traditions of the Moslem community. The United Nations did not overlook this important matter and stipulated in the Partition Resolution that "the family law and personal status of the various minorities and other religious interests, including endowments, shall be respected." [43]

Israeli authorities, however, placed Moslem religious affairs under the control of the Israeli Jewish Ministry of Religious Affairs and appointed an Israeli Jew to administer and control *waqf* properties. This is not all – Revenue accruing from *waqf* property intended for religious and charitable purposes, is now collected by the Israeli authorities and channelled into general government revenue. The persons and institutions who were to benefit from these 'endowments' are deprived of their benefits; and the 'dispositions of the founders' – maintained and preserved as a sacred trust until the creation of Israel – have thus been violated, if not altogether obliterated. These actions are in flagrant violation of Israel's international obligations and constitute an act of repression of the religious rights and freedoms of the Moslem community.*

Denial of Equal Political Rights to Arab Citizens

According to recognized principles of democratic government and practices in all civilized countries, minorities are free to establish their own political parties and to adopt the platform they desire. In Parliament and the Cabinet they are usually represented in proportion to their voting strength.

In the Israeli-occupied territory of Palestine, however, the Arab minority is not permitted to exercise its political rights and prerogatives in the same manner and to the same extent as is the Jewish majority. Although the United Nations Partition Resolution of 1947 makes it an imperative condition that the 'Jewish state' shall constitutionally *guarantee* "to all persons equal and non-discriminatory rights in political matters," the Israeli authorities have denied these rights to their Arab minority.

According to Israeli sources the Moslem and Christian Arab citizens comprise eleven per cent of the total population of the country. As such, they have an undisputed right to representation in all branches of the Israeli government. Nevertheless, they are prevented from forming their own political parties. For election to Parliament, an Arab candidate must run on the ticket of one of the

* According to a report published in the *Jerusalem Post* (Israel) of 1February, 1966, "All Moslem religious endowment properties (waqf) in Jaffa will be transferred to the Custodian of Absentee Property, including a 40-dunum (ten acre) cemetery plot . . ."
The judge in the case is reported to have said that "an Amendment to the Absentee Property Law explicitly vested ownership of *waqf* properties in the hands of the Custodian."

existing Jewish parties and must abide by its platform whether he agrees with its principles or not. Attempts were made by some of the Arab leaders to organize an Arab front which would be entrusted with safeguarding the rights and interests of the Moslem and Christian Arab communities. The Israeli authorities took steps to thwart the efforts of the sponsors, by withholding travel permits to the meeting place. In addition, the sponsors were required to report to the Police stations at certain inconvenient hours of the day to ensure their non-attendance. Such action was unjustified and humiliating, particularly when it is usually taken against criminals whose surveillance becomes necessary 'in the interests of public security.'

Dr. Harold E. Fey, former Senior Editor of the *Christian Century*, wrote: "The Arabs have no alternative but to elect those who are nominated for them. They do not have an independent party and are prevented from forming one." Dr. Fey went on to say that the Arabs "do not deny that Israel may be a democracy for the majority, but they know it is something less than that for the minority, the Class B citizens." [44]

The Arabs are not only prevented from forming their own political parties; they are also deprived of their full share of political representation. The Israeli Parliament has 120 seats of which six are occupied by Arabs sitting as members of Jewish parties. As such, they are not in a position to protect Arab rights and interests, especially when these clash with the policy of the Jewish majority. When an Arab member of Parliament is courageous enough to table an objection in the interests of the Arab minority, his voice is the only one heard in favour, even within his own party.

The presence of these Arab members of Parliament enables Zionist propaganda to tell the world that the Arabs of Israel enjoy full political freedom. This creates the false impression that Israel fulfills all of the requirements of a democratic state.

A comparison with the situation in nearby Jordan – which, incidentally, is described by Israel as far from being a democratic country – will reveal a totally different picture. In Jordan, the Christian inhabitants comprise less than ten per cent of a total population of 2,100,000 persons. According to their numerical strength, Christians are entitled to three out of the forty seats in both Houses of Parliament. Instead, they occupy six seats.

Another analogy may be drawn from the executive and administrative branches of government. In Israel, the Cabinet does not include a single Arab Minister. There are no Arabs holding the post of under–secretary or director of a department. Their number in the general government services is insignificant. In contrast, Jordan has two Cabinet posts occupied by Christians – one representing the East Bank and the other the West Bank. In addition, there are many Christians who hold the office of under–secretary, director of a department and other senior positions. Christian representation in the general services far exceeds the ratio based on population.

Arab Minority Protests

In May 1958, certain sections of the American press carried a news item about a revolt which had broken out in Nazareth and in the villages of *Kafr Yasif* and *Um El-Fahm.* In reporting the incident, the press conveyed the impression that the so-called 'revolt' was inspired and led by communists, consequently, the true causes of the unrest remained unknown to the outside world.

What actually happened was that the Arab inhabitants tried to take advantage of the *May Day* celebrations to declare publicly their indignation and to protest the oppressive and discriminate conditions under which they lived. Israeli forces charged the unarmed demonstrators with clubs and rifles. In the ensuing scuffle, seventeen persons were wounded and about 350 arrested.

Each year on 10 December, the Israelis celebrate the anniversary of 'Human Rights Day' with speeches explaining and extolling the principles embodied in the Universal Declaration of Human Rights. In 1958, the Arab minority took advantage of the occasion to remind the Israelis, in a lengthy memoradum addressed to the Israeli President and the Secretary-General of the United Nations, that while Israel was celebrating its adherence to the principles of the Declaration of Human Rights, it was, in practice, consistently violating its provisions for the Arab minority. The petitioners called upon the Israeli authorities to remove the oppressive and discriminative laws and practices, imposed upon the Arab minority and to treat the Arabs with a spirit consistent with the principles in the Universal Declaration of Human Rights.[45]

Summation of Israeli Violations

To sum up: the Israelis are guilty of violating the basic principles regarding minority rights, as laid down in the United Nations Charter, the Universal Declaration of Human Rights and the Partition Resolution. The following summary pinpoints the abuse of these international obligations:

1– "*No person shall be subjected to arbitrary . . . exile*" – Israel has expelled about 35,000 of the Arab inhabitants from their homes and villages to other parts of the country and refuses to allow them to return.

2– Guarantees "*to all persons equal and non-discriminatory rights*"–
Israel has placed the Arab minority in a class 'B' category; restricted their movement; discriminated against them in employment, in political representations, in government service, in education, in health facilities, etc.

3– "*Everyone has the right to freedom of movement and residence within the borders of the state*" –
Israel has prohibited the free movement of the Arab minority and imposes forced residence on some for the least cause.

4– "*Everyone has the right to leave any country, including his own, and to return to his country*" –
Israel prevents the travel of an Arab outside the country unless he undertakes to sign away his right of return.

5– "*No expropriation of land owned by an Arab in the Jewish state shall be allowed except for public purposes*"–
Israel has so far expropriated 1,250,000 dunums of fertile Arab land and is in the process of confiscating more;

6– "*Palestine citizens residing in Palestine . . . shall, upon recognition of independence, become citizens of the state*"–

Israel, while granting immediate citizenship rights to a Jew the moment he steps on Palestine soil, withholds such rights from the Arab inhabitants who have been born and live there;

7– *The control and administration of Waqf (pious foundation property) "shall be exercised in accordance with religious law and the dispositions of the founders"–*
Israel has taken over such properties and is utilizing the proceeds from the sale or lease thereof for the settlement of new Jewish immigrants, contrary to the "dispositions of the founders."

Commenting on Israel's treatment of non-Jews, James Warburg, former banker and writer on international affairs, said: "Nothing could be more tragic than to witness the creation of a Jewish state in which the non-Jewish minorities are treated as second-class citizens – in which neither a Jew's Christian wife nor their children can be buried in the same cemetery as their father." Warburg then remarked: "It is one thing to create a much-needed refuge for the persecuted and oppressed. It is quite another thing to create a new chauvinistic nationalism and a state based in part upon medieval theocratic bigotry and in part upon the Nazi-exploited myth of the existence of a Jewish race." [46]

With this record, Israel's claim to be a democratic nation in which all citizens enjoy equal rights and freedoms is without foundation. What is written into a constitution or law is meaningless, unless the implementation is consistent with the spirit. All men are equal before God. It is a sin to withhold what God in his Goodness has given to man. Of this sin, the Israelis are profoundly guilty.

XII Violations and Aggression

Violation and defiance of U. N. authority

The state of Israel came into being as a result of an act of the United Nations and, as such, the Israelis are obligated to the World Organization to respect and comply, *unreservedly,* with all its principles and stipulations. But no sooner was the 'Jewish state' established, when the Israelis began to violate the provisions of the very resolution which brought their 'state' into existence and all subsequent resolutions calling upon the Israelis to do certain things.

The principal resolutions which stand unimplemented against the Israeli record are:

(1) *No.* 181 *(II) of* 29 *November* 1947 (on partition) – defining the territory of the 'Jewish state' and providing guarantees for the rights of the Arab inhabitants.

(2) *No.* 194 *(III) of* 11 *December* 1948 (on refugees) – providing for the exercise of the right of the refugees to make a free choice between return to their homes and compensation.

(3) *No.* 303 *(IV) of* 9 *December* 1949 (on Jerusalem) – declaring the Holy City a *corpus separatum* under United Nations jurisdiction.

(4) *No.* 394 *(V) of* 14 *December* 1950 (on rights, property and interests of the refugees) – directing the Conciliation Commission on measures for "the protection of the rights, property and interests of the refugees" pending final settlement.

(5) *No.* 273 *(III) of* 11 *May* 1949 (on admission of Israel to membership of U.N.) – The United Nations "*decided* to admit Israel into membership of the United Nations" after it had taken "*note* of the declarations and explanations made by the representative of the Govern-

ment of Israel before the *ad hoc* Political Committee in respect of the implementation of its resolutions of 29 November 1947 (on territory) and 11 December 1948 (on refugees)."

Israeli arguments for non-compliance with their obligations under the Charter and non-implementation of the provisions of the resolutions cited, are: The Arab States having attacked the state of Israel, the Israelis are no longer bound by the Partition Resolution; territory won in battle beyond that assigned to the 'Jewish state' under the Partition Plan is not returnable. On the internationalization of Jerusalem, the Israelis reacted by declaring the Holy City the 'capital' of Israel with retrospective effect to 15 May 1948.

As regards the refugees, the Israelis claim that having abandoned their homes and lands of their own free will, the refugees have thereby forfeited their rights of return and to reclaim their property.

As for "the protection of the rights, property and interests of the refugees," the Israelis regard any United Nations control over property situated in Israel as derogatory to the sovereignty of the 'Jewish state' and interference in the internal affairs of a member-state.

In the light of the chronological order of events of the period, the Israeli arguments are neither logical nor reasonable. It will be recalled that Arab rejection of the partition plan was in 1947 for obviously legitimate reasons; the entry of the Arab armies into Palestine was in May 1948; hostilities ceased in July 1948; the United Nations' call to Israel to permit the refugees to return to their homes was in December 1948; the 'Lausanne Protocol' by which both parties agreed to settle their dispute on the basis of the resolution of 29 November 1947 (on territory) and resolution of 11 December 1948 (on refugees) was signed on 12 May 1949; and last but not least, Israeli implementation of these two resolutions was made a condition for Israel's admission into membership of the United Nations.

The fact that agreement was reached after the cessation of

hostilities rendered immaterial the positions and actions of either party during the period which preceded the date of the signing of the 'Lausanne Protocol' and Israel's declaration of readiness to implement the said resolutions. In effect, the agreement meant that whatever the causes or the responsibilities, these were to be ignored as both parties lent their attention to a settlement based on the 'Protocol' signed at Lausanne, Switzerland. But the Israelis after achieving their objective, decided to repudiate their obligations.

While ignoring their failure to implement five standing resolutions, the Israelis arrogantly accuse the United Arab Republic of violating the one sole resolution which stands unimplemented against any Arab State. This is a Security Council resolution No. 95 (1951) of 1 September 1951 – (S 2322) calling upon Egypt "to terminate the restrictions on the passage of international commercial shipping and goods through the Suez Canal wherever bound and to cease all interference with shipping."

The resolution, the last in the string of unimplemented resolutions, was adopted despite the strong objection of some of the Council members. The representative of India, for example, stressed that "the Security Council is not the most appropriate body for the adjudication of questions involving complicated legal aspects;"[1] the representative of China said: "The draft seems to have assumed the validity of the claim that the measures adopted by Egypt in the Suez Canal are in violation of the general international law and the provisions of the Suez Canal Convention and the Armistice Agreement. In our opinion, this is a point to be proved. Armistice is the first step to peace, but does not mean the termination of a state of war ... It is unreasonable to suppose or assume that the neutralization of the Suez Canal cancels every right of the territorial Power;"[2] the representative of the United Kingdom, in introducing the draft resolution admitted that it did not take all the factors into consideration, [3] yet he presented his proposal.

In the light of these comments in the Security Council, is it not reasonable to conclude that the resolution was based on political rather than on legal considerations ?

The Suez Canal controversy is but one aspect of the Palestine

Problem and no single aspect can be resolved outside an overall settlement. That the Suez Canal dispute is a part of the Palestine issue was recognized by the late Secretary-General Dag Hammarskjold when he said: "The issue has important legal aspects which may be considered as meriting further clarification, but it is also part of the general Palestine problem." [4]

Arab attitude on the resolution on Suez Canal and the Palestine problem, may be summed up in the statement made by President Nasser in an interview with two U.S. correspondents on 8 October 1959: "The resolutions concerning Palestine," he said, "are an indivisible entity – the right of the refugees to return to their homeland; their right to their properties or compensation for their properties; and their right to the Palestine territory cannot be be divided ... We are ready," he went on, "to accept a United Nations board or commission to put (all) resolutions into effect for both Israel and us. But it would be unfair if only we are asked to implement the resolution on our side while Israel does not implement those on her side."

At no time have the Israelis shown similar willingness to implement resolutions standing against them. On the contrary, their policy has been reflected in their deeds and declarations from time to time, such as:

"FORCE OF ARMS, NOT FORMAL RESOLUTIONS WILL DECIDE THE ISSUE." [5]

"THESE RESOLUTIONS NO LONGER LIVE, NOR WILL THEY RISE AGAIN." [6]

"ALL THAT WE HAVE TAKEN WE SHALL HOLD." [7]

The Armistice Demarcation Line

The four General Armistice Agreements prescribe in identical terms that "No element of the land, sea or air military or paramilitary forces of either Party, including non-regular forces, shall commit any warlike or hostile act against the military or paramilitary forces of the other Party, or against civilians in territory under the control of that Party; or shall advance beyond or pass over for any purposes whatsoever the Armistice Demarcation Lines ... or enter into or pass the air space of that other Party." Further on, the Agreements provide that "The basic purpose of the Armistice Demarcation Lines is to delineate the lines beyond which the armed forces of the respective Parties shall not move." [8]

Right from the start this invisible armistice demarcation line invited trouble. While the General Armistice Agreements prescribe that their provisions were "dictated exclusively by military and not by political considerations," anyone familiar with the land topography of Palestine, can easily see that the reverse was the result. The line appears to have been drawn to meet political pressures and considerations rather than military necessities. It coincided almost to the minutest detail with what the Zionists demanded from the British Mandatory Government in 1946 as the minimum boundaries of the 'Jewish state' which they were willing to accept. The armistice demarcation line separated Arab villages from their fertile lands in the coastal and other plains and included in the Israeli-held territory lands through which the railway line and principal highways ran whether or not this damaged Arab interests. One sad example has been the fate of the Arab town of Qalqilya in the central sector. This town was one of the most prosperous in Palestine, owning extensive orange groves and serving as one of the main vegetable markets of the country. The demarcation line severed all its orange groves in favour of Israel, leaving it a bulging peninsula, landless except for its rocky areas towards the east and its inhabitants helpless as they watched the Israelis gather the fruits of the trees they and their forefathers had planted and tended for generations for export to world markets while they languished in distress and poverty.

With conditions being what they are along the entire length of the demarcation line, it is no wonder that the Arab villagers attempt, from time to time, to cross over to 'steal' what legitimately belongs to them and in the process lose their lives. It is only natural for such conditions to create a situation of revenge by those who lose their dear ones after having lost their lands and means of livelihood.

Commenting on such a unique situation, a former resident of Israel now in the United States cited the "acts of cruelty and manifestations of demoralization which are now occuring in Israel, particularly in the army, in its treatment of Arab refugees and 'infiltrees'," said, "an average from five to seven such 'infiltrees' are being shot by Israeli soldiers every week as a matter of military routine." [9] This atrocity was confirmed by the *New York Times* which reported, "a total of 394 Arab infiltrees killed, 227 wounded and 2,595 captured in 1952." [10]

The only protest against such treatment came from Israeli poet Nathan Alterman. Writing in *Davar,* official organ of the Israeli Labour Party, the poet pointed out, "Jews have always been notoriously lax in their attitude towards illegal crossing of frontiers, false passports and other small formal offenses against the state and never looked upon them as moral issues, certainly not as crimes punishable by death." Alterman then exclaims with indignation: "Oh you Knesset members; you former passport forgers; you infiltrees, grand-children of infiltrees, how quickly you have learned the new morality of militarism!" [11]

The Israeli plea is that their military raids across the armistice demarcation line constitute 'retaliation'. If the actual facts of the Palestine problem were considered, it would become evident that the term is wrongly applied. According to the dictionary, 'retaliation' means "return like for like, evil for evil"; and the word 'reprisal' – often used as describing Israeli actions – means "to procure redress of grievances." Since it was the Arabs, not the Jews, who were the first sufferers through expulsion and dispossession by force of arms and are being prevented from returning, it follows with reason that their efforts to retrieve their rights and possessions, by whatever means, should more accurately be classified as 'retaliation' and 'reprisal' against Israeli 'provocation'.

Whatever the merits or demerits of the Israeli argument, the fact remains that by taking the law into their own hands and crossing over the armistice demarcation line by military force, the Israelis have violated their obligations under the United Nations Charter, the truce order of the Security Council of 15 July 1948, [12] and the provisions of the General Armistice Agreements.

The philosophy of so-called Israeli 'retaliation' has been examined by the Security Council each time an attack by the Israelis had taken place and has been condemned in the statements made by the majority of the Council members, as well as in Security Council and Mixed Armistice Commission resolutions. For example, in its resolution of 19 January 1956, the Security Council proclaimed that the alleged 'provocation' which Israel claimed had prompted its attack on Syrian territory "in no way justifies the Israeli action." The resolution proceeded to "remind" Israel that the Council had "already condemned military action in breach of the General Armistice Agreements, whether or not taken by way of retaliation." [13]

During the discussion in the Security Council of a second attack by Israeli military forces on Syrian territory on 16 March 1962, the British representative strongly condemned the Israeli "delibrate attack" and demanded that their leaders drop their "policy of violence" in favour of cooperation with the United Nations; [14] The late U.S. Ambassador Adlai Stevenson also rapped the Israelis for reverting to military actions which flagrantly violated United Nations resolutions. "This policy," he said "contributed to the rapid rise of tensions in the Middle East during 1955 and 1956 and it can no more be countenanced today than it was then."[15] It is worthy to note that the report of the Chief of Staff on the incident was that there was no evidence to support the Israeli charge that the attack on Syria was necessary to destroy a fortified post in self-defence. He said his observers found no evidence of any such post "either existing or destroyed" when they inspected the the area. [16]

If the members of the Security Council had hoped that by their statements and resolutions the Israelis – would cease their aggression across the armistice demarcation line, they were very much mistaken. The Council was once again seized with the problem of Israeli aggression on the village of Sammu' on 13 November 1966. Condemnation of the Israeli action was in this case universal. The representative of the United Kingdom said it "constituted a flagrant violation of our Charter and of the Israel–Jordan Armistice Agreement; it has done nothing to enchance the security of Israeli citizens or the reputation of Israel." [17]

The Representative of the United States was more vocal. He said his Government condemns the raid "deeming it in clear violation of the solemn obligations undertaken by Israel in the General Armistice Agreements. And what makes it of course most deplorable," he added, "is the tragic toll in human lives of this inexcusable action." He went on to say, "The Government of Israel carried out (with the support of tanks, armoured vehicles, heavy weapons and aircraft) a raid into Jordan the nature of which and whose consequences in human lives and in destruction far surpass the cumulative total of the various acts of terrorism conducted against the frontiers of Israel." He compared this latest Israeli aggression with "the retaliatory action at Qibya taken by the armed forces of Israel on 14–15 October 1953," the brutality of which also received world condemnation.

The fact that the Israeli action was naked aggression devoid of any justification, is borne out by the testimony of the United States representative in his statement which followed. He said: "My Government is confident that the Government of the Kingdom of Jordan in good faith fully adheres to and respects its obligations under the General Armistice. Its record of cooperation with the United Nations peace-keeping machinery in the Middle East speaks for itself, " he concluded. [18]

The Representative of France intervened also "to condemn unequivocally the military action planned and carried out by the Israeli authorities." He remarked, "What is difficult to understand is that an attack which has proved to be so deadly was launched against a country which is respectful of its international obligations." [19]

The U.S.S.R. Representative told the Council that by its "direct military attack on a densely populated part of Jordan, Israel had flagrantly and brutally violated the most important provision of the United Nations and this alone deserves our condemnation." He described the attack as "lawlessness and brigandage" and "an open and arrogant challenge to the Security Council." [20]

Following these and other condemnations, the Security Council adopted a resolution on 25 November censuring "Israel for this large-scale military action in violation of the United Nations Charter and of the General Armistice Agreement between Israel and Jordan;" and emphasizing "to Israel that actions of military reprisal cannot be tolerated and that if they are repeated, the Security Council will have to consider further and more effective steps as envisaged in the Charter to ensure against the repetition of such acts." [21]

By this time, the Israelis had gotten used to Security Council 'condemnations' and 'censures', which meant very little to them. For on 7 April 1967, Israeli jet planes attacked Syrian positions and flew as far as Damascus bombing villages and causing loss of life and much damage. One would have expected the Security Council would immediately invoke its warning of "further and more effective steps" against Israel. Instead complete silence prevailed in the chambers of the United Nations. Such attitude did little to deter the Israelis from more serious aggressions or to enhance the authority and prestige of the United Nations.

Classification of violations

Violations of the General Armistice Agreements may be classified under two main categories:

(1) Individual crossings of the armistice demarcation line; and
(2) Crossings by the regular armed forces – planned and organized under government supervision and control.

The majority of the violations under category (1) have been committed by the Palestine Arabs, particularly by the inhabitants of the villages falling along the armistice demarcation line who could see – as they still do – their homes, orchards, groves and fields, but are prevented from entering them. It was only natural for some of them to sneak back to their homes and fields in order to retrieve some of their belongings or to 'steal' their own crops and fruits for their starving families. Others were child shepherds who wandered innocently across the 'line' unaware that they were committing a violation.

Had the armistice demarcation line been drawn to follow village boundaries rather than made to sever all fertile Arab lands in favour of Israel, the problems which have since arisen and which continue to plague conditions on the armistice demarcation line might well have been minimized. Reporting to the Security Council on the situation, the Chief of Staff said: "The problem is particularly difficult because the demarcation line is long – about 620 kilometres – and because it divides the former mandated territory of Palestine haphazardly, separating, for instance, many Arab villages from their lands." [22]

Despite these difficulties, the Arab States made every effort within their power to curb crossings in order to reduce the unnecessary loss of human life. This is attested to by Commander E.H. Hutchison, who said: "During my three years on the Jordan-Israel Mixed Armistice Commission, I watched Jordan's attitude towards border control change from one of mild interest to a keen determination to put a stop to infiltration." [23] This was further affirmed in 1966 by the Representatives of the United States and France both of whom paid tribute to Jordan's respect for her international obligations. [24]

As regards violations under category (2), it is a matter of United Nations record that all such attacks have been by the Israeli regular armed forces. No Arab State has ever been brought before either the Mixed Armistice Commission or the Security Council accused of an attack by its regular armed forces on Israeli-held territory. This is confirmed by the testimony of the Chief of Staff before the Security Council on 9 November 1953. Asked "how many Israeli attacks were carried out by Israeli military forces in retaliation to the total violations by Israelis," General Bennike replied: "Of the 21 resolutions condemning Israel, adopted by the Israeli-Jordan Mixed Armistice Commission, four refer to action by 'Israeli armed groups', one to 'armed Israelis', four to 'Israeli forces', one to 'Israeli regular forces', one to 'Israeli troops', one to 'Israeli soldiers', one to 'an officer and Israeli security forces', one to 'Israeli armoured cars', and one to 'Israeli regular army'. The answer to your question is sixteen." [25]

The General was then asked to indicate whether there were "any organized attacks by the Arab Legion against Israeli settlements or villages"; and "Did the Arab Legion engage during the truce in any mass murders or mass destructions." To this he replied: "Jordan regular forces were condemned by the Mixed Armistice Commission for three violations of the General Armistice Agreement none of which was an organized attack by the Arab Legion against an Israeli settlement or village." [26]

Israeli aggression

The acts of aggression committed by the Israelis after the signing of the Armistice in 1949 are too numerous to enumerate. They range from army patrol and aircraft crossings of the 'lines' for reconnaissance purposes to murder and destruction of villages. What is significant about these aggressions is that the attacks are carefully planned and meticulously carried out by the *regular forces* of the Israeli army under Government instructions.

The United Nations has not published at any time statistics on the violations committed and casualties suffered by the parties to the General Armistice Agreements as one would have expected it to do. Such official statistics are no doubt vital to determine the relative responsibility of the parties for the unrest and tension prevailing in the area and in order to dispel the distortions created by the one-sided propaganda alleging that Arab 'infiltration' – the so-called root of the problem – has, over the years, inflicted heavy losses on the Israelis which they could neither tolerate nor allow to pass unpunished.

However, a fairly accurate appraisal of responsibility may be gathered from the individual independent tabulations published by Commander E.H. Hutchison for the period June 1949 to 15 October 1954 when he served on the Israeli-Jordan Mixed Armistice Commission and by General E.L.M. Burns for the period 1 January

1955 to 39 September 1956 when he was Chief of Staff. It is unfortunate that figures for all fronts since 1949 and for the period beyond September 1956 have not been made public by other members of the United Nations Truce Supervision Organization who came before or followed Commander Hutchison and General Burns in their cycles of duty.

Commander Hutchison stated that during the period under his review, [27] the Israelis were condemned for 95 violations and the Jordanians for 60 violations – a ratio of two to one. In regard to those killed and wounded, the verified figures were:

	Killed	*Wounded*
Israelis	34	57
Jordanians	127	118

Here the ratio was for every one Israeli killed there were four killed on the Jordan side.

General Burns' comparative figures for the four sectors along the armistice demarcation line in respect of the period under his review, [28] were:

	Killed	*Wounded*
Israelis	121	332
Arabs	496	419

Here also the ratio for the twenty-one-month period works out at four Arabs killed for every one Israeli. This does not, however, include the 18 Israelis and 48 Jordanians reported killed as a result of the Israeli attack on the town of Qalqilya on 10/11 October 1956; nor the casualties suffered following the Israeli invasion of Egypt on 29 October 1956. Civilian losses within the Gaza Strip during the Israeli occupation were estimated by neutral sources to have run into the thousands.

If the above figures of condemnation and casualties are any criterion for the purpose of fixing responsibility, then one is led to the obvious conclusion that it is the Israelis – not the Arabs – who are the principal violators of the General Armistice Agreements and the aggressors responsible for the tension along the armistice demarcation line. This conclusion is also arrived at by General Carl Von Horn who replaced General Burns as Chief of

Staff. He said: "... it was Israeli policy to maintain a situation 'pregnant' with threats of Arab attacks. It seemed to all of us in U.N.T.S.O. that there were two reasons why this suited them. First, it ensured a high state of readiness and efficiency within their own Army, which showed a marked tendency towards internal disputes immediately tension relaxed. Second, it enabled them to make sure that their 'plight' received the maximum amount of attention in foreign and particularly American newspapers, with the natural corollary that sympathy, aid and money continued to flow into Israel in substantial quantities." [29]

According to the records of the United Nations, the Israeli armed forces launched over forty military attacks in one form or another on Arab territory between the date of the signing of the General Armistice Agreements and April 1967. The following is a list of the principal attacks as a result of which there has been loss of life and damage to property. These have been either condemned by the Mixed Armistice Commission or censured by the Security Council:

1. Aerial bombardment of El-Himmeh (Syria) on 5 April 1951. [30]
2. The villages of Falame and Rantis (Jordan) attacked on 28/29 January 1953. [31]
3. The villages of Idna, Surif and Wadi Fukin (Jordan) attacked on 11 August 1953. [32]
4. An Arab Bedouin encampment south of the Gaza Strip attacked by air and ground forces in the summer of 1953. [33]
5. The villages of Qibya, Shuqba and Budrus (Jordan) attacked on 14/15 October 1953. [34] 75 people were killed; the villages were completely demolished.
6. The village of Nahhalin (Jordan) attacked on 28/29 March 1954. [35] 14 people were killed; the village was demolished.
7. The Arab Legion camp in 'Azzun (Jordan) attacked on 27/28 June 1954. [36]
8. The village of Beit Liqya (Jordan) attacked on 1/2

September 1954 [37]

9. Syrian territory attacked on 8/9 December 1954. [38]
10. The Gaza Strip attacked on 8 February 1955. [39] 38 people were killed and 31 others wounded.
11. The Gaza Strip was attacked and the Egyptian post on Hill 79 was occupied on 22 August 1955. [40]
12. Khan Yunis and Bani Suheila (Gaza Strip) were attacked on 31 August / 1 September 1955. [41] 46 people were killed and 50 others wounded.
13. Syrian territory was attacked on 22/23 October 1955. [42]
14. Kuntilla post (Sinai Peninsula) was attacked on 28 October 1955. [43]
15. Sabha post (Sinai Peninsula) was attacked on 2/3 November 1955. [44] 50 people were killed and 40 men taken prisoners.
16. El-Buteiha and El-Koursi area (Syria) attacked on 11/12 December 1955. [45] 50 people killed and 28 taken prisoners.
17. Egyptian patrols in the Gaza Strip attacked on 16/17 August 1956. [46]
18. Umm el-Rihan (Jordan) attacked on 28 August 1956. [47]
19. The village of Rahwa (Jordan) attacked on 11 September 1956. [48]
20. The village of Gharandal (Jordan) attacked on 13 September 1956. [49]
21. The villages of Sharafa and Wadi Fukin (Jordan) attacked on 25/26 September 1956. [50]
22. The villages of Qalqilya, 'Azzum, Nabi Elias and Khan Sufin (Jordan) attacked on 10/11 October 1956. [51] 48 people killed and 31 others wounded.
23. The invasion of Egypt began on 29 October 1956. [52]
24. The village of El-Tawafiq (Syria) was attacked on 1 February 1962. [53] The village was razed to the ground.
25. Syrian territory along the shores of Lake Tiberias was attacked on 16 March 1962. [54]
26. The villages of Nukheila, Abbasieh and Tell el-Aziziyat

(Syria) were attacked from the air and ground artillery on 13 November 1964. [55]

27. The towns of Jenin and Qalqilya and the village of Manshiyat near Jisr el-Majami' (Jordan) were attacked on 27 May 1965. [56] Four people killed and seven others wounded. A number of houses demolished.
28. The villages of Houla and Meis el-Jabal (Lebanon) were attacked on 28/29 October 1965. [57] One woman killed and two houses and three village cisterns demolished.
29. Syrian territory was bombed from the air by jet planes on 14 July 1966. [58] Jet fighters shelled Syrian positions, killing one woman and wounding nine civilians.
30. The village of Sammu' (Jordan) was attacked on 13 November 1966. [59] 18 killed, 130 wounded and 125 houses, including the school, clinic and mosque demolished.
31. On 7 April 1967, Israeli planes penetrated deep into Syrian territory and attacked Syrian targets. [60]

The Qibya attack

Commenting on the Qibya attack of 1953, Father Ralph Gorman, an American Roman Catholic Priest who spent many years in Jerusalem, said: "Terror was a political weapon of the Nazis and is still used by the Communists. But neither Nazis nor Communists ever used terror in a more cold-blooded and wanton manner than the Israelis in the massacre of Qibya."

"The official report of the Palestine Truce Supervisor," he pointed out, "removed any possible doubt that the Israelis, themselves in large part refugees from Hitler's terror, were perpetrators of this horrible slaughter of innocent men, women and children. It also reveals that it was an official act of the state, carried out by an official organ, the army," he added.

The Reverend Father then went on to describe the attack. He said: "The evening of October 14 was like any other for the 1500 inhabitants of the peaceful village until at 9.30 all hell let loose.

Mortar shells began exploding from artillery that had been carefully aimed from Israel before dark. After the town had been partly demolished and many of its inhabitants buried in the rubble of falling homes or blown up to bits by exploding shells, half a battalion of the regular Israeli army moved in and surrounded the village to cut off escape. "Then followed," he said, "an orgy of murder that would be incredible if it had not been verified by reliable neutral testimony. Women and children as well as men were murdered deliberately, systematically and in cold-blood."

Father Gorman then stated, "The only response the Israelis have made to outraged protests of the civilized world has been one of defiance and self-justification. The Prime Minister excused the murderers. Israeli newspapers openly gloated over the deed and even American Zionists showed little concern other than a fear that American dollars might not continue to flow as freely as before into the coffers of the new state." [61]

The Diary of Moshe Sharett, acting Prime Minister at the time of the Qibya massacre, published in October 1965 by his son in rebuttal to certain statements made by Ben Gurion against his father, are most revealing of the manner in which the dastardly attack was planned. The excerpts from the Diary begin with 14 October 1953, the day the raid took place. Sharett writes in regard to the incident which precipitated the massacre: ". . . Today the Mixed Armistice Commission roundly condemned the killing (of a woman and two children at Yahud). *Even the Jordanian delegates voted in favour of the resolution. They took upon themselves to prevent such atrocities in the future. Under such circumstances, is it wise to retaliate?"* Sharett enquires.

Sharett then comments: "I came to the conclusion that we are again confronted with a situation like that other time when I had a raid called off and in so doing broke off the vicious circle of bloody revenge for a fortnight and more. If we retaliate, we only make the marauder bands' job easier and give the authorities an excuse to do something. I called Lavon (Defence Minister) and told him what I thought. He said he would consult B.G." (Ben Gurion).

The diary continues: "In the afternoon, during a meeting

with Lavon and others in connection with developments in the North, an Army representative brought Lavon a note from the UNTSO Chief of Staff Gen. Vagn Bennike, saying that *the Commander of the Jordan Legion, Glubb Pasha, had asked for police bloodhounds to cross over from Israel to track down the Yahu murderers.* Sharett then states that after Lavon read the note, the Army man asked: "Any change in plans?" Lavon answered: "No change." [62]

From this diary, it will be seen that the Jordan Government after being satisfied that the killings were the work of its citizens, went so far as to ask for Israeli blood-hounds to follow the murderers inside Jordan territory. Notwithstanding the sincerity of the Jordan Government, the Israelis made 'no change' in their plans for the massacre of the innocent inhabitants of Qibya.

The 'El-Fateh' and 'El-Asifa' Organizations

Little is known outside the Arab world about *El-Fateh* and *El-'Asifa* except what the Zionist and Israeli press claim them to be–a group of marauders, saboteurs, cut-throats bent on creating trouble for 'little Israel'. But if one were to investigate the causes which led up to their creation and studied the objectives of the organization in relation to similar movements which spring up in times of stress, a logical explanation for their deeds may be arrived at.

The letters of the word *Fateh* are made up of the Arabic initials of the term 'Palestine Liberation Movement' if read backwards; and the word *'Asifa* stands for 'Striking Force' of the mother organization. *Fateh* came into existence in January 1965; and its members are a group of dedicated young Palestinians who have experienced the Palestine tragedy but were not responsible for it.

The principles of the organization are no different in any way to liberation movements established in any other country, namely, to remove the evils and injustices imposed upon the indigenous inhabitants by imperialist or colonialist Powers and to regain the people's God-given right of freedom and security to which they are fully entitled.

In a way one can easily compare the set-up of this Arab organization with those of the four Zionist underground movements of British Mandate days, namely, *Hagana* (Defence), *Palmach* (Striking Force), *Irgun Zvei Leumi* (Jewish Resistance Movement) and *Stern Gang* (Freedom Fighters) but with one basic difference. The Zionist groups were organized to wrest a country from its original inhabitants using political intrigue, influence and pressures abroad and brute force, massacres, expulsions and dispossessions in Palestine. The objectives of the Palestine Arabs, on the other hand, are to regain possession of their rights and property and to liberate their homeland from the invader. Surely these are lofty motives; and those who saw nothing wrong in the actions of the Zionist groups prior to 1948, have no right now to frown if similar methods are used by the Palestine Arabs to undo the injustice and harm they suffered at the hands of their enemies.

While the movement may not be officially sanctioned by the Arab Governments and is in fact even opposed by some, it undoubtedly has the moral support of the people as the only means to liberate Palestine and bring justice and peace to the Holy Land, particularly since all peaceful approaches have failed to restore to the Palestine Arabs their usurped rights in their homeland.

It should be noted that the loss of contact with homeland and property since 1948 through terror and armed force does not in any way derogate the right of an individual or change the character of the guilty and aggrieved parties. Having been denied a peaceful return to their homes and property for almost two decades, the Palestine Arabs believe the only way left open to them is to take punitive measures against those who expelled and dispossessed them. Their so-called 'infiltration' should therefore more accurately be called 'reprisal and retaliation' against Israeli 'provocation and infiltration' as a means "to procure redress of grievances" suffered by them at the hands of the Zionists. To describe the Palestine Arabs as the aggressors and the Israelis as the victims is a misnomer. It is like condemning the police and courts of law for administering justice and absolving the criminal of his crime!

Admittedly, no peace-loving person can honestly condone

aggression for whatever reason and from whatever source; but man's patience is not inexhaustable in the face of a stubborn adversary. The Palestine Arabs have used every peaceful approach. They appealed to the United Nations, to the Western Powers and to world opinion, with no avail. Under such circumstances, they have no alternative but to take the law into their own hands. It is difficult to convince a wronged people that their methods of applying "evil for evil" in an endeavor "to procure redress of grievances" are sinful.

Equation between Nazism and Zionism

Whenever and wherever Jews are mistreated, the conscience of humanity, as a whole is revolted. The world is made to hear a great deal about the heartless persecutions of tyrants; and every form of retaliation – from condemnation to boycott – is applied against the offender on a wide scale.

But the world has not heard about the equally cruel, equally heartless mistreatment of the Palestine Arabs by the no less ruthless Zionists before and after the creation of the state of Israel in 1948.

If the same principles of human justice were to be applied in both instances, the relationship between both evils would be easily discernable.

A comparison between what happened to the Palestine Arabs at the hands of the Zionists and the treatment of the Jews of Europe during the era of Nazi persecution will explain how close Zionism is to Nazism. The Zionists, in their treatment of the Palestine Arabs, repeated the Nazi treatment of the Jews, in their short cut to their goal of a 'state' in the Holy Land.

An earlier analogy between the two '*isms*' was aptly drawn by the eminent British historian Arnold Toynbee in his monumental works, A Study of History. He said: "The Jews' immediate reaction to their own experience was to become persecutors in their turn for the first time since A. D. 135 and this at the first opportunity that had arisen for them to inflict on other human beings who had done the Jews no injury, but who happened to be weaker than they were, some of the wrongs and sufferings that had been inflicted on the Jews ..." Toynbee added: "In A.D. 1948, the Jews knew, from personal experience, what they were doing; and it was their supreme tragedy that the lesson learned by them from their encounter with the Nazi Gentiles should have been not to eschew but to imitate some of the evil deeds that the Nazis had committed against the Jews." [63]

Since the Zionists and Israelis vehemently protest the equation made between Nazism and Zionism, it is only fair to compare notes to allow the reader to arrive at his own conclusions:

Nazism was based on an exclusive national fanaticism, racial discrimination, and the loyalty of Germans outside Germany to Nazism.	Zionism is based on an exclusive Jewish nationalism, racial discrimination, and the loyalty of Jews outside Israel to Zionism and Israel.
The Nazis have been condemned for the migration, sufferings and deaths of European Jewry.	The Zionists committed massacres and brought untold sufferings to over one million Palestine Arabs.
The Nazis drove Jews into concentration camps or forced them to leave the country as refugees. They, however, allowed them to take their belongings with them.	The Israelis drove the Arabs out of their homes with nothing but the clothes they wore. They live as refugees, while the Israelis enjoy their homes, lands and belongings.
The Nazis enacted discriminatory laws against the Jews, deprived them of means of livelihood and treated them as 'second-class' citizens.	The Israelis enacted discriminatory laws against the Arabs, deprived them of livelihood, confiscated their lands, and treat those living among them as 'second-class' citizens.
Laws enacted by the Allied Powers to redress the wrong done to the Jews were implemented in their entirety.	U.N. resolutions calling on Israel to restore private property and pay compensation for loss of or damage to property remain unimplemented.

The West German Government paid reparations to Israel, granted indemity to individual Jews, and where possible, restored private property.

The Israelis confiscated and disposed of private Arab property; they refused to pay even the rents and profits derived from these properties.

Jews are able to return to Germany and regain possession of their property which it is said they were 'forced to sell'.

The Palestine Arabs are not permitted to return or even to claim their property which was 'seized'.

Nazi leaders were hanged by the Allies for crimes against humanity. Adolph Eichmann was hanged and cremated by the Israelis under a unique 'law' enacted after the commission of Eichmann's crimes, for deeds committed before Israel was established and not on Israeli-held soil. Having accepted 'reparations' from West Germany, the Israelis would appear to have forfeited any claim to punish Nazi criminals.

David Ben Gurion, Menachim Beigin, with their other Zionist collaborators, committed no less atrocious crimes against the Palestine Arabs. Instead of being made to pay for these with their lives, as did the Nazi criminals, they are received with respect and honour in the Capitals of the world as 'heroes' for establishing a 'Jewish state'.

The German people's conscience was burdened with Nazi horrors and every effort is still being made at retribution.

The Israeli conscience remains very much dead as over one million human beings rot in refugee camps, suffering deprivation, humiliation and frustration.

The difference between the West German Government and the Israeli so-called 'government' is that whereas the former has replaced a despotic Nazi regime, assessed human and moral obligations and made amends, the latter has shirked all human responsibility and imitated Nazi methods because this helped to establish a 'Jewish state'.

After the lapse of fifteen years since the downfall of Hitler and after the Israeli Government had accepted blood-money for the crimes of Hitler, running into hundreds of millions of dollars, Adolph Eichman was kidnapped and brought to trial in Jerusalem under circumstances which have been described as 'lawless'. He paid with his life for his implication in crimes against the Jews. Ironically, the judge in this case – Israel – was guilty of no less atrocious crimes against the Palestine Arabs. There is a well-known principle of law which says, "he who seeks justice must come into court with clean hands." Are Israel's hands clean? And who will pass judgement on Israel? Chaim Weizmann, first president of the 'Jewish state', gave the answer in 1948: "I am certain," he said, "that the world will judge the Jewish state by what it will do with the Arabs." [64] That Judgement is long overdue!

Meanwhile, a voice of truth has been heard from Israel. This voice drew a parallel between what Eichmann had committed and what his judges are guilty of:

> "With deep sorrow and shame we ask: Does Israel, which for 13 years has been imposing exile and misery on hundreds of thousands of men, women and children whose only guilt is that they are Arabs; which has deprived her Arab inhabitants of elementary human rights, confiscated most of their lands and forces them to beg for a permit for every move in the country.
> "Does the Israel of Qibya, Gaza, Kafr Qasem and the wanton attacks on Egypt have the moral right to sit in judgment?
> "Israeli leaders and newspapermen vehementlv denounce those Germans who were silent during the beastly Nazi reign. Even German liberals and leftists became Nazis, it is said.
> "But how do the Jews in Israel behave? Do they not approve – not tacitly, but quite loudly – the inhuman actions of their government? Are there many Jewish houses in Israel that do not harbour Arab property? Do not the Kibutsim build *socialism* on robbed Arab land?
> "What a spectacle: In the City of the Prophets and under the eyes of Humanity, they are sitting in judgment!" [65]

Persecution, discrimination, oppression – whether directed

against Jews or Arabs – are equally abhorent. The Arabs of Deir Yasin, of Qibya, of Kafr Qasem, of Gaza and many other places, who were massacred in cold-blood by the Zionists and Israelis; the nearly million Arabs who were terrorized from their homes and forced to lead lives of misery and hopelessness in refugee camps; the Arabs whose liberties and properties were 'seized' and whose fundamental rights were suppressed and usurped; are these Arabs not human beings? Are they not equally worthy of sympathy and consideration as were the innocent Jewish victims of Nazism?

If the Christian peoples still have a conscience, how can human standards of love and justice be applied differently to Jews and Arabs?

The world conscience as a whole and that of world Jewry in particular, has remained unmoved by the crimes that were committed against the Palestine Arabs. Little, if any, concern has been shown by world Jewry over the injustices their co-religionists in so-called 'Israel' have inflicted upon the Moslem and Christian inhabitants of the Holy Land.

It is strange indeed to see the indifference shown toward the sufferings of others at the hands of the victims of yesteryear. It is more surprising that those who have been so quick to condemn the persecution and humiliation of the Jews have not seen fit to do so concerning the expelled Palestine Arabs.

Nearly two decades have passed and the Palestine Arabs are still waiting for world conscience to be aroused to their plight. They appear to be waiting in vain.

XIII | *Israel and the United States*

Israel's favoured position

The state of Israel is often referred to as the 'favoured child' or the 'creation' of the United States and as such, its continued existence and well-being are regarded as the responsibility of that country.

There is much truth in this statement. Had it not been for the active part played by the White House in 1947 and 1948, the 'Jewish state' would never have come into being; the Palestine tragedy, with all its human miseries, would not have occurred; the present tension and instability in the Middle East would not have arisen; and the United States traditional position of respect and trust in the Arab world would not have been damaged. The Senate Committee on Foreign Relations, after hearing the views on American foreign policy of retired Foreign Service officers, who had done service in the Middle East, declared: "It was unanimously agreed that the manner in which Israel was created had an unfortunate effect on our relationship with the Arab nations."[1] Since this declaration was made, these relations have deteriorated considerably.

There are many who recognize the error of early American judgement and consider the creation of the 'Jewish state' a mistake. But instead of attempting to redress the wrong committed, they lull themselves into a 'sweep–it–under–the–rug' attitude and rely on time to heal Arab wounds and bring the two peoples together, forgetting that at no time has it been possible to fraternize between right and wrong. This short-sighted policy has not only proved dangerous; it has encouraged the Israelis into believing that whatever they do and no matter how far they go in their intransigence and defiance of their international obligations and human decency, the United States – Government and people – would always be there to lend them the support they need. Even when the world was brought to the brink of a general war as a result of Israel's aggression against Egypt in 1956, General Eisenhower, who first took a firm stand that Israel must not be allowed to benefit from her aggression, was later compelled to retract from his position and arranged for the passage of Israeli ships through the Gulf of Aqaba – then denied them – in return for Israeli willingness to withdraw from the Sinai Peninsula and the Gaza Strip. This enabled David Ben Gurion subsequently to declare, we went out to open the Gulf for our ships and we got it. When Israeli Prime Minister Levi Eshkol declared in 1967 that the U.S. Sixth Fleet was in the Mediterranean to protect Israel against Arab Aggression, the statement was not flatly denied by the U.S. Government as one would have expected. The weak attempts of U.S. ambassadors in Arab countries to ally Arab fears had the opposite effect of confirming Arab suspicions.

Israel's strength in the United States is the complex of American Zionist organizations. Even though card-carrying Zionists represent – by Zionism's own figures – less than 10% of the American Jews, the movement is highly organized, munificently financed and closely disciplined. The economic pressures, social ostracism and excommunication the Zionists are able to exercise over Jews who may fall out of line with their policies, has had the effect of cowing American Jewry – with very few exceptions – into submission. And American Jews, wittingly or unwittingly, while striking an 'I am not a Zionist, but . . .' attitude, utilize their wealth, influence and economic standing in the country to advance Israeli objectives, placing them above United States interest and security.

With this power, the Zionists have been able to make great inroads into American life – in the Houses of Congress, in the Government, in mass media of information, in churches and educational institutions. Dr. Harry N. Howard, Professor of Middle East Studies at the American University, Washington, D.C., attributes Zionist success to the erroneous belief that United States and Israeli interests are identical. He states:

"Despite the obvious evidence to the contrary over the years, there is an implicit, if rationalized, assumption on the part of American Zionists and the Israelis that there is some peculiar, unique identity of interests between the United States and Israel which does not and cannot obtain between the United States and any other country ... The rationalization is employed to support the contention that, somehow or other, the United States should support Israel, whatever its policies in the Middle East.

"Israel, it is said, is the 'natural' ally of the United States, a kind of Western outpost on the Eastern Mediterranean. The idea antedates the establishment of the state of Israel, going back at least as far as the Balfour Declaration in November 1917 when, among other things, a Jewish 'homeland' was to serve British imperial interests in the neighbourhood of the Suez Canal. In later years, it was to become a 'little bastion' of 'embattled democracy' in the 'hostile' and 'feudal' Arab world, said to be anti-democratic, anti-Western and anti-American. Constant appeals for political and financial support have been based on this rationalization of a unique identity of interests and the presumed natural antagonism between the United States and the Arab States, leaving aside the exploitation of a common religio-ethical heritage and liberal and humanitarian principles.

"To implement the assumption, great pressures, sometimes incredible and much propaganda are brought to bear on the United States Government and public opinion through the Zionist apparatus, now clearly shown to be inseparably linked with the Jewish Agency, duly registered as the agent of a foreign principal.* While these have a long history, it was only

* In 1963, the U.S. Foreign Relations Committee conducted an investigation into the 'foreign agent' aspect of American Zionist groups in the United States for the purpose of checking abuse. The report of the Committee disclosed, according to sworn testimony, the firm control maintained by the Jewish Agency for Israel in Jerusalem over Zionist and some 'non-Zionist' activities in the United States. Large sums, obtained mainly from the United Jewish Appeal, were funnelled back to the United States from Israel. *The money was used to support the indoctrination of U.S. Jews themselves in Zionist politics and 'culture'.*

> during the period of 1942-1946 that it was decided to make the United States the Zionist power base in the diplomatic manouvers and campaigns which led to the establishment of the state of Israel during 1947-1948." [2]

U.S. political support

In any issue before the United Nations, the United States invariably adopts the Israeli position. For example, whereas the United States Representative at the United Nations will annually sponsor a resolution calling upon the Israelis to implement paragraph 11 of United Nations resolution 194 (III) of 11 December 1948 giving the Arab refugees the choice between repatriation and compensation, in practice, the United States Government will resist any United Nations pressure on Israel for implementation. But it will use every opportunity to support Zionist and Israeli demands on the Soviet Union to permit the immigration of Russian Jews to Palestine!

Here is the paradoxical example of the United States, always

Senator William F. Fulbright, the Chairman of the Committee, referred to the Zionist operation as a 'conduit' through which more than $1,000,000 a year passed for political lobbying and propaganda in the United States – all from *tax-free funds raised ostensibly for humanitarian purposes*.

The Senate Record, which runs into some 220 pages, disclosed that:

1. More than $5,000,000 of mainly United Jewish Appeal Funds were returned to the United States from Israel in five-and-a-half years for political lobbying and propaganda purposes.
2. Some $300,000 of United Jewish Appeal funds were used to gain control of the Jewish Telegraphic Agency ('news' and propaganda distributor to the Jewish press).
3. United Jewish Appeal funds, returned through 'foreign agent' channels, were used to create and maintain the Presidents Conference of Major Jewish Organizations (Union of American Hebrew Congregations, Bnai Brith, etc.).
4. The Synagogue Council of America received funds as did the Zionist loyybist I.L. Kenen (to the latter alone, $38,000 in one year).
5. Christian supporters of Zionism were given tours of Israel and were paid to run the American Christian Palestine Committee (succeeded by the American Christian Association for Israel). [3]

a champion of the authority of the United Nations, taking up a double-standard stand in the Arab-Israeli conflict and encouraging Israeli defiance of the World Organization.

This dual position was disclosed further in the presence of the author in a U.S. policy statement by a Deputy Secretary of State before the Mid-American Conference at Stillwater, Oklahoma, on 8 May 1964. The Washington official, speaking on the question of the Arab refugees, told his audience, "against great odds, Israel has built a thriving economy, a sound social structure and a stable, domestic government. Does it not deserve our admiration and our friendship? At the least," he continued, "should we not refrain from trying to force that country to make concessions which it believes would weaken its economy and social structure and endanger its security? We certainly have to think twice or thrice about these questions and to weigh carefully whether what we urge Israel to do would in fact injure it." The Deputy Secretary of State then added: "Israel is a friend of the United States and of the West. It has a Western outlook, uninfluenced by the communists. One of our major policy objectives is to persuade more countries to adopt this attitude." [4]

Another illustration of the U.S. Government's favouritism towards Israel is in its constant opposition to Arab annual demands before the United Nations for "the establishment of appropriate and effective machinery for safe-guarding the property rights of the Arab refugees of Palestine, " pending a final settlement. The request did not call for a full restoration of Arab rights in Palestine. It merely sought to preserve the Arab refugees' property rights. It did not threaten the existence of Israel, but, admittedly, might cause her some enbarrassment – embarrassment in contrast to the destruction and elimination of a whole Arab country! The Arab proposal lost, years in succession, only because U.S. behind-the-scene pressures were brought to bear on the smaller nations in the General Assembly not to vote for the proposal.

The effect on the Arab world of the United States stand was one of deep disappointment and profound resentment. One Arab delegate at the United Nations explained Arab reaction by declaring: "The Soviet Union, although a communist country, was prepared to respect private ownership as a system for other countries whereas the United States, a capitalist country, opposed property rights!" [5]

Even when it comes to border incidents before the Security Council, the United States position is one-sided. For example, where the incident is an attack on Arab territory by Israel's regular armed forces and as a result of which there has been much loss of Arab life, the resolution is mild and worded in such a way as to place responsibility on both sides, describing the incident as 'regretable'. Where, however, the incident is one of suspected 'infiltration' and Arab governmental responsibility was only presumed, the U.S. representative, while admitting that the judgement of the United States was inspired only by 'circumstantial' evidence, described the incident with such harsh words as "In all justice and in the interests of law and order in international affairs, we believe this reprehensible act of murder on August 20 (1964) deserves the strongest condemnation."

When interviewed on television, the Israeli Ambassador in Washington expressed satisfaction at the statement; former Israeli Foreign Minister Golda Meir, assailed the Soviet Union for refusing to go along with the U.S. resolution of condemnation, whose representative explained that there was not conclusive evidence that the Arab government was responsible for the incident.

Moral support

The encouragement given Israel from time to time, without considering the injustices inflicted upon the Palestine Arabs, has no limits. The Deputy Secretary of State just quoted also told his audience that the United States considered "Israel is a refuge for Jews from countries where they have been endangered, oppressed, suffered discrimination. U.S. public opinion," he said "influenced by our strong Biblical tradition, has considered it our duty to support the establishment and maintenance of this refuge." [6] "While the U.S. has been unwilling to give them special immigration privileges," it was willing to do so at Arab expense.

United States moral support for Israel is also expressed in other ways. For example, Israel's Day of Independence is celebrated in the United States as if the 'Jewish state' were the 51st state of the Union. No other country in the world enjoys this favoured treatment. Mayors of the larger cities proclaim the day as 'Israel Independence Day', hoist the Zionist flag and send greetings to Israeli leaders and Zionist gatherings. Even the President of the United States is expected to take cognizance of the occasion and to send his felicitations.

In 1964, President Johnson, speaking at a $ 250–plate dinner sponsored by the Chaim Weizmann Institute at the Waldorf Astoria Hotel in New York, was reported to have paid "tribute to Israel's development." He told his audience of 1,500 guests that "at its birth in 1948, this tiny nation faced monumental problems of economic survival. Only a fifth of its meagre territory," he said, "was fit for cultivation. Yet it was called upon to sustain a population that doubled in ten years."

The source of the President's erroneous information is obvious. The question which he did not know was the fact that the overwhelming portion of this so-called 'tiny' nation's 'meagre territory' does not belong rightfully to the Israelis, but to the Moslem and Christian inhabitants of the Holy Land who were expelled and dispossessed of their legal and legitimate rights; and the 'developments' referred to are only possible through the political, moral and financial support of the United States.

For the President of the United States to be placed in the position of condoning the plunder of other people's rights and possessions, to ignore the great human sufferings of innocent people which has lasted for nearly two decades and to lavish words of praise and encouragement on the aggressors, is hardly in keeping with the principles on which United States democracy and freedom were founded. Arab reaction to this attitude is one of bewilderment and disappointment.

Commenting on the publicity given to Israel's achievements in occupied Palestine – achievements which politicians in the United

States hasten to applaud in their bid for the 'Jewish vote' – Richard J. Marquardt, in a letter to the press enquires with wonder: "How much longer will the American public be exposed to this kind of sentimental mythology? I recognize," he said, "that many persons of the Jewish faith need to have repeated to them the stories of Israel's 'miracles' and of that country's legendary figures. They apparently have a deep need for heroic symbols with which to identify. This is quite understandable," he concedes. "But what of the remaining 97 per cent of the American population?" he asks. Marquardt then suggests that "our appetite for these highly biased tales is not an insatiable one," and he comments, "I, for one, am bored to distraction with Israel, its 'spectacular accomplishments', its bond drives, its strident appeals, its constantly hammering propaganda, a blatant mixture of bathos and boasting . . . With some three-and-a-half billion dollars available to it from various foreign sources since its creation, why shouldn't Israel have accomplished something?" Marquardt enquires. [7]

Those who applaud Israel's so-called achievements forget that the Israelis have unlimited financial resources to draw on. Any country with such extraordinary potential might even do better. However, can Israel's accomplishments be looked upon as truly worthy, considering the sufferings inflicted upon other human beings and the dangers the 'Jewish state' poses to world peace? A noted Professor from Canada aptly remarked, "The material achievements of Zionism have tended to blind the eyes of many in the West to its real character, just as the material achievements of Nazism and Facism blinded many to the evil inherent in those creeds. The destructive character of Zionism," he pointed out, "arises from the fact that, like the rabid nationalisms already mentioned, it is determined to do something for its adherents, no matter what the cost to other people." The Professor then warns: "For countries of the Western world to link their Middle East policies in any way with support of such an 'ism' is to court disaster." [8]

Military aid

There is ample evidence that the U.S. Government, prior to

the creation of the state of Israel in 1948, closed its eyes to the smuggling of arms and ammunition out of the country for the Zionist underground terrorists in Palestine and allowed funds to be donated *tax-free,* that were used for the purchase of illicit arms from Czechoslovakia and other Communist countries.

When Israel came into being, the United States at first either supplied the Israelis, secretly, with military equipment or encouraged Canada and European nations to do so, pretending all the time its 'impartiality' in the conflict between Arabs and Israelis. Then in 1962, the U.S. Government appeared to have thrown caution to the winds and began an 'open door' policy for Israel but still insisting that it was impartial. That year, the sale of 'Hawk' missiles was announced; in February 1966, 200 Patton tanks were delivered;* and in May 1966, the Israelis received 'tactical' aircraft of the Douglas Skyhawk light-bomber type. It was claimed by some U.S. Administration officials that they were hopeful, "the sale of some attack jet bombers to Israel would at least temporarily halt American involvement in the Middle Eastern arms race." [9] But they did not elaborate.

The effect of this latest transaction on the Israelis was one of elation. The Military Correspondent of the Israeli English-language newspaper, the *Jerusalem Post,* reported: "The addition to the Israel Air Force of a number of Douglas Skyhawk light bombers gives it an important new striking force." According to experts, the Skyhawk is said to be "one of the best and most efficient of its types now in the service ... As a light bomber, this type of plane does not need the speed of interceptors, relying on hedge-hopping maneuverability and which is termed 'counter-measures' to combat enemy interception ... The plane," it is said, "has been used in combat in Vietnam and elsewhere and is a particular favourite of the U.S. Navy and Marines who operate it from aircraft carriers." [10]

The U.S. Government explains that its supply of military equipment to Israel is merely to keep the balance of military power

* There is evidence to prove that Patton tanks were used in the Israeli attack on the village of Sammu' on 13 November 1966 for which Israel was strongly condemned.

in the Middle East and thus to maintain peace.

The Arabs do not share this view. In the first place, is it conceivable that parity in military strength between two million Jews and 100 million Arabs could really be maintained for very long? In effect, the United States was creating for the Arabs in the Middle East the same situation it so vehemently decried in the Caribbean in 1962. The United States would never see justice in a balance of power between it and Cuba; yet it sought to impose on the Arabs a formula it would not accept for itself.

In the second place, the argument that the military equipment was for defensive purposes is unconvincing. A 'defensive' weapon must be judged by the character of the state possessing it, not by its range and calibre. Castro also claimed that the Russian missiles in Cuba were for defence! In its record at the United Nations, Israel is known to have been condemned over forty times for aggression against Arab territory by its regular armed forces. It continues to threaten to attack and destroy any works which the Arab States might carry out for the utilization of the headwaters of the River Jordan in Lebanon and Syria; in fact, in July 1966, the Israelis did attack these works using the same U.S. jet light bombers supplied to Israel only a few months before. This attack resulted in the death of one woman and the wounding of nine civilians. For this deed – admitted before the Security Council – the Israelis were not even censured.

Under such circumstances, is it not natural for the Arab States to feel that Israel has been placed in the advantageous position of being able to ensure the success of its aggressions, by bringing into operation American equipment against Arab defences? Are not the Arabs justified in their concern over U.S. arms in Israel, as Americans were over the presence of Russian missiles in Cuba?

The Arabs believe that the decision to sell military equipment to Israel is prompted by strong Zionist pressure and by the fate of the so-called 'Jewish vote'. For example, the announcement of the sale of the 'Hawk' missiles in 1962 was made to American Zionist leaders before it was made public and the timing was about one month before the elections. Again, Arabs watched their rights and destiny sacrificed on the altar of American domestic politics, without regard for principle or equity.

But the supply of jet light bombers might not have been influenced only by the approaching elections. There is reason to believe that President Johnson was anxious for Jewish support for his policies in Vietnam.

According to the *Jewish Telegraphic Agency,* President Johnson is reported to be disturbed by the lack of support for his Vietnam policy in the American Jewish Community at a time when he is taking steps to aid Israel. [11]

Arab reaction to the sale of the Skyhawk jets to Israel was reflected in an *Editorial* which appeared in the *Daily Star* of Beirut, Lebanon. The writer said: "The disclosure of a United States agreement to sell Israel a small number of tactical jet bombers came at a critical time for American policy in the Middle East and may prove detrimental to U.S. interests in the Arab World." The Paper added: "The United States decision to provide Israel with the A-4 Skyhawk, a light-weight attack bomber, comes as a departure from American policy not to be directly involved in the arms race in the Middle East ... Direct U.S. involvement in the arms race," it was pointed out, "will support Arab assertions that the American Administration cannot identify itself except with Israel in the area and thus, if the Arabs are to expect international support, they must look elsewhere. What gain had the U.S. envisaged when it agreed to the deal is anybody's guess. If anything, it spells short-sightedness and tactlessness."

The writer went on to say, "American assertions that they are only trying to maintain an arms balance between the Arabs and Israel can never be accepted by the Arabs. It has always been the case that Israel has chosen to attack a single Arab state – as in the recent case of Jordan – without the Arab Governments replying in unison. Thus, in these cases, Israel, with the American arms it has been receiving stands superior to the Arab state concerned. How then can a balance be maintained? What logic is it to place all the Arab Governments on one side of the balance and Israel, a nation of two million, on the other? U.S. policy-makers should find themselves a better role in the Middle East than the present one," the Editorial concluded. [12]

It was disclosed in 1965, prior to the missile deal in 1962, that the United States Government had in 1960, supported the 'free gift' of arms to Israel by the West German Government. On the day of disclosure, it was revealed that at least 80 per cent of the shipment had already been delivered.

According to the *New York Times,* "In Washington, the State Department acknowledged that West Germany had informed the United States in advance about its secret agreement to supply Israel with arms, including American-made tanks and that the United States had given its approval. The arms shipments were suspended when President Nasser denounced them," the paper said. [13]

The extent of American involvement in the arms deal appears to have exceeded mere 'approval'. The *New York Times* later reported that "a high United States official made the appeal directly to Chancellor Ludwig Erhard last summer to ship arms to Israel. The Chancellor agreed reluctantly to ship a large quantity of surplus tanks to Israel." [14]

But this belated and embarrassing admission appears not to have satisfied the West German Government which, through its Press Chief, Karl Gunther von Hase, complained that "the United States support for West Germany in its difficulties in the Middle East had been given reluctantly. We do not hide the fact," he added, "that a statement on its part in this whole affair was only gradually wrung out of the American Government." [15]

A pertinent commentary on United States Middle East policy appeared during the critical days in an *Editorial* in the *Chicago Tribune* of March 23, 1965, under the title "The Rewards of Duplicity," which is worth quoting:

> "West Germany's diplomatic dilemma in the Near East is troublesome enough even without recognizing our part in bringing it about.
> *As matters stand, it is to a large extent our problem, too, because it was under pressure from our government that West*

> *Germany agreed secretly to provide military supplies to Israel...* (*emphasis added*)
>
> "Our financial columnist, Eliot Janeway, has suggested that the Russians are stirring up the trouble in the hope of forcing us into a Near-Eastern Viet Nam which would be less embarrassing to the Communists than the imbroglio in southeast Asia. Both Russia and China would be glad to see Western influence eliminated from the Arab world and this is just what would happen if the West were to commit itself to Israel's side in a war against the Arabs.
>
> "Mr. Janeway may very well be right. But if the Russians are trying to embarrass us in the Near East, we have made the job as easy as possible for them by our own double-dealing in that area...
>
> "One of the easiest ways to get into trouble is not to know where you're going and it doesn't look as if we do. We'd be better off if we hadn't meddled in the Near East at all." [16]

The United States Government wants the Arabs to believe that United States policy toward the Arab States and Israel is one of impartiality. The Arabs would welcome this. But when some see themselves threatened, from time to time, with the curtailment of food supplies – for which, incidentally, they pay; when they see the Israelis enjoying, not only political, moral, military and financial support, but also the advantage of United States pressure on other nations for secret military aid to Israel, it is difficult to sustain faith in the good intentions of the United States.

This double-standard policy can only lead to greater estrangement between the Arabs and the United States and cause grave dangers in the Middle East – a situation which must be deplored by all those who are anxious to see an improvement in Arab-American relations and the easing of tensions in a strategic oil-rich region of the globe.

Instead of trying to maintain an unrealistic parity in military strength between the Israelis and the Arab States, in order to appease a minority group whose 'votes' are desired and whose influence is apparently too strong to resist, the United States would do well, for its own sake, to heed a warning at this belated hour, given by Dr. W.T. Stace, Professor of Philosophy at Princeton University, as far back as 1947 when the future of Palestine was being discussed. He enquired: "Do we want peace or don't we? If we do, then there is only one way to get it. We have to cease deciding international issues by considerations of vote-catching, self-interests, power, greed, prejudice, passion and more or less base emotions disguised under the name of patriotism. We have to begin," he advised, "to decide them impartially by reason and the principles of justice." [17] This advice, like many which came before and after it, went unheeded and if today the Middle East is suffering from turmoil and unrest, it is all due to the causes which Mr. Stace had described.

Financial aid

United States financial aid to Israel falls into three categories, namely, direct governmental aid; donations from American Jewry; and income from the sale of Israeli bonds. The total amount realized from these sources during the years 1948 to 1965 is estimated to have exceeded three-and-half billion dollars. It is no secret that without United States financial aid pouring annually into its coffers, Israel would not be able to exist as a state for six months. And this aid is not of a temporary or periodical nature; world Jewry has been put on notice that it will have to go on and increase as the years go by.

Commenting on the assistance the Israelis are receiving from abroad and Israel's ability to survive, Eugene Van Cleef, Professor Emeritus of Geography at the Ohio State University, said: "Neither the natural resources of Israel nor the determination of its people to survive are adequate to sustain the country at the level it has set for itself." Taking the year 1960 as an example, Van Cleef pointed out, "aside from borrowings which helped to maintain the people, (that year) funds consisted of $ 299,500,000" which entered the country from various sources. "Of one thing we may be certain," he said, "Israel pursues a very precarious existence. Her imports are nearly two and one-half to three times as large as her exports and the differential cannot be balanced by the rendering of services. Per capita imports in 1960 were $ 234, compared with her per capita exports of $ 99." [18]

The aid Israel receives from the United States under the three headings just mentioned is:

1. *Governmental* – According to a U.S. Aid Financial Report, covering the period 1949 to 1963, "the total value of all U.S. dollar programmes (to Israel) was $ 1,002,600,000."[19] To this should be added the 1964 and 1965 grants of $116,200,000 [20] – making a total of $ 1,118,800,000 for 1949–1965. This is estimated to be the highest per capita on record.

To this may be added a conservative figure of some $ 25,000,000 per annum (or $ 450,000,000 for 1948–1965) which the United States Government forfeited in the way of income tax on United Jewish Appeal contributions going to the Tel Aviv Government and which sums are, strictly speaking not being utilized for charitable purposes but to maintain a 'state'.

2. *United Jewish Appeal* – The funds raised *tax-free* by the United Jewish Appeal in the United States between 1946 and 1963, of which the bulk went to Israel, is said to have totalled $1,489,000,000. In addition, the Israelis conduct other private drives in the United States on behalf of Hadassah, the Hebrew University, Technion, Histadrut, the Weizmann Institute, etc., etc. These bring in tens of millions of dollars annually.

Disclosure of how part of these *tax-free* dollars is being used for profit-making, came to light in a publication of the American Council for Judaism. Under the title *Profit from U.S. Relief Funds,* the Council pointed out that "Few contributors to the United Jewish Appeal know that the Jewish Agency for Israel – recipient of 80% of UJA dollars going abroad – has IL. 150,763,332 invested in profit-making corporations. These 'relief' dollars go into El Al Airlines, Zim–Israel Navigation Co. and construction, agricultural and other firms operating on a profit basis. Last month" (September 1965), "S.Z. Shragai, head of the Jewish Agency's immigration department, offered British Zionists new apartments in Israel for $ 100 to $ 333 down, paying off the rest with a loan from the

Jewish Agency for 30 years at 6% . . ." [21]

Meanwhile, the Jewish National Fund – another veteran Zionist fund-raising mechanism operating in the United States – was accused of diverting relief funds for other profit-making ventures. This accusation was made by the *Jerusalem Post* (Israel) newspaper. It wrote: "The Jewish National Fund is diverting funds contributed by world Jewry for reclamation work into setting up joint contracting companies with private firms." It complained that "These companies receive the bulk of J.N.F. work – although their work is more expensive according to the managers of a large contracting firm." The Paper then comments that it was not known "if the J.N.F. was legally entitled to engage in private contracting, but pointed out that even if so, it was unethical to take donations from abroad and use it to set up such companies." [22]

Commenting on these *tax-free* donations, James Warburg, a prominent financier of the U.S. Jewish community, enquired: "Why should all contributions to the United Jewish Appeal be tax-deductible when so large a proportion of them flow directly or indirectly into the hands of a foreign government which openly engages in propaganda attempting to influence the policy of the Government of the United States?" [23]

Another comment on the methods used to obtain these *tax-free* 'donations' comes from the late Henry Hurwitz, a prominent Jewish writer. Hurwitz said: ". . . as is well known, a very large proportion of the supposedly *voluntary* philanthropic donations are extracted from business and professional men on threats of punitive economic and social sanctions. This must be described as what it is – a species of terrorism. Such terrorism has become a most effective technique in large Jewish fund-raising." [24]

In 1958, Senator E. Flanders of Vermont saw the dangers in Israeli policies in the Middle East and recognized that the funds which go to Israel from the United States in the form of charity are utilized for other than charitable causes. He therefore presented the Senate with a resolution in the following terms:

> "Whereas the unrest in the Arab world is caused primarily by the forcible occupation of Arab land by

the government of Israel; and
"Whereas the expansion of the population of Israel threatens an added seizure of Arab territory; and
"Whereas the over-population of Israel is largely financed by tax-free contributions from American citizens;
"Therefore, be it
"Resolved, that the Treasury investigate the uses to which tax-free contributions of American citizens are put when sent to Israel, to see whether they tend to exacerbate Middle East turmoil rather than relieve unavoidable distress to the end that the tax-free status may be justified or withdrawn." [25]

It was no surprise to see the failure of the draft resolution. Zionist influence in both Houses of Congress is too strong to permit the passage of any resolution detrimental to the interests of Israel!

3. *Sale of Israeli Bonds*:– Following the establishment of the state of Israel in 1948, the Israelis were granted the unique privilege of floating bond drives in the United States – a privilege not accorded to any other nation.

As a result, four Israeli bond issues have been floated since 1951: Independence Issue, Development Issue, Second Development Issue and Third Development Issue. Sales of the Third Development Issue began on March 1, 1964.

Floatation of the Independence Issue for a three-year period, from May 1954 to May 1957, resulted in sales of $ 145.5 million. The second issue, the Development Issue, was floated for a five-year period from 1954 to 1959 and resulted in sales of $ 234.1 million. Sales of the third issue were $ 293.7 million in 1964, the end of the five-year period of floatation. Sales of the fourth issue began on March 1, 1964; at the end of 1964 $ 72.8 million of this issuc had been sold.

From the inception of sales of bonds, in May 1951, through November 1964, $ 61.0 million worth of the bonds were surrendered in Israel for pounds by the Jewish Agency for Israel. In 1964, $ 5.2 million worth of bonds were received by UJA in payment of individual pledges. This was a decrease from the 1963 bond 'turn-ins' of $ 6.7 million.

The Third Development Issue provides that a bond must be held for a period of at least two years before a charitable institution may surrender it in Israel for Israeli pounds. As a result, these bonds may not be used in payment of pledges during this two-year period.

Redemption of the Twelve Year Dollar Savings Bonds of the Independence Issue began on May 1, 1963 and redemption of the Ten-Year Dollar Savings Bonds of the Development Issue began on April 1, 1964. The appreciated value of bonds of both issues maturing from May 1, 1963, to the end of 1964 is $ 66.8 million. This amount includes $ 29.5 million of Independence Issue Bonds which matured during 1964 and $ 13.6 million Development Issue Bonds which matured during 1964. [26]

Total sales for all bonds issued between 1951 and 1964 have exceeded the sum of $840 million by the end of 1965; the amount realized from the sale of bonds during 1965, amounted to $ 90.5 million. [27]

A substantial portion of the monies received by bond holders upon redemption of their matured bonds was reinvested in State of Israel bonds sold in 1963 and later years. [28]

Efforts are being made to maintain the present annual level of sales. Whereas the Israelis appear to meet their commitments in regard to the Bond Issues which mature, they are actually taking with the left hand what they hand out with the right! And so the vicious circle goes on.

Arab concern over United States aid to Israel is only in so far as it affects Arab rights and security. United States aid has encouraged the Israelis to follow a policy of defiance and intransigence and has given them the financial resources and the moral support for aggressive actions against the territories of the neighbouring Arab States.

It has been proved, beyond the shadow of a doubt, that the *tax-free* dollars – in addition to being used to influence United States policy-makers "to follow courses of action beneficial to special interests but with potentially catastrophic consequences for the nation as a whole," as Senator William Fulbright told the Senate in

September 1960 [29] – are being utilized to maintain one of the largest per capita aggressive military machine in the world, including the construction of a $ 700,000,000 nuclear reactor capable of producing an atom bomb. Failure of the U.S. Government to insist upon the separation of funds for charitable purposes from funds for a military build-up, may, ultimately, lead to disaster.

4. *West German 'reparations' to Israel* – American aid to Israel is not confined to the United States. Pressure was brought to bear on the West German Government in 1950 to share in responsibility for the maintenance of Israel's existence. At the time, the West German people were living under a cloud of the Nazi era; and, anxious to atone for Hitler's crimes against the Jews, the Bonn Government was willing to pay 'reparations' to the state of Israel if only Germany could be relieved of the 'guilt complex' under which it laboured and to absolve its future generations from blame.*

This German weakness was apparent and was exploited by both the United States - which had voluntarily assumed responsibility for Israel's well-being - and the Israelis who saw in West Germany the means to extract funds in order to consolidate their precarious existence. Consequently, in 1952, an agreement was concluded between the Bonn Government and the Israeli authorities whereby the latter, by 10 March 1966, had received in yearly instalments a total of 3,450 million Marks (about $862 million) in reparations.** [30]

If reparations could compensate for the crimes committed by

---

* Public opinion in Israel, it was reported, has made it clear, "no Israeli Government could permit itself the onus of absolving Germany from its moral debt to the Jewish people by tacit admission that relations with Bonn can now be pursued on a 'normal' basis." [31] Prime Minister Levi Eshkol, commenting on West German 'reparations' to Israel, said: "For us this is not reconciliation but only re-imbursement for a small part of the property plundered from the Jews of Europe during the Nazi era." [32]

** Claims have also been made on East Germany to pay 'reparations' to Israel. But, in the absence of the effectiveness of United States influence over that country, East Germany has flatly refused to respond.
Another source which attracted Israeli attention was Austria. Claims for 'reparations' have been proferred, but so far they have not been met.

the Nazis against humanity, then it would have been more appropriate and closer to reason for monies due to people who had died intestate to go to the Jewish communities of the countries from which the victims came to be used to re-establish the Jewish community which remained alive after the Nazi cataclysm, rather than to be paid to a 'state' which did not exist at the time the crimes were committed and to which the victims were not in any way related. The only link between the victims and the Israelis was Judaism and neither in international nor common law, does religion grant inheritance rights.

In 1960, with the end of the 1952 Agreement approaching and Israeli financial needs increasing, United States pressure was once again brought into play. A semi-secret agreement was reached between then Prime Minister David Ben Gurion and the late Chancellor Konrad Adanauer, both of whom were visiting in *New York*. The terms of the agreement were said – but later denied by the West German Government – to involve the payment by West Germany to Israel of $ 500,000,000 within ten years. The disclosure of the existence of the agreement resulted in the breaking off of diplomatic relations between ten Arab States and the Bonn Government, as the latter attempted to appease the Israeli Government by recognition and the exchange of ambassadors which actually took place in 1965. The Israelis were not satisfied with Bonn's new offers of aid and insisted on the fulfilment of the original agreement. Negotiations ensued and on 12 May 1966, agreement was finally, reached whereby Germany agreed to grant aid to Israel on a yearly basis, the first starting on 1 April 1966 with "a long-term credit of 160 million Marks (about $40 million)." Repayment to be made "up to twenty years with interest varying from zero to three per cent. The accord," it is said, "delays repayment up to seven years." [33] It is understood that a 'gentleman's agreement' was also agreed upon whereby the Israelis would receive from West Germany economic aid on an annual basis, each instalment to be decided on its merits.

In addition to what the state of Israel received from West Germany as its share of 'reparations' for Nazi crimes against the

Jews, individual indemnification was also made. According to the *New York Times,* in 1959 alone, "about $ 60,000,000 in individual restitution and indemnification payments have been sent to Israelis." The Paper estimated that "nearly 400,000 claims for individual damages have been filed by Israelis"; it disclosed that "since the first payments began in 1954, a total of $ 186,000,000 has been granted. At least $ 250,000,000 more is hoped for (in Israel) before the West German Government's programme is finished," the *New York Times* pointed out.

The Paper then explained that "the individual payments are made for personal injuries, for time spent in concentration camps, for loss of earning ability, or for loss of professional careers resulting from Nazi actions. They are also made for loss of personal and business property." [34]

It is reliably reported that the amount of indemnification paid out to individual Jews in Israel by the end of 1965 was in the neighbourhood of $525,000,000. However, Dr. Nahum Goldmann, President of the World Zionist Organization, disclosed, "about 12,000 million marks (about $ 3,000 million) still remain to be paid out on personal restitution claims." He asserted that he had discussed the matter with Israeli Finance Minister Pinhas Sapir and that a group of Israeli and West German experts were soon to meet to discuss ways of expediting the matter. [35]

The Arabs do not begrudge restitution or reparation being made to Jewish victims of Nazi beastiality. But they expect justice to be applied without discrimination. The Israelis – Government and people – who have received, and continue to receive, these benefits from West Germany, forget that they too owe a debt to the Palestine Arabs. Individual Palestine Arabs suffered atrocities and material losses at the hands of the Israelis, similar to those for which the Israelis are receiving compensation. One does not expect the Israelis to be so benevolent since they were the perpetrators of the crime, but the United States Government, which took so much interest in the welfare and well-being of the 'Jewish state', could have employed the same pressures on the Israelis it used on the Bonn Government.

Since the creation of the 'Jewish state', the Israelis have been receiving financial aid from the United States on an unprecedented scale in comparison to the size of its population or the extent of the territory of the country. Yet its annual trade deficit is reported to have exceeded, in 1965, $450,000,000 while every facet of its economy is heavily subsidized to enable its trade to enter foreign markets.

Israel's financial difficulties have been greatly aggravated since the fulfilment of the 'reparations' agreement with West Germany. Hence their concern to renew the arrangement with the Bonn Government on a permanent basis. Its replacement by 'economic aid' is not likely to alleviate Israel's precarious situation. Israeli leaders have therefore cautioned American Jewry that the 'state' will continue to need financial assistance at an increasing rate for many years to come. United Jewish Appeal Survey Missions from the United States visited Israel in 1965 and again in 1966 to consider the extent of financial aid needed to maintain the 'Jewish state'. Their initial conclusion was reported to be one of *grave concern.*

Aid through exploitation of Arab property

Another source of aid is through the exploitation of Arab refugee property in Israeli-occupied territory. By obstructing the appointment of a custodian to administer Arab property and paying the proceeds therefrom to the Arab owners who are now in refugee camps, the United States has provided the Israelis with an additional source of income, probably in the hope that they might some day become self-sufficient and so relieve the United States of part of its involvement.

It is difficult to estimate with any degree of accuracy what the capital value of Arab property in occupied Palestine is, or the annual income derived therefrom. But it is safe to say that the former runs into the billions of dollars and the annual income into the hundreds of millions of dollars. Arab losses in Palestine include agricultural lands, farmsteads, cattle, machinery, city properties, contents of private homes and business premises, motor vehicles, plants, etc. – in short, the patrimony of an entire nation. Some of these properties have been sold; others are leased annually; and the proceeds from both transactions are spent on the settlement of new Jewish immigrants of whom few were ever 'refugees'.

Israel's self-sufficiency

Despite all what the United States is doing for the 'Jewish state'; despite future German 'economic' aid; and despite the incomes derived from 'seized' Arab property, the Israeli effort to reach self-sufficiency in food production can never materialize. While they have been able, gradually, to bring under cultivation all confiscated cultivable land and claim annual increases in production, the saturation point is about to be reached. The marginal land remaining available capable of improvement is not as extensive as the Israelis would have one believe. The lands of the southern Negeb, comprising over half the territory of the Israeli-occupied part of Palestine, are mainly 'arid wilderness' and will continue to be so despite statements to the contrary. The *New York Times* confirms this view and describes the territory as "true desert", and remarks, "all the water in the world would not help." [36] It is therefore safe to say that neither now nor in the near or distant future will Israel's food production reach the level required to accommodate Israel's policy of unrestricted Jewish immigration.

The Israelis claim that they now produce 70% of their food needs. But this was the maximum which experts estimated during the British Mandate Palestine agricultural production could reach with highly improved methods and normal increases in population. This percentage will, however, soon begin to dwindle as more and more agricultural land is taken up for new housing schemes to accommodate the Jews lured into the Palestine 'ghetto' under the 'ingathering' policy and more and more mouths have to be fed.

The Israelis will shortly be faced with one of two alternatives. Either to limit or prohibit immigration altogether or to have another go at expansion into further Arab territory. The latter is the most likely to be attempted so long as United States favouritism towards Israel is what it is.

Even the optimist must regard the future of Israel in the Middle East with foreboding. For American Jewry, it means more and more money; for the Arabs, it means more tension, more danger, greater alterness and arming; and for the United States, it means the loss of much needed friends, more tension and greater instability in a vital and strategic oil-rich area of the Middle East, with all their consequences of graver dangers to United States interests, security and world peace.

Israelis sabotage American installations

Despite all what the United States has done and is still doing for Israel; and not content with what Zionist pressure groups are doing to influence U.S. foreign policy on Palestine in their favour, the Israelis resort also to criminal tactics to reach their goals.

The best illustration of Israel's attempt to sabotage American interests is in the events which precipitated what later became known as the *Lavon Affair*. This case will go down in history as one of the most despicable acts in international intrigue in modern times. The facts are:

In 1954, relations between the United States, Egypt and the rest of the Arab world were progressing steadily in a spirit of amicable cordiality. Cultural and economic agreements between the strategically located Arab World and the United States were under discussion. These developments irritated the Israelis who feared the possible loss of American moral and financial support of the 'Jewish state'. Zionist propaganda against the Arabs in the United States was deemed insufficient. It was felt that something dramatic had to be done to arouse the enmity of the American people against the Arabs. Consequently, an espionage ring was formed in Egypt, composed mainly of Egyptian Zionist Jews, with headquarters in Paris . *Its orders were to bomb official United States offices, burn United States Information Agency libraries and eventually attack American personnel working in Egypt.*

In November of that year, several bomb incidents took place against United States installations; in December, the Egyptian police luckily arrested the culprits red-handed. The ring-leader committed suicide, two agents were tried and condemned to death after they had confessed and the rest were sentenced to various terms of imprisonment.* [37]

It is distressing indeed that the press in the United States did not report on the incident. To do so, would have exposed Israel's vicious character and the dangers it poses to American interests and security in the Middle East. Israel, instead, continues to be pictured as the best friend the United States ever had in the Middle East.

Yet, when a group of Congolese and African students, opposed to Tshombe, attacked the U.S. library in Cairo in 1965, the American press was quick to condemn the deed as the responsibility of the United Arab Republic. Certain members of Congress expressed their hostility to President Nasser in no mild language and demanded that President Johnson should cut off the sale of surplus wheat to the U.A.R.

And when the U.A.R. took prompt measures to expel the African students who were responsible for the riot, apologized for the incident and offered (and the U.S. Government accepted) suitable accomodation on the Nile for the use of the library; while President Nasser, personally, contributed 1,000 volumes to the new library as a gesture of goodwill and regret, the American press did not see fit to consider the matter as 'news-worthy'.**

The impact of the Arab-Israeli conflict on Arab-American

* This incident should serve as reminder that ten years earlier, the Zionists in Palestine made a similar attempt to inflame British feelings against the Egyptians, when they sent their agents to Cairo to assassinate Secretary of State Lord Moyne, in November 1944. As fate would have it, the assassins in that case also, were caught and made to pay with their lives for their dastardly deed.

** The new library was opened on 3 October, 1965 – eleven months after its destruction – and the opening ceremony was attended by Egyptian Deputy Prime Minister for Culture, Dr. Mohammed Abdul Kader Hatem, as the relations can never be minimized or belittled. Arabs do sometimes ponder if American foreign policy regarding Palestine is developed and pursued on the basis of the merits of the question. On the basis of American interests and principles of justice and morality, or on aims primarily motivated by domestic political considerations. As long as the Arab-Israeli conflict is consistently introduced into American domestic politics, as long as American politicians continue to outbid each other in catering to the so-called 'Jewish vote', as long as American foreign policy-makers are subjected mercilessly to Zionist pressures whenever they want to make a move that might be contrary to the interests of Israel, Arab-American relations will continue to suffer and the prestige of the Communist bloc – among the masses in the Arab world at least - will find favour and be enhanced.

representative of President Nasser and by U.S. Ambassador Lucius D. Battle. In his address, Ambassador Battle "expressed thanks to President Nasser and the U.A.R. for making available the building for the library at the nimnial cost of one pound ($2.80) yearly until a permanent location for the library is found." [38]

XIV *Impact of Israel on Arab World*

The impact of the creation of the state of Israel on the Arab world and the dangers it poses to Arab territories and security, are not sufficiently recognized in international circles. Hence the Arabs are often accused of obstinacy and advised to be more realistic and reconcile themselves to the fact that Israel is there to stay and that they must learn to live with it.

The matter is not as simple as all that. It is not only what the Israelis have done so far in Palestine that worries the Arabs, but what they also plan to do in the future. The United States will not accept Red China and rejects any suggestion of co-existence because of the latter's record of aggression in trying to impose its ideology on other peoples. The United States regards Communism a threat to the American way of life and will fight to keep it out even from countries far removed from the American continent. The war in Vietnam is a case in point, as was Korea before it.

The Palestine problem is much more involved. It is not a case of fear of the imposition of an ideology foreign to the Arab way of life. Here strangers came and turned the Arab inhabitants out and took over their homeland and possessions. They established themselves into a state and talk of 'ingathering' all the Jews of the world into this small patch of territory as a first step towards their bid for a Zionist 'empire' to stretch from the 'Nile to the Euphrates'. They claim the land as part of their so-called ancient 'biblical' and 'historical' domain.

The Zionist programme, though generally known since the time of Herzl, has recently been confirmed through the publication by the U.S. State Department of certain confidential documents relating to the year 1943. In an on-the-spot report from the Middle East dated 3 May 1943, a personal representative of President Roosevelt, Patrick J. Hurley, was reported to have made the following statement to the President:

"For its part, the Zionist Organization in Palestine has indicated its commitment to an enlarged programme for:

1. a sovereign Jewish state which would embrace Palestine and probably Transjordania;
2. an eventual transfer of the Arab population from Palestine to Iraq; and
3. Jewish leadership for the whole Middle East in the fields of economic development and control." [1]

The first objective has been partly realized; the second has been mostly realized by expulsions and dispossession; and the third is fortunately blocked by the Arab States' determination not to recognize the state of Israel and to strengthen their economic blockade of the intruder.

It is indeed tragic to observe that the U.S. Government should have been aware, since 1943, of these Zionist machinations and yet to have lent support to Zionist policies towards Palestine at the United Nations and to the state of Israel after its formation, with its resultant damage to United States prestige and interests in the Middle East, not to mention the tension and instability it has created!

Jewish Immigration

'Ingathering of the exiles', the name for Israel's immigration, is a blend of nineteenth and twentieth-century immigration of economic origin with a semi-religious Messianic idea of redemption, based on the nationalistic assumption that all Jews the world over are 'exiles' and must, sooner or later, 'return' to their so-called historic 'Biblical' homeland.

In accordance with this ideology, or prophecy, which incidentally colours most policies of Israel, the Jewish Agency and the World Zionist movement began a feverish activity of transferring large numbers of Jews to Palestine territory from the time of the very inception of the State. The economic absorptive capacity of the country and the welfare of the immigrants, which are determining factors in most other immigration policies, were dismissed as of secondary importance. The primary purpose was to bring over as a matter of urgency, as many immigrants as possible in order to build the 'state'.

'Ingathering' began even before the formal establishment of the state of Israel with the illegal immigration from Europe to Palestine during the last years of World War II in defiance of the British Mandatory Power. The period of illegal immigration was followed after Israel was established by the big rush of Jewish refugees from German and Polish camps, which brought to the new 'state' approximately 350,000 Jewish immigrants during the years 1948-1950 and practically emptied all Jewish refugee camps in Europe. Since then, 'Ingathering' has lost its usefulness and humanitarian character and has become a political movement, kept alive by propaganda and by the desperate need of the Israeli Government to fill the vacuum created by the flight of the Palestine Arabs from their homes and to create a *fait accompli* of an occupied country.[2]

This Israeli policy of unlimited immigration, without regard to the absorptive capacity of the country, has raised the Jewish population of the Israeli-occupied part of Palestine from 650,000 in 1948 to 2,239,200 by the end of 1964 [3] and to over 2,500,000 in 1966.

The Arabs view this Jewish invasion of Palestine with grave concern because of the dangers it poses to adjacent Arab territories as a result of over-crowding. There are no signs of controlling it. On the contrary, every effort is being made to increase it. This is confirmed by the various statements made by the Israeli leaders from time to time. For example, in 1959, David Ben Gurion declared that "the right to exist, the power to exist and the motive for existence of the state of Israel lie in mass immigration." [4] The Director General of the Ministry of Defence, one of Ben Gurion's chief lieutenants at the time, in a speech delivered on Rumanian immigration, said: "The greater the population of Israel, the greater will be her army. A million soldiers will safeguard the state of Israel against any Arab attack. No Arab country will dare to attack Israel if her army will be a million strong." [5]

The entry of more immigrants into Palestine territory, coupled with the offensive policy of the Israeli leaders, constitutes the threat of permanent displacement for the Palestine Arabs – a situation which can only aggravate the Palestine problem and make a peaceful solution highly improbable.

Arab fears of Jewish immigration are not mere illusions but real. The dangers resulting therefrom were also foreseen by the late U.N. Mediator Count Bernadotte as far back as 1948. He reported to the Security Council shortly before his assassination, "It could not be ignored that unrestricted immigration to the Jewish area of Palestine might, over a period of years, give rise to a population pressure and to economic and political disturbances which would justify present Arab fears of ultimate Jewish expansion in the Near East." Bernadotte recognized at the time the dangers to Arab interests of Israel's unlimited immigration policy for he pointed out, "It can scarcely be ignored that Jewish immigration into the Jewish area of Palestine concerns not only the Jewish people and territory but also the neighbouring Arab world."[6] Despite this warning and Arab objections, the United Nations has not been moved to arrest this military build-up in the Middle East.

That this Jewish immigration is not an humanitarian movement is fully recognized. Moshe Menuhin, himself a Jew, is as puzzled as the Arabs about the alleged 'plight of Jews in other countries'. Commenting on a report by the New York Correspondent of the London *Jewish Chronicle* in its issue of December 13, 1963, that the 'tidal wave' of immigration to Israel and the plight of Jews in thirty other countries have pushed the fund raising targets to record levels, Menuhin enquires: "Who are these immigrants? Are they really persecuted Jewish refugees who are being rescued? If so, why don't we know something about them through the American newspapers? Or is it just plain Jewish man-power 'ingathered' into Israel to build up the 'Jewish homeland'?"

The author then points out that, "Originally, the problem of persecuted Jewish refugees in 1945-1948 – the problem of the victims of Nazi beastiality – '*had*' to remain unsolved, in order to insure the creation of the 'Jewish' state in Palestine in 1948.

Remember," Menuhin recalls, "the incredible story of President Roosevelt sending his friend Morris L. Ernst on a successful mission to England to persuade the British Government to take part of the displaced persons and then the outcry of Roosevelt : "Nothing doing on the programme... We can't put it over because the dominant vocal Jewish leadership of America won't stand for it'. Now it appears," he said, "that the 'problems' of the 'Jewish homeland' cannot be solved unless there takes place a forced draft of Western free-world immigrants for the 'ingathering of the exiles'." [7]

There are unfortunately people who, out of ignorance, follow the Zionist propaganda line and argue that the Jews have no place to go to and that Palestine is their only salvation. But, why do they have to go anywhere when one considers conditions in the world today? At no time since the downfall of Hitler have the Jews been more secure, enjoying equal rights and privileges with their fellow-citizens and generally exercising greater freedoms than they are at present. This belated recognition of human rights may be attributable in a large measure to the fact that the horrors of the Second World War have finally had their impact on human nature to abhor and reject persecution, oppression and discrimination against other people as a way of life. Consequently, religious persecution has now become something of the past; and racial discrimination in the few countries where it still exists is well on the way out.

That being the case, why should the Jews feel they must flee their homelands? Why do they need a 'refuge' and if so, now from whom? Was it through persecution in the United States that Golda Meir (former Israeli Foreign Minister) left her home in Wisconsin? Was it discrimination which made Abba Eban (Israeli Foreign Minister) leave his South African abode? Was it because of oppression that Walter Eytan (Director of the Foreign Office) fled England? None of these obviously occurred and no Jew who has reached the Palestine shores after 1945 can honestly say he fled from danger. It was only the greed for power of a small group of adventurers who cared little about what is good for the Jews, or other people, so long as they could establish a 'state' – a state which has turned out to be a second 'ghetto' in Palestine at the cost of great suffering to other people. The Talmudic quote ignored by the Israelis is so true:

"Woe to him that buildeth a town with blood
and establishes a city by iniquity!" [8]

Israeli Expansion

On the face of it, Zionism began with the seemingly innocuous objective of securing a *refuge* for the persecuted Jews of Europe. But when it obtained a foothold in Palestine, through the Balfour Declaration, it began to clamour for *statehood* and when it achieved this 'statehood', it began to plan for expansion.

The limits of *Eretz Israel* as loosely defined by the Zionist movement, coincide with the ancient biblical and historical boundaries of the so-called *Promised Land,* namely, from 'the Nile to the Euphrates' – to include the Sinai Peninsula, Jordan, Lebanon and parts of Syria, Iraq and even Saudi Arabia.

Each time the Arabs draw attention to the dangers to Arab territories of Israeli policies of expansion, they are met with an emphatic denial of any such intention. The Zionist-Israeli propaganda machine belittles the Arab accusation as a mere illusion and claims that all they now wish, after having robbed the Palestine Arabs of homes and property, is 'to live in peace with their Arab neighbours'.

The Arabs have never had any doubts of Zionist intentions in Palestine, they were always aware that these included, as a first step, the establishment of a 'Jewish state' to be followed by territorial expansion at a time of their own chosing. British officials in Palestine during the period of the Mandate also saw this very clearly. Even before the Mandate was announced, the Chief Military Administrator in Palestine saw fit to report to his Government that the Zionists "appear bent on committing the temporary military Administration to a partialist policy before the issue of the Mandate. It is manifestly impossible," the report continued, "to please partisans who officially claim nothing more than a 'National Home' but in reality will be satisfied with nothing less than a 'Jewish state'." [9]

Commenting on this report, Michel Ionides, who spent many years in the Middle East in the services of the Trans-Jordan and Iraqi Governments, said: "The Arabs were up against stiff odds. Officially, a Jewish state was not intended. The British Government had said so and the Zionists did nothing to remove that belief. The Arabs saw the tongue in the Zionist cheek, the British public did not." [10] Today the Arabs see a step further, the West does not.

From conversations the author had with leading Americans in the United States, he gathered the general impression that the U.S. Sixth Fleet was in the Mediterranean to protect Israel. One person who had spent two weeks with the Fleet in 1963, remarked, "the officers and men were anti-Israel because they did not see why they should roam the seas for the sake of Israel."

The Israelis held that the only way to have the Fleet withdrawn was to ensure that the Israelis become strong enough to look after themselves. To be able to be so, the Israelis are said to argue that they should be allowed to make certain boundary adjustments. These are:

(1) Occupation of the West Bank of the Jordan, this, they claim, would make it impossible for the Arabs to attack Israel from the east. At present, they say, they are vulnerable from every point where the Jordan hills overlook the Israeli plains. In the central sector, in case of conflict, the country could be split in two since the width of the 'state' was only ten miles.

(2) Occupation of the Gaza Strip and, if not the whole of the Sinai Peninsula, then at least that part which the Israelis had asked to be ceded to them in return for their withdrawal from Sinai in 1956. That strip was to run southward from El Arish to the Gulf of Aqaba thence to Sharm Esh-Sheikh. This territory, they argue, they require for colonization as a security measure, freedom of passage of Israeli shipping through the Strait of Tiran and eventually for the construction of a canal to parallel the Suez Canal.

(3) Occupation of those portions of Lebanese and Syrian

territory to include the headwaters of the River Jordan and a portion of the River Litani to ensure that Israel has an ample water supply for its development and progress.

If the Western world is naive enough to believe Zionist and Israeli statements, the Arabs – out of bitter experience – will not once again be fooled. The Zionists have always claimed that they wished to live in peace with the Arabs in Palestine where, they said, there was room for both peoples to live side by side; but events have shown that such 'peace' was dependant upon, not only the establishment of a 'Jewish state' in Palestine, but that the Palestine Arabs shall not be there to enjoy the promised 'peace' within their homeland but watch it from neighbouring Arab territories as *refugees.*

Now that the 'Jewish state' has been established, the Israelis once again hold out the 'olive branch', this time not to the Palestine Arabs but to the surrounding Arab States, in the hope that this false overture will be accepted until such time as they are ready to slice off a still further piece of Arab territory.

If Israeli denials of an expansionist policy are to be believed, how is one to reconcile between such denials and Israeli declarations, actions, and planning which confront the Arabs from time to time? Here are a few illustrations:

(1) *Mr. Ben Gurion,* writing in the Israeli Yearbooks, asserted that the state "has been resurrected in the western *part* of the land" of Israel and that independence has been reached "in *a part* of our small country." He added: "Every state consists of a land and a people. Israel is no exception, but it is a state identical neither with its land nor with its people. It has already been said that when the State was established, it held only six per cent of the Jewish people remaining alive after the Nazi cataclysm. It must now be said that it has been established in only *a portion of the Land of Israel.* Even those who are dubious as to the restoration of the historical frontiers, as fixed and crystallized from the beginning of time, will hardly deny the anomaly of the boundaries of the new State." [11]

(2) *David Ben Gurion*, on another occasion, stated: "I accept to form the Cabinet on one condition and that is, to utilize all

nature of the Problem. Furthermore, the armistice demarcation lines – which specify Arab–Israeli relationship – were not shown on the maps attached to the survey, to indicate how the Israeli reservoir and water-pipes would cut across the boundaries between the Arab and Jewish states under the United Nations Partition Plan of 1947. The 'proposal' regarded the political entities in the area as mere territories in a water–shed which were required to pool their energies and their water resources for the improvement of their economic conditions regardless of the political situation. In short, the Johnston 'proposal' concentrated chiefly on a solution of Israel's water problems to make possible the immigration and integration of several millions of new immigrants into the Negeb – thus consolidating Israel's economic and military power and enabling it to embark upon further expansion into neighbouring Arab territory. No consideration whatsoever was given to what was to become of the Palestine Arabs, whose lands the Israelis intended to irrigate under the Johnston 'proposal'. Under such circumstances, is it reasonable to expect the Arab States to acquiesce in such a one-sided scheme?

To augment their argument, the Israelis further claim that since Syria and Jordan were utilizing the waters of the Yarmuk River solely to Arab advantage, they have every right to divert the waters of the Jordan to whatever area they saw fit.

One important factor the Israelis fail to reveal. The Arab Yarmuk project is designed *not to divert* but to *put to better use* the waters of the River entirely *within* the river-bed in the Jordan Valley. Not one drop of water is being pumped out of the area and not one foot of Jewish-owned land is being deprived of its water. The Israeli project, on the other hand, takes away the Jordan waters *outside* the river-bed some 150 miles away to the Negeb and before the needs of Arab land in the Jordan Valley have been satisfied. Whereas the Arab action is logical and permissible under international law, the Israeli action is not.

A further argument the Israelis use to win public support, is that their plans are no more than a scheme to carry water from within Israel's own borders to irrigate 'the neglected parched and desert lands of the Negeb' – situated also within its own territory – that Arab opposition was unjustified and was merely designed to create trouble for Israel.

On the face of it, the Israeli approach might appear innocent. But apart from its irrigation aspects, the project has great political implications which can neither be ignored nor minimized. These are:

1- To utilize every tract of land and thus make it impossible for the Palestine Arabs to return to their homes and lands;
2- To make room for a greater influx of Jewish immigrants in order to provide the necessary manpower to expand further into Arab territory and realize the Zionist dream of an 'empire' from the 'Nile to the Euphrates';
3- To render ineffective all United Nations resolutions and directives on Palestine.

The Arab point of view is that Israel's diversion of the waters of the River Jordan is not a simple water project 'within its own borders' to irrigate land legally owned by Jews in Palestine, which the Arab States are attempting to obstruct by what some misinformed writers have described as a 'dog-in-the-manger' attitude. Much more is at stake than the public has been given to understand. The Israeli scheme involves the rights and property of individual Palestine Arabs who have been expelled and dispossessed of their lands by force of arms, as well as the rights and interests of Arab cultivators in the Jordan Valley.

The Arab States' refusal to participate with the Israelis in any irrigation scheme put forward by United States experts, or to acquiesce in Israel's present unilateral action, is basic and stems from the fact that the River Jordan project is an integral part of the Palestine Problem as a whole. It must be treated within an overall solution of that problem, not nibbled at, to serve the interests of Israel alone. *Any Arab agreement at this stage, will mean signing away the rights of the Palestine Arabs in their homeland and will be interpreted as an implied acceptance of the present armistice demarcation line as the permanent boundaries of Israel.*

Israeli tactics have, from time to time, attempted to obtain advantages by political pressures and influences outside an overall settlement of the Palestine Problem, such as passage of Israeli shipping through the Suez Canal and now a *de facto* recognition of the 'armistice demarcation lines' as the permanent boundaries of the 'Jewish State' once the River Jordan diversion project is agreed to. But Arab conviction has invariably held – and will continue to hold – that all of these matters are side issues of the main Palestine conflict and cannot be dealt with piecemeal. They are all part of the Palestine Arabs' right to their homeland. And until Arab rights are redeemed, the Arabs will not cease to oppose, with all the means at their disposal, any project which detrimentally affects the Palestine Arabs' rights and interests.

It will be recalled that the division of the waters of the River Jordan between the Arab States and Israel outside an overall solution of the Palestine Problem was regarded by the United Nations Economic Survey Mission as not feasible. The Survey Mission visited the Middle East in 1949 with the aim of examining the possibility of an economic approach to the Palestine Problem. In its recommendations, the Survey Mission had this to say about the development of the Jordan Valley:

> "In the absence of a peace settlement between Israel and adjoining countries on outstanding issues involving repatriation and compensation of Arab refugees and territorial boundaries, it is unrealistic to suppose that agreement on the complex question of international water rights could be negotiated among the parties... Whatever promise the full development of the Jordan River system may hold for better living and economic productivity in the Middle East, this must await a mutual desire to create and share benefits from a better use of waters now denied to all parties. Engineering, technical and financial assistance in this problem must assume peace and co-operation before men and money can be applied to the development of the Jordan River system as a whole." [17]

There is also one further reason which must not be lost sight of. The River Jordan has always had great sentimental and spiritual significance to mankind because of its association with the life of Christ and the Message of Salvation He brought to the world.

Never did it occur to anyone that this Biblical waterway which, since time immemorial, has brought inspiration, comfort and plenty to the people who lived along its banks, would one day become a source of irritation and strife. No one ever dreamed that its peaceful waters – the waters which were blessed by the First Baptism – would bring the spectre of war into the area.

"Diversion of the Jordan River waters," warned His Beatitude Orthodox Ecumenical Patriarch Athenagoras on 11 January, 1964, following his historic meeting in Jerusalem with His Holiness Pope Paul VI, "will be a source of grief and sorrow throughout the world. He told newsmen that "Orthodox Christians are gravely concerned over the diversion question and want the River in which Christ was baptized to continue its flow."

It should not only be the Orthodox Eastern Church that should feel concerned over what is happening, but the whole of Christendom must decry the desercration of one of its holiest shrines.

The Arabs – Moslems and Christians – are deeply affected by the Israeli action, not only by reason of the River's religious and historic significance, but also because of the material damage already suffered by the farmers of the Jordan Valley, whose very existence has been jeopardized and the dangers it presents to general Arab rights and security.

To sum up, Arab opposition to the Israeli Jordan River project rests on three fundamental factors:

1- The land on which the reservoir has been constructed, the territory through which the pipeline passes and the lands in the Negeb it proposes to irrigate, are all or mostly Arab-owned; *while parts of the scheme fall outside the territory allotted to the 'Jewish State' under the Partition Resolution and present Israeli occupation is subject to the provisions of the Armistice Agreements.*

   It should be noted that the U.N. Resolution establishing the state of Israel guaranteed the integrity of Arab rights and property. Section 8 of Chapter 2 distinctly stipulates that "no expropriation of land owned by an Arab in the possible means to expand towards the south." [12]

(3) *Moshe Dayan,* as Chief of Staff of the Israeli Army, declared: "It lies upon the people's shoulder to prepare for the war, but it lies upon the Israeli army to carry out the fight with the ultimate object of erecting the Israeli *Empire.*" [13]

(4) *Menahem Beigin,* Leader of the *Herut* Party: "I deeply believe in launching preventive war against the Arab States without further hesitation. By doing so, we will achieve two targets: firstly, the annihilation of the Arab power; and secondly, the expansion of our territory." [14]

(5) Another spokesman of the *Herut* Party, declared in New York in 1956: "Peace with the Arab countries is *impossible* with the present boundaries of Israel which leave Israel open to attack." He advised that "Israel should take the offensive immediately and capture strategic points along its border, including the Gaza Strip and then should take over the British backed Kingdom of Jordan." [15]

(6) *Dr. Chaim Weizmann,* President of the World Zionist Organization for most of three decades and first Israeli President, during his visit to Jerusalem on 1 December, 1948, told his audience: "Do not worry because part of Jerusalem is not now within the state. All will come to pass in peace. Again I counsel patience." He went on to say: "Fear not, my friends – the old synagogues will be rebuilt anew and the way to the Wailing Wall will be opened again. With your blood and sacrifices you have renewed the covenant of old. Jerusalem is ours by virtue of the blood which your sons shed defending it." [16]

Such statements, coming as they did from the Israeli leaders, can mean one thing and only one thing – Expansion! The Prime Minister refers to the '*state* of Israel' as established in 'a portion of the *Land* of Israel'; the Israeli Chief of Staff calls for a fight to establish 'the Israeli *Empire*'; and the *Herut* Party calls for the occupation of the Gaza Strip and the Hashemite Kingdom of Jordan.

The situation along the Israeli–Syrian armistice demarcation line at the time of writing is pregnant with danger. It has all the signs of Israeli plans for expansion, using the 'fedaiyeen' raids as an excuse. There are two reasons which make an imminent Israeli attack plausible: The first is that inter-Arab differences are at their highest and therefore the Arabs are presently weakest militarily to resist any thrust which the Israelis might make; and the second is that the 1968 United States presidential elections are approaching. The Israelis may feel that American Zionists are now strong enough to make the 'Jewish vote' a factor to prevent a repetition of United States interference to dislodge them, as President Eisenhower did in 1956.

The River Jordan

A further Israeli encroachment on Arab rights took place through the diversion of the waters of the River Jordan. The project, which cost some $150 million, took ten years to complete. Pumping started in August 1964.

The Israelis maintain that their project conforms in every respect with what became known as the *'Johnston Plan'*, and as such, is, in their view, permissible.

This is inaccurate. There is no such thing as a *'Johnston Plan'*. Mr. Johnston made it clear, when he first visited the Middle East, that it was not a 'plan', or even a 'scheme', he was submitting to the parties, but a mere *proposal,* "a broad conception," he said, "of what might be done, offered as a basis for discussion and negotiation." The 'proposal' suggested that 60% of the water should go to Lebanon, Syria and Jordan and the remaining 40% to the Israelis.

Mr. Johnston, as the emissary of President Eisenhower, was received by the Arab States and listened to with respect, befitting the position he held. But this does not mean that his 'proposal' was binding upon the Arabs. It was carefully considered and rejected, not only because of its technical deficiencies, but mainly because it attempted to liquidate the Palestine Problem by means of economic formulae and prescriptions. The cardinal sin of the proposal lay in the fact that it completely ignored the political

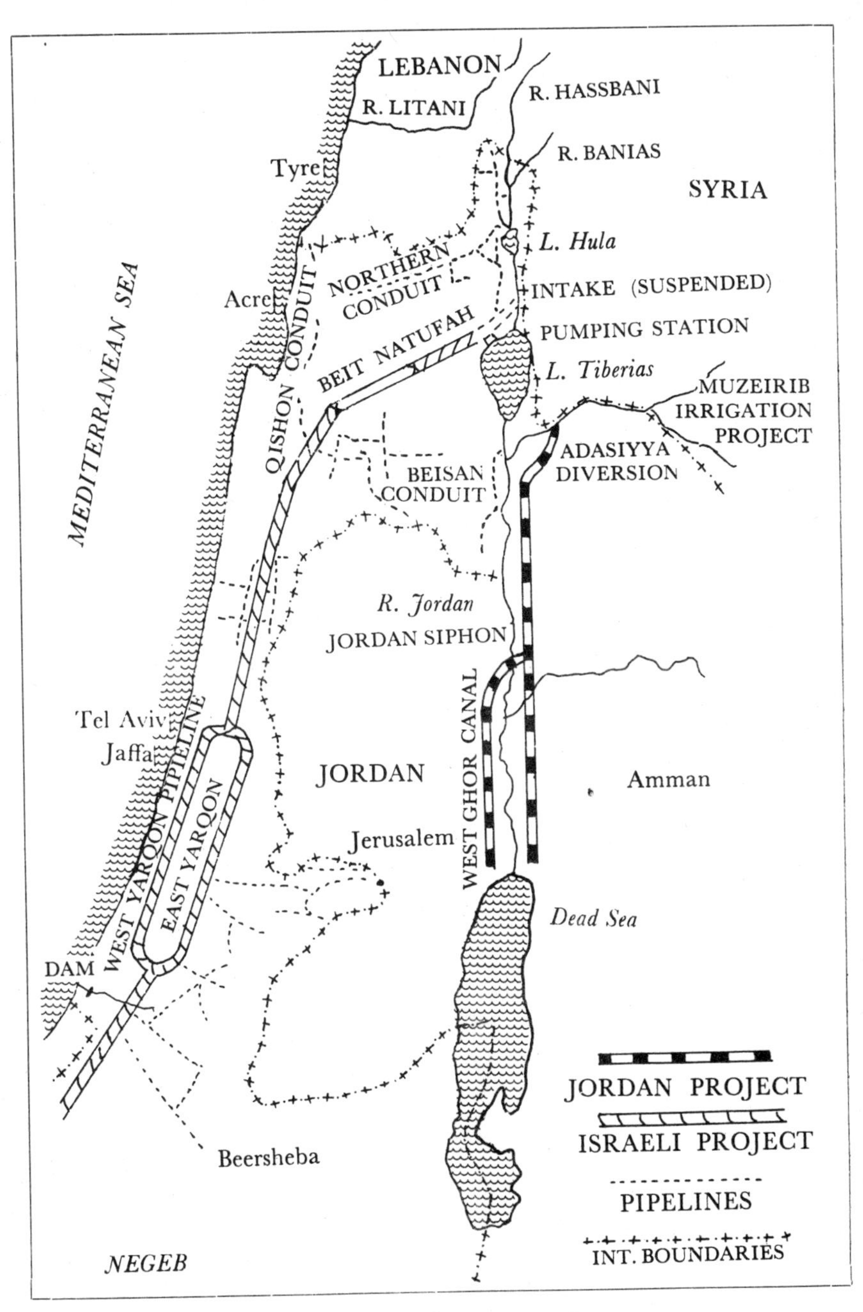

River Jordan Projects

'Jewish State' shall be allowed except for public purposes." The Section goes on to prescribe that "in all cases of expropriation full compensation as fixed by the Supreme Court shall be paid previous to dispossession."

The Israelis have neither justly 'expropriated' the land nor offered or paid the Arab owners 'compensation as fixed by the Supreme Court.' They simply *seized* it.

On the other hand, the Armistice Agreements preclude the parties from acquiring any benefits from the armistice. It is prescribed that "no provision of this Agreement shall in any way prejudice the rights, claims and positions of either Party hereto in the ultimate peaceful settlement of the Palestine question, the provisions of this Agreement being dictated exclusively by military and not by political, considerations."

It will, therefore, be seen that the Israelis are not free to carry out projects of a permanent nature in territory outside the boundaries of the 'Jewish state', as delineated in the Partition Plan and now held under Armistice Agreements. Since Israel's unilateral action does 'prejudice the rights, claims and positions' of the Palestine Arab land-owners and gives the Israelis a military advantage through increased immigration and in other ways, it is in direct violation of the provisions of the Agreements.

2- The main waters of the River Jordan originate in Lebanon and Syria; and beyond the Sea of Galilee, the River forms the boundary between Palestine and Jordan. Its waters have been used from time immemorial to cultivate lands in the Jordan Valley and not beyond.

Removal of water from within the Israeli-occupied part of Palestine for irrigation of land not in the immediate vicinity of the river-bed but some 150 miles away, has deprived the Arab cultivators in the Jordan Valley of their sustenance, has increased salinity and with a depleted flow, if not cut off altogether, will dry up the Dead Sea within a period of from 70 to 100 years.

According to Oppenheim, a leading jurist in international law, "the flow of ... international rivers is not within the arbitrary power of one of the riparian states, for it is a rule of International Law that no state is allowed to alter the natural conditions of its own territory to the disadvantage of the natural conditions of the territory of a neighbouring state. For this reason, a state is not only forbidden to stop or divert the flow of a river which runs from its own to a neighbouring state, but likewise to make such use of the water of the river as either causes danger to the neighbouring state or prevents it from making proper use of the flow of the river on its part." [18]

3- Israeli sources declare, the River Jordan project is intended to provide space for new Jewish immigrants. The entry of more immigrants into Palestine constitutes a serious threat of permanent displacement of the Palestine Arabs – a situation which can only aggravate the Palestine controversy.

To meet the new Israeli threat, Arab kings and heads of state met thrice in summit conferences to consider the dangerous situation arising out of the Israeli action and the steps to be taken to safeguard Arab rights and interests. Among the measures adopted was a decision to implement recommendations of the League of Arab States to utilize, to Arab advantage, the headwaters of the River Jordan, which originate in Lebanon and Syria. Underlying the Arab Summit decisions were two major considerations:

The *first*, of a positive nature, seeking to benefit the Arab riparians in Lebanon, Syria and Jordan whose right to utilize their own waters, on their own soil, has priority over whatever new claim another party may put forward. The *second*, a negative one, is to deny the Israelis – regarded as an alien and aggressive creation whose alleged title to Palestine is derived from military conquest – the use of Arab waters which would consolidate further their hold over Arab lands in occupied Palestine and increase their potential to undertake new military adventures in neighbouring Arab countries.

The implementation of the Arab plans have been postponed; but this postponement does not mean that the Arabs are going to sit back and allow their rights to be infringed upon and their future security threatened. The Israelis claim to be within their rights in diverting the waters of the Jordan within the territory under their control. By the same logic, the Arabs believe they have every right to take whatever measures they deem necessary to utilize, for the benefit of Arab lands, the headwaters of the River Jordan which originate in Lebanon and Syria.

The Israelis have threatened that if the headwaters of the River Jordan are tampered with, they will regard this as a provocation and go to war. If war does come to the Middle East, it will be the Israelis, not the Arab States, who will have started it. Responsibility will then rest on the shoulders of the United Nations and those Powers which have encouraged the Israelis in their present dangerous venture.

The possibility of war may have been averted for the present, but certainly not eliminated. The dangers grow closer as the Israelis move from one encroachment to another without consideration of risks. Pinhas Sapir, the Israeli Finance Minister, discloses that "in addition to irrigation, the plan provides at a later stage for the generation of hydro-electric power. This," he says, "is to be derived from a canal connecting the Mediterranean (near Haifa) with the Dead Sea and utilizing the drop of 390 metres between the two seas to drive the power turbines. This canal" the writer states, "would also compensate the Dead Sea for the diversion of the Jordan into the irrigation system." He points out that "this hydro-electric scheme has already emerged from the stage of theoretical speculation into the more tangible form of engineering calculations and design."

Sapir then explains that the "preliminary studies for the scheme have been prepared for the Water Planning Authority of Israel by Messers Hayes and Cotton who have wide experience of similar engineering projects in the United States. According to their calculations, the scheme could ultimately generate 1,500,000,000 Kwh. per year. In their opinion this is an eminently sound practical enterprise both from the engineering and economic points of view. With this abundant and cheap source of power to drive the irrigation pumps and turn the wheels of industry, the country could rapidly advance to a new era of prosperity," it is claimed. [19]

From a development point of view, the scheme may look innocent, feasible and profitable. But such unilateral action without consideration to what damage may occur to the interests of others, is fraught with grave dangers. It must be noted that once the salt waters of the Mediterranean have done their job of generating electricity for Israel, they will enter Arab lands and Arab territory and destroy what little sweet water remains in the Jordan Valley for use by the Arab farmers on both banks of the River. That the Arab States would be willing to accept this new aggression without taking measures to protect their lands is doubtful.

The Arab boycott

One of the most misunderstood aspects of the Palestine Problem is the Arab boycott of the state of Israel. From time to time, the Zionists launch campaigns to distort and misconstrue this legitimate weapon of self-defence, in order to undermine economic relations between foreign companies and Arab countries and to disrupt friendly relations between the Arabs and other countries. These Zionist sources have spread the myth that the Arab boycott is 'anti-Semitic' in purpose and intent, applied on purely emotional and prejudicial grounds, nothing could be further from the truth.

The Arab boycott of Israel – launched by the League of Arab States in May 1951 – is basically a defensive measure, worldwide in its scope and not limited to any one country. It seeks to protect the Arab States from the threat of Israeli expansion and to prevent the domination of international Zionist capital over Arab national economy. The boycott is legitimate, legal and peaceful; *it is not directed against Jews because they are Jews*. In a way, the Arab boycott of Israel may be compared with the United States boycott of Cuba, even though the dangers Cuba presents to United States interests and security are not as great as those the Israelis pose to Arab rights, security and interests.

The Arab States have officially affirmed that they will never discriminate against Jewish individuals or firms which respect the Arab boycott against Israel. A statement issued by the General Union of the Arab Chambers of Commerce, Industry and Agriculture reaffirms this position in the following words:

> "The Arab boycott is directed against *Israel* , but *not* against the Jewish people. Indeed, there are many Jewish citizens living in most of the Arab States who are unmolested and prosperous.
>
> "Jewish firms outside Israel receive from the Arabs the same treatment as non-Jewish firms. There is no discrimination. Any firms, irrespective of the creed or race of its owners, shareholders, or managers will be able to deal with the Arab countries, so long as it does not breach the regulations of the Arab boycott of Israel."

The purpose of the Arab boycott is to limit the economic power of a state with avowed plans to expand at the expense of Arab territory and Arab interests.

Because of Israel's continuing acts of outright aggression, the Arab States have found it imperative to maintain and strengthen an economic boycott against Israel as an elementary measure of self-defence. The Arab boycott applies to the firms – regardless of their nationality – which engage in the following practices:

1. Firms which have branch factories in Israel.
2. Firms which have assembly plants in Israel, or firms whose agents assemble their products in Israel.
3. Firms which have agencies or main offices in Israel for their Middle Eastern operations.
4. Firms which give patents, trade marks, copyrights, etc., to Israeli companies.
5. Firms (and private or public organizations) which purchase shares in Israeli companies or factories.

6. Technical or consultant firms which offer their services to Israel.
7. Airplanes which fly to Israel. These planes may not fly in air space over Arab territory.

The boycott of firms which bolster Israel, militarily or economically, is within the accepted principles and practices of international law. Trade is a contract and a contract is the law which binds two parties. According to the principles of free will, each party to a contract has the right to specify conditions and terms and it is the right of the other party to accept or reject them as it sees fit. In such a situation, it cannot be said that either party has exerted pressure or force, nor can it be said that the contract constitutes interference in the internal affairs of any foreign country.

The Arab States do not wish to undermine the interests of any foreign firm or its investors. They immediately get in touch with any firm reported to have dealings with Israel in order to obtain clarification with regard to the nature and extent of these dealings. If the dealings are of a purely commercial nature, the subject is immediately closed. If the association tends *to strengthen Israel economically and to bolster its military potential,* the firm in question is informed that its dealings with Israel are detrimental to the interests and security of the Arab States. The firm is also informed that the laws of the Arab States forbid dealing with it because a state of war exists between Israel and the Arab countries. The firm is then free to decide whether it wants to deal with the Arab States and terminate its association with Israel, or to terminate its relations with the Arab States.

One other false accusation levelled against the Arabs is that the Saudi Arabian Government prohibits the entry of Americans of the Jewish faith into its country. On 13 August, 1956, the Saudi Arabian Embassy in Washington, D.C., issued the following statement clarifying its position with regard to the entry of Americans of the Jewish faith into Saudi Arabia:

> "The Saudi Arabian Government, it must be made clear, does not discriminate against anybody on the basis of race, colour, or creed. *The fact is that only Zionists – regardless of their faith or*

nationality – are not permitted entry into Saudi Arabia. Indeed, American non-Zionist Jews have been welcomed into the country. The attitude of the Saudi Arabian Government toward Zionists is dictated by considerations of national security and safety."

Little or no publicity was given to this declaration. The public remained uninformed, as the Zionist propaganda machine continues its attacks depicting that Saudi Arabia discriminates against 'Americans of the Jewish faith'.

These Saudi Arabian security measures are not alien to the United States Government, which refuses admission to persons who are, or ever were, members of a Communist party, irrespective of their religion or nationality. This is a sovereign right that cannot be questioned.

Ben Gurion's statement that "when a Jew in America or South Africa speaks of 'our government' to his 'fellow Jews', he usually means the government of Israel; while the Jewish public in various countries view the Israeli ambassador as their own representative,"[20] justifies Saudi Arabia's policy of baring Zionists from its country. World Jewry has not denied the Israeli claim and it is not for the Arabs to disavow it.

Writing in the *Jewish Newsletter* (New York), Elias Koussa, a Christian Arab living in Haifa, drew a parallel between the treatment of the Arab minority and Zionist protests against the non-employment of Zionist-Jews by ARAMCO (Arabian-American Oil Co.) when he said: "It is surprising how the American Zionists strongly oppose discrimination by Aramco against the Jews and yet enthusiastically support, or at least acquiesce, in the discrimination exercised by Israel against its Arab citizens. For the last eleven years, they have been suffering from serious discriminatory practices by the military rule imposed on racial grounds, in all areas predominantly inhabited by Arabs."

He went on to say: "the usual explanation put forth by the responsible leaders, Israelis and Zionists, for the imposition and preservation of the rule, is that it is a security precaution necessitated by the atmosphere of enmity surrounding the country."

Koussa, however, points out that "assuming the explanation is genuine and correct, it is, *a fortiori,* a stronger justification for the Saudi policy of excluding Jews from employment by ARAMCO, "because a state of war still exists between Saudi Arabia and Israel." He added, "It is thus reasonable to infer that in the view of these American propagandists, discrimination is permissible and lawful when exercised against the Arabs, objectionable and undemocratic when applied to the Jews. But what is sauce for the goose is sauce for the gander."

The Haifa advocate concludes by remarking: "Ironically enough, the boycott of which the American Zionists and Israel complain with much ado, is a weapon which the Arabs learned from the Zionist Jews themselves. It was first invoked during the mandatory regime by the Jewish Agency, the Keren Kayemeth, the Keren Hayesod, the Histadruth and by nearly every Jewish institution of importance, e.g., the Palestine Electric Corporation and the Anglo-Palestine Bank, etc. In these political and commercial organizations, it was a rule of procedure that no Arab should be employed. The Jews considered the boycott fully justified and lawful. Now it has become unlawful and undemocratic because it is being used by the Arabs against the Jews. Such is the sense of American Zionists!" [21]

Those who condemn the Arab boycott of Israel, would do well to recall the Zionist boycott of Hitlerite Germany which began in 1933 – shortly after Hitler came to power. A leading American Zionist, broadcasting from New York, described the Zionist campaign of boycott against Germany as "two-fold – defensive and constructive." He said, "What we are proposing and have already gone far towards doing, is to prosecute a purely defensive economic boycott that will undermine the Hitler regime and bring the German people to their senses by destroying their export trade on which their very existence depends." He went on to say, "Each of you, Jew and Gentile alike, who has not already enlisted in this sacred war should do so now and here. It is not sufficient that you buy no goods made in Germany. You must refuse to deal with any merchant or shopkeeper who sells any German-made goods or who patronizes German ships or shipping." He concluded by asking his audience of Jews and millions of non-Jewish friends to help "drive the last nail in the coffin of bigotry and fanaticism that has dared raise its ugly head to slander, belie and disgrace twentieth century civilization." [22]

Whereas Hitler had, in 1933, not yet committed any atrocities against the Jews, the Arab boycott came into operation in 1951, after the Israelis had, in 1948, committed massacres, atrocities explusions and dispossessions against the Palestine Arabs. It should be noted that Arab boycott objectives are no different to the early Zionist objectives, namely, they are "defensive and constructive," intended to "undermine the (Israeli) regime ... by destroying their export trade on which their very existence depends."

XV Peace or War

It can be safely deduced from the preceding Chapters that all efforts to settle the Palestine Problem peacefully have failed. The Israelis, who have taken everything, persist in their refusal to give back anything; and the Palestine Arabs, who have lost everything, are not prepared to forego any of their natural rights. Consequently, the matter stands deadlocked.

The United Nations, on the other hand, has shelved the issue among its 'chronic' problems. It now intervenes only when a border incident occurs, or to vote annual funds to maintain the hapless victims of the tragedy in refugee camps. This laxity on the part of the World Body to shoulder its responsibilities, has stiffened Israeli policy into the attitude: "All that we have taken we shall hold." [1]

The passage of time will not obliterate the rights of the individual to home, property and country. These rights are recognized as a sacred trust; and provision for their respect has been incorporated in the Universal Declaration of Human Rights and accepted by almost all nations. Furthermore, the will of the majority and its right to self-determination form the corner-stone of the United Nations Charter.

Thus, when U.N. Mediator Count Bernadotte reported to the General Assembly in 1948, "no settlement can be just and complete if recognition is not accorded to the right of the Arab refugee to return to the home from which he has been dislodged..." [2] he was merely reminding the World Organization of its solemn duty under its own instruments; and when British historian Arnold Toynbee pointed out that justice for Palestine demands "the vindication of people's rights and the righting of their wrongs..." [3] he was also explaining to the Great Powers what is expected of them.

These laudable principles of justice and protection of human rights are annually applauded in speeches from the rostrum of the

United Nations and in high official declarations. But when it comes to applying them equally to all mankind, the prejudice and vested interests of the strong against the weak become apparent. Such was the case in Palestine. Those Powers which laid down the rule of freedom and equality for all peoples, were the first to break it; and those who screamed loudest in support of the right of self-determination for certain European countries, were the first to suppress it in Palestine.

There are people who deplore the Palestine tragedy on humanitarian grounds and also see in it a threat to world peace. Some of them point out that it is the responsibility of the United Nations and they urge for implementation of its resolutions with determination and courage; others consider Israel should be pressured to take back if only a token number of refugees as a gesture of her goodwill; and others still feel that a bi-national state might be the answer to a settlement and peace. None of these proposals found any response because the Israelis are unwilling to accept any compromise short of the *status quo* – the rule of the accomplished fact.

Israel's peace offers

It is not the call to negotiate peace that will bring peace, but the earnest will and honest acceptance of the principles on which peace can be negotiated. In the case of Palestine, these principles are:

1. That it must be admitted that a grave injustice has been committed against the people of Palestine;
2. That the community of nations must recognize its responsibility in this and that it must fulfill those responsibilities whatever the consequences;
3. That measures to redress the wrong and correct the injustice must be taken.

Israel's offers for peace with the Arabs do not fulfill any of these requirements. As such, they have been rightly described as "far from real peace as blatant propaganda is from the truth. It has been shouted so loudly and so often by Ben Gurion and other Israeli leaders since 1948, that it is well on the way to becoming a *cliché* of the century." [4]

Ironically, the Israelis will, as occasion demands, shed crocodile tears over the plight of the Palestine Arab refugees, giving the impression that they too feel concern over down-trodden and distressed people. This display of false sympathy was voiced in an *Editorial* published in the Israeli English-language semi-official newspaper, the *Jerusalem Post,* on the occasion of consideration of the Report of the Commissioner-General of the United Nations Relief and Works Agency for Palestine. The *Editorial* stated: "Next to the Arab refugee populations themselves, who continue to labour under so many disabilities in the Arab countries in which they have been living for almost eighteen years, probably nobody is as interested in seeing their problem finally solved as the State and Government of Israel." The writer then points out, "There is, first of all, a human responsibility for disrupted lives, a condition with which every generation of Jews has been painfully familiar and also a national responsibility . . ." [5]

If the Israelis were truly sincere in their expressions of concern over the 'disrupted lives' of the Palestine Arab refugees, why do they not begin by doing something to alleviate the sufferings they had inflicted upon them? The Israelis occupy and exploit their property and have plundered their possessions; they refuse even to turn over to them the rents and profits derived from Arab property and homes, pending a final settlement. Instead they allow them to rot in refugee camps for nearly two decades on the charity of the United Nations. Even towards that charity they will not contribute a cent.

Material benefits are certainly not what the Arabs of Palestine want. But a genuine and tangible expression of regret through material restitution is one way towards reducing hatred and bitterness between people and creating a congenial atmosphere for compromise.

It has, however, been established that peace is not the Israeli objective. Each time the Israelis talk about peace, they do so in the hope that the Arab States will be lulled into a false sense of security and then attack them. To illustrate:

1. On 9 January, 1952, Aba Eban told the United Nations: "... the Arab and Israel peoples, united by so many bonds ... may yet make this region the scene of civilization worthy of its ancient and medieval past."
   On 28 January, the Jordan villages of *Falama* and *Rantis* were attacked.
2. On 28 September, 1953, Aba Eban told the United Nations: "My Government continues to uphold the vision of the Middle East at peace within itself, uniting the efforts of its two kindred peoples to heal the wounds of aggressive violence ..."
   On 14 October, the brutal attack on *Qibya* took place where 42 civilians were killed, 4 men and 38 women and children were wounded and a mosque, school and 40 houses destroyed.
3. On 11 December, 1953, then Foreign Minister the late Moshe Sharett, declared: "There is also a major problem of our relations with the Arab States around us. All I can say on this is that the conclusion of permanent peace between us depends on them alone – on our part we are always ready for it."
   On 28 March, 1954, the Jordan village of *Nahhalin* was attacked under circumstances similar to those at *Qibya*.
4. In January 1955, Moshe Dayan, then Chief of Staff of the Israeli forces, said : "Israel has no aggressive designs against her neighbours."
   On 28 February, an attack was made on *Gaza* in which 38 persons were killed and 31 wounded.
5. On 14 August, 1955, Ben Gurion declared: "We must faithfully observe the conditions of the Armistice Agreements ... We must ... strive incessantly for relations of peace between Israel and the Arab States."
   On 31 August, *Khan Yunis* and *Bani Suheila,* in the Gaza Strip, were attacked and the 'Demilitarized Zone' was occupied.

6. On 21 March, 1956, Moshe Sharett said: "... since the summer of 1948, we have made one attempt after another to induce our neighbours to enter into negotiations with us that might lead to a peace settlement."
   In April, *Deir El-Balah, Gaza* and *Khan Yunis* were attacked, 59 civilians were killed and 102 wounded.
7. On 2 July, 1956, Golda Meir said: "I should like to survey some of the basic considerations that guide our foreign policy. First and foremost comes peace; ... Our policy has ... always been one of peace."
   On 10 October, the village of *Qalqilya,* in Jordan was attacked; and
   On 29 October, the invasion of the *Sinai Peninsula* began.

The Israelis may want peace, but they want this peace on their own terms. These include:

The abrogation of all United Nations Resolutions on Palestine where they favour the Palestine Arabs;

Legalization of the crime of exiling and dispossessing an entire nation;

Resettlement of the Palestine Arabs in Arab countries;

Recognition of Israel as a sovereign state with the present 'armistice demarcation lines' as its permanent boundaries for the time being;

Removal of the Arab boycott and the prohibition of passage of Israeli shipping through the Suez Canal.

Do the Israelis really expect the Arabs to be so naive as to accept such conditions? Or that serious-minded people in the world could consider peace on such terms as logical, feasible and just? Are they not the terms of unconditional surrender?

Under such circumstances and in the light of past experience, the Arabs regard these Israeli 'peace offers' as dishonest and inconsistent with justice and reason, not worthy of any consideration.

Arab Attitude

The establishment of the state of Israel has created tension and instability in the Middle East in three ways:

1. It created a refugee problem of over one million people who have added greatly to the existing social, economic and political difficulties of adjacent Arab countries. So long as a wronged people remain deprived of their elemental rights in homes and country, they will continue to be a source of danger in the countries they inhabit and will serve as fertile soil for subversion and unrest. If conditions appear quiet in refugee camps, it is only because of the stringent measures adopted by the host governments and the refugees' dependence on the Arab States to do all they can to regain for them their usurped rights in their homeland.
2. The creation of the state of Israel in the heart of the Arab World has severed the territorial continuity of the region – thus cutting off land communication between Arab territories in Asia from those in Africa and making contact between them more difficult.
3. Israel has already provided adequate proof of its aggressive intentions by its periodical attacks and annexations of territory beyond that assigned to the 'Jewish state' under the Partition Plan. Its invasion of Egypt, in 1956, in an attempt to annex the Sinai Peninsula, makes it highly imperative for the Arab States to keep themselves well armed and alert at all times.

The Arab States cannot be accused of having at any time repudiated their obligations as members of the United Nations. They continued to abide by their undertakings under the 'Lausanne Protocol' of 1949. But Israeli obstinacy since that date has convinced the Arab States that nothing can be gained through either the Palestine Conciliation Commission or by direct negotiation. The Arab position was clearly explained by President Nasser during a televised interview with the Chief Correspondent of the Canadian Broadcasting and Television Service in 1960 and has not altered since. The President said:

> "The whole (Arab-Israeli) issue has been in the hands of the United Nations for years. Israel's answer to the question was the explusion of more than one million Arabs from their homes in 1948 and repeated violation

> of all resolutions made by the United Nations calling for the restoration to the Palestine Arabs of their usurped rights."

Asked whether negotiations could serve a useful purpose, the President pointed out that negotiations were impossible, "for, in the first place, the Israeli aggressions against Arab lands and Arab rights still continue, while the leaders of Israel have shown no signs of repentance. In the second place, we do not trust the leaders of Israel. A few days before Egypt was attacked in 1956, the Israeli Premier declared in the Knesseth that he was willing to fly to meet me for the sake of peace, while at that particular moment he was up to his ears in preparation for the tripartite aggression on our country."

The chances of Arab recognition of the state of Israel simply do not exist now, or in the future. To understand this Arab attitude former U.S. Ambassador to the U.A.R. Dr. John S. Badeau has put it this way:

> "This is not too different from the American attitude toward China, for we refuse to admit diplomatically the *de facto* existence of Red China. This has become an emotional issue in American life; and the suggestion . . . that steps might be taken toward recognition, was criticized not only on political grounds, but much more on moral grounds. The suggestion was even made that these were irresponsible 'pink-tinged Americans' because they insisted on raising the issue of Red China.
>
> "I find that the Arab reaction to Israel becomes understandable in terms of the American experience." [6]

The Arab States have ultimately reached the conclusion that any salvation for Palestine must come primarily through the efforts and sacrifices of the Palestine Arabs themselves. Arab kings and heads of state, meeting in their first Summit Conference in January 1964, finally acquiesced in the Palestine Arabs' demand to be allowed to organize themselves and to plan their own strategy for the liberation of their homeland. They also decided to give the Palestine Arabs every support and assistance.

A Palestine Liberation Organization was then formed and entrusted with the task of mobolizing the People of Palestine in their forth-coming struggle to liberate their homeland. According to the approved Constitution, the liberation of Palestine is deemed to be a defensive measure, necessitated by the needs of self-defence – a right provided for and upheld in the Charter of the United Nations. The Organization has declared its readiness to befriend all nations that love freedom, justice and peace; and urges all such nations to support and assist the People of Palestine in their struggle to restore what legitimately belongs to them in their own country and to enable them to exercise their national sovereignty and freedom.

The Israelis have charged that these objectives are aggressive, aimed at the sovereignty of the state of Israel; they protested to the United Nations, describing them as a source of danger to Israeli security.

If the term 'aggression' can be applied to the aims of an Organization which calls for regaining what rightfully belongs to the Palestine Arabs and what was taken from them by force of arms, the Arabs believe that the same definition would be a mild way to describe the Zionist invasion of Palestine by alien Jews who had never lived or even seen Palestine before; the massacres and atrocities committed against the Palestine Arabs; and the explusions and dispossession of those who had lived and owned its soil for centuries.

Those who condoned Zionist methods in Palestine in ousting the original Arab inhabitants, must be equally prepared to justify the employment of similar methods to dislodge those who usurped Arab rights, property and interests. They must also be prepared to admit the propriety of Arab application to the Israelis of Ben Gurion's formula of conquest – "Force of arms, not formal resolutions will determine the issue."

Every Palestine Arab – Moslem and Christian, old and young – is behind the aims of the Palestine Liberation Organization. Nothing short of full rights in homes and country is acceptable. The Palestine Arabs have waited for two decades to regain their rights; they are prepared to go on waiting for their day of deliverance.

To understand the attitude of the individual Arab toward peace with Israel, a young refugee girl aptly expressed it in a Christmas Message to the world from Jerusalem in these words:

"We believe in Peace,
We support Peace;
But we will not 'make' Peace.
We were never the aggressors;
We were the victims.
We cannot make Peace
With the very enemies of Peace." [7]

Conclusion

In the final analysis, Israeli obstinacy and United Nations impotence to administer justice to the Palestine Arabs, drives one to the conclusion that war over Palestine has become inevitable. People cannot be left, from one generation to another, to rot in refugee camps with the constant threat from the United States that relief measures cannot go on for ever; nor can the Arab states continue to be dressed in armour because of the aggressive element which has been planted in their midst, watching and waiting for the opportunity to detach more territory from the Arab homeland.

The surest way toward a solution short of war is for the Powers which created the Problem in the first instance to take the same road with the same enthusiasm and zeal and return both Arabs and Jews to their own homelands.

Some consider this course impracticable and costly. But it will prove in the long run more sensible and less costly than war. Zionist opposition to such a move will no doubt be violent. This can be overcome more easily than many think. The state of Israel has been maintained by monies from abroad. Withhold such funds until the Israeli leaders submit to reason; and then utilize the funds to settle the Jews in happier environments.

As things stand at present, conditions in Israel are not as rosy as the Zionists paint them. Strong differences exist between the Ashkenazi and Sephardic communities which indicate that religion alone is not sufficient to bring the two communities together. Their different cultures, different languages and different ways of life and thinking will always be a hindrance to good living. Israel's communal troubles are presently eclipsed because of the Arab-Israeli conflict. Unity is maintained only through fear of an outside force.

Under such circumstances, it will be no hardship – perhaps even a blessing – for Jews who had emigrated to Palestine after 1947 to return to their countries of origin or to any other country of their choice. They still speak the languages of those countries; they still belong to the same culture and way of life; and there is nothing to differentiate them from the Gentile communities among whom they were born and lived, except their refusal to become assimilated. In fact, they would be more at home in Czechoslovakia, Hungary, Rumania, Poland, South Africa, the United States, Russia, etc., than the Palestine Arabs would be in Arab countries.

Those who remain in Palestine would be only those who are willing to live and share with the Palestine Arabs the responsibilities and privileges of citizenship and the Holy Land will once again have peace.

But the course just outlined needs statesmen, not politicians. It needs men of courage, conscience, wisdom and determination. Where are these men to be found? As Ellen G. White put it:

"THE GREATEST WANT OF THE WORLD
IS THE WANT OF MEN –
MEN WHO WILL NOT BE BOUGHT OR SOLD,
MEN WHO IN THEIR INMOST SOULS
ARE TRUE AND HONEST,
MEN WHO DO NOT FEAR TO CALL
SIN BY ITS RIGHT NAME,
MEN WHOSE CONSCIENCE IS AS TRUE TO DUTY
AS THE NEEDLE TO THE POLE,
MEN WHO WILL STAND FOR THE RIGHT
THOUGH THE HEAVENS FALL!"

XVI | *The 1967 Aggression*

The printing of this book had reached its final stages the day the Israeli forces invaded the Sinai Peninsula on 5 June 1967 for the second time. This Chapter is intended to provide a brief comment on whether the new situation, which has arisen as a result of the Israeli occupation of the West Bank of the Jordan, the Gaza Strip, the Sinai Peninsula and parts of Syria has altered – or will alter – in any way the basic issues of the Palestine problem; whether the Arab attitude towards the state of Israel is likely to soften or stiffen; the manner in which the Palestine problem has been handled by the United Nations since 1948; the position of the United States and Britain in the dispute; and the chances, if any, for peace under the changed conditions.

It is believed that had the United Nations followed up the ceasefire orders of the Security Council of 1948 with a permanent solution in due time, the 1967 war would not have occurred and the new tragedies inflicted upon the innocent inhabitants of the occupied territories would have been avoided. To become a refugee once in a lifetime is bad enough; to become one a second time within the span of twenty years, is incredible.

The event which led to the war on 5 June 1967 was allegedly the closure of the Strait of Tiran to Israeli shipping. While this may have been the immediate excuse, to understand the implications involved, it is important to search for the underlying causes. It is misleading to assume that the controversy is one over the 'innocent passage' of Israeli shipping through the Gulf of Aqaba; or over the question as to whether or not the Strait of Tiran is an international waterway. Had the problem been so simple, a solution could easily have been found by referring the case to the International Court of Justice.

The causes of the Arab–Israeli conflict, of which the Gulf of Aqaba controversy is but a side issue, are far deeper than that.

The preceding chapters have placed before the reader evidence on how the problem arose, the forces responsible for the conflict and what ought to be done to bring 'peace with justice' to the troubled Holy Land and the region. A proper understanding of the problem is therefore not only essential but obligatory upon those in charge of information media in order to bring the truth to the public and on those Powers on whose shoulders the responsibility for world peace rests. To continue to follow a 'sweep-it-under-the-rug' policy, or to treat the conflict as a chronic case with which the world must learn to live, or to confine treatment merely to the immediate causes without touching the disease itself, is to court disaster.

Although the war lasted for hardly four days, the extent of human suffering; the losses of tens of thousands of lives; the extensive damage done, particularly to the Holy City of Jerusalem; the wholesale plunder of homes and business premises in Jerusalem; the number of persons who fled their homes or are being driven out by the Israeli forces; and the casualties caused by the Israeli use of napalm bombs against civilians fleeing from danger zones, make the tragedy far worse than that of 1948.

It is difficult to understand how the world conscience could show concern over material things, such as passage of shipping through waterways and ignore the sufferings and tragedies of human beings, simply because the aggressor in this case happens to be Israel. The revulsion with which Hitler's crimes against the Jews are still being viewed, as compared with the apathy with which Israeli crimes against the Moslem and Christian inhabitants of the Holy Land are being received in the Christian world, leave the Arab cold with disappointment and suspicion that Christianity as practised in the West might, after all, not be a *religion* of love, charity and justice, but a *convenience* where the precepts of the faith are used to serve selfish interests, material benefits and political advantages.

To suggest that the U.A.R. was planning to attack Israel is ludicrous. There is ample evidence to show that the Israelis had been preparing for an attack on Syria long before President Nasser had asked the United Nations Emergency Force to leave the Gaza

Strip and Sharm Esh-Sheikh. The movement of U.A.R. troops into the non-militarized Sinai Peninsula was a defensive measure to counter-balance the Israeli build-up on the Syrian borders and in order to deter aggression. He made that clear not only in his official pronouncements but also in answer to messages he received from President Johnson. The pact signed with Jordan a few days before the Israeli attack began was – like those with Syria and Iraq – to provide *collective* security against Israeli aggression. Whether President Johnson had made similar approaches and received similar assurances from the Israeli leaders is not known. If he did, then it is not clear how he could have failed to condemn the Israeli action when it came. The United States representative at the United Nations even went so far as to obstruct any condemnation of Israel by the Security Council. One can only wonder at such an attitude, especially when it is compared with U.S. attitudes towards nations less involved in aggressive actions.

The Israelis may have proven by their swift treacherous action their military superiority over the Arab armies, but this does not mean that the Arab spirit to regain what they believe is rightfully theirs has been broken. It remains as indomitable as ever. The Israelis may have won a military victory, but they are certainly far from winning the peace they seek. If there had been a gleam of hope in the past of an Arab-Israeli rapprochement, that possibility has now vanished and the gap between the Arab and the Israeli has become wider and the wound deeper. What kind of presence do the Israelis expect in Palestine when they have to rely all the time on might and not on right? David Ben Gurion is known to often quote the Bible. Has it ever occurred to him to remind his colleagues of the passage which warns: 'He who conquers by the sword shall fall by the sword'?

What effect the Israeli military conquest will have in the long run on the future of the Middle East, on Arab relations with the United States and Britain for championing the Israeli cause so ardently and on world peace, is still too early to predict. Much depends, however, on the future attitudes of these two Powers. Will they continue to insist on a solution, using Israeli military successes as a bargaining point? Or will they change to one of moral courage to deal squarely with the problem by first demanding immediate Israeli withdrawal and then tackling the basic issue without fear or favour with a view to bringing 'peace with justice' to the Middle East?

The United States – with the United Kingdom in its wake – appears to have settled on the first course. It rejected the only logical proposal that of the Soviet Union in the Security Council to condemn the aggressor, order a cease-fire and demand simultaneous withdrawal behind the 1949 lines. And when the Soviet Union requested the Secretary General to convene a special session of the General Assembly, the United States opposed the request but agreed to participate. The only other nation to oppose a special session was Israel. The fartherest the United States was willing to go at this stage was for the Security Council merely to order a cease-fire, with no pressure for immediate implementation. Such an attitude is not in accord with United States policies in other cases where the aggressor has been required to remove all traces of his aggression before 'peace talks' can even be entertained. China's entry into membership of the United Nations continues to be barred by the United States because of her part in the war in Korea in 1953.

United States opposition in the Security Council has thus allowed the Israelis to remain in occupation of Arab territories, assuring them breathing space and freedom of action to expel and dispossess the already-once-before-dispossessed Arab inhabitants and to alter the physical features of many Arab villages by razing them to the ground as they did with others in 1948 to prevent the return of the Arab inhabitants and claiming later that there were no longer homes to which they could return. Whereas prompt action could reduce human suffering and material losses, the longer the Israelis remain in occupation the more difficult it would become to dislodge them and restore to the hapless inhabitants the conditions which prevailed before the attack.

The reason the United States gives for its rejection of Israeli withdrawal at this juncture is that conditions in the Middle East would return to what they were before the conflict began and no nearer to permanent peace, which, it claims, is what is now desired.

Such an argument lacks both logic and reason. In the first place, a permanent settlement of the Palestine problem on the basis of the 'accomplished fact' that could not be brought about within twenty years, would certainly drag on for years even if all the requirements for peace were presently congenial, which they are not. This would, in effect, mean that the Israelis would remain in occupation of the territory they encroached upon and probably eventually annex it as they did with the extra territory held under armistice agreements. In the circumstances, the Arab residents of the occupied territories would be subjected to the indignities and discrimination of Israeli rule and those outside would be obliged to lead the life of refugees. Such a one-side imposition is preposterous and is certainly not conducive to peace.

In the second place, the approach is inconsistent with the oft declared policy of "U.S. 'commitments' guaranteeing the territorial integrity of states in the Middle East against any violation of frontiers or armistice lines." This unilateral undertaking was reinforced on 25 May 1950 with the signing of the Tripartite Declaration whereby the United States, the United Kingdom and France voluntarily agreed to maintain the *status quo* in the Middle East. It is true the invasion of Egypt in 1956 nullified the agreement between the three Powers because of the involvement of Britain and France in the attack on Egypt, but the United States did not abrogate its self-imposed responsibilities thereunder. On the contrary, American leaders continued to remind the Arabs on every occasion of United States 'commitments' not to allow a change in frontiers or armistice lines by force. "These must be freely negotiated," was the United States slogan. President Johnson – like the two Presidents who preceded him – made this United States position clear; and only a few days before the Israeli attack, he repeated the 'commitment'. Naturally, in the face of such constant warnings by a Great Power, if for no other reason, the Arab States were not likely to start a war and get involved in battle with the United States. As events later showed, the warning turned out to be for the benefit of the Israelis.

In the third place, United States opposition at the United Nations is contrary to the warning contained in Security Council resolution condemning Israel for the attack on the Jordan village of Sammu' on 13 November 1966. That resolution "emphasized to Israel that actions of military reprisal cannot be tolerated and that if they are repeated, the Security Council will have to consider further and more effective steps as envisaged in the Charter against the repetition of such acts"* If an act of the magnitude of the Israeli aggression of 5 June 1967 is not worthy of 'further and more effective steps' what is?

Ironically, this resolution was sponsored by the United States and if it was honestly meant, then the United States by reason of its declarations and commitments, has become doubly responsible to act – both inside and outside the United Nations – to dislodge the Israelis. To leave them in possession of the territories they have occupied until the Arabs are willing to negotiate for permanent peace and to expect the Arabs to agree to come to the conference table with a dagger stuck in their back and a pistol pointed to their head, virtually means unconditional surrender on Israeli terms. This is a curious parallel to the United States position in Vietnam where the North Vietnamese are being asked to start negotiations for peace while United States bombers are still pounding away at Hanoi. The North Vietnamese response has, quite naturally, been negative.

To consider 'peace' or even a 'solution' of the Palestine Problem in such an atmosphere is, in effect, to call for a total failure of the objective the United States says it has in mind. At any rate, the annexation of the Old City of Jerusalem to the Israeli–held Sector, leaves no room for a peace dialogue with the Israelis.

It should further be noted that to allow the Israelis to hold on to territory occupied by force of arms will encourage other nations to solve their territorial problems by launching a *blitzkreig* against the territory of another nation and getting away with it. If the Israelis have been able to do it, why cannot other

* See Security Council resolution S/228 of 25 November 1966.

nations? The dangers of creating such a precedent need hardly be stressed.

The Arab States accuse the United States and Britain of collusion with Israel. Both Governments emphatically deny this. Just as the 'Suez Canal Conspiracy' came to light gradually after 1956, so also will the happenings before and during the June 1967 war become known in due time. But in the meantime, military experts indicate that Israel could not have possibly carried out a round-the-clock attack on twenty-five airfields in the United Arab Republic, covering distances of some 2,500 mile, and in addition attacked targets in far-off Iraq and Latikia and covered the Syrian and Jordan fronts all at once without receiving additional aircraft and having closer bases on land and aircraft carriers at sea from which to operate. Even if this were possible, the experts point out that this vast air operation could not have remained undetected by the U.S. Sixth Fleet and the British warships in the Mediterranean. The U.S. ship *Liberty*, torpedoed by the Israelis soon after the attack began, was only 15 miles away from shore. It was later admitted that the ship had been 'spying' and if so, surely it was in a position to know what was going on. The fact that neither the U.S. Sixth Fleet nor the British ships warned the U.A.R. of the impending attack, means one of two things: Either the radar instruments of both fleets are obsolete, or that there was enough collusion to allow the surprise attack to succeed. To any fair-minded person, the latter would be the more convincing. The very fact that the United States warned the U.A.R. not to fire the first shot and later supported the Israeli position is in itself collusion.

But coming back to the problem on the political level, here again it is difficult to discount collusion. By not fulfilling its guarantees of 'territorial integrity'; by refusing to recognize and condemn the Israeli aggression; by voting against a resolution for immediate Israeli withdrawal; and by abstaining on the annexation of the Old City of Jerusalem to the Israeli-held Sector – all these provide convincing evidence of United States partiality. The testimony of Father Ralph Gorman, C. P., who lived in Jerusalem for many years and had occasion to study the situation on the spot, reinforces such a conclusion. Writing in *The Sign* (USA) magazine of November 1951, Father Gorman stated: "The Arabs are no fools. They realize what is being prepared for them – with American approval and money. They know," he added, "that the sword is aimed at them and that, unless Zionist plans are frustrated, they will be driven back step by step into the desert – their lands, homes, vineyards and farms taken over by an alien people brought from the ends of the earth for this purpose." So when Israeli Prime Minister Levi Eshkol and his Defence Minister Moshe Dayan declared that the Israelis "have reached their natural boundary on the River Jordan and that they will never leave Jerusalem," they were merely carrying out their plans of expansion and confident of United States 'approval and money'.*

With such a 'sword' hanging over their heads and an insatiable enemy eyeing further Arab territory, Arab homes and Arab property, is it any wonder that the Arabs reject all peace overtures by the Israelis; supect American intentions towards them; and remain adamant in their determination to resist all attempts of encroachment on the Arab homeland?

The United States has lost because of its partial attitude in the present conflict. It would be better advised – if it is really interested in peace and the return of its own position of prestige and interests in the Arab world – to re-appraise its policy towards the two belligerents and follow one of impartiality based on principles of equity and justice. It is only in this way that it will be possible for the United States to regain the confidence of the Arabs and enlist their cooperation for the good of the Middle East, the United States and world peace. The fact that a presidential election year is approaching should not allow certain American politicians to sacrifice American interests on the altar of domestic politics and the 'Jewish vote'.

The United Nations failed in 1948 to bring peace to the Middle

* For Israeli policy of expansion, with particular reference to the annexation of the West Bank of the Jordan, the Gaza Strip, the Sinai Peninsula and the headwaters of the River Jordan, see Chapter XIV, pp. 280-282

East because it took no decisive action to ensure implementation of its own resolutions. The 1948 cease–fire order gave the Israelis the breathing space they needed to regroup their forces, replenish their supplies in men and material, strengthen their defences and improve their offensive potentialities in readiness for the second round. When the war was resumed, the Israelis emerged stronger and better equipped, able to penetrate deeper into Arab territory, expelling and dispossessing, in the process, the Arab inhabitants.

Acceptance of the cease-fire order by the Arab States in 1948 turned out to be a great mistake for which they are now paying dearly. But then they had faith in the U.N. Charter and the ability of the world Organization to do justice. The Security Council had earlier requested the Secretary General to convoke a special session of the General Assembly to reconsider the question of 'the future government of Palestine.' The Arabs then expected an equitable solution of the Palestine problem since partition was being avoided. But as things turned out, the General Assembly took no further steps, while the Security Council issued an order for a permanent cease-fire and called upon the parties to conclude an armistice. That armistice did not give the Israelis a right to the territories occupied by force of arms, but in the course of time, the Israelis annexed these territories to their 'state' in their programme of expansion. *

In 1956, the Israelis – taking advantage of the dispute between Egypt, on the one hand and Britain and France, on the other, over the nationalization of the Suez Canal – conspired with the two Great Powers and attacked Egypt on 29 October 1956. Their prizes were to be, if the attack succeeded: The British would return to the occupation of the Suez Canal zone; the French would benefit by the overthrow of President Nasser and thereby end Egyptian support for the Algerians; and the Israelis would annex the Sinia Peninsula to their 'state' in their second round for the establishment of an 'empire' from the 'Nile to the Euphrates', as the Zionist Movement envisaged from the start.

The calculations of the three colluding partners back-fired,

* See Chapter VIII, pp. 116–155.

as the United States Government was then not in a position to permit aggression without getting involved in a third world war. While the Israelis were openly warned that their withdrawal from the Sinai Peninsula and the Gaza Strip must be 'unconditional' and that they must not be allowed to benefit from their aggression, it appears that President Eisenhower had made a secret promise to the Israelis – which the Israelis later divulged – assuring them that their withdrawal to behind the armistice demarcation lines would be compensated by free passage through the Gulf of Aqaba.* He kept his word. This turned out to be a great mistake and the spark which ignited the present war.

In the special session of the General Assembly which convened to deal with the Israeli invasion, Mr. Lester Pearson, then Representative of Canada, proposed the formation of a United Nations Emergency Force for such period as will enable the General Assembly to find a permanent solution for the Palestine problem. The proposal was approved; Mr. Pearson received the Nobel Prize as his reward; and the United Nations sat back allowing ten years to go by without doing anything. When U.N. Secretary General U Thant was criticized for having pulled out the United Nations Emergency Force so quickly, he quite rightly retorted, ten years for a temporary peace force was long enough.

The impotence of the United Nations and the double-dealing of the American President are responsible for the 1967 war, the critical situation which has since developed and the great human sufferings that have resulted. Had the cease-fire order of 1948 been followed by serious action to settle the Palestine problem, the Israeli attack on Egypt in 1956 would not have taken place; and had the United Nations acted in full on Mr. Pearson's proposal to use the presence of the Emergency Force as a temporary peace-keeping force while a sincere effort was being made for a permanent solution for the Palestine problem, the 1967 war would not have broken out.

The problem now before the world is, what to do next? President Johnson, speaking before the National Foreign Policy

---

* *Ibid*, pp. 146–152.

Conference for Educators in Washington on 19 June 1967, said that the United States was 'committed' to "a peace based on five principles." These principles – later embodied in a draft resolution submitted to the General Assembly – were:

A. Mutual recognition of the political independence and territorial integrity of all countries in the area, encompassing recognized boundaries and other arrangements, including disengagement and withdrawal of forces, that will give them security against terror, destruction and war;

B. Freedom of innocent maritime passage;

C. Just and equitable solution of the refugee problem;

D. Registration and limitation of arms shipments into the area;

E. Recognition of the right of all sovereign nations to exist in peace and security.

While the plan might appear to some reasonable, to the Arabs it is totally inacceptable because the five points presented are not just in principle. In the first placc, apart from its ambiguity, the plan does not, as a first essential step, recognize and condemn aggression and demand immediate withdrawal. By not doing so, it places the aggressor in the advantageous position of using the occupied territory as a bargaining weapon. Israeli Foreign Minister Abba Eban has already announced that Israel would not consider itself bound by any General Assembly resolution which might call upon his Government to withdraw from the territory occupied. With such an attitude, it is difficult to see how 'peace talks' could even begin.

In the second place, President Johnson's proposals give equal validity to Zionist *claims* and Arab *rights* in Palestine which the Arabs absolutely deny on the grounds that such assumption is inconsistent with the principles which govern the rights of people to their homeland. At the same time, the proposals, in effect, confirm Israeli seizure of Arab homes, Arab lands and an Arab homeland.

Furthermore, President Johnson's proposals are a departure

from the proclaimed policy of the United States after World War II, when that country emerged as the champion of freedom and undertook upon itself to uphold peace, prevent the use of force and to guarantee the political independence and territorial integrity of all freedom-loving nations. For example, in 1953, when the North Koreans attempted to occupy South Korea by force of arms, the United States – under the flag of the United Nations – went to war, driving the North Koreans back to behind the 38th Parallel. And when the Viet Cong in South Vietnam attempted – with the help of the North Vietnamese – to change the order of things in the country with a view to uniting the two Vietnams into one state, the United States immediately took up arms and involved itself in a war from which it is now unable to extricate itself. All this sacrifice in men and money, the United States tells the world, it has undertaken in the interests of freedom, the rights of peoples and world peace. Another example of United States inconsistency is in the insistence of that Government on condemnation of the Soviet Union for its action in Hungary in 1956.

If the United States were really sincere in its claims and regards its obligations applicable to all nations without favour, then the Israelis should never have been allowed to start the war; and once started, the United States is now morally 'committed' to prevent Israeli aggression and encroachment on the territories of the neighbouring Arab states, using force, if necessary, to dislodge them as it did in Korea and continues to do in Vietnam. But to remain passive and then to come forward with proposals wholly in the interests of the aggressor, reflects unkindly on the intentions of the United States towards the Arabs, to say the least.

In order to find common ground between the draft resolution of the Soviet Union for condemnation, withdrawal and compensation and the United States five-point proposals, the non-aligned nations, led by Yugoslavia, submitted a draft resolution dropping the 'condemnation' and 'compensation' clauses and concentrating on immediate unconditional Israeli withdrawal.

The Latin American countries, inspired by the United States, countered with a draft resolution tying up Israeli withdrawal with negotiations for permanent peace. In other words, the Israelis were to remain in the occupied territories until peace was signed.

In the voting which followed on 4 July 1967, both resolutions failed to obtain the two-thirds majority. The position thus remained deadlocked.

Failure of the United Nations to condemn aggression and to order immediate Israeli withdrawal from territories occupied by force of arms, has dealt a severe blow to the principles of peace enunciated in the United Nations Charter. By its lack of action, the United Nations has created a precedent for those nations which believe in force and thus exposed itself and its principles to ridicule. Instead of bringing peace to the war-torn Middle East and avoiding a world conflagration, it has set the stage for a more bloody struggle in the future. The Great Powers which used their influence to block the passage of a resolution based on the provisions of the United Nations Charter, have done a disservice to the cause of peace and to the prestige of the Organization towards which all nations look for safety, independence and freedom.

For peace in the Middle East to succeed, it must be freely negotiated. In the case of Palestine – notwithstanding United States opposition – there are only two courses of action open to the United Nations: one immediate; the other to follow. These are:

The first is to show no favouritism to either party and to condemn aggression and the use of force on *principle* as the United Nations Charter stipulates; to demand and ensure immediate withdrawal to behind the 1949 armistice demarcation lines, as occurred in Korea in 1953 and is today being demanded in Vietnam; to order the payment of compensation for losses sustained by the civilian population in lives and property, as the Israelis demanded and received from the Federal German Republic for crimes committed by the Nazis against the Jews; and to punish the guilty for atrocities and crimes committed against humanity, as occurred at Nuremberg. What is needed to bring peace is the implementation of the principles established by the Democracies and to apply them equally to friend and foe.

The second step - once the tragedies of the immediate aggression have been dispensed with and tempers have been allowed to cool down – is to re-open the entire Question of Palestine and to consider how best to redress the wrong done to the Palestine Arabs and to prescribe the manner in which they should be enabled to re-enter and to regain possession of their rights and property in their homeland.

Unless these steps are taken with courage, wisdom and determination, the present crisis will flare up again in the not too distant future. It is more than likely that the conflict then will not be confined to the Middle East.

This Chapter would be incomplete without the following eyewitness report by the author on the tragedies suffered by the inhabitants of the West Bank of the Jordan :

Standing on the east bank of the River, the author was appalled by the scene which met his eyes. A mass of humanity in thousands was wading through the waters of the river - some beneath, others between, the debris of the bombed Abdullah (formerly Allenby) Bridge, with still others being hurriedly pushed - sometimes by a volley of over-head shots - to speed them on their way to join the unhappy procession.

Young men and women were seen leading the blind, the aged, the infirm and the helpless; while babies and little children were being passed overhead from one person to another like bundles. At one time, the spectacle looked like the eager multitudes described in the Holy Bible which flocked to the same waters of the River Jordan two thousand years before to be baptized by John the Baptist; but a closer look into the horrified faces of the crowd, brought one back to reality and the scene looked more like the chaotic flight of the Russians in the film *Dr. Zhivago.*

The east bank of the river swarmed with people - refugees searching for each other or trying to decide where to go; people from Amman anxiously hoping to find or get news of their loved ones in Jerusalem; foreign correspondents taking pictures to write their 'stories'. In short, misery was rampant. In contrast, on the west bank of the river stood a group of Israeli soldiers, including a rabbi in skull-cap, idly watching this great human calamity and enjoying its every detail as they giggled, pointed at people who slipped into the water or bumped their heads against the iron beams and laughed heartily. The sight was exasperating and enough to turn one's stomach with disgust. This display of lack of human feelings and pleasure over human misery recalled the stories so often related of the Nazis enjoying the sight of Jews being led to their deaths.

Talking to a few, one woman said that her group came from a village near Jerusalem. They were summoned to gather in the village square and then herded into trucks and driven to a spot between Jericho and the River Jordan, shown the direction of the river and speeded on their way by a few shots. But the story of Muhammad Esh-Sheikh Naser, sixty years of age, a well-to-do man of Tulkarm, father of nine children, is worth relating because it is the story of the majority. He began: It was 1 p.m. on June 7 when the town was stormed by Israeli troops who first ordered people indoors. At. 7 p.m., the inhabitants were told to gather in the town square where he found some 15,000 had already arrived. They were assured that they would be delayed only until a census of the population had been taken. But at 10 p.m., trucks arrived and they were ordered into them. They appealed and begged to be allowed to remain in their homes and when this was refused, they asked to be allowed to at least take a few of their belongings, but with no avail. They were driven a short distance out of town told to get out and not to try to walk back. They spent the night with the sky for cover. The next morning they walked eastward to the nearest Arab village seeking shelter and food. At 4 p.m. the loud speaker of the mosque was used to summon them to get into the trucks which had just arrived. They were driven to a short distance of Nablus and again told to get out. They were unable to enter the town because of the curfew and were therefore obliged to spend a second night in the open. On the third day, they were driven to a solitary place in the Jordan Valley some ten miles from the River Jordan, shown the direction of the river and told to start walking, sending a few volleys among them to speed them on their way. The ten-mile walk in the mid-day sun without food or water was too much for many who either died or were left dying from sheer exhaustion or thirst. There was nothing the others could do but to abandon them, a prey to wild animals. This was reminscent of the 25-mile walk of the inhabitants of Ramle and Lydda in 1948, when hundreds of old and young children did not make it to Ramallah and their bodies were left behind for the jackals.

When these stragglers finally made it to the river, they found that its waters had swelled because the Israelis had earlier opened the dikes at the mouth of Lake Tiberias. Some of the men carried the children, while others helped the womenfolk. Many were unable to make the crossing or slipped in the process and got carried away by the current.

Asked how many of his group he thought had lost their lives during the exodus, Muhammad Esh-Sheikh Naser replied that a number of the young men had been shot in the town square; others in their homes; some of the old, the feeble and weak died by the wayside; and some were carried away by the river current. He was unable to give any estimate, but said that the number was not small.

The most gruesome and heart-breaking experience was the visit to the victims of the Israeli napalm bombs. Some were burned beyond recongition; others had burns that will disfigure or maim them for life; but the saddest sight of all was that of two innocent children between the ages of 6 and 7 years lying helpless in bed with burns all over their faces and bodies. The look of disbelief in their eyes, as if to enquire: what was all this about, why it had to happen and why it had to be them, was pathetic. One foreign correspondent no doubt badly shaken, suddenly burst out: "What is the difference between this and the ovens of Hitler's Germany?" This remark was not surprising. Anyone seeing the sight could not but be reminded of the comment by British historian Arnold Toynbee, so aptly put in 1948 in less wicked circumstances: ... the Jews knew, from personal experience what they were doing; and it was their supreme tragedy that the lesson learned by them from their encounter with the Nazi Gentiles should have been not to eschew but to imitate some of the evil deeds that the Nazis had committed against the Jews."

The number of persons who either fled or were driven out had reached at the time of writing the figure of 150,000 with more thousands arriving every day. It is expected that, unless the United Nations does something to order immediate Israeli withdrawal, the total figure is likely to reach half-a-million.

The Government of Jordan is using all its resources and facilities to find shelter and food for these distressed people. Some are housed in schools – five families in a 12x12 foot room squatting on the ground with nothing to sit or sleep on except the bare floor; others are accommodated in tents or hastily erected shacks; others found accommodation with friends or relatives; while the majority roam aimlessly from one spot to another. The task facing the Jordan Government is enormous; and the Government needs all the help it can get from friendly governments and peoples of good will. What the future has in store for this new set of exiles, is at present difficult to forecast. The immediate need, however, is to alleviate their sufferings.

Epilogue | *Reflections of a Palestinian*

It is common to human nature to look back over past accomplishments, successes and failures. Some reflections bring satisfaction and pride; others sorrow and sadness; others regret; others still might create an emotion of bitterness and probably hate; and others perhaps wonder or bewilderment.

Reflections into the past do not generally occur to the young. Their minds are set more on the future as they plan and build 'castles in the air.' But those who have passed middle age, seldom look ahead for fear that the future might remind them of the inevitable. They are therefore inclined to relive the past as they leaf through its pages, sorting out the pleasant memories from the unpleasant and try to figure out why they had not done even better in their lives, or where they had failed.

Some of my own reflections have been to find answers to certain questions, such as, what is it in human nature that makes man generally so wicked? Is it the animal instinct for survival? Or is it the eagerness for power and possession that makes the strong enslave the weak? Why cannot man follow the precept of 'live and let live', all sharing in God's blessings and mercies during his short stay on earth? What kind of patriotism is this that makes man go to war to kill another whom he does not know, had never seen and who had done him no personal injury? And is man really sincere when he declares his willingness to sacrifice his own life so that others may be free and lead a better life? Is it not all downright hypocracy on the part of world leaders to cover up for their selfishness and greed for power and fame?

In war man claims he is fighting for a principle, for democracy, for the freedom of mankind, for a safer and better world, for a happier way of life, free from fear and want. This was said during World War I; it was said again during World War II; repeated during the Korean war; and now in the undeclared war in Vietnam.

It will no doubt continue to be proclaimed each time there is a conflict until the end of time. Ironically, once the war is over, each nation goes its own way to lick its wounds and to start all over again to practice the same injustices which brought about the previous conflict, forgetting all about the human sacrifices and material losses suffered by both sides and the promises and pledges given in the hour of need.

But bringing my reflections closer home, as a Palestinian, ours are of a unique but sad character, because they have not ended happily but the tragedy goes on. During my early childhood, I was witness to the non-fulfilment of promises and pledges given to the Arabs during World War I. The second phase of my life was fostered by constant fear of uprooting and loss of home and possessions to strangers being brought into the country with the ultimate intention of replacing the Arab inhabitants. The third found me and my family the victims of an unprecedented act of expulsion and dispossession. Man's wickedness against man could not have been practised in a more brutal manner.

As I now look back over the past, I am unable to find anything I had done that might deserve such cruel punishment. I believe I led an orderly and honest life; I brought up my family in a God-fearing way; I did harm to no one; I helped others as best as I could. In short, I tried to live by the teachings of my Christian faith: "Love thy neighbour as thyself" and "Do to others as you would others do to you." Notwithstanding my efforts at upright living, I found myself, overnight, homeless, penniless, my only worldly possession the suit I stood in, with family refugee in one country and I in another and relatives and friends widely scattered sharing our fate and sufferings. The home I constructed with my honest earnings over the years and the furniture I assembled to make life more comfortable for my family, were taken away and given to strangers to me in language, culture and religion. After nineteen years, I am not recovered from my perplexity as I ask myself: "Why Palestine? why?".

My reflections also take me back tenderly to Jerusalem and my home. I remember Jerusalem, the cradle of Judaism, Christianity and Islam, the city from which the light of salvation shone forth into the darkness of the world. I remember Jerusalem, the Holy City, the home of peace and inspiration and my home. I remember Jerusalem, the place of prayer, of communion with God, who forgives and protects.

I remember the open fields around the walls of the Old City, where so often the shepherds watched their flocks by night. I remember Solomon's Quarries, which extend to a great depth under the Old City. I remember how, as children, we used to peep into the endless dark of that cave, daring not to go more than a few yards for fear that the unknown would devour us.

I remember the pealing of the church bells to remind the Christian of his faith, the voice of the muezzin high up in his minaret calling to Islam's sons to prayer, the Jew wending his way at sunrise and sunset to the synagogue – all to offer to the Almighty prayer for His blessing and thanks-giving for the peace and beauty of the Holy City.

I remember my playmates of over fifty years ago – Moslems, Christians and Jews. I even remember a childhood brawl between my Moslem and Jewish friends and how a passerby stopped to separate the fighting boys. I remember the storm of accusations which poured from the boys' lips, but the Good Samaritan reminded them that they were cousins, the 'seed of Abraham', and told them how unbecoming it was that they should fight when they ought to love and tolerate each other. I remember how we all smiled and forgot our troubles and were soon gaily back at our game. That night – how vividly I remember! I asked my mother: "If my Moslem and Jewish playmates are really cousins to each other, what am I, a Christian, to both of them?" My mother replied: "Those who have accepted Christ as their Saviour are equally the children of Abraham and therefore you are a brother to both your friends."

I remember how we children looked forward to the yearly community festivities. In the Spring, Moslem, Christian and Jew alike took part in the Moslem pilgrimage to the tomb of the prophet Moses and watched with delight and excitement the dance of the *dervishes* to the chanting of heroic songs and banner waving. In the summer, Moslem, Christian and Jew alike flocked to the Valley to take part in the Jewish celebrations at the tomb of Sadik Shameon. And in the Autumn Moslem, Christian and Jew alike picnicked in the gardens around the tomb of the Holy Virgin Mary, near Gethsemane, where the Christian community spent a day and a night singing and rejoicing. I remember how at the end of each festival I walked home with my toys and sweets, regretful that the feast had come to an end.

Ours was indeed a Holy City, a city of peace, love and brotherhood, where the stranger could find shelter, the pilgrim loving care and the faithful salvation.

I remember my home, its walls and fences and the trees and shrubs I planted and tended with my own hands; and I enquire: Who are those people who live in my house? What right have they to be there? Why will they not even pay rent for their forced occupation? In how many homes are my precious belongings now scattered after they had been plundered and robbed? Who is now eating off my dining-room table? Sitting on my sofas, couches and chairs? Sleeping in our beds? Playing our piano? Using our library and kitchen utensils? Who gathers the grapes off my vine? The fruits off my trees? Who plucks my flowers? Who feeds my canaries? Are the strangers' children using my children's swings, sand-boxes and toys?* And then I come up with a question of wonder: How do they feel to live in robbed homes and stolen property? Do they ever suffer from a feeling of guilt or shame at what they have done? Or is it all part of their nature and dead conscience?

---

* David Pinsky, the famous Yiddish-American dramatist and story writer from Israel, "tells of one Israeli woman, a mother of two children who occcupied the home of a former well-to-do Arab family. The house was spacious; the garden well kept. One day the children discovered a closet full of toys which belonged to the children of the exiled Arab family. The children were overjoyed with their find and began to play noisily with the toys. But the mother was suddenly struck by the thought that her children were playing with the toys of Arab children who were now exiled and homeless. She began to brood. Where were those children whose toys were being played with by her own children? Have they a roof over their heads? A bed to sleep in or a toy to

My thoughts then carry me through the nineteen years of my exile, the countries I have been to, the homes in the United States I visited and the different peoples I met. With nothing but the memories of my past, I have silently watched people take interest in their homes, their occupations, their friends, their pleasures and their plans for the future. I have watched them celebrate Christmas with the same joy and happiness we used to celebrate ours in Jerusalem around the Christmas Tree with our children and their cousins and friends gathered in bliss and rejoicing over the Birth of the Child Who was like unto them.

In my reflections I often wished these carefree good people would for once at least put themselves in my place and imagine their feelings if they were to be deprived of country, home, property, family, relatives and friends. Would they rebel against such tyranny? Would they fight to regain what is rightfully theirs? Or would they meekly – as the Palestinians are now being asked – 'bless those who persecute them' and heed the threats of their persecutors to keep the peace and not to disturb the development and exploitation by strangers of our homes and fields or else . . . ?

But then, why expect people who are comfortable in life, have their families around them, their homes intact, their pleasures to enjoy and free from fear and want, to worry about the sufferings and deprivations of others even if only by thinking about them? Was this not the attitude of the so-called 'world humanitarian' – Eleanor Roosevelt – when she passed through Jerusalem in 1951 on her way to the Israeli-occupied Sector of the City? Invited by an American lady-resident of Jerusalem to visit a refugee camp and see for herself the pathetic plight of the Moslem and Christian inhabitants of the Holy Land who filled the countryside and sur-

play with? What right have her children to be happy at the expense of the unhappiness of others? She ordered the children to put the toys back into the closet and forbade them to play with them. But this did not restore her peace of mind. What right had she and her family to occupy a house which does not belong to her? Is she not doing to the Arabs what the Nazis did to her and her family?" (*Voice of Dissent*, by William Zukerman, Bookman Associates, Inc., New York, 1964, p. 141) rounding caves, she replied with all candour and without the least compassion or emotion that she did not come to the Middle East to see the Arab refugees but her friends in Israel. Callously she added that there were refugees all over the world and the Palestine Arabs were not worse off. That was a sad moment for humanity and a sorry one for the United States whose 'humanitarianism' the former first lady so badly represented!

My reflections include those who were instrumental in the creation of the state of Israel at the cost of great human suffering to others and also those who today continue to block every move to right the wrong committed. Can their political career or material benefits be so important to them that they have become devoid of all human feeling or integrity, willing to sell their conscience for 'thirty pieces of silver' as Judas sold Christ two-thousand years before? Is it not a tragedy that people who have committed or helped in the perpetration of a crime should continue to lead a normal life while their victims suffer deprivation, frustration and anguish? Is it possible that they will escape punishment for ever? Or will it some day come true that "the sins of the fathers shall be visited upon the children"?

God's mills grind slow and the day *will* come when the Moslem and Christian inhabitants of the Holy land *will* return to their homes and the nightmare of the twenty, thirty or even one-hundred years will pass. Judging from the past history of the Holy Land, this is bound to happen. The Zionist invasion is not the first. Romans, Greeks, the Crusades and others have crossed the Mediterranean and they have come to the edge of our desert. But always, after bearing patiently with them for a while, the desert has risen in protest and it has pressed them back into the sea. The Arabian desert is bound to rebel again and the Zionist intruders will be cast into the sea from whence they came and we shall have peace again in the Holy land.

References

Chapter I — Introduction (pp. 1 - 8)

1. U.N. Document S/888.
2. Ben Gurion, David, *Rebirth and Destiny of Israel,* (New York: The Philosophical Library, 1954), p. 419
3. Israeli Government *Yearbook* 1952, pp. 63, 65
4. Statement by Menachem Beigin in the Israeli Parliament on October 12 1955.
5. Quoted from the Hope Simpson Report – *Cmd.* 3686, pp. 53–54
6. *New York Times,* 6 December 1953
7. Translated from the Israeli Hebrew language Magazine *Ner,* January-February 1961, and published in the American Council for Judaism Magazine *Issues,* Fall 1961, p. 19

Chapter II — Historical Background (pp. 9 - 25)

1. Luke, Charles & Keith-Roach, Edward, *Handbook of Palestine and Transjordan,* (London: MacMillan, 1930), pp. 233-234.
2. *Jewish Life,* (A bi-monthly magazine of the Union of Orthodox Jewish Congregations of America), October 1960, pp. 21–31.
3. Jeffries, Joseph M.N., *Palestine: The Reality,* (New York: Longmans, Green & Co. 1939), pp. 237–238.
4. Howard, Harry N., *The King-Crane Commission,*(Beirut: Khayats,1963),p.5.
5. *Cmd.* 5957 – Hussein-McMahon Correspondence 1915–1916, Letter No. 1, dated 14 July 1915.
6. *Ibid,* Letter No. 4 dated 24 October 1915.
7. *Cmd.* 5974: Annex C, pp. 30–38.
8. Woodward, E.L. & Butler, R., *Documents on British Foreign Policy,* 1919–1939, Ist. ser., Vol. 4, pp. 241–251.
9. Antonius, George, *The Arab Awakening,* (London: Hamish Hamilton, 1938), p. 248.
10. Lloyd George, David, *Memoirs of the Peace Conference,* (New Haven : Yale University Press, 1939), pp. 664–665.
11. *Ibid.*
12. Herzl, Theodor, *The Jewish State,* (New York: American Zionist Emergency Council, 1946), p. 92.
13. Malcolm, James, *Origins of the Balfour Declaration,*(Zionist Archives),pp.2–3,

14. Wise, Stephen, & De Haas, Jacob, *The Great Betrayal*,(New York:Brentano's, 1930) p. 288.
15. Lloyd George, *Memoirs of the Peace Conference*, Vol. 11, p. 738.
16. *Cmd.* 5479 – Palestine Royal (Peel) Commission Report, p, 17
17. Palestine: *A Survey of Palestine* 1945 – 1946, p.1.
18. Antonius, *The Arab Awakening*, p. 268.
19. Jeffries, *Palestine: The Reality*, pp. 216–217.
20. Antonius, *The Arab Awakening*, pp. 433–434.
21. Jeffries, *Palestine: The Reality*, pp. 237–238.
22. *Ibid*, pp. 234–235,
23. Hoover, Herbert, *Ordeal of Woodrow Wilson*,(New York: McGraw-Hill Book Co., 1958), pp. 23, 25.
24. Miller, David Hunter, *My Diary at the Conference of Paris*, (New York: 1924), Vol. III.
25. U.S. Dept. of State, *Papers Relating to the Foreign Relations of the U.S.* – The Paris Peace Conference 1919, pp. 785–786.
(Quoted in *The King-Crane Commission*, by Harry N. Howard, p. 20)
26. Jeffries, *Palestine: The Reality*, pp. 237–238.
27. Howard, *The King-Crane Commission*, pp. 349–352.

Chapter III — Palestine and the Jews (pp. 26 - 39)

1. *Israel According to Holy Scriptures*, (Cedar Rapid: Ingram Press), pp. 11–15.
2. *Ibid*, pp. 6–9.
3. *Ibid*, pp. 29–31.
4. *Ibid*, p. 28.
5. *Ibid*, pp. 35, 45.
6. *Ibid*, pp. 19–25.
7. From the 'Secret' Documents released by the British Government: Paper No. CAB. 24/24 – *The Anti-Semitism of the Present Government*, by Sir Edwin S. Montagu, Secretary of State for India, dated 23 August 1917.
8. Shapiro, Harry L., *The Jewish People: A Biographical History*, (UNESCO, 1960), pp. 74–75.
9. American Council for Judaism, *Issues* Magazine, (New York: Winter 1965–66), pp. 21–23.
10. Litvin, Baruch, *The Jewish Identity*, Edited by Sidney Hoenig, Feldheim. (Quoted in the *Jerusalem Post* (Israel), 14 September 1966).
11. From a Review of the book *The Jewish Identity*, in an article entitled *Who is a Jew Today*, published in the *Jerusalem Post* (Israel), 14 September 1966.
12. Glubb, Sir John Bagot, *A Soldier with the Arabs*, (London: Hodder & Stoughton, 1957), p. 446.

REFERENCES

Chapter IV — The Zionist Movement (pp. 41 - 54)

1. Stein, Leonard, *Zionism,* (London: Kegan Paul, Trench, Trubner and Co., Ltd., 1932), p. 62.
2. William E. Hocking, Alford Professor Emeritus of Philosophy, Harvard University – Letter published in *New York Times,* 23 March 1944.
3. American Council for Judaism, *Issues* magazine, Fall 1961, pp. 91–92.
4. U.S. Congressional Record, 86th Congress, 2nd Session, Vol. 106, No. 78, April 29, 1960.
5. Hearing before the Committee on Foreign Relations, U.S. Senate, 88th Congress, lst Session, Part, 9, May 23, 1963.
6. *The Jewish Chronicle* (London), 8 April 1960.
7. Israeli Government *Yearbook* 1959–1960, January 1960, p. 94.
8. *Issues* Magazine, Spring 1966, p. 54.
9. Ben Gurion, *Rebirth and Destiny of Israel,* p. 489
10. *Jewish Newsletter* (New York), 9 January 1961.
11. *New York Times,* 18 May 1961.
12. Israeli Government *Yearbook* 1953–1954, p. 35
13. *Issues* Magazine, Spring 1962, p. 7
14. *The Jewish Chronicle* (London), 24 March, 1961.
15. Mallison Jr., W.T., *The Zionist-Israel Juridical claims to constitute 'The Jewish People' nationality entity and to confer membership in it: Appraisal in Public International Law,* (Washington, DC: 1964), Vol. 32, No. 5, Appendix B, p. 1075.
16. Quoted by Ian Gilmour in the *Spectator* Magazine, 24 June 1960
17. *New York Times,* 7 May, 1961.
18. From a letter by Richard J. Marquardt, published in *Holiday* Magazine of March 1963.
19. *Jewish Newsletter,* 9 January 1961.
20. Menuhin, Moshe, *The Decadence of Judaism in Our Time,* (New York: Exposition Press, 1965), pp. 400–401
21. *Jerusalem Post,* 14 January, 1966, p. 8
22. Lilienthal, Alfred, *What Price Israel?* (Chicago: Henry Regnery, 1953), p. 207
23. Kimche, Jon and David, *Both Sides of the Hill,* (London: Secker & Warburg, 1960), pp. 20,31.
24. *The Spectator* (London) Magazine, 22 July 1960.
25. Ernest, Morris L., *So Far So Good,* (New York : Harper & Bros., 1952), pp. 176–177.
26. American Council for Judaism, *The Council News,* May 1950, p. 2.
27. *The Spectator* Magazine, 22 July 1960.
28. Crossman, Richard, *Palestine Mission: A Personal Record,* (New York: Harper and Brothers, 1947), p. 47

29. *Jewish Newsletter*, 18 May, 1959
30. *The Spectator* Magazine, 24 June 1960

Chapter V — Palestine Under Mandate (pp. 55 - 75)

1. League of Nations, *Responsibilities of the League arising out of Article 22 (Mandates)*, No. 20/48/161, Annex I, p. 5.
2. *Cmd.* 1785 – Text in *A Survey of Palestine* 1945–1946, pp. 5–6.
3. Jeffries, *Palestine: The Reality*, p. 314.
4. Barbour, Neville, *Nisi Dominus*, (London: George G. Harrap & Co., Ltd., 1946), p. 97.
5. Report not published. Mentioned in *A Survey of Palestine* 1946, p. 17.
6. *Cmd.* 1540 – See *A Survey of Palestine* 1945–1946, p. 18.
7. *Cmd.* 3530 – *Ibid*, pp. 24–25.
8. *Cmd.* 5479 – *Ibid*, p. 38.
9. Ziff, William, *The Rape of Palestine*, (New York: Longmans, Green & Co., 1938), p. 171.
10. *Cmd.* 1700 – *'The Churchill Memorandum'*, dated 3 June 1922.
11. *Cmd.* 3692 – *The 'Passifield White Paper'*, dated October 1930.
12. *Cmd.* 6019 – *The* 1939 *White Paper (Known as the 'MacDonald White Paper')* dated 17 May 1939.
13. Palestine: *A Survey of Palestine* 1945–1946, p. 54.
14. *Ibid*, p. 57.
15. Royal Institute of International Affairs, *Great Britain and Palestine* 1915–1945, (New York and London: Oxford University Press, 1946), p. 128.
16. R.I.I.A., *The Middle East (2nd Edition)*, p. 36.
17. ESCO Foundation for Palestine, Inc,. *Palestine: A Study of Jewish, Arab and British Policies*, (New Haven: Yale University Press, 1947), Vol. II, p. 1085.
18. R.I.I.A., *Great Britain and Palestine* 1915–1945, pp. 139–140.
19. *Cmd. 6873* – Statement of Information relating to acts of Violence, 24 July 1946.
20. Palestine: *A Survey of Palestine* 1945–1946, p. 33.
21. *Ibid*, p. 58.
22. *Ibid*, pp. 67–68.
23. *Ibid*, p. 73.
24. Marlowe, S.H., *The Seat of Pilate*, (London: Cresset Press, 1959), p. 183.
25. Zaar, Isaac, *Rescue and Liberation : America's part in the birth of Israel*, (New York: Bloch Publishing Co., 1954), p. 115.
26. Palestine: *A Survey of Palestine* 1945–1946, p. 73.
27. Palestine: *Supplementary Memorandum to UNSCOP*, p. 14.
28. Koestler, Arthur, *Promise and Fulfilment*, (London: Macmillan & Co., 1949), p. 88.

29. Palestine: *Supplementary Memorandum to UNSCOP,* p. 24.
30. *New York Times,* 1 August 1947, i: 8.
31. *Cmd. 6873.*
32. Palestine: *Supplementary Memorandum to UNSCOP,* p. 58
33. *Ibid,* p. 57 .
34. *Ibid,* p. 56 .
35. Zaar, *Rescue and Liberation* , pp. 241–242.
36. *Cmd.* 7088 – Proposals for the Future of Palestine.
37. Palestine: *Supplementary Memorandum to UNSCOP,* p. 27.

Chapter VI — Palestine Problem before the U.N. (pp. 76 - 99)

1. U.N. Document A/364, Add. 1: Supplement No. 11, Annex 11, p.l.
2. *Ibid,* Annex II (pp.1–2): Documents A/287, A/288, A/289, A/290 and A/291.
3. Official Records of First Special Session of General Assembly, Vol. II, p. 12.
4. *Ibid,* p. 81.
5. *Ibid,* Vol. I, p. 23.
6. *Ibid,* pp. 59–60.
7. U.N. Document A/310: Resolution No. 104 (S–1).
8. *Ibid,* Resolution No. 105 (S–1).
9. Official Records of First Special Session of General Assembly Vol. III, pp. 183–184.
10. *Ibid,* pp. 345ff.
11. *Ibid,* Vol. 1, pp. 122–177. See also U.N. Document A/310: Resolution No. 106 (S–1) of 15 May 1947.
12. U.N. Document A/364. Add. 1, Vol. II, Annexes, Annex 5, p. 5
13. *Ibid,* Annex 18, p. 16.
14. *Ibid,* Vol. 1.
15. U.N. Document A/516: Report of *Ad Hoc* Committee on Palestine, pp. 2–19
16. U.N. Document A/AC./14/34 of 19 November 1947.
17. U.N. Document A/AC./14/32 of 11 November 1947.
18. Official Records of Second Session of General Assembly, Vol. 11, p. 1632.
19. *Ibid,* Summary records of meetings of *Ad Hoc* Committee of 25 September to 25 November 1947, pp. 150, 199-201.
20. *Ibid,* Vol. II, Annex 33, p. 1633.
21. *Ibid,* p. 1634.
22. *Ibid.*
23. *Ibid,* p. 1637.
24. U.N. Document A/516.
25. U.N. Document A/364.
26. Official Records of Second Session of General Assembly (12th meeting), Vol. II, pp. 1313-1314.

27. *Ibid,* p. 1312.
28. *Ibid,* p. 1319.
29. *Ibid,* p. 1357.
30. *Ibid,* p. 1365.
31. *Ibid,* pp. 1367–1369.
32. *Ibid,* p. 1314.
33. *Ibid* (128th meeting), pp. 1424–1425: U.N. Resolution 181 (II) of 29 November 1947.
34. *Ibid,* p. 1426.
35. Lilienthal, *What Price Israel?* pp. 72–73
36. Bethman, Erich W., *Decisive Years in Palestine* 1918–1948, (Washington DC: American Friends of the Middle East, 1959), p.35.
37. Millis, Walter (Ed.), *The Forrestal Diaries,* (New York: The Viking Press, 1951), p. 344
38. *Ibid,* p. 345.
39. Lilienthal, *What Price Israel?* p. 64.
40. *Ibid,* p. 124.
41. Neuman, Emanuel, in *American Zionist,* 5 February 1953.
42. U.S. Congressional Record, 18 December 1947, p. 1176.
43. Quotations from Drew Pearson. Reproduced in *Chicago Daily Tribune,* 9 February 1948, Part 2, 8:1.
44. Welles, Sumner, *We Need Not Fail,* (Boston: Houghton Mifflin, 1948), p. 63.
45. Millis, *The Forrestal Diaries,* p. 363.
46. Calculated on the basis of the figures in the *Village Statistics,* published by the Palestine Government in 1945 and the maps showing the 1947 partition and the 1949 armistice demarcation line.
47. Menuhin, *The Decadence of Judaism in Our Time.* From the statement about the author.
48. *Ibid,* p. 114.
49. *Ibid,* p. 115.
50. U.N. Resolution No. 181 (II) of 29 November 1947.

Chapter VII — Strife, War, Truce (pp. 100 - 115)

1. U.N. Resolution of Partition No. 181 (II) of 29 November 1947.
2. U.N. Official Records of General Assembly: Plenary Session, 14 May 1948.
3. Bethmann, *Decisive Years in Palestine* 1919–1948, p. 41.
4. Glubb, *A Soldier with the Arabs,* p. 302.
5. Jewish Telegraphic Agency, *Daily News Bulletin,* 26 April 1963.
6. Glubb, *A Soldier with the Arabs,* p. 81.
7. From an article by Nathan Chofshi in *Jewish Newsletter,* 9 February 1959.
8. Glubb, *A Soldier with the Arabs,* p. 251.

9. Kimche, Jon, *The Seven Fallen Pillars,* (New York: F.A. Praeger, 1953), p. 228.
10. Joseph, Dov, *The Faithful City: The Seige of Jerusalem* 1948 (New York: Simon and Schuster, 1960), p. 71.
11. Toynbee, Arnold, *A Study of History,* (London: Oxford University Press, 1953–1954), Vol. VIII, p. 290.
12. Beigin, Menachem, *The Revolt: Story of the Irgun,* (New York: Henry Schuman, 1951), (Quoted by the *Jewish Newsletter,* 3 October, 1960).
13. Glubb, *A Soldier with the Arabs,* p. 99.
14. O'Ballance, Edgar, *The Arab-Israeli War* 1948, (New York: F.A. Praeger, 1957), p. 209.
15. *Jewish Newsletter,* 3 October 1960,
16. O'Ballance, *The Arab-Israeli War,* 1948, p. 64.
17. Ben Gurion, *Rebirth and Destiny of Israel,* p. 296.
18. *Ibid,* pp. 291–292.
19. Beigin, *The Revolt: Story of the Irgun,* p. 162.
20. *Ibid,* p. 348.
21. Weizmann, Chaim, *Trial and Error* (London: East and West Library, 1950), p. 556.
22. McDonald, James, *My Mission, to Israel,* (New York: Simon and Schuster, 1951), p. 176.
23. U.N. Library Document UNX. 956.9 – A/658.
24. Glubb, *A Soldier with the Arabs,* p. 302.
25. U.N. Document S/773: Resolution 49 (1948) of 22 May 1948.
26. U.N. Document S/801: Resolution 50 (1948) of 29 May 1948.
27. Kimche, *The Seven Fallen Pillars,* pp. 249–250.
28. Ben Gurion, *Rebirth and Destiny of Israel,* p. 247.
29. Glubb, *A Soldier with the Arabs,* p. 81.
30. *Jewish Newsletter,* 9 February 1959.
31. *Ibid,* 19 May 1958.
32. Glubb, *A Soldier with the Arabs,* p. 251.
33. From an article by Erskine Childers entitled *The Other Exodus,* published in the *Spectator* (London) Magazine, 12 May 1961.

Chapter VIII — The Armistice (pp. 116 - 155)

1. See U.N. Document S/902: Resolution No. 54 (1948)
2. U.N. Document S/1080: Resolution No. 62 (1948)
3. With Egypt on 24 February 1949 – U.N. Document S/1264/Rev. 1
   With Lebanon on 23 March 1949 – U.N. Document S/1296/Rev. 1
   With Jordan on 3 April 1949 – U.N. Document S/1302/Rev. 1
   With Syria on 20 July 1949 – U.N. Document S/1353/Rev. 1

4. Oppenheim, L., *International Law,* (London: Longmans, Green & Co., 1963), Lauterpacht Edditions, Vol. II, pp. 546-547.
5. U.N. Document S/1376, II: Resolution No. 73 (1949) of 11 August 1949.
6. See map annexed to U.N. Document S/1353/Rev. 1.
7. U.N. Document S/PV. 635, pp. 27–28.
8. U.N. Document S/2049, Section IV. para. 3.
9. U.N. Document S/2088, para. 8.
10. U.N. resolution 93 (1951) of 18 May 1951.
11. U.N. Document S/2157: Resolution No. 93 (1951) of 18 May 1951.
12. See Report dated 26 June 1951 – U.N. Document S/2213, Part II, paras. 14 & 17.
13. See Report dated 16 August 1951 – U.N. Document S/2300, para. 9.
14. See Report dated 6 November 1951 – U.N. Document S/2389, paras. 14 & 16.
15. See report dated 30 October 1952 – U.N. Document S/2833, paras. 50 & 58.
16. See paragraph IV:55 of Report by General Vagn Bennike before Security Council at its meeting on 27 October 1953.
17. See General Bennike's report to the Security Council at its meeting of 27 October 1953.
18. U.N. Document S/3343, Annex C.
19. U.N. Document S/3343, para. 18
20. U.N. Document S/3596, Annex VII, para. 1
21. Horn, General Carl Von, *Soldiering for Peace,* (London: Cassell & Co., Ltd, 1966), p. 75
22. *Ibid,* p. 123.
23. *Ibid,* p. 124.
24. Ibid, p. 263.
25. *Ibid,* p. 85,
26. Ibid, p. 263.
27. Ibid, pp. 264–265.
28. See agreement dated 7 July 1948 signed between the Military Commanders of Jordan and Israel, (Quote at end of p. 128).
29. Hutchison, E.H., *Violent Truce,*(New York: Devin-Adair Co., 1956), pp. 20–29.
30. Ibid, pp. 40-41
31. *Ibid,* pp. 87–88 .
32. Burns, E.L.M., *Between Arab and Israelis,* (New York: Ivan Obolensky, Inc., 1963), p. 158.
33. U.N. Document S/3942: Resolution No. 127 (1958).
34. U.N. Document A/1873, p. 55, para. 514.
35. *Ibid,* p. 57, para. 535.
36. *Ibid,* p. 57, para. 541.
37. *Ibid,* p. 60, para. 567.
38. U.N. Document S/1797.

39. U.N. Document S/1907: Resolution No. 89 (1950).
40. U.N. Document S/PV. 635, pp. 27–28.
41. U.N. Document S/3103.
42. U.N. Document S/3596, Section V.
43. U.N. Document S/PV. 635, p. 36.
44. U.N. Document S/3596, Annex VIII.
45. U.N. Document S/3638, para. 10.
46. U.N. Document S/3659, Annex, Section II, paras. 1,9 and 10.
47. U.N. Document S/1264/Rev.1, Articles II:2 and V:3
48. For text of communiqué, see *United States Policy in the Middle East (Documents)*, (Washington DC: Dept. of State, 1957), pp. 135–136.
49. *Jewish Observer,* 9 November 1956.
50. Burns, *Between Arab and Israeli,* p. 180
51. *New York Times,* 8 November 1956.
52. *Ibid.*
53. Burns, *Between Arab and Israeli,* p. 184.
54. U.N. Document A/3354: Resolution No. 997 (ES-I).
55. Burns, *Between Arab and Israeli,* p. 243.
56. See Proclamation by President Kennedy dated October 23, 1962– U.S. Dept. of State *Bulletin,* Vol. XLVII, No. 1220 (November 20, 1962), p. 717 (No. 3504:27, Federal Register, 10401).
57. U.N. Document S/902: Resolution No. 54 (1948) of 15 July 1948.
58. U.N. Document S/1044: Decision adopted at 367th meeting.
59. U.N. Document S/1070: Resolution 61 (1948) of 4 November 1948.
60. U.N. Document A/1264/Rev. 1, p. 11
61. *Ibid.* p. 3
62. Horn, *Soldiering for Peace,* pp. 282–283.

Chapter IX — U.N. Efforts for a Settlement. (pp. 156 - 168)

1. U.N. Document A/648, *Report of U.N. Mediator,* paras. 5 and 6.
2. Bethmann, *Decisive Years in Palestine* 1919–1948, p. 49.
3. Menuhin, *The Decadence of Judaism in Our Time,* pp. 129–130.
4. U.N. Document A/648, p. 14.
5. U.N. Resolution 194 (III) of 11 December 1948.
6. U.N. Document A/SPC/SR. 433 of 19 October 1965 – Official Records of Spcial Political Committee.
7. U.N. Resolution 394 (V) of 14 December 1950.
8. U.N. Document A/927 of 21 June 1949.
9. *Ibid,* para. 10 and annex.
10. *Ibid,* paras. 24–29.
11. *Ibid,* paras. 32–33.

12. U.N. Official Records of First Committee of Third Session, 23 and 29 November 1948.
13. Israeli Government *Yearbook* 1950, pp. 140–142.
14. U.N. Resolution 273 (III) of 11 May 1949.
15. Israeli Government *Yearbook* 1950, pp. 43–45.
16. U.N. Official Records of Trusteeship Council, Second Special Session, 20 December 1949 – Resolution No. 114 (II) of 9 December 1949.
17. Ben Gurion, *Rebirth and Destiny of Israel*, p. 362.

Chapter X — The Arab Refugee Problem (pp. 169 - 189)

1. U.N. Document A/4121.
2. U.N. Document A/3686.
3. U.N. Document A/SPC/PV. 199, p. 26.
4. U.N. Document A/5813 – UNRWA Report for period I July 1963 to 30 June 1964, pp. 1–4.
5. U.N. Document A/6013 – UNRWA Report for period I July 1964 to 30 June 1965, pp. 4–5.
6. U.N. Document A/6313 – UNRWA Report for period 1 July 1965 to 30 June 1966, p. 3, para. 5.
7. *New York Times* (Sunday edition), 11 December 1966, Section E.3.
8. U.N. Document A/5813, p. 5, para. 21
9. U.N. Document A/6313, Table 2, p. 43.
10. U.N. Document A/6013, p. 57.
11. U.N. Document A/6313, Table 5, p. 46.
12. *Ibid*, pp. 33–34.
13. *Ibid*, paras. 54–55, p. 16; Table 17, p. 56.
14. *Ibid*, para 33, p. 10; Table 22, p. 70.
15. U.N. Document A/4478, p. 10.
16. U.N. Provisional Summary Record of Special Political Committee, No. A/SPC/SR. 437, dated 26 October 1965, pp. 3–4.
17. *U.N. Document* A/SPC/SR. 442, dated 2 November 1965, p. 5.
18. Draft – Resolution No. A/SPC/L.128 of 9 November 1966–U.N. Document A/6506 of 15 November , 1966.
19. *U.N. Document* A/SPC/SR. 456, dated 18 November 1965, p.2.
20. A/SPC/SR. 457, dated 19 November 1965, pp. 6–7.
21. U.N. Document GA/AH/356 of 22 November 1955.
22. U.N. Press Release PAL/861; UNRWA *Newsletter*, February 1961,
23. Israeli Government *Yearbook* 1950, pp. 44–45.
24. U.N. Document A/3931, para. 4.
25. Toynbee, *A Study of History*, Vol. VIII, p. 290.
26. From a lecture and subsequent debate between Prof. Toynbee and Israeli

ambassador at McGill University, Montreal, Canada, January 1961.
27. *Jewish Newsletter,* 1 December 1958.
28. *Ibid,* 1 December 1958, and 14 December 1959.

Chapter XI — Arabs Under Israeli Rule (pp. 190 - 225)

1. Jewish Agency for Palestine, *Statements and Memoranda,* pp. 71–72.
2. Israeli Government, *Laws of State of Israel,* (English) Vol. I, Ordinances, 1948, p. 5
3. Toynbee, *A Study of History,* Vol. VIII, p. 289.
4. Letter dated 10 November, 1960, addressed to the President of the U.N. General Assembly by a group of Arab leaders in Israel.
5. *New York Times,* 22 September, 1961.
6. *Ibid,* 26 September, 1961.
7. *Statistical Abstract of Israel* 1965, pp. 38–39.
8. Israeli Government, *Laws of the State of Israel,* Vol. I, p. 8
9. Israeli Government, *Collection of Regulations,* 1949, pp. 169–170.
10. *Palestine Gazette* No. 1442 of 27 September, 1945, Supplement No. 2, pp. 1055–1098.
11. *Jerusalem Post,* 7 November 1966.
12. *Ibid,* 9 November 1966.
13. Peretz, Don, *Israel and the Palestine Arabs,* (Washington, D.C.: The Middle East Institute, 1958), pp. 95–96.
14. U.N. Document A/519, p. 138.
15. Israeli Government *Yearbook* 1952, pp. 207–210.
16. Peretz, *Israel and the Palestine Arabs,* p. 125.
17. *Haaretz* (Israeli) Newspaper, 3 April, 1953.
18. *American Mercury* Magazine, August 1957.
19. *Jewish Newsletter*
20. *Ner* Magazine, September-October 1953.
21. *Jewish Newsletter,* 29 June, 1959.
22. U.N. Security Council Records, S/1302 / Rev. 1 of 20 June, 1949, Article VI, para. 6
23. *Jewish Newsletter,* 15 April, 1957.
24. *Ibid,* 13 May 1957.
25. *Ibid,* 8 July 1958.
26. *New York Times,* 13 October, 1958.
27. *Ibid,* 17 October, 1958.
28. *New York Herald Tribune,* 27 February, 1959.
29. *Jewish Newsletter,* 3 November, 1958.
30. U.N. Partition Resolution 181 (II) of 29 November, 1947, Ch. 2 Article 8.
31. From an Article entitled *How Israel Treats Her Arabs* published in the *American Mercury* Magazine, August 1957.

32. *The Abandoned Areas Ordinance* 1949, State of Israel Laws, Vol. I, pp. 25–26. *The Absentee Property Regulations* 1948, Jerusalem Post, 19 December 1948. *The Emergency Regulations* (*Cultivation of Waste Lands*) 1948–1949, State of Israel Laws, Vol II , pp. 70–77.
33. Peretz, *Israel and the Palestine Arabs,* p. 152.
34. Text published in *Middle East Journal,* Vol. VII, No. 3, Summer 1953 pp. 358–360.
35. Peretz, *Israel and the Palestine Arabs*, p. 172.
36. From an Article entitled *We Accuse!* published in *Haaretz,* 14 January, 1955
37. From an Article entitled *The Arabs Among Us* published in *Haaretz,* 14 January, 1955
38. *Ibid,* 7 January, 1955.
39. Peretz, *Israel and the Palestine Arabs,* pp. 178–179.
40. *The Christian Century* Magazine, 13 January, 1954.
41. Palestine: *Bentwich Compilation of Laws and Regulations,* Vol. 2, pp. 398–402.
42. Palestine: *A Survey of Palestine,* 1945–1946, Vol. I, Chapter I, p. 6.
43. U.N. Partition Resolution 181 (II) of 29 November 1947, Chapter 2, Article 4.
44. *The Christian Century* Magazine, 13 January, 1954.
45. Memorandum published in *Wahdat Al-Jubha* (Haifa), 6 February, 1959
46. From a speech delivered at Mishkan Israel Synagogue, New Haven, Connecticut, on 27 November, 1959 (See *Jewish Newsletter,* November 30, 1959).

Chapter XII — Violations and Aggression (pp. 226 - 248)

1. U.N. Security Council Records: 553rd meeting, p. 30.
2. *Ibid,* pp. 10–11.
3. *Ibid,* 552nd meeting, p. 3.
4. U.N. Secretary-General's Report for 1958 – 1959, p. 5.
5. Ben Gurion, *Rebirth and Destiny of Israel,* pp. 227,232.
6. As quoted in the *Jewish Observer and Middle East Review,* Vol. IV, No. 18, 6 May 1955, p. 3
7. Ben Gurion, *Rebirth and Destiny of Israel,* p. 247.
8. Articles II:2 and V:3 of Armistice Agreement with Egypt; and Articles III: 2 and IV: 2 of Agreements with Lebanon, Jordan and Syria.
9. *Forward* (New York) newspaper, 27 December 1952.
10. *New York Times,* 2 January 1953.
11. Zukerman, William, *Voice of Dissent,* (New York: Bookman Associates, Inc., 1964), pp. 33–34.
13. U.N. Document S/902: Resolution No. 54 (1948).
13. U.N. Document S/3538: Resolution No. 111 (1956)
14. U.N. Document S/PV. 1003 of 5 April 1962., pp. 16,21.

15. U.N. Document S/PV. 999 of 28 March 1962, p. 42.
16. U.N. Document S/PV. 1001 of 4 April 1962, p.1
17. U.N. Document S/PV. 1320 of 16 November 1966.
18. *Ibid.*
19. U.N. Document S/PV. 1321 of 16 November 1966.
20. *Ibid.*
21. Security Council resolution S/228 (1966)
of 25 November 1966.
22. U.N. Document S/PV. 630, p. 14, para. 59.
23. Hutchison, *Violent Truce,* p. 102.
24. U.N. Documents S/PV, 1320 & S/PV. 1321 of 16 November 1966.
25. U.N. Document S/PV. 635, p. 41.
26. *Ibid,* pp. 41–42.
27. Hutchison, *Violent Truce,* pp. 91–92.
28. Burns, *Between Arab and Israeli,* pp. 173–174.
29. Horn, *Soldiering for Peace,* p. 96.
30. U.N. Document S/2157: Resolution No. 93 (1951) of 18 May 1951.
31. U.N. Document S/PV. 630, para. 13.
32. *Ibid,* para. 17.
33. *Ibid,* para, 48.
34. *Ibid,* para. 25; also U.N. Document S/3139/Rev. 2: Resolution No. 101 (1953) of 24 November 1953.
35. U.N. Document S/3251, para. 11.
36. U.N. Doocument S/3290, para. 8.
37. *Ibid,* paras. 1–7 and Annex.
38. U.N. Document S/3516, Appendix I,
39. See U.N. Documents S/3373 and A/2935, paras. 33–43;
also U.N. Document S/3378: Resolution No. 106 (1955) of 29 March 1955.
40. U.N. Document S/3430, para. 2 .
41. *Ibid,* para. 16.
42. U.N. Document S/3516, Appendix II.
43. *Ibid.*
44. *Ibid,* see also report in *New York Times,* 4 November 1955.
45. U.N. Document S/3516, paras. 1–10;
also U.N. Document S/3538; Resolution No. 111 (1956) of 19 Jannuary 1956.
46. U.N. Document S/3638, paras. 6–10.
47. U.N. Document S/3660, para. 6 .
48. *Ibid.*
49. *Ibid.* para. 2.
50. *Ibid,* para. 7.
51. U.N. Document S/3685 & Corr. 1, paras. 1–21.
52. See General Assembly Resolutions Nos. 997 (ES-1) to 1003 (ES–I) and

Nos. 1120 (XI), 1123 (XI) to 1125 (XI).
53. U.N. Document S/5111: Resolution No. 171 (1962) of 9 April 1962.
54. U.N. Document S/5102, p. 40, para. 32.
55. See U.N. Document S/6248 of 19 March 1965.
56. See U.N. Document S/6390 of 28 May 1965.
57. See U.N. Document S/6898 of 11 November 1965.
58. See U.N. Document S/7412 of 18 July 1966.
59. Security Council Resolution S/228 (1966) of 25 November 1966.
60. See U.N. Document S/7843 of 7 April 1967.
61. From an *Editorial* in *Sign* Magazine (A Catholic publication in U.S.A.), December 1953.
62. From the excerpts from the Diary of Moshe Sharett, published in *Ma'ariv* (Hebrew) newspaper and reproduced in the *Jerusalem Post* (Israel), 31 October 1965.
63. Toynbee, *A Study od History,* Vol. VIII, pp. 289–290.
64. Weizmann, *Trial and Error,* p. 566.
65. From a news item about the *Third Force Movement in Israel,* published under the title *A Messenger from Israel* in the *Jewish Newsletter* (New York), 1 May 1961.

Chapter XIII — Israel and the United States (pp. 249 - 274)

1. U.S. Resolution No. 31, 86th Congress, lst Session, 15 June 1959, p. 57.
2. From an article published in *Issues* Magazine,
Summer 1964, pp. 15–16.
3. See Record of Hearings of Meetings of Committee on Foreign Relations, U.S. Senate, 88th Congress, lst Session, Part 9, 23 May 1963, pp. 1211–1424 & 1695–1782.
4. From a U.S. policy speech by the Hon. John D. Jernegan, of the Dept. of State on 8 May 1964.
5. U.N. Document A/SPC/SR, 252 of 19 April, 1961.
6. Statement made by the Hon. John D. Jernegan. See Ref. No. 4.
7. From letter published in *Holiday* Magazine, March 1963.
8. From an article by Professor Fred. V. Winnett entitled "Why the West should stop supporting Israel", published In *McGill Magazine* (Montreal, Canada), 18 January 1958.
9. *Near East Report* (Washington DC), May 1966 (Quoted from the *New York Times,* May 1966).
10. *The Jerusalem Post* (Israel), 22 May 1966, from an article "Israel getting versatile."
11. From the *Near East Report,* ,
Vol. X, No. 19, 20 September 1966.

12. *The Daily Star* (Beirut), 24 May 1966.
13. *New York Times,* 18 February 1965.
14. *Ibid,* 20 February 1965.
15. *Ibid,*
16. From an Editorial, published in the *Chicago Tribune,* 23 March 1965.
17. From an article by Professor W.T. Stace, published in the *Atlantic Monthly,* No. 4, February 1947.
18. From an article published in the *Middle East Journal,* (Washington DC), Summer 1964, pp. 311–312.
19. From Financial Report by AID Representative in Israel (John E. De Wilde), American Embassy, Tel Aviv, 26 July 1963.
20. *Near East Report* Supplement to May 1966 issue, p. B. 15.
21. American Council for Judaism (New York), *Brief,* October 1965.
22. *Jerusalem Post* (Israel), 13 September 1965.
23, *Jewish Newsletter,* 30 November 1959.
24. Menuhin, *The Decadence of Judaism in Our Time,* p. 367.
25. U.S. Congressional Record and Proceedings, 85th Congress, 2nd Session, 18 July 1958.
26. *American Jewish Yearbook* 1965, p. 241.
27. Israeli Government, *Israeli D gest,* Vol. IX, No. 1, 14 January 1966, p. 2
28. *American Jewish Yearbook* 1965, p. 242.
29. U.S. Congressional Record, 86th Congress, 2nd Session, Vol. 106, No. 78, 29 April 1960.
30. *The German Tribune,* No. 210, 9 April 1966, p. 2 .
31. *Jerusalem Post,* 25 February 1966, p. 9.
32. *The German Tribune,* 24 September 1966, pp. 1–2 (Quoted from *Hannoversche Presse,* 15 September 1966)
33. *Jerusalem Post,* 3 May 1966.
34. *New York Times,* 18 October 1959.
35. *Jerusalem Post,* 19 April 1966
36. *New York Times,* 10 February 1958.
37. See Article by Rev. Humphrey Walz, published in *The Jewish Newsletter,* 6 March 1961.
38. *The Daily Star* (Beirut), 5 October 1965.

Chapter XIV — Impact of Israel on Arab World (pp. 275-297)

1. United States: *Foreign Relations of the United States* 1943: *The Near East and Africa,* (Washington, DC, 1964), Vol. IV, pp. 776–777.
2. From an Editorial by William Zukerman, published in the *Jewish Newsletter.* Reproduced in his book *Voice of Dissent,* pp. 200–201.
3. Israeli Government *Statistical Abstract* 1965, No. 16, p. 27.

4. *Issues* Magazine, Spring 1959, p. 25.
5. *Jewish Telegraphic Agency,* 6 February 1959.
(Quoted in the *Jewish Newsletter,* 23 February 1959).
6. U.N. Security Council Document No. S/888.
7. Menuhin, *The Decadence of Judaism in Our Time,* p. 433.
8. The Talmud, *Habakkuk,* 2:12.
9. Kirk, George E., *A Short History of the Middle East,*(London:Methuen, 1948), pp. 156–157.
10. Ionides, Michael, *Divide and Lose: The Arab Revolt* 1955–1958. (London: Geoffrey Bles, 1960), p. 43.
11. Israeli Government *Yearbook* 1951–1952, p. 64; and *Yearbook* 1952, pp. 63 and 65.
12. From a speech delivered at a meeting of *Mapai* Party at Beersheba in 1952.
13. From a statement broadcast on the Arabic programme, Israel radio, 12 February 1952.
14. From a statement made in the Israeli Parliament on 12 October 1955.
15. *New York Times,* 25 January 1956.
16. Joseph, *The Embattled C ty,* pp. 322–323.
17. Rizk, Edward, *The River Jordan,* (New York: The Arab Information Center, 1964), p. 20.
18. Lauterpacht, L., (Ed.), *International Law* 1955, p. 474.
19. Sapir, Pinhas, *The Development of Israel,* Israel in the Middle East, No. 3–5, Vol. IV (24), December 1952, pp. 62–63.
20. Israeli Government *Yearbook* 1953–1954, p. 35.
21. *Jewish Newsletter,* 13 July 1950.
22. From a radio broadcast by Samuel Untermeyer over station WABC (New York), 6 August 1933.

Chapter XV — Peace or War (pp. 298 - 307)

1. Ben Gurion, *Rebirth and Destiny of Israel,* p. 247.
2. U.N. Document A/648, p. 5 .
3. Toynbee, Arnold, *The West and the Arabs,* Encyclopedia Britannica: Yearbook 1959.
4. *Jewish Newsletter,* 10 October 1960.
5. *Jerusalem Post* (Israel), 10 October 1965.
6. From an article entitled *Advice to a Traveller,*
Published in *Issues* (New York) Magazine, Summer 1960, p. 30.
7. From an article by Suhaila Saleh, published in the Special Christmas Issue 1964 of the *Jerusalem Times* (Jordan).

Index

I

J

K